The Vestry Book

OF

Christ Church Parish

This edition is limited to 500 copies,
of which this is

No. 404

Chamberlayne

CHRIST CHURCH AS IT APPEARS TODAY

The Vestry Book of
Christ Church Parish
Middlesex County
Virginia

1663-1767

❧ C. G. Chamberlayne ❧

HERITAGE BOOKS
2019

HERITAGE BOOKS

AN IMPRINT OF HERITAGE BOOKS, INC.

Books, CDs, and more—Worldwide

For our listing of thousands of titles see our website
at
www.HeritageBooks.com

A Facsimile Reprint
Published 2019 by
HERITAGE BOOKS, INC.
Publishing Division
5810 Ruatan Street
Berwyn Heights, Md. 20740

International Standard Book Numbers
Paperbound: 978-0-7884-0806-9
Clothbound: 978-0-7884-6046-3

TO

MY WIFE

ELIZABETH BOLLING CHAMBERLAYNE,

to whose encouragement and help whatever of worthwhile
achievement in this and every other effort of mine
is mainly due, I dedicate this book.

C. G. CHAMBERLAYNE

Preface

The MS. volume hereinafter reproduced contains the earliest records of Christ Church Parish, Middlesex County, Virginia. In fact it antedates by several years the establishment of the parish, which took place in the year 1666.

From the year 1767, the date of the last official entry in it, until some time subsequent to the publication of Bishop Meade's *Old Churches, Ministers and Families of Virginia,* the volume appears to have been in the possession of the descendants of Col. Edmund Berkeley [Meade, *Old Churches, etc.,* Vol. I, page 371, Note]. Later, but at just what date is unknown to the transcriber, it was "presented to the Library of the Theo. Sem. of Va. by William N. Berkeley, of Aldie, Loudoun Co. Va." [Pencilled note on first of four blank leaves preceding first page of the MS. volume]. For many years it has been one of the cherished possessions of that library. Permission to transcribe and publish it was given to the undersigned by the late Rt. Rev. Robt. A. Gibson, D. D., President of the Board of Trustees of the Seminary.

The MS. volume is a folio 14 inches tall by 9 inches wide, and contains 316 pages. In addition to the note referred to above, there is a second pencilled note on the last of the blank leaves preceding the MS. proper, to the following effect:

"This Record begins in 1663 & ends 1767

1663
———
104

P. Slaughter".

The entry on page 316 of the MS. (the last page) is in ink. It is undated and unsigned. The handwriting is similar to—the transcriber cannot say that it is identical with—that of the pencilled note referred to above and signed P. Slaughter.

As clearly appears from the records, Christ Church Parish was established in the year 1666. The first entry in the MS. Vestry Book of the parish is, however, dated Nov. 19, 1663. This entry has to do with a vestry meeting for the Parish of Lancaster. To the question that naturally arises, how it happens that the Vestry Book of Christ Church Parish, Middlesex County, begins with entries recording the minutes of vestry meetings of Lancaster Parish, the answer is as follows.

Lancaster County embraced originally land on both sides of the Rappahannock [*Hening,* Vol. I, page 550, March 13, 1659-60 "Whereas it appeares that there was levied for Sir William Berkeley upon the county of Lancaster (which then included the whole river of Rappahannock) twelve thousand six hundred pounds of tobacco", etc.]. In 1664 that part of the county lying south of the Rappahannock contained two parishes, Lancaster Parish and Peanckatanck Parish [*Vestry Book,* page 2], which were served by one minister, Mr. Morris. In 1665 [*Vestry Book,* page 4] it was a question whether the two parishes should remain separate organizations or be merged into one parish. On January 29, 1666, a general vestry for all that part of Lancaster County lying south of the Rappahannock was held, at which meeting it was agreed upon that "yᵉ Two prishes Formerly called Lancaster and Peanckatank from hence forth be United as one, and called Christ Church prish." Accordingly the date January 29, 1666 may be taken as that of the beginning of Christ Church Parish, Middlesex County. Confirming the action of this general vestry, the Grand Assembly at their session beginning October 23, 1666, passed the following Act: *"Whereas* the parishes of Lancaster and Pyankatank having formerly been united and since divided into two parishes, by that division became more sensible of the inconveniency and charge, have petitioned to be reunited, it is accordingly ordered that their petition be granted and the parishes reunited and to be called by the name of Christ Church Parish [*Hening,* Vol. II, page 252].

Now as far back as 1675 Christ Church Parish and Middlesex County were in a certain sense synonymous terms [*Vestry Book,* page 23, where the accounts of the parish levy are headed "Middlefex County Dʳ Parish Levy"]. Certainly from fairly early times in their history the two districts were coterminous [*Vestry Book,* pages 148 and 150, where the limits of the first and last precincts for processioning are given as "the Lower end of this County" and "the Upper end of the County" respectively]. In the absence then of direct proof to the contrary, it would not be unnatural to suppose that county and parish had been established at one and the same date. This was for some time the supposition of the undersigned, but, as will appear, it was an erroneous one. Though the Parish of Christ Church was formed in 1666, it was two years (more or less) thereafter that Middlesex County was established. The proof of this statement is as follows.

In *Hening* we have no Act of Assembly establishing Middlesex County. However, we have an early reference to the county under the date April 20, 1670 [*Hening,* Vol. II, pages 509-510]. But we can trace the county back still further. In the records in the Virginia Land Office we find three entries recording grants of land in Middlesex County made by Sir William Berkeley, Knt., Governor, to Mr. Richard Parrott, Mr. Richard Whittaker, and Mr. Tho. Tugwell, respectively. The grants to Mr. Parrot and Mr. Whittaker are both dated Feb. 5, 1669 (which *might* mean 1670) ; that to Mr. Tugwell is dated Oct. 30, 1669. Middlesex County was then in existence in the year 1669.

In the Lancaster County Order Book for 1666-1680 occurs —under date of July 10, 1667—the following interesting entry (which, so far as the present writer knows, has never before been published) : "A peticon being this day presented to this Court under the hands of some of the inhabitants of yᵉ *South side of yᵉ riv in this County desireing that evry other Court might bee kept on the sᵈ *South side in answer to yᵉ sᵈ peticon

---

* In each case the word was originally written North. This word North was then scratched through once or twice with a pen, and the word South was written immediately above it. The fourth time the word was used it was left as originally written, though obviously South was meant.—C. G. C.

this Court do declare that †[x x x x] it very iust & reasonable that the Court be continued where it hath for many yeares past been †[x] kept & that if yᵉ *South side of this County shalbe pleased to devide from †[x] & make a County on ye **North side, they are left to their owne libtie (?) when they think fitt."

From the above transcript from the records of Lancaster County it is evident that certainly so late as July 10, 1667, the inhabitants of Lancaster County living south of the Rappahannock (i. e., in what is now Middlesex County) were not even seriously contemplating taking steps to have their district made into a separate county. Doubtless, however, the curt refusal of the Court of Lancaster County to consent to their petition to have every other meeting of the court held on the south side of the river, coupled with the gentle hint that if they did not like the existing state of affairs, they were at liberty to go ahead and organize a county of their own, was one of the causes of the movement which soon took place to have a new county (Middlesex) created.

In *The Randolph Manuscript* [*The Virginia Magazine of History and Biography,* Vol. XVII, October, 1909, No. 4, page 341] occurs—under date of September 27, 1667—the following entry: "Whereas there is an Order for making a Bridge over §Dragon Swamp the North side of which is in Lancaster County and the other side where the bridge will come uncertain whether in Gloster or New Kent County It is proposed that all the three counties may contribute toward making the said bridge."

The above excerpt from *The Randolph Manuscript* conclusively proves that what is now Middlesex County was in September, 1667, still a part of Lancaster County.

---

† These six words are illegible.—C. G. C.
* See note on preceding page.
** Obviously a mistake for South.—C. G. C.
§ Note—from *The Virginia Magazine of History and Biography* "Lancaster County then included both sides of the Rappahannock. The Dragon lies between the present counties of Gloucester and King and Queen (formerly a part of New Kent—C. G. C.) on the south and Middlesex and Essex on the north."

Finally in the Christ Church Parish Vestry Books occurs— under date of September 16, 1668—the following entry [*Vestry Book,* page 13] : "It is Agreed upon That yᵉ Petition Should be Delivered by the Conſent of the Piſh to the Grand Aſ-sembly for the Rattification of yᵉ former Act Made for the County of Lancaſter to be Divided into two Countys."

From the above excerpt from the Christ Church Parish Vestry Book three facts are evident: (1) that some time between Sept. 27, 1667 and Sept. 16, 1668 the Grand Assembly had taken at least some provisional action looking to the for-mation of a new county (Middlesex) out of territory then in-cluded in Lancaster County; (2) that something was still lacking in that action to make it completely effective, for the territory south of the Rappahannock was not yet a fully estab-lished separate county; and (3) the inhabitants of the south side were now desirous of having the new county (Middlesex) finally and without further delay established.

In view of the foregoing facts: (1) that Middlesex County is first mentioned by name in *Hening* under the date April 20, 1670; (2) that the records in the Virginia Land Office carry the county back no further than to Oct. 30, 1669 (or at earliest to Feb. 5, 1669) ; (3) that under the date July 10, 1667, the Lancaster County Order Book refers to the south side of the Rappahannock as being in Lancaster County; (4) that under the date Sept. 27, 1667, *The Randolph Manuscript* refers to the north side of the Dragon Swamp (now Middlesex County) as being in Lancaster County; and (5) finally that on Sept. 16, 1668, the vestry of Christ Church agree that a petition for the rattification of a former act for the division of the County of Lancaster be forwarded to the Grand Assembly ———— it can be taken as possible that Middlesex County was (at least provisionally or in some sense) established between Sept. 27, 1667, and Sept. 16, 1668; as highly probable that it was finally established some time between Sept. 27, 1667 and Feb. 5, 1669; and as certain that it was established between Sept. 27, 1667 and Oct. 30, 1669.

It is, of course, entirely possible that future researches made in England or in this country will bring to light some document definitely determining the date (year, month, and day) of the establishment of Middlesex County; and it is to be hoped that a research to that end will be instituted. Meanwhile the question as to the date of the establishment of Middlesex County stands as above indicated.

In conclusion, a personal word or two. Needless to say, there are inaccuracies in this publication; in view of the nature of the work it could hardly be otherwise. However, the transcriber trusts that the inaccuracies are few and unimportant, and that the printed volume is as nearly perfect a reproduction of the original record as could be made with types. The curious on this point can, if they wish, check up on the transcriber by comparing the latter's work with the original MS. volume (in the Library of the Theological Seminary, at Alexandria) or with the official photostatic copy of the original (in the Archives Department of the State Library, Richmond, Virginia).

The mechanical difficulties involved in the reproduction of the MS. in print seemed at first sight almost insuperable. That they have for the most part been so successfully overcome is due entirely to the skill and efforts of Mr. Edwin L. Levy, of the Old Dominion Press, to whom the transcriber wishes now to express his thanks for personal courtesies extending over a period of many months. He also wishes to acknowledge here his indebtedness to Dr. W. G. Stanard, of the Virginia Historical Society, and to Dr. H. R. McIlwaine, of the Virginia State Library, for helpful suggestions during the progress of the work, and to Mr. Barton Palmer, of Christchurch School, Christchurch, Va., for the photograph of the "Old Tombs at Christ Church", a cut of which appears opposite page 175.

For further information in regard to Christ Church Parish and to Middlesex County the interested reader is referred to the following publications:

Hening, *Statutes at Large;* New York, 1823.

Howe, *Historical Collections of Virginia;* Charleston, 1846.

Meade, *Old Churches, Ministers and Families of Virginia;* 2nd Edition, Philadelphia, 1872.

The Parish Register of Christ Church, Middlesex County, Va., from 1653 *to* 1812; Richmond, Va., 1897.

Colonial Churches; Richmond, Va., 1907 (Articles on Christ Church, Lancaster County, Virginia, by Dr. W. G. Stanard, and Christ Church, Middlesex County, Virginia, by the Rev. John Moncure, D. D.)

C. G. CHAMBERLAYNE.

Richmond, Va., October 31, 1927.

The Vestry Book

.. of ...

Christ Church Parish

Middlesex County, Virginia, 1663-1767

———

November y 19, 1663.

Att a Vestrey held for the Pish of Lancaster at yᵉ house of Mʳ Henry Corbin &c.

Whereas it doth appeare That There is an Act of Assembly Injoy [   ] all pʳishes to keepe a perfect Register of all Christnings Burials & [   ] as by the Said Act will more at large appeare——In obedience [   ] we yᵉ Vestry of Lancʳ Pʳish being yᵉ Majoʳ part of us now mett [   ] Doe hereby authoriſe and Appoint Mʳ Henry Corbin To keepe a [   ] Register of Every Thing required by yᵉ Said Act for This Ensuein [   ] And it is further Agreed That Every Vestry Man Shall Take [   ] Charge of the sᵈ Register for a whole Yeare, If a Clerk be not provided in yᵉ Intrim.

It is further Ordered That There be Levyed upon yᵉ Pʳish fo[   ] The Defraying of Mʳ Henry Corbins Charge in Two Assem[   ] Suñe of Foure Thousand Seven hundred Fourty and Thre[ ] pounds of Tobacco, and That yᵉ Sheriff is Desired to Collect [   ] Same, and Mʳ Cuthbert Potter is hereby appointed to pʳf[   ] The List for This Pʳish.

Cuthbert Potter	John Vause	
Abra : Weekes	Henry Corbin	Vestrymen
Thomas Willis	Richard Perrott	
Robert Chowning		

The Vestry Mens Oath &c

I A B As I doe Acknowledge my Selfe a True Soñe of the Church of England, Soe I doe believe The Articles of Faith there profeſs [   ] and doe oblidge myselfe to be conformable to yᵉ Doctrine and Disipline There Taught and Established, and That as Vestry Man for this Pish of Christ Church I will well and Truely performe m[   ] Duty Therein, being Directed by the Laws and Customes of This Cuntrey, and the Cannons of yᵉ Church of England, Soe Far as They will Suite with our preſent Capacity, And This I Shall Senſeerely do According to the best of my Knowledge Skill an[   ] Cuning, Without feare favour or partiallity, and Soe helpe me God.

(2)   Fr [   ] 4

Januy 1664*

Att a Vestry held at yᵉ house of Mʳ Henry Corbin It was There agreed and Ordered That Mʳ Henry Corbin Mʳ Richard Perrott and Mʳ Cuthbert Potter, or any Two of Them Meete and Treat and Conclude wᵗʰ Such persons as The Vestry of Peanckatanck hath or Shall appoint to Meete and Treat Concerning The Settlement and payment of Mʳ Morris (a Minister now come to Reside wᵗʰ us) and what yᵉ Said Thre persons, or any Two of them Shall Agree and Conclude Upon wᵗʰ yᵉ persons appointed by The Vestry of Peanckatanck and the Said Morris, We doe In the behalfe of yᵉ Pish allowe and Confirme

	Abrã. Weekes	Robᵗ Chowning
Present	Edwᵈ Boswell	John Vause
	Tho. Willis	Henry Thacker
	Nichᵒ Cock	

---

* Written in black ink between the lines. The writing is evidently that of a later hand. From the similarity of the handwriting to that of the pencilled note on the last of the four inserted blank sheets at the front of the volume I suppose it was written by Dr. Philip Slaughter. —C. G. C.

Aprill 31ᵗʰ 1665

Att a Vestry held at yᵉ House of Henry Nicholls

	Mʳ Henry Corbin	Mʳ Robert Chowning
Present	Mʳ John Curtis	Mʳ Nichᵒ Cock
	Mʳ Cuthbert Potter	Mʳ Thomas Willis
	Mʳ Edwᵈ Boswell	Mʳ Abrā. Weekes

It being Judged the place formerly Determined by a Vestry to Build the Church upon, was most Inconvenient to the Generallity of the People, and would be of Exterordinary Charge, upon better Conſideration it was now Unanimously Agreed for yᵉ Final Determination where yᵉ Church Should be built, That Lotts Should be Cast whether on the North or South Side of Sunderland Creek The Lott falling on the North Side It was accordingly Ordered and Decreed to be built on the Land of Mʳ Rowland Burnham Decᵈ with the approbation of Mʳ Henry Corbin now in possession of the Said Devidend, and Mʳ John Curtis and Mʳ Abrā. Weekes Church Wardens were Ordered to agree wᵗʰ Workmen wᵗʰ all Convenient Expedition for the building of yᵉ Said Church in Such Decent mañer & Form as is usuall, and that They provide all Things fitting, and to be Satt[   ] (3) And paid out of [   ]

Agreed by reason the Church was built on yᵉ North Side, That Mʳ Henry Corbin Mʳ Richard Perrott Mʳ Abraham Weekes Mʳ Jnᵒ Haslewood Mʳ Nichᵒ Cock Mʳ Robert Chowning, Doe Each of Them This pʳsent yeare Marke a Cow Calfe for yᵉ use of yᵉ Pish and to keepe it w[   ] Equall Care as Theire owne Till it be Two yeares old, and Then all of them that Shalbe liveing, and Theire Encrease if any to be Disposed of by yᵉ Vestry as a Stock for yᵉ Pish, and yᵉ Marke of the Said Calfe to be onely a Crop on yᵉ Right Eare.

It was further Ordered at that Meeting for yᵉ more Certaine and Convenient Meeting of yᵉ People, That Henry Nicholls have Six hundred pounds of Tobacco allowed him out of his Leveys for the use of his house for one Yeare, till a Church be built & Finished.

Sep 26ᵗʰ 1665

At a Vestry held at yᵉ house of Mʳ Henry Corbin

Present	Mʳ Henry Corbin	Mʳ Tho. Willis
	Mʳ Richard Perrott	Mʳ John Vause
	Mʳ John Curtis	Mʳ Robt. Chowning
	Mʳ Cuth: Potter	Mʳ Boswell
	Mʳ Abrã. Weekes	Mʳ Thacker
		Mʳ Cock

It was there Unanimously Agreed Upon good Consideration That Mʳ Henry Corbin and Mʳ Cuth. Potter doe Treat wᵗʰ The Vestry of Peanckatanck or wᵗʰ whome They Shall appoint for yᵉ Firme Settleing of yᵉ Bounds of our Pish, or the Uniteing of both Pʳishes into one Upon Such Termes as They Shall Think Fitt and what yᵉ Said Mʳ Corbin and Mʳ Potter Shall accord wᵗʰ Them, we Shall rattafie allow and Confirme.

It was also ordered yᵗ the Church wardens Take a list of a [ ] The Tythables and lay yᵉ Levey for yᵉ Minister for 8000ˡᵇ of Tobacco and Caske, and 17000ˡᵇ of Tobacco for yᵉ building of a Churc[ ] according to yᵉ Modall of yᵉ Middle-plantacoñ Church in all Respects, at yᵉ place agreed upon, And that yᵉ Church wardens pay to mʳ Morris 6000ˡᵇ of Tobacco, and 2000 To Mʳ Henry Corbin for Money lent him as ℔ ordʳ of yᵉ Vestry, and yᵗ Mʳ Jnᵒ Curtis who hath Undertaken yᵉ building of yᵉ Said Church be paid the 17000ˡᵇ of Tobacco and Caske.

(4)   It was Then Ordered yᵗ the Churchwardens Se and receive all Fines Due to yᵉ Pʳish according to Law, and to give an accᵗ to yᵉ Next Vestry.

It was also Ordered That Henry Pickett have Foure Hundred pounds pounds of Tobacco paid him to Cure a Scald head of a Childe now in his Keepeing of William Baldwins Decᵈ and that yᵉ next Vestry the Said Childe being Cast on the Pʳish be Bound to yᵉ Said Pickett according to Law.

Mʳ Curtis is Desired to Record these Orders.

November 19ᵗʰ 1665

Att a Vestry held for yᵉ Parish of Lancaster &c

It was Then Ordered yᵗ Mʳ John Curtis Church Warden for yᵉ lower part of yᵉ Said Pish Doe levey and receive The Leveys Due from all Tythable pʳsons wᵗʰin his pʳsincts of this pʳish, Vizᵗ wᵗʰin yᵉ Same bounds it was levyed for Mʳ Cole Minister to both pʳishes, and is according to an Ordʳ of yᵉ County Court at yᵉ request of yᵉ Pishonoʳˢ of Peanckatanck Dated yᵉ last day of 7ᵇʳ 1657 for yᵉ Finall End of all Differences, and if yᵉ Said Curtis conceives any late Seated Plantacoñ wᵗʰin our bounds, Demands The Leveys of Them, but forbeare yᵉ receiving of it.

	Henry Corbin	John Haslewood
Vestrymen	Richard Perrott	Tho Willis
	Cuth Potter	Nichᵉ Cock
	Abrā. Weekes	John Vause

(5) At a Generall Vestry for y South Side of L[   ]
[]oun[]y held at yᵉ house of Sʳ Henry Chichley January 29ᵗʰ 1666 for Christ Church Pish.

Impʳˢ We doe accord and Agree that yᵉ Two pʳishes Formerly called Lancaster and Peanckatanck from henceforth be united as one, and called Christ Church pʳish

Itm That a Mother Church be built in yᵉ Small Indian Field next yᵉ head of Capt. Brocas his ground. It being Adjudged by us to be about yᵉ Middle of yᵉ pʳish

Itm That yᵉ Mother Church be called by the Name of Christ Church

Itm That the late reputed* pʳish of Pyancketancke doe this yeare Levey to the late Reputed Bounds, Includeing the Thickett Plantacoñ and Harwoods Pattent and noe more, for the repaire of theire Church and other Contingencies.

Itm That the late pʳish of Lancaster Doe Levey to the late reputed bound [   ] for the building of Theire Chappell of Eaſe, and Theire other contingeſes The Thicket onely Excepted

Itm That the Mother Church be forthwith built by the Undertakers Capᵗ Cuth: Potter and Mʳ John Appleton and that They

---

* This word is half erased in the record.—C. G. C.

be equally joyn[ ] in yᵉ Trouble of receiveing the whole Levey with the Foure Church-Wardens, and they be hereby Impowered to receive Thirty Thousand weight of Tobacco and Caske this pʳsent yeare within yᵉ aforesaid pʳish and that present and Due payment be made Thereof to the Undertakers, alsoe that Sixteene Thousand weight of Tobacco and Caske be alſo Levied and due payment be made Thereof to Mʳ Richard Morris Parson of yᵉ Said Pish.

Itm. That the whole Levey be laid at Eighty Five pounds of Tobacco ₱ pole, and the overplus when yᵉ aforesaid Sumes are paid, if any, The Collectoʳˢ to be accomptable for yᵉ same

Itm. That Thirty Seven pounds of Tobacco and Caske ₱ pole be Levyed and Collected by the Churchwardens of yᵉ late Reputed pʳish of Lancast[ ] for building of theire Chappell of Ease

Itm. It is Unanimously Agreed That Mʳ Morris, if he please, Continue Minister of our pʳish, and have the Same Maintenance as las[ ] yeare allowed, but is opinions that he be not Inducted, and that Sʳ Gray Skipwith, Mʳ Dudley Mʳ Leach Mʳ Potter Mʳ Perrott Mʳ Curt[ ] Mʳ Weekes or any Five of them, are appointed to Treat wᵗʰ Mʳ Morri[ ] In that affaire

Itm That Mʳ Corbin be appointed and Requested to take Bond of the Undertakers for building the Mother Church, In every respect to be done and Finished according to the Middle plantacoñ Church, To be finished in Six Months, Glass and Iron worke convenient Time to be given for its Transportation out of England   Itm

(6)   Itm. It is Agreed That Majoʳ Genʳ¹¹ Robert Smith and Henry Corbin Esqʳ be requested to move to the Assembly for Continueing the Union of the Two late Parishes of Pyancktanke and Lancaster.

Sʳ Gray Skipwith

	Mʳ Robert Smith	Richard Perrott
	Patrick Miller	Cuth. Potter
Vestrymen	Edwᵈ Boswell	John Curtis
	Willᵐ Butcher	John Appleton
	Richᵈ Thacker	Wᵐ Dudley

Anthony Elliott   Geo. Wadding
Henry Thacker   Wᵐ Leach
Henry Corbin   John Needles

At a Vestry held at Christ Church yᵉ last Day of December
Anno 1666

Impʳˢ It was then Ordered that Marmaduk Hornſbee
who had ⸝Undertaken to build the Chappell in the Uper
Precints of the Said Pish be released and Discharged from
his obligacoñ, And that Mʳ Abrã. Weekes doe with the Tobacco that is already Leveyed and in his hand Indeavoʳ to
Finish the said Chappell, and for wᵗ further Charge he Shalbe
at in finishing of it, to be pᵈ at the Charge of the whole Parish

Itm̃. It is Ordered and Agreed That Mʳ Cuthbert Potter doe
Finish the Mother Church In the most Decent Manner he
Shall Think Fitt and when it is finished Some of this Vestry
be appointed to vew the Middle plantation Church and this,
and for wᵗ Charge the Said Potter hath been at more then he
was Obliged too in Compleatly Finishing the Said Work, to be
Considered by this Vestry, and Sattisfaction made him for
the Same.

Itm̃. It is ordered that Fourty Foure pounds of Tobacco ℔
pole be Raiſed and Leveyed on Each Tythable in the Said Pish
according to the Number of Tythables now in the County
List, and that all other perſons Tythable and omitted in the
County List doe pay accordingly, allowance for Caske being
made them According to Custome, And that all Families who
pay not a full hogshead be obliged to bring theire percells to
Convenient places where The Collectoʳˢ Shall appoint There to
be packed in hhᵈˢ And who Shalbe Deficient therein to pay
Double Leveys for his Contempt

Itm̃. That Mʳ George Wading and Mʳ Robert Beverley are
appointed Church Wardens this Yeare at yʳ Request of Mʳ
Morris, And they to Collect the Leveys in the lower Pcincts
of this Pish

(7) Itm̃. That Mʳ John Haslewood and Mʳ Humphrey
Jones are appointed Church Wardens this Yeare And They to

Collect yᵉ Leveys in the uper precincts All According to the late bounds of Lancaster and Pyanckatanke

Itm̃. It is Ordered and Agreed That for wᵗ arrears are Due on the last yea[ ] Levey be Collected and paid this Yeare, And where there is Action for it, They doe Distrayne for the Same

Itm̃. It is Ordered that Mʳ Christopher Wormeley Mʳ Humphrey Jones and Mʳ Robert Beverley be added to This Vestry, They takeing the Oath of Allegiance Supremacie.

Itm̃. It is Ordered that a Vestry doe meete at this Church on the 30ᵗʰ of Janʳʸ next.

Itm̃. It is Ordered and Deſired that Mʳ Cuth. Potter doe Record These Severall Orders and attest them Under his owe hand which Shalbe accompted Authenticke

	Sʳ Gray Skipwith	Majoʳ Genʳˡˡ Robᵗ Smith
	Henry Corbin Esqʳ	Mʳ Abrã. Weekes
	Mʳ Cuth. Potter	Mʳ Henry Thacker
Vestrymen	Mʳ Robᵗ Chowning	Mʳ John Vause
	Mʳ Tho. Willis	Mʳ Jnᵒ Needles
	Mʳ Jnᵒ Haslewood	Mʳ Nichᵒ Cock
	Mʳ Geo. Wading	Mʳ Patrick Miller

At a Vestry held for Christ Church Pish the 30ᵗʰ of January An. 1666.

Present

Majoʳ Genʳˡˡ Robᵗ Smith	Henry Corbin Esqʳ	
Mʳ Cuth. Potter	Mʳ Jnᵒ Curtis	
Capᵗ Ch. Wormeley	Mʳ Wᵐ Leach	
Mʳ Jnᵒ Needles	Mʳ Wᵐ Dudley	Vestrymen
Mʳ Geo: Wading	Mʳ Robᵗ Beverly	
Mʳ Hum̃: Jones	Mʳ Henry Thacker	
Mʳ Tho: Willis	Mʳ Wᵐ Butcher	

Impʳˢ Capᵗ Chr Wormeley Mʳ Humphrey Jones Mʳ Robᵗ Beverley and Mʳ Bucher did According to yᵉ Ordʳ of the last Vestry Take the Oath of Allegience Supremicie, as Also the Oath of Conformity to the Church of England, According to Ordʳ of the Goʳ and Councill Itm̃

(8) Itm. Upon the petⁿ of John Blaike a poore Decriped Man of This p^rish. It was Ordered that a 1000^{lb} of Tobacco & Cask be paid him out of This Yeares Levey Towards The Maintenance of his Wife and Family

Itm. It is Ordered that John Humphryes be paid a 1000^{lb} of Tobacco and Cask out of this Yeares levey for Officiating as Clerke.

Itm. Mr Richard Morris haveing Served this Pish as Minister according to Agreement is Ordered to have 16000^{lb} of Tobacco and Caske conveniently paid him by the Several Church Wardens, for wch They are to take his full Discharge

Itm. It is Ordered that* by this Vestry that Mr Richard Morris be Difmist from being our Minister any longer

Itm. It is Ordered that Mr Gabriell Comberland Doe Serve At This Church as Reader this Enfueing Yeare, And that he Doe Duely read Divine Service Each Sabboth Day in ye foreNoon 'till we can be provided of a Minister, for wch he is to have a 1000^{lb} of Tobacco and Caske

Itm. It is Ordered that John Humphryes Doe Serve as Reader at ye lower Chapell this Ensueing Yeare, And That he Doe Duely Reade Divine Service Each Sabboth day In the fore Noone 'till we Can be provided of a Minister for wch he is to have a 1000^{lb} of Tobacco and Caske

Itm. It is Ordered Mr Richard Hughs Doe Serve as Reader of the Uper Chappell this Ensueing Yeare, And that he doe Duely Reade Divine Service Each Sabboth Day in the Forenoon 'till we can be provided of a Minister for wch he is to have 1000^{lb} of Tobacco and Caske

Itm. This Vestry Takeing into Consideration our p^rsent want of a Minister have Ordered and Desired Majo^r Gen^{rll} Robert Smith and Henry Corbin Esqr to Write to Mr Richard Perrott now in England to procure us a Minister to come over upon Such Tearmes as they Shall Judge Convenient, or to Treat wth any other on that affaire as Occafion Shall p^rsent.

Itm. Upon the request of Mr Humphry Jones. It is Ordered

---

* This word is half erased in the record.—C. G. C.

by this Vestry That he Collect the Levyes In the Uper p^rcinques of this Pish.

Itm̃. It is ordered that a Vestry do meete at this Church on the last Day of March next

(9) At a Vestry held for Christ Church Pish the 9th Day of June 1667

Present	Majo^r Gen^{rll} Robt Smith	Henry Corbin Esqr
	Lieu^t Coll° Cuth. Potter	Mr Wm Leach
	Capt Chr Wormeley	Mr Henry Thacker
	Mr John Needles	Mr Wm Bucher
	Mr Geo. Wading	M^r Jn° Haslewood
	Mr Hum̃. Jones	Mr Nich° Cock

Vestrymen

It is Ordered that Do^r Rose be paid 5000 weight of Tobacco provided that he make a perfect Cure of Jn° Blake a poore Decriped Man of this p^rish.

Thomas Worth is Ordered to be Read^r at the Mother Church This Ensueing Yeare and Ordered to be paid a 1000 Weight of Tobacco

At a Vestry held for Christ Church the 27th Day of Octo^{br} 1667

	Majo^r Gen^{rll} Robt Smith	Mr Wm Bucher
Psent	Lt Coll° Cuth. Potter	Henry Corbin Esqr
	Mr Tho Willis	Lt John Needles
		Mr Robert Beverley

Vestrymen

It was Ordered and Desired that Mr Potter & Mr Willis Should Treat wth and Imploy Coll° John Catlitt and Mr George Morris in Surveying of Some Adjacent Lands for the finding out a Convenient Gleabe for this pish, According to the Ord^r of the hon^{rble} Govo^r and Councill, And that the Owners of any Such Lands have Notice if They please to be there & to Certify Theire proceedings Therein to ye next Vestry, And that the Said Surveyo^{rs} be paid out of this Yeares Levey

It is Ordered that ye Vestry doe meete at This Church for the laying of the Levey on the 12th of Novem^{br} next

November the 12th 1667

A full Vestry not meeting This Day According to Appointment The laying of the Levey is Deferred to the 20 Day of this Month where all are Desired to be

(10)   At a Vestry held for Christ Church Pish the 20 Day of November 1667

Psent	Majo^r Gen^{rll} Robt Smith	Henry Corbin Esqr
	Lt Coll^o Cuth: Potter	Mr John Needles
	Mr Wm Leach	Mr John Curtis
	Mr Abrā. Weekes	Mr Wm Bucher
	Mr Patrick Miller	Mr John Scarbrough

It is Ordered that Ten pounds of Tobacco ℔ pole be raised and Levyed upon Each Tythable in this p^{r}ish this Ensueing Yeare

It is Ordered that ye Sheriff doe Collect and Receive The Levey This Yeare And that he be Allowed Five ℔ Cent for his Collection and noe more, In regard he hath promised to Receive it ye next Yeare upon ye Same Sallery

It is Ordered that the said Sheriff doe pay out of this Yeares Levey one Thousand pounds of Tobacco and Cask to m^r Richd Hughs for his officiateing as Reader at the Uper Chappell In the Uper Psinq^s of this p^{r}ish This last Yeare

It is Ordered that Jno Humphryes be paid One Thousand pounds of Tobacco and Caske out of this Levey for his officiateing as Reader at ye Chappell in the Uper Psinq^s of this Pish this last Year

It is Ordered that Coll^o Jno Catlett and Mr Geo: Morris be paid Twelve hundred pounds of Tobacco in Caske for Surveying Some Adjacent Lands for the finding a convenient Gleabe for this parish According to an Ord^r of the Honourable the Govo^r and Counſell

It is Ordered that a Vestry doe meete at this Church in the Christmas holy Dayes when Mr Superias is Expected to give us a Sermon

It is Ordered that Mr Henry Thacker and Mr Nicholas Cock Doe View the Middle Plantacoñ Church and make Report to this Vestry how much it is Short of this Church In workmanship, And that allowance be made the Undertaker Accordingly.

(11)   At a Vestry held for Christ Church Pish the 15th Day of February 1667

Psent   Majo^r Gen^{rll} Robert Smith

Henry Corbin Esqr	Mr Abrã. Weekes
Coll^o Cuth Potter	Mr Robt Beverly
Capt Chr Wormeley	Mr Jno Vause
Mr Jno Needles	Mr Jno Curtis &c

Vestrymen

Thomas Spicer is Ordered to be Reader at this Christ Church This Ensueing Yeare, and Ordered to have 1000^{lb} of Tobacco and Caske

It is Ordered that the lower pish have liberty to keepe There owne Reader, or any other that they Shall Approve of

Mr Weekes Acquainting ye Vestry that Mr Morgaine being Sick, The Vestry have ordered him to furnish him wth a Barrill of Corne

At a Vestry held for Christ Church Pish The 14th of June 1668

Present

Majo^r Gen^{rll} Robert Smith

Lt Coll^o Cuth Potter	Mr Tho. Willis	
Capt Chr Wormeley	Mr Perrott	Veſtrymen
Lt John Needles	Mr Haslewood	
Mr Jno Vause	Mr Wading	

It was then Ordered that a Vestry Should meete at this Church on Wedneſday being ye 17th of this Instant to Treat And Conclude wth Mr Shepherd to Serve the Pish as Minister for this Enſueing Yeare, The whole Vestry or Soe many as Shall then meete.

(12)   At a Vestry held for Christ Church Pish This 17th Day of June 1668

Present   Major Genrll Robt Smith   Mr Wm Bucher
               Lt Collo Cuth. Potter   Mr Wading
               Capt Chr Wormeley   Mr Jno Curtis
               Lt Jno Needles
                         Vestrymen

Upon a Treaty wth Mr Shephard It was Agreed he Should
Serve This Pish 'till the Middle of December next, And to
have halfe a Yeares Allowance, According to the Act of Aſsembly, To Serve the whole Parrish.

At a Vestry held for Christ Church Pish This 16th of Sep-
tembr 1668

Present   Major Genrll Robert Smith
               And 15 more Vestry Men &c.

Itm. It is Agreed upon That ye Petition Should be Delivered
by the Conſent of the Pish to the Grand Aſsembly for the Rattification of ye former Act Made for the County of Lancaster
to be Divided into Two Countys.

At a Vestry for Chrst Church Pish This 16th of November
1688

Present   Sr Gray Skipwith   Mr Geo: Wading
               Major Genrll R. Smith   Mr Jno Curtis
               Henry Corbin Esqr   Mr Tho: Willis
               Mr Jno Haslewood   Mr Tho. Chowning
               Mr Willm Leach   Mr Wm Bucher
               Mr Jno Needles
                         Vestrymen

It is Ordered by the Vestry That all perquisets or Mariages
That Mr Hughs have done Since Mr Shepherd hath been
here That Mr Hughs make Sattisfaction to Mr Shepherd for
it or thoſe that it is Due from

It is Ordered that Mr Shepherd be allowed 6 Tythables to the
prortion of the Pish Levey this Yeare &c.   It

(13)   It is further Ordered That Mr Shepherd have the use
of the Horse as long as he Stayes wth us. And that 2000lb of
Tobacco be Levyed to pay for him.

It is Ordered that Mr Perrott be paid 5610lb of Tobacco upon
his accompt.

It is Ordered that M͏ʳ Morrey be paid 1000ˡᵇ of Tobacco by the Governͬˢ Order

It is Ordered that yᵉ Three Clerks be paid 3000ˡᵇ of Tobacco, Equall proportion

It is Ordered that 46ˡᵇ of Tobacco ℔ pole be raised and Levyed On Each Tythable in this Pish this Psent Yeare for Defraying The Pish Charge And that the Sher. Doe Collect, and make paymͭ Accordingly, Sallery and Caske being Included.

At a Vestry held for Christ Church Pish this first Of December 1668

Psent Majoͬ Genͬˡˡ Robert Smith &c.

It is Ordered by this Vestry That M͏ʳ Shepherd Doe Continue our Minister this Enſueing Yeare (if he pleaſe) And to have Allowed him 16000ˡᵇ of Tobacco and Caske wᵗʰ all perqᵗˢ And yͭ to be in full of all Demands for that Yeare from yᵉ Pish, And to begin the 10ᵗʰ of this Pͬsent Decemᵇʳ

It is Ordered that yᵉ Vestry doe Meete the 28ᵗʰ of December 1668 At This Church

At a Vestry held for Christ Church Pish this 28ᵗʰ of December 1668

Present Majoͬ Genͬˡˡ Robert Smith &c

It is Ordered and Agreed upon by this Vestry That M͏ʳ Shepherd be paid 1300ˡᵇ of Tobaccoe the next Yeare, The Tobacco to be levyed upon all yᵉ Vestry Each proportion, and noe other

It is Ordered that yᵉ Vestry doe meete at This Church &c

It

(14)   It is Ordered that M͏ʳ Dudley and M͏ʳ Miller be Church Wardens for Pyanckatanck

It is Ordered that M͏ʳ Willis and M͏ʳ Reeves be Church Wardens for the Great Church

It is Ordered that M͏ʳ Chowning and M͏ʳ Cock be Church Wardens for yᵉ Upper Chapˡˡ

It is Ordered yͭ the Vestry Doe meete at this Church the first of March

At a Vestry held for Christ Church the 11ᵗʰ of May 1669

Present Majoͬ Generˡˡ Robert Smith &c

It is Ordered that ye hon^{rble} Majo^r Gener^{ll} Doe Send this
pre∫ent Yeare for Ornaments for this great Church, as he
and Mr Shepherd sees Fitt &c

At a Vestry held for Christ Church Pish 21th of No^{br} 1670

Present	Sr Henry Chichley	Majo^r Gen^{rll} Robt Smith
	Capt Chr. Wormeley	Do^r Walter Whittaker
	Mr Robt Beverly	Mr Hum̃. Jones
Vestrymen	Mr Henry Thacker	Mr Jno Scarbrough
	Mr Wm Dudley	Mr Wm Gordin
	Mr Jno Needles	Mr Tho Warwick
	Coll^o Cuth. Potter	

It is Ordered by this p^rsent Vestry that all Such p^rsons As
have not paid one hundred pounds of Tobacco to the Collecto^{rs}
for Mr Shepherd According to the Ord^r of Vestry wch beareth
Date from the first of December 1668.— That all Such as
have Denied paym^t to pay forthwth the Said one hundred
pounds of Tobacco to Mr Robt Beverley If Denyed, he is hereby Impowered for to Distrayne

It is Ordered that ye Vestry Do Meete the Day after the next
Court In Dec^{br} next En∫ueing

It is Agreed upon by this p^rsent Vestry for the Future That
if but Foure or Five of the Vestry doe Meete, That They Shall
doe all Such Bu∫ines as belongs to the Pish without Staying
for any other.

(15) At a Vestry held for Christ Church Pish ye 3th of May
1670

Present	Majo^r Gen^{rll} Robt Smith	Mr Hum̃. Jones
	Henry Corbin Esqr	Mr Jno Needles
	Mr Jno Haslewood	Mr Abrã Weekes
	Mr Richd Perrott	Mr John Vause
	Mr Walter Whittaker	Mr Robt Chowning
	Capt Chr. Wormeley	Mr Jno Scarbrough
	Mr Henry Thacker	

Vestrymen

This Vestry Mr Richard Robinson was chosen to be one of
ye Vestry And Sworne

It is Ordered that John Smith Doe Continue Reader at the uper Chap[ll]

It is Ordered that M[r] Shepherd Doe Continue Our Minister This Enſueing Yeare if he please, And to be paid as form[rly] Sixteene Thouſand pounds of Tobacco, for officiateing in the parish one whole Yeare from y[e] time his last Yeare was out, And to be paid all p[rq][ts] formerly Due, and for y[e] Time to Come, And to be Esteemed Minister as to all Dues, As if he were Inducted.

It is Ordered That M[r] Thomas Warwick be Church Warden for y[e] Uper Chap[ll] and to goe forthw[th] before Coll[o] Corbin And be Sworne

It is Ordered that M[r] William Gorden be Church Warden for The great Church, And to goe before S[r] Henry Chichley to be Sworn [ ]

It is Ordered that M[r] William Dudley be Church Warden For y[e] lower Chap[ll] and to goe w[th]in Ten dayes before Majo[r] Gen[rll] Smith There to be Sworne

This Day the Vestry have Desired S[r] Henry Chichley to be one of the Vestry

(16)   At a Vestry held for Christ Church Pish November 7[th] 1671

Present	Majo[r] Gen[rll] Rob[t] Smith	S[r] Henry Chichley
	L[t] Coll[o] Cuth. Potter	Henry Corbin Esq[r]
	Cap[t] Chr Wormeley	M[r] Rich[d] Perrott
	M[r] John Haslewood	M[r] Huṁ. Jones
	M[r] Abrā. Weekes	M[r] W[m] Gordon
	M[r] Rich[d] Robinson	M[r] Tho. Warwick
18 Vestrymen	M[r] W[m] Dudley	M[r] Jn[o] Scarbrough
	M[r] John Vause	Do[r] Whittaker
	M[r] Henry Thacker	M[r] Rob[t] Beverly

It is Ordered that M[r] Jn[o] Vause be Church Warden for The Great Church in y[e] room of M[r] W[m] Gordon

It is Ordered that M[r] Nich[o] Cock be Church warden In the Roome of M[r] Thomas Warwick, And also that M[r] William Dudley Continue Church Warden at Pyanckatanke this Ensueing yeare.

It is Ordered that Mr Jno Vause goe before Sr Henry Chichley to be Sworne

It is Ordered that Mr Nich^o Cock goe before Coll^o Corbin There to be Sworne

This Vestry findeing y^t many Servants for ye Time past haveing been Accused of Fornication, have Immediately after theire Freedome Absented themselves out of ye County and thereby Escaped There Due punishment or Fine Imposed by Law for Such offence Have therefore thought fitt to Order, and doe Accordingly ord^r That from hence forward all & every Master and M^{rs} or M^r or Mistre∫ses that either now have in theire Service, or for the time to come Shall happen to have any Man Servant already reputed, or shall herafter be reputed to be the Father of a Bastard Childe, Every Such Master & Mistre∫s Shall be, and are hereby Injoyned to Carry before Some one or more of the Magestrates of this p^{r}ish, every Such Servt Soe Reputed as aforesaid, before he Shall discharge the Said Servt of his Services,or Shall pay him his Freedome Corne or Cloaths, upon the penalty of paying the Pish Five hundred pounds of Tobacco & Caske unles the Servt So brought before the Majestrate or Majestrates be by him or them Acquitted from the Accusation of Such Crime

(17) It is Ordered that George Axe be Reader of Pyanckatancke Church This En∫ueing Yeare to Reade Divine Service every Sabbath Day, and to keepe ye Church Dcent and Cleane And to be paid for his officiateing one Thousand pounds of Tobacco & Caske

It is Ordered that John Smith doe continue Reader at the Uper Chap^{ll} and to be paid as formerly.

It is Ordered that John Wortham doe Continue Reader at The Great Church This En∫ueing Yeare And be paid as formerly

It is Ordered that noe Tobacco be paid unto Mr Beverly for The use of Do^r Rose Untill John Blaikes Leggs be perfectly Cured

It is Ordered that Mr Shepherd be paid 16,000^{lb} of Tobacco & Cask

It is Ordered that Mr Dudley be paid 10,000^{lb} of Tobacco & Cask

To John Smith 1000. To David Barwick 1000. To Jno Wortham 1000^{lb} of Tobacco and Caske

It is Ordered that Mr Shepherd be paid 16000^{lb} of Tobacco & Caske yearly for Soe long as he Shall Continue our Minister for the Future.

It is Ordered that Mr Shepherd Doe Agree wth a Carpen^{tr} for to Repaire the Dwelling houſeing to make them convenient to live in At ye plantation that formerly was Mr Allex^{r} Smiths

It is Ordered That John Wortham be paid 396^{lb} of Tobacco and Caske for Attendance At ye Vestry and Washing the Church Lynen

It is Ordered y^{t} Robert Thompson be paid 500^{lb} of Tob^{o} & Caske

It is Ordered y^{t} Capt Robert Beverly be paid 690^{lb} of Tobacco for Surveying ye Gleab & Writeing ye Deede

It is Ordered y^{t} Mr Richard Robinson be paid 10000^{lb} of Tobacco

(18) At a Vestry held for ye Pish of Christ Church 5th of 9^{br} 1672

Psent	Sr Henry Chichley k^{t}	Coll^{o} Chr: Wormeley
	Henry Corbin Esqr	Capt Robt Beverley
	Mr Richd Perrott	Mr Richd Robinson
	Coll^{o} Cuth. Potter	Mr Jno Vause

It is Ordered that Majo^{r} John Burnham and Capt Ralph Wormeley be Added to ye Vestry and Sworne Accordingly

Sr Henry Chichley doth promiſe to Secure a convenient parcell of Land to ye great Church (Viz^{t}) That wch is the Church yard and y^{t} whereon ye Stable Standeth

It is Ordered That Mr Shepherd doe Agree wth a Carpenter And other Workmen, to fitt and finish his Dwelling house at the Parish Charge And to build a Quarter for his Servants, & not to put ye Parish to any more Charge for Carpen^{trs} worke for ye Future

These may Certifie that it was ye Govo^{rs} oppinion, And Accordingly ye Vestrys order y^{t} Mr Shepherd was to be paid

It is ordered ... [illegible] ... hundred pounds
of Tobacco for or by reason of a Bastard Child ... the ... Thomas
being ... to the next Court

It is ordered yt Thomas Sherlding and Jno Sutton serv.ts to Majr [illegible]
Smith be fined Each of 500l of Tobacco for or by reason of [illegible]
... a Bastard Childe, And yt Sherly and yt Mothers of yt [illegible]
Children be brought to ye next Court held for Midd: County by [illegible]

It is ordered that Coll.o Potter be paid wt Money is due to him [illegible]
... Coll. Robert Smith ——— This ord.r Revoked this day ———

This day did Majr John Burnham and Coll.o Ralph Wormeley take
the oath of Conformity to ye Church of England ———

It is Ordered that Coll.o Potter be paid fowre thousand pounds of
Tobacco and Cask, and five pounds sterling Money out of what is
due to ye parish from Majr Genl Smith for Ornaments for ye
Church and for ye ffont ———

Christ Church Parish Charges ———

	lb Tobo
To mr John Shephard Minister ———	16000
To John Wortham Clerk ———	1400
To John Smith Clerk ———	1000
To George Ayer Clerk ———	1000
To mr William Dudley for Compleating ye Charges ———	10000
To Andrew Williamson for worke done ———	150
To Wine for ye Communion ———	65
To 4 Hooks and 5 Henges ———	100
To Timber and Nailes ———	60
To Nursing a Bastard Childe, ye reputed father being named Thomas Sherlding	200
To John Macknorett for ffencing ye Church yard ———	400
To mr Shepard for worke done by ye Gleab house ———	490
To Robert Thompson a poore Man ———	500
To David ... for 2 parish Children, to Tax one from ... Whittakers, ye other from Coll.o Wormleys	400
To mr Wm Dudley for Comm. Wine ———	200
To other Charges omitted wth Cask and Sallery ———	36960
	3570
Totall	46530

for Burialls in y⁰ Church and Chancell, preaching Funerall Sermons, and other p'quisites Customarily paid y⁰ Minister As if he were Inducted, And yᵗ he was to have for breaking up y⁰ Ground there, Fourty Shillings, for a Majistrate or his Wife, and 20ˢ Shillings for a Child belonging to Them. And Thre pound for all other p'sons, This was y⁰ Govern'ˢ oppinion to y⁰ best of Collᵒ Corbins Remembrance   Therefore it is ordered by y⁰ Vestry abovenamed yᵗ Mʳ Shepherd have all perquisits justly due from mʳ Geo: Reeves or any other p'son, wᵗſoever According to y⁰ Go'ˢ opinion.

It is ordered yᵗ mʳ Robert Beverly doe Detaine in his hand Five hundred pounds Tobacco of George Andertons for or by reaſon of a Bastard Childe

Ordered that Collᵒ Cuth. Potter doe Detaine in his Custody Five hundred pounds of Tobᵒ of Richard Shippeys, for or by reason of a Bastard Childe

Ordered that Edward Michaell be Fined 500ˡᵇ of Tobᵒ for or by reason of a Bastard Childe.

(19)   It is ordered that Jane Watts be Fined Five hundred pounds of Tobacco for or by reason of a Baſtard Childe, And that y⁰ Sherriff bring her to y⁰ next Court

It is ordered yᵗ Thomas Scheilding and Jnᵒ Sutton serv'ˢ to Majoʳ Gen'¹¹ Smith be fined Each of them 500ˡᵇ of Tobacco, for or by reason of either of them a Bastard Childe, And yᵗ They and y⁰ Mothers of Theire Children be brought to y⁰ next Court held for Midx County by y⁰ Sherif

It is ordered that Collᵒ Potter be paid wᵗ Money is due to the Pish from Majoʳ Gen'¹¹ Robert Smith. This ordʳ Revoked this Day.

This Day did Majoʳ John Burnham and Collᵒ Ralph Wormeley take the oath of Conformity according to y⁰ Church of England

It is Ordered that Collᵒ Potter be paid Foure Thousand pounds of Tobacco and Cask, and Five pounds Sterling Money out of what is Due to y⁰ parish from Majoʳ Gen'¹¹ Smith for Ornaments for y⁰ Church and for a Funt

Christ Church Parish Charge

	lb Tob°
To M[r] John Shepherd Minister	16000
To John Wortham Clerk	1400
To John Smith Clerk	1000
To George Axe Clerk	1000
To m[r] William Dudley for Compleating y[e] Chappell	10000
To Andrew Williamson for work done	150
To Wine for y[e] Comunion	65
To 4 Hooks and 5 Henges	100
To Timber and Nailes	60
To Nursing a Bastard Childe, y[e] reputed father Is named Thomas Sheilding	200
To John Macknerett for Cleaning y[e] Church Yard	400
To m[r] Shepard for work done to y[e] Gleab house	490
To Robert Thompson a poore Man	500
To David Barrick for 2 p[r]ish Children, to Say one from Do[r] Whittakers, y[e] other from Coll[o] Wormleys	400
To m[r] W[m] Dudley for Com. Wine	200

[*]	36960
To other Charges omitted, w[th] Cask and Sallery	9576

	Totall	46536

```
(2
3(8
95(5
46936    81½   Pish Levey
5711    61½   Publique & County
57       ----
        143    p[r] pole
```

(20) At a Vestry held for Christ Church Pish 25th of No[br] 1673

---

* A remarkable piece of addition.—C. G. C.

Present	Henry Corbin Esqr	M^r Jn° Vause
	Lt Coll° Chr Wormley	M R Robinson
	Capt Robt Beverley	Mr Hum. Jones
	m^r Richd Perrott	Mr Wm Dudly
Vestrymen	m^r Abrā. Weekes	Mr Nich° Cock
	m^r Henry Thacker	M^r Jn° Needles

It is ordered by this p^rsent Vestry that Mr John Shepherd be paid 16000^{lb} of Tobacco and Cask by ye Sheriff wthout Any Discount.

It is ordered that m^r John Shepherd be paid 5030^{lb} of Tob° According to his Accompt for building and repaireing the Severall hou∫es at ye Gleab, And is hereby obliged to leave The Dwelling hou∫e and Quarter in as good repaire at his Departure from ye Gleab as now when finished

It is ordered that m^r Richard Robinson be paid 8655^{lb} of Tobacco According to his Accompt ℔ Covering ye Church wth Shingles, and mending ye payles about ye Church Yard, and other Charges

It is ordered that m^r Nich° Cock be paid 3200^{lb} of Tobacco for Shingling ye Uper Chappell, and payling in ye Yard, and for Nailes towards ye Worke.

It is ordered that m^r William Dudley be paid 400^{lb} of Tob° for payling in ye Church Yard and makeing ye Horse Block

Ordered that Majo^r Gen^{rll} Robt Smith be paid 1200^{lb} of Tob° for keeping a Bastard Childe

Ordered that old Thompson be paid 500^{lb} of Tobacco.

Ordered that Jn° Macknerent be paid 290^{lb} of Tobacco for Cleaning ye Church Yard.

It is Ordered That Jn° Wortham be paid 1400^{lb} of Tobacco

Ordered that Geo. Axe be paid 1000^{lb} Tobacco

Ordered y^t John Williams be paid 1000^{lb} Tobacco

(21) 1674-5 It is ordered that Fifty Five pounds of Tobacco ℔ pole be Levyed for quitting the parish Charge this p^rsent Yeare

It is ordered That m^r John Shepherd be paid Sixteen Thousand pounds of Tobacco and Caske for his being Minister to this pish This Yeare

It is ordered that m^r Robert Beverly be Collecter of the Pish Leveys, And be Allowed Five in ye hundred for ye Collection

It is ordered that Henry Corbin Esqr be paid Three hundred Fourty and foure pounds of Tobacco & Cask for 1^{lb} 14^s 4^d Disbursted for Glass————It is ordered that Jno Wortham be paid Five hundred pounds of Tobacco and Caske for being reader this halfe Yeare And that he Continue Reader at ye Great Church this Enſueing Yeare, And he is hereby ordered to read pryers Every Sunday when there is noe Sermon, And take care to keepe The Church in all Decency and hand-ſomeneſs.

It is ordered that Francis Bridge be paid one Thousand pounds of Tobacco and Caske for being reader at ye uper Chappell, And that he continue Reader There this Enſuing Yeare

It is ordered that Mr Miller be pd Fourty five pounds of To-bacco for Soe much disburſted for Comunion Wine

It is ordered that Mr Jno Lindſey be Reader at ye Uper Chappell

1675 It is Ordered by this p^rsent Vestry That all Masters of Families that have p^rmitted, or Shall p^rmitt theire Serv^{ts} To be Married To pay the Minister and Clerks theire Due And that ye Collecto^{rs} Collects it and to Distraine if denyed And Likewise for all p^rquisits w^tsoever Due

It is ordered that Mr Shepherd have a Preſentation to The Right honer^{ble} the Govo^r That he may Thereby obtaine his In-duction, that he be paid for ye Future According To Law, This by the Majo^r part of ye Vestry.

It is ordered that Mr Henry Thacker & Mr John Vause Shall goe and View the late plantation of Mr Allex. Smythe wth The houſing belonging thereto, And also to Treat wth Mr Robinson About ye price of it, And give Report of it to ye next Vestry

It

(22)   It is ordered that John Wortham be omitted payin his owne particular Levey as long as he continues Reader at ye Great Church

Ordered that Jn° Smith Continue reader at yᵉ Uper Chappell this Enſueing Yeare, And to keepe it Decently and handſomely To be paid one Thousand pounds of Tobacco

It is ordered the Sheriff Demand and Receive of Mʳ James Blackmore Five hundred pounds of Tobacco for Fines Due to yᵉ parish, he becoming Security for Gregory Gibbs

It is ord'd that Mʳ William Dudley be paid next Yeare Five hundred pounds of Tobacco and Caske

It is ordered that Mʳ James Blackmore pay unto Mʳ William Dudley 1200ˡᵇ of Tobacco, wᶜʰ is in his Custody

Middleſex County Dʳ Parish Levey

To Mʳ John Sheppherd	16000
To his Gleabe putting in good repaire	5030
To Mʳ Richard Robinson Ch. Warden as ℈ his Accoᵗ	6655
To yᵉ Thre Clerkes	3400
To old Mackneret	200
To Mʳ Nichᵒ Cock as ℈ his Accompᵗ	3700
To old Thompson	500
To Mʳ Dudley Ch. Warden	400
To a parish Childe at Slopers	1200
To Mʳ Shepherds Tythables	960
	38045
Cask at 10 ℈ cent	3804
	41849
Sallery at 5 ℈ Cent	2093
	43942
Credᵗ as ℈ other Side	1400
Totall	42542

(23)   1676 It is ordered by this pʳsent Veſtry That Mʳ John Shepherd be paid 16000ˡᵇ of Tobacco & Caske   16000

It is ordered that Mr George Axe be paid one Thousand
    pounds of Tobacco & Caske   1000

It is ordered that George Williams be p^d one Thouſand
    pounds of Tobacco and Caske   1000

It is ordered that John Wortham be p^d Fourteen hundred
    pounds of Tobacco and Caske   1400

It is ordered that Henry Corbin Esqr be p^d 190^{lb} of
    Tobacco and Cask for 15^s Short laid in ye County
    Levey   190

It is ordered that Robert Thompson a reall poore old
    Man be p^d 1000

It is ordered that John Mackernet be paid   400

It is ordered that Mr Jno Shepherd be p^d ℔ a Tythable   100

It is ordered that Mr Shepherd be p^d for Roleing Tobacco
    to Convenient Landing   170

It is ordered that Sr Henry Chichley be p^d Two Thous^d
    pounds of Tobacco & Caske for New Shingling y^e
    Church And payling and posting ye Church Yard   2000

It is ordered that Sr Henry Chichley be p^d for Nailes
    for ye Church and Church Yard   125

                                lb :   23385

It is ordered that Mr George Axe be reader at ye Uper Chappell

It is ordered that Capt Ralph Wormeley be Ch. Warden in
the Roome of Sr Henry Chichley

And Capt Whittaker and Esqr Corbin in ye roome of M^r
Dudley and m^r Cock

M^o Some of the Former Vestrys were Defaced in the old
Booke and Some were wanting, But from hence forward all
are perfect &c.

(24) At a Vestry held at Christ Church 8th Day of May 1677

Psent	Mr Jno Shepherd Clerk	
	Sr Henry Chichley	Mr Richd Perrott S^r
	Capt Ralph Wormely	Capt Walter Whitaker
	Coll^o Chr. Wormly	Mr Richd Perrott Junr
Vestrymen	Majo^r Robt Beverly	Majo^r John Burnham

Mr Richd Robinſon   Mr Abrā. Weekes
Mr John Vauſe   Mr Humphrey Jones
Mr John Needles   Mr Francis Bridge

It is ordered that mr George Axe be reader & Clerk for Christ Church

It is ordered that mr John Coggin be Reader for ye lower Chappell

It is ordered that Mr Richard Perrott Junr be Ch. Warden in ye place of Collo Christopr Wormeley, And Mr Francis Bridge in the Roome of Capt Ralph Wormeley, And Lt Collo Jno Burnham In ye Roome of Mr Richard Perrott Senr

It is ordered that Mr John Sheppard Clerk, be pd his full Dues in Tobacco as formerly, for ye Yeare 1676, And that altho he was Compelled Sometime to leave ye Pish by meanes and Armed Force of Ill Disposed prsons Then in Rebellion, That he be paid his full Dues as formerly for this prsent yeare At ye Expiration Thereof.

Mr Humphrey Jones out his pious Zeale and love to ye Church Hath beſtowed a Silver Bowle of about 14 ounces Weight, and a Pewter Flagon, and a pewter plate, for Comunion plate Engraven According to this Marke X for the uſe of Christ Church Uper Chappell

It is ordered by this prsent Vestry that wt Just Dues, or other Lawfull prquisits are left Unpayed to Mr Sheppard for the yeare 1675 that ye Ch. wardens take Effectuall care to ſee the Same forthwth pd him.

(25) At a Vestry held ye 20th of Novembr 1677 At ye Houſe of Mr Richard Robinson for Christ Church Pish

Psent   Mr John Sheppard, Clerk
                 Sr Henry Chichley Kt   Capt Walter Whittaker
                 Major Gen¹¹ Robt. Smith Mr Richd Perrott Senr
Vestrymen Collo Chr Wormeley   Mr Richd Perrot Junr
                 Lt Collo Jno Burnham   Mr Abrā. Weekes
                 Capt Ralph Wormeley   Mr Fra. Bridge
                 Mr Richard Robinson   Mr Jno Needles
                 Mr John Vause

lb. Tob°

It is ordered that Mr John Sheppard be paid for this
    Yeare And the last Yeare as formerly   32000
It is ordered that George Axe be p^d for This Yeare and
    ye last as formerly   2000
It is ordered that George Williams be p^d for this Yeare
    and the last Yeare as Formerly   2000
It is ordered that Mr John Cocking be p^d for
    Serving the Great Church this p^rsent Yeare   1400
It is ordered that Capt Ralph Wormeley be p^d for keeping
    of Strastows Bastard Childe Ten Monthes   1000
It is ordered that M^r Frā. Bridge be p^d for Disburſtm^{ts}
    upon a Bastard Childe   75
It is ordered that John Blake be p^d for Cleaning Christ
    Church and Church Yard   200
It is ordered that Wm Perry be p^d for Entertaineing a
    poore Stranger   100
Ordered that John Blake be p^d for Keeping of a Baſtard
    Childe of a Servant Maydes liveing with Cap. Ra.
    Wormely   500
Ordered that Mr Richard Perrott Junr be p^d for y^e
    Chest At ye Lower Chappell   300
Ordered that Lt Coll^o Burnham be p^d for ye Chest y^t
    he hath provided for ye Uper Chappell   160

                                     lb   39735

It is ordered that 31½ pounds of   Cask 10 ℔ Ct   3973
Tobacco be Defrayed for paying of   Sall 5 ℔ Ct   2185
the Pish Charge this Psent yeare

                                     lb   45893

Ordered that Majo^r Robt Beverly be p^d ye next yeare 497^{1b}
Tobacco & Caske for Dischargeing & paying Pish Levys be-
longing to m^r John Shepard Clerk this yeare

    (26) (Blank)

    (27) At a Vestry held at Christ Church the 22th of Octo^{br}
1678

Psent   Mr John Sheppard Minister
Sr Henry Chichley K^t   Mr Richd Robinson
Coll^o Chr. Wormeley   Mr John Vauſe
Capt Walter Whittaker Mr Hum̃. Jones   Veſtrymen
Mr Richd Perrott Junr   Mr John Needles

It is ordered by this p^rsent Vestry that all ye Gentlemen of the
Vestry doe meete (by publique Notice given) upon the 5th
Day of November next here at Christ Church, And y^t all
Gen^tmen of of ye Vestry that Shall be Absent wthout Lawfull
Excuse, Shalbe Fined Two hundred pounds of Tobacco, And
So to be Fined for the future for all Such Neglects.

(28)   At a Vestry held at Christ Church the 5th of Novem^{br}
1678

Psent   Mr Jno Shepard Minister
Majo^r Gen^{rll} Robert Smith   Mr Richd Perrott, Senr
Coll^o Chr. Wormeley   Mr Abrã. Weekes
Capt Walter Whittaker   Mr Richd Robinson
Majo^r John Burnham   Mr Jno Vause
Majo^r Robert Beverley   Mr Richd Perrott Junr
Lt Jno Needles   Mr Hum̃ Jones

It is Ordered by this p^rsent Vestry y^t the pious gift of Ralph
Wormely Esqr of a large Silver Flaggon for Com̃union plate
Subscribed (Christ Church in ye County of Middlesex) be
Recorded, And that it Shall Remaine for the Use of the Said
Church for Ever
It is ordered by this p^rsent Vestry that ye Severall Ch. wardens
for the Two yeares Last past make Strict Inquirey w^t Fines
are Due in theire Severall precincts, for Basterdy, And that
they give an Accompt of the Same The next Court held for this
County
It is ordered y^t Mr John Sheppard be paid for this yeare
         Sixteen Thouſand pounds of Tob^o and Caske   16000
It is ordered that Mr Geo: Axe Cl of the Lower Chap^{ll}
         be paid for his Service this Yeare   1000
It is ordered that John Coging Shalbe p^d for his
         Service In officiating as Cl. at Christ Church   700

It is ordered y^t Joseph Harvie Shalbe p^d for halfe
    a yeares officiateing as Cl. at Christ Church   700
It is ordered y^t John Collins Shalbe p^d for officiateing
    As Cl. of ye uper Chappell a whole yeare   1000
It is ordered by this p^rsent Vestry that John Blake be
    paid for Cleaneing ye Great Church yard as Sex-
    ton This p^rsent yeare   400
    It is ordered by this p^rsent Vestry y^t Coll^o Chr Wormeley
Majo^r Robt Beverley Mr Nich^o Cock & Mr John Stamper or
any Thre of them, be Requested to View ye worke done on
the Lower Chappell by Mr Richard Perrott Junr order that
they will give Theire Report according to the best of theire
Judgments of the Same, ye next Court held for this County
and y^t they meete for ye Same at ye houſe of Mr Robert Beverley ye 9th of this Instant November

                                                            It

    (29)   It is ordered that David Barwick be paid for
Accomedation of Dyeting of ye Two Carpenters for 5
Monthes Time, which were at Worke in ye Repaireing
of the Uper Chappell   1000
    It is ordered that 17250^lb of Tobacco & Caske be Col-
lected for ye Reimbursting Mr Richard Perrott Junr
for worke done to the Lower Chappell, And to remaine
in ye Collecto^rs hands 'till ye Report of what Vallew y^e
worke done is) be given by the gentlemen appointed by
ye Same and ye Judgm^t of ye Vestry paſs Thereon   17250
    It is ordered that Mr William Poole Chirurg^a to be
paid for his Attendance and paines Taken about ye Cure
of Robt Main[11]   2000
    It is ordered that Majo^r Robert Beverley be p^d for
Nailes and Timber for ye Lower Chap[11] as ℔ his accompt   2597
    It is ordered that Mr Robert Price be paid for keeping
a Bastard Child Two Monthes, at ye rate of 1000 a yeare   167
    It is ordered by this p^rsent Vestry That Capt Walter
Whittaker be Church Warden for ye Lower Pcincts this
p^rsent yeare, And y^t Mr John Vause be Ch : Warden for

yᵉ Middle Pcincts, And yᵗ mʳ Abraham Weekes be Ch.
Warden for the Uper Pcincts, this Psent Yeare

It is ordered yᵗ mʳ John Sheppard be pᵈ for Roleing
of Inconvenient Tobacco   250

It is ordered that Jnᵒ Blake be pᵈ for keeping a Bastard
Childe a Twelve moneth   1200

It is ordered by this pʳsent Vestry That whereas there
was an orderer Entred at a Vestry held 25ᵗʰ of Noᵇʳ
1673 That mʳ Jnᵒ Sheppard Minister Should leave yᵉ
Gleabe houſes in as good Repaire as when Finished, its
to be Understood of yᵉ 25 foot Dwelling houſe, Cloſset
& Shed, and a Quarter Repaired, The Cauſualtys of
Violent Gusts and Fire Excepted. And for wᵗ other
houſes he builds at his one proper Charge, he nor the
next Incumbent Shalbe obliged to keepe Repaired

It is ordered yᵗ mʳ Jnᵒ Sheppard be paid for plaiſtering of his Dwelling house build by yᵉ Pish   600

It is ordered yᵗ Joseph Harvie be Clerke, and to officiate at the grᵗ Church & Chappells, and to keepe them
Cleane, and to have for his Sallery Two Thousand
pounds of Tobᵒ & Caske

It is ordered that Jnᵒ Blake be paid for Looking after
and keeping Cleane yᵉ Lower Chappell   200

                                        Turn over

(30) It is ordered yᵗ mʳ Jnᵒ Sheppard pay no Pish
Levey for his 5 Servants at yᵉ Glebe. They being Dis-
counted in yᵉ last Levey

Christ Church Parrish, Middlesex County, Dr. Nobʳ 5ᵗʰ 1678

To Mʳ John Sheppard   16000
To George Axe   1000
To John Cogin   700
To Joseph Harvie   700
To Jnᵒ Collins   1000
To John Blake   400
To David Barwick   1000
To Mʳ Richard Perrott Junʳ To remaine in yᵉ Collectoʳˢ
    hands untill further order of yᵉ Veſtry   17250

To Mr William Poole, Aſsigned to Majo^r Robt Beverley 2000
To Majo^r Robert Beverley 2597
To Mr Robert Price 167
To Mr John Sheppard 250
To John Blake 1200
To Mr John Sheppard 600
To John Blake 200
                                              45064
          Caske at 10 ꝑ Cent   4506
                                              49570
          Sallery at 5 ꝑ Cent   2479
                                              52049

52049   The Number of Tythables, M^r Jn°
 111   Shepards 5 Serv^ts Excep^td from pay-
───   ing any part of ye parish Tythes, is
52160   652

     4
     52100(80^lb   The Levey ꝑ pole is Eighty
     0522   The overplus will be (111)
     05

(31)   At a Vestry held at Christ Church the 5th of Novem^br
1679
     Psent
     Sr Henry Chichley Kt Govern^r   Mr Humphrey Jones
     Majo^r Gen^rll Robert Smyth   Coll. X Wormeley
     Ralph Wormeley Esqr   Mr Richd Robinson
     Majo^r John Burnham   Mr John Vause

It is ordered by this p^rsent Vestry that Mr Christoph^r Robinson and Mr Matthew Kemp be added to this Vestry and Accordingly to be Sworne at the next Vestry held at this Church
It is ordered that Mr Richard Robinson be Ch. Warden for this
Middle precincts, Mr Humphrey Jones for ye Upper Pcinque,
and Mr John Man for ye Lower Pcinque

It is ordered that Mr John Vause Late Ch. Warden
of this Pcincqe be p^d Nineteene hundred and Ninety
pounds of Tobacco and Caske   1990

It is ordered by this Psent Vestry that m^r John Sheppard be p^d Sixteen Thousand pounds of Tobacco and Caske   16000

It is ordered by this p^rsent Vestry that Joseph Harvie be paid Two Thousand pounds of Tobacco and Caske for This last yeares Sallery   2000

It is ordered by this p^rsent Vestry that Mr Joseph Harvie Continue Clerk the Enſueing yeare.

Mem^{dm} That Mr John Sheppard did demand his Sallery of 16000^{lb} of Tobacco and Caske, And the Vestrys opinion was that he was not to be paid 'till ye Publique Levey was Collected. Against wch he objected, that ye Ch. Wardens ought to Collect it, or himſelfe would, the uſuall Sallery being Allowed.

It is ordered that John Blalke be paid for keeping a Bastard Child Evleven Moneths, and is to keepe the Same until next Court for   1000

It is ordered that Rebecca Goodridge be p^d for keeping a B : Childe   860

It is ordered that Andrew Roſs for cleaneing ye Church Yard and bilding a Horse block be paid   100

It is ordered that Daniell Long be Allowed   400

		lb	22350
There was 3 Tythables	Cash at 10 ₱ Cent		2235
of Mr Sheppards Deducted	Sallery at 5 ₱ Ct		1129
Rest 607 Tythables &c			
	Totall		25814

(32)   At a Vestry held at Christ Church the 15th of Decem^{br} 1679

	Majo^r Gen^{rll} Robert Smith	Mr John Vause
	Capt. Ralph Wormeley Esqr	Mr Humphrey Jones
	Coll^o Christo^r Wormeley	Mr John Man
Psent	Capt Walter Whittaker	Mr Chr Robinſon
	Majo^r Robert Beverley	Mr Matt. Kemp
	Mr Richd Robinson	

It is ordered by this pʳsent Vestry That mʳ John Sheppard Minister Shall for the Future be paid according to Act of Aſsembly.

(33)   At a Vestry held for Christ Church Pish Middlesex At the houſe of mʳ Richard Robinson the 5ᵗʰ of Octoᵇʳ 1680.

Psent   Mʳ Jn° Sheppard Miniſter

Majoʳ Genʳˡˡ Robert Smith	Majoʳ Robᵗ Beverley
Ralph Wormely Esqʳ	Mʳ Richᵈ Robinson
Mʳ Richᵈ Perrott Senʳ	Mʳ Hum. Jones
Mʳ Abrã. Weekes	Mʳ John Man
Coll° Chr Wormeley	Mʳ Chr Robinson
Capᵗ Walter Whittaker	Mʳ Matthew Kemp

Veſtrymen

It is ordered by this Psent Vestry that Mʳ Robert Smith be Added to the Vestry, and Accordingly to be forthwith Sworne, And was alſoe Sworne his Day.

It is ordered by this pʳsent Vestry that Anthony Slauter be paid for Nursing Henry Normans Orphin Childe foure Monhs, Ending his Day, Foure hundred pounds of Tobacco and Cask   400

It is ordered that Mʳ Humphrey Jones be paid for Two Forms for yᵉ uper Chappell   80

It is ordered that Thomas Mins be paid for Nurſing a Bastʳd Child of a woman Servant belonging to Majoʳ Genʳˡˡ Robert Smith Ending in Xemb. next   1000

It is ordered that Mʳ Alexandʳ Smith for his w°man Servant Nursing of a bastard Child of her Body begotten by one of Sᵈ Smiths Servants, yᵉ yeare Ending in Aprˡˡ next   1000

It is ordered that Thomas Norman be paid for Nursing a bastard Child of a Woman Servᵗ of mʳ Jn° Sheppard, Ending in January next   1000

It is ordered that Nich° West be pᵈ for keeping of a Bastard Child belonging to mʳ Richᵈ Perrott Senʳ Servant The yeare ending in november next   1000

It is ordered y[t] m[r] John Sheppard be p[d] Sixteen
Thousand pounds of Tobacco and Cask for this p[r]sent
Yeare   16000

It is ordered that Joseph Harvie be paid Two Thous-
and pounds of Tobacco and Cask for this Psent yeare   2000

   (2   _____
T(2   22480
556   Cash at 8 ₱ Cent   1799
764(3   _____
25493 (38 ₱ pole y[e] Pish   24279
6655   180 ₱ pole y[e] County   Sallery at 5 ₱ Ct   1214
66 ——   _____
   lb 218 ₱ pole in all   lb.   25493

668 Tythables, out of w[ch] M[r] Shepard is
allowed 3 Tythables. 665 Tythables in all.

Turn over

(34) It is ordered by this p[r]sent Vestry that m[r] Joseph
Harvie Continue Clerk for the Enſueing yeare.

Mem[dm] That there is Short Levyed 113[lb] of Tobacco, w[ch]
will be Due to Cap[t] Whittaker y[e] next yeare.

It is ordered that Majo[r] Robert Beverley be Ch. Warden
This Enſueing yeare for y[e] Lower p[r]sinqe.

It is ordered that m[r] X. Robinson be Ch. Warden this yeare
for the middle p[r]sinq[r]

It is ordered that m[r] Nich[o] Cock be Ch. Warden this yeare
for y[e] Uper p[r]sinque.

At a Vestry held the 7[th] of November 1681. At the house
of m[r] Robinson for Christ Church parish.

	M[r] Richard Perrott, Sen[r]	M[r] Rich[d] Robinson
	Majo[r] Gen[rll] Robert Smith	M[r] Hum̃. Jones
Psent	Coll[o] Chr Wormeley	M[r] John Man
	Cap[t] Walter Whittaker	L[t] John Needles
	Majo[r] Ro[b] Beverley	M[r] Chr Robinson
	M[r] Abrã Weekes	M[r] Robert Smith Jun[r]

lb

It is ordered by this p[r]sent Vestry that M[r] John
Sheppard be paid y[e] Sum̃e of   16000

It is ordered by this p^rsent Vestry that Joseph Harvie
be paid   2000
It is ordered that Mr Christo^r Robinson p^rsent Ch.
Warden be paid as ℔ Accompt   6450
It is ordered that Mr William Poole be paid for keep-
ing of one Mary Teston a poore Impotent Pson   1000
It is ordered that Christop^r Edey be paid for keeping
Matthew Jones   500
It is ordered that Richard Watts be paid for Maintence
This p^rsent Yeare   1000
It is ordered that Majo^r Gen^{r11} Robert Smith be paid
for Keeping of a bastard Child of Katherine Etrages   1000
It is ordered that Allexand^r Smith be paid for keep-
ing of a Baſtard Child   1000
It is ordered that Joseph Hopkins be paid for keeping
a Bastard Child Seven Monthes   600

                                                                    29550
(35)   Brought from over Leafe   29550
It is ordered that Thomas Spencer be paid for keep-
ing a Baſtard Child a Yeare   1000
It is ordered that Majo^r Robert Beverly be p^d for
his Charge in Repaireing the Lower Chappell   2000

                                                          lb   32550
                  Cask at 8 ℔ Cent comes to   2604

Tythables 657   35154
                  Sallery at 5 ℔ Cent comes to   1758

                                            Totall lb   36912

β(1
4ᴑ
4ᴑβ(2
ᴑ4ᴑ(ᴑ
βᴑ9ᴒ12   (56 ℔ pole & 120 over
ᴑβ77
ᴑβ

It is ordered that m^r Joseph Harvie Continue Clerk of This Pish this Ensueing yeare.

Capt Henry Creeke out of his pious zeal and love to the Church, hath Beſtowed and given upon the 17th Day of Aprill Last 1681. upon the uper Chappell of Ease to Christ Church in Middlesex County Viz^t one Silver Trencher plate, weighing about   ounces, Ingraven wth the Coate of Armes of Henry Corbin Esqr upon the Inside of the Brim Thereof And on the out Side of the bottom thereof, is Ingraven (the name of Henry Corbin Esqr) Also one Damask Table Cloath, and two Damask Napkins, all wch are Marked I-C being for ye use of the Coñunion Table of the Said Chappell, and there Soe to Remaine for Ever &c.

Nota   That ye Table Cloath and Two Napkins are in ye Custody of m^r Huñ. Jones.

(36) At a Vestry held the Pñ̃o January 1682 At ye house of m^r Richard Robinson for Christ Church Pish

Psent   Mr Jno Sheppard Minister

    Mr Richd Perrott Senr Mr Abrã Weekes
    Coll^o Chr. Wormeley   Mr Richd Robinson
    Capt Walter Whittaker   Mr Richd Perrott Jn^r
                                     Mr Chr. Robinson

	lb
It is ordered by this Psent Vestry that Mr John Shepard be paid	16000
It is ordered that Joseph Harvie be paid	2000
It is ordered that m^r Christop^r Robinson be paid for a Bastard Child nurst by Tho. Normans Wife	2000
It is ordered that m^r Chr. Robinson be p^d for a Baſtard Child nurst by Anth^o Slauters wife	1000
It is ordered that Ditto m^r Robinson be p^d for a Bastard Child nurst by m^r Alexand^r Smith	1000
It is ordered that Anth^o Slauter be p^d for nursing of a bastard Child	500
It is ordered that Majo^r Gen^{rll} Robert Smith be p^d for nursing of a bastard Child kept one yeare Ending ye 25th of January	1000

It is ordered that Majoʳ Genʳˡˡ Robert Smith be paid
for keeping of a bastard Child from yᵉ 19ᵗʰ of Sepᵗ last
to this Day   300
It is ordered that mʳ Jnᵒ Sheppard be pᵈ for 3 Levys
Due to him last Yeare   369
It is ordered that mʳ John Sheppard be pᵈ for 3
Leveys this pʳsent Yeare   413
It is ordered that William Watts be paid   500
It is ordered yᵗ yᵉ Sheriff be pᵈ for wᵗ was Short
Levied in yᵉ County Court   358
     1   ——————
   49 (9   25941
   507 (o
   29418   (48 ℔ pole is Pish Charge   Cask at 8 ℔ Cent 2076
   6111   139 Is yᵉ County Charge   Sallery at 5 ℔ Ct. 1401
   61   ——   ——————
       187 ℔ pole in all   lb   29418

(37)   At a Vestry held at Christ Church for Christ Church
Pish In Middlesex County the 31ᵗʰ of March 1682/3

Psent

Mʳ Jnᵒ Sheppard Minister

Mʳ Richᵈ Perrott Senʳ   Mʳ Richᵈ Robinson
Collᵒ Chr Wormeley   Mʳ Matthew Kemp

Veſtrymen

Whereas by a former ordʳ of Vestry held at Christ Church
the 21ᵗʰ of Novembʳ 1670 it was then Concluded that if Foure
or Five of the Gentlemen of the Vestry did meete at time appointed, that They Should doe all buſineſses belonging to the
parrish without Staying for any other, It is Therefore ordered
by this pʳsent Vestry that mʳ Oswald Cary mʳ Robert Dudley,
Mʳ Allexandʳ Smith & Mʳ Robert Price have Notice by the
Clerk of this parish to be present the 27ᵗʰ Inſtant, to be Sworne
Vestrymen for the said parish.

It is ordered by this pʳsent Vestry that all the Gentlemen
of the Vestry belonging to this parish have notice to Appeare
the 27ᵗʰ Inſtant, At wᶜʰ Tyme a Vestry is Intended to be held
in this place.

(38)   At a Vestry held At Christ Church for Christ Church
Parish In Midd^x County the 27th of March 1683.

Psent

Mr Jno Sheppard Minister

Majo^r Gen^{rll} Robt Smith   Mr Robt Smith Junr
Mr Richd Perrott Senr   Mr Richd Robinson
Coll° Chr Wormeley   Mr Matthew Kemp
Coll° Cuth. Potter   Mr Oswald Cary both
                                Mr Robert Price Sworn
                                   this Day Veſtrymen

It is ordered by this p^rsent Vestry that m^r Chr Robinson
Doe Continue Church Warden for this Middle precinq.

It is ordered that m^r Nich^o Cock be Ch. Warden for the
Uper precinq, And that they both come the next Court held
for this County then to be Sworne.

It is ordered that Joseph Harvie do Rake and burn the
Leaves about the Thre Churches, and to Endeavo^r to Secure
them from Fire, And he to be Allowed five hundred pounds
of Tobacco and Caske for the Same Yearly, besides his yearly
Sallery.

It is ordered that m^r Christop^r Robinson present Ch. Warden Doe Spedily Repaire the Great Church according to
order Under Written Viz^t That ye Earth be firmly Ram'd,
under the Sells, and a Convenient pent house made to keepe
the Raine off them, that the Shingles be all taken off, and the
Lathes also ript off, and every Shingle now nailed on, with
one good Naile upon the Covering, That the pailes about the
Church Yard be well Repaired, and new posts of Casnutt or
Locus be Sett in ye roome of the old, That the Church be
plaiſtered where wanting, and as Soone a Conveniently may,
New pavement laid in the Chancell and Alley.

It is also ordered by this p^rsent Vestry that m^r Matthew
Kemp and m^r Nich^o Cock Doe Such repaires to the Chappells
in theire precinqs as Shalbe needfull.

Mr Matthew Kemp was this Day Sworne Church Warden
for the Lower precinq.

(39) At a Vestry held at Christ Church for Christ Church parish In Middlesex County the 20ᵗʰ of July 1683.

Present

	Ralph Wormeley Esqʳ	Collº Cuthbert Potter
	Mʳ Richᵈ Perrott Senʳ	Mʳ Robert Smith
Vestrymen	Collº Chr Wormeley	Mʳ Chr Robinson
	Capᵗ Walter Whittaker	Mʳ Nicholas Cock
	Mʳ Richᵈ Robinson	

It is ordered by this pʳsent Vestry that Doʳ William Poole takes home to his house the Pson of Christopʳ Goulder of this parish, and to use the Utmost of his Endeavoʳ to Cure him of his Blindneſs, and in Case that Doʳ Poole Should make a Cure thereof, Then the Said Doʳ Poole is to have for the Cure Two Thousand pounds of Tobacco & Caske, But in Caſe he Doth not Cure yᵉ Said Christopʳ Goulder, That then the Said Doʳ Poole is to have but Reasonable Sattisfaction for his Trouble.

It is ordered by this pʳsent Vestry that Joseph Harvie be omitted from paying of his owne pʳsonall Levey for the Time he Shall Continue Clerk &c.

It is ordered by this pʳsent Vestry that Whereas it hath pleased Almighty God to take [unto himselfe]* out of this life mʳ John Sheppard our late Worthy Minister, And this Veſtry and the whole parish Deſireing to have his place Supplied wᵗʰ a Gentleman of good life and Doctrine, and a True Sone of the Church of England And they Knowing of none Such at pʳsent in this Cuntry but have Beniffices—It is therefore unanimously Agreed by the Vestry that the honorᵇˡᵉ Ralph Wormeley Esqʳ and mʳ Robert Smith be Deſired and Impowered to Write in the name of this Vestry to the honorᵇˡᵉ the Lady Agatha Chichley and Majoʳ Genʳˡˡ Robert Smith who it is hoped are now Safe in London, To Request them or Either of them That they will please to take the Trouble to procure a fitt minister in England to Come over and Supply

---

* Note: The words enclosed in brackets were partly erased from, but are still legible in, the original.—C. G. C.

the place of m[r] Sheppard, For whose better Incouragement this Vestry doe promiſe and Accordingly Resolve that they will Entertaine noe Minister in the Said parish (Except for the present Time onely) untill they have an acco[t] from those hon[rble] Psons, And that they will Willingly accep[t] and Receive into this Pish Such Minister as they Shall perswade to Come and Recocomend to this Vestry, And that Such Minister Shall have beſide y[e] Gleabe Land and plantation (wch containes 400 acres of Land) The Suñe of Sixteene Thousand pounds of Tob[o] & Caske yearly p[d] him by this Pish, besides all perq[ts] and other proffits wch have bin Enjoyed by our Said Worthy Minister M[r] John Sheppard.

(40)   At a Vestry held the 6th of November 1683 At the house of m[r] Richard Robinson for Christ Church parish In Middlesex County &c.

Present

	M[r] Rich[d] Perrott Sen[r]	m[r] Robert Smith
	Coll[o] Chr Wormeley	m[r] Matthew Kemp
Vestrymen	Cap[t] Walter Whittaker	m[r] Rich[d] Robinson
	Coll[o] Cuthbert Potter	m[r] Robert Price
	m[r] Abrã Weekes	m[r] Alexand[r] Smith
	m[r] Nicholas Cock	m[r] Robert Dudley

It is ordered by this p[r]sent Vestry that m[r] Richard Robinson be Church Warden In the absence of m[r] Xph[r] Robinson untill his Returne.

It is ordered by this p[r]sent Vestry that m[r] Allexander Smith and m[r] Robert Dudley be added to this Vestry, & They both p[r]sonally appearing was this Day accordingly Sworne &c.

It is ordered that Richard Watts a poore old Decripped Man be all allowed for Mentaineance   lb   500

It is ordered That Jane Privett be allowed for mentainance   500

It is ordered that Do[r] William Poole be allowed towards his Trouble and Care Taken wth Christop[r] Goulder towards the bringing him to his Sight (w[ch] was loost)   1000

It is ordered that Doctor Robert Boodle be Allowed
Towards the Cure of William Stone a poore Decripped
and VIserated man, Still under the hands of y⁰ s⁴
Do⁰ Boodle   1000

It is ordered that M⁰ Robert Smith be paid for Keeping a Bastard Childe of William Walters, begotten of
Kath. Lestridge, named Elizabeth for 10 m⁰ time to
this Day after the Rate of a 1000: a yeare   833

It is ordered that m⁰ Oswald Cary doe furnish & Supply William Stone a poore Decriped and VIcerated Man
now at Do⁰ Boodles wᵗʰ one Cotten Suite, one paire of
Shoos one paire of Stockins and Two Shirts, and he to
be allowed   200

It is ordered that Thomas Norman be pᵈ for Keeping a
parish Child 1000ˡᵇ of Tobacco, & he to keepe the said Child
'till the po. Jan⁰ next   1000

                                                                  5033
(41)   Brought from the other Side   5033

It is ordered that m⁰ Robert Smith be paid for keeping
of a bastard Child of William Walters begotten of Katherine Leſtridge Termed   for a Yeare   1000

It is ordered that 4000ˡᵇ of Tobacco for the Church
worke to be done by Edward Evans be Levyed & to Remaine in the hands of m⁰ Richard Robinson Ch. Warden
'till the Worke be Finished   4000

It is ordered that 500ˡᵇ of Tobacco be Levied for
Nailes for the Church worke & to Remaine in the hands
of the above Said Church Warden   500

It is ordered that Joseph Harvie be paid for his Sallery
and looking after all the Churches & Church Yards   2500
It is ordered that m⁰ John Sheppard Decᵈ be allowed
his whole Sallery   16,000

It is ordered that m⁰ Superious (Minister) be
Allowed for preaching   1000

It is ordered that John Davis be allowed for his
preaching   1000

(2		31,033
$(5	Caske at 8 ₩	
1₮	Cent is	2,482
2$(6		
35₮32 (58½ The parrish ₩ pole		33,515
6122 26 The County ₩ pole	Sallery at 5 ₩	
6.1 ———	Cent is	1,676
84½ ₩ pole Together		
	lb	35,191
To mr Sheppards 3 Tythables abated	250	
To Cask for that 250 Comes to	20	
To Sallery for 270 Comes to	27	0297
Short in the County Levey		0264
	Totall lb	35,752

It is ordered that the Sheriff of this County Doe
Collect the parish Charge being 58½ ₩ pole.

(42)   At a Vestry held at Chriſt Church for Chriſt Church
Piſh In Middleſex County this 26ᵗʰ Novembʳ 1683

Present

The Honorᵇˡᵉ Ralph Wormeley Esqʳ   Collᵒ Cuthbert Potter
Collᵒ Chr. Wormeley   Mʳ John Man
Capᵗ Walter Whittaker   Mʳ Matthew Kemp
Mʳ Robert Smith   Mʳ Richᵈ Robinſon
                      mʳ Allexandʳ Smith

It is ordered by this Veſtry That Upon a Treaty with Mʳ
Duell Pead, That he Should officiate in this parish as Minister
a Whole Twelve Month, And to have Sixteen Thousand pounds
of Tobacco and Caske with all Pquisitts and the uſe of the
Gleabe Lands for the said Time.

(43)   Virginia — By his Excellency —
Whereas by act of Aſsembly It is Enacted that noe pʳson
Shalbe Capacitated in any Respect wᵗſoever to grant or Iſsue

forth Lycences for the Solemnization of Marriages, Unless
those that I Shall Depute for y^t purpose, or the first in
Comifsion for y^t County where ye parties to be Married do
Inhabit, which act being of too large a Lattitude Severall In-
conveniences & Abufes have been Occafioned thereby Divers
Juftices and others prefumeing to Grant Lycences when they
are not thereto quallified, I Therefore Francis Lord Howard
Barron of Effingham his Majesties L^t and Govorn^r Gen^{rll} of
Virginia (for Divers and Sundry Caufes me Thereunto Move-
ing, but more Efpecially that the Intent of the aforesaid act
be put in Effectuall Execution, and all others afsertained of
theire Juft Dues, and p^{r}ties to be Married fully advifed who
are Impowered to grant Lycences) Have Therefore Thought
Fit and doe hereby Lycence permit and allow Coll^o Thomas
Pate (being well afsured of his Integrity) and him onely, to
grant Lycences for Marriages In the Counties of Gloster and
Middlefex Giveing and hereby Granting unto the said Coll^o
Thomas Pate all p^{r}qufits and Emoluments which already have,
or doe accrue from, the Twenty Eight Day of Septem^{br} laft
to the Twenty Eight day of Septem^{br} which shalbe in the yeare
of our Lord God one Thousand Six hundred Eighty and
Foure, with power alfo to Demand Recieve and Call to accompt
all those who have from the Twenty Eight of Septem^{br} laft
Granted Lycences for Marriages in ye aforesaid Counties,
who upon Rendering theire Respective Accompts I doe hereby
order and Appoint That they pay the produce of such Dues
and p^{r}qufits to the said Coll^o Thomas Pate Upon ye penalty
of ye Forfeiture of w^t is provided against Thofe that prefume
to grant Lycences Contrary to act, and wthout any other qualli-
fication And for the more Effectuall putting in Execution
of this my Comifion or Derivate power, I doe hereby appoint
order and require That noe Orthodox Minister, or perfon
w^{t}foever for the Future, prefume to Celebrate or Solemnize
the Rites of Mattrimony in the aforesaid Counties wthout
Either the publication of the banns according to the Confti-
tutions of the Church of England, or Lycence from the aforesaid Coll^o Thomas Pate and him onely, upon penalty of For-

feiting what is provided by act againſt those Miniſters that presume to Marry wᵗʰout publication of Banns or Lycence, With power likewiſe to Substitute one or more under him in the aforesaid Counties or Either of them to (44) To Grant Lycences for the Same, And to the Intent that this my Com̄iſsion may be fully Known in the aforesaid Counties, and full Notification Thereof made, I doe hereby order & appoint that the Same be publiquely Read in the Respective parishes of the aforesaid Counties, and Regiſtered in the Severall Regiſters, Given under my hand and Seale this Twentieth Day of February—168¾ Annoq Regni Regis Caroli Secundi 36°.

Effingham

(45) At a Vestry held the 2ᵗʰ of June 1684 at the houſe of Mʳ Richard Robinson for Christ Church parish In Middleſex County.

Present

	Mʳ Richᵈ Perrott Senʳ	Mʳ Richᵈ Robinson
mʳ Duell	Capᵗ Walter Whittaker	Mʳ Oswald Cary
Pead	Mʳ Robert Smith	Mʳ Alexandʳ Smith
Minister	Collᵒ Cuthbert Potter	Mʳ Robert Dudley
	Mʳ Humphry Jones	Mʳ Robᵗ Price
	Mʳ Nathaniell Kemp	Mʳ John Wortham
	Mʳ John Man	Mʳ William Daniel

Mʳ William Churchill

It is ordered by this pʳsent Vestry That mʳ John Wortham mʳ William Daniell and mʳ William Churchill be Added to this Veſtry, and they all Thre this Day pʳsonally Appearing was likewise this Day Accordingly Sworne Members Thereof.

It is ordered by this pʳsent Vestry that yᵉ Com̄union Table at the Great Church and alſo at both Chappells be Railed in, as Convenient as poſsible may be; wᵗʰout Obstructing any paſsage, and that there be Benches and Forms provided for all the Thre Churches, for Convenience of Seating the people, and that Each Respective Church Warden in his Respective place Se it done and performed with all Expedition &c.

Memorandᵐ That Mʳ Duell Pead our pʳsent Miniſter out of his pious Intentions to the good of the Sōles of his Flock,

Mentioned that the blefsed Sacrament of the Lords Supper
(too much neglected) might for the Future be more Frequently
Adminiftered and attended. To this Intent he the aforesaid
mʳ Pead propounded the Monthly obfervation thereof, That
is to say, on the first Sunday in yᵉ Month according to Courfe,
That the Congregation Should Afsemble to Divine Service at
the Mother Church, Then there the Sacrament of the Lords
Supper Should be Celebrated, and moreover that this great
Solemn Miftry might as well Worthily as Frequently be ob-
served he the said mʳ Pead did then Frackly and Freely
promise a Sermon at the Said Church Monthly, that is to say
on the Satterday in the afternoone afore the Giveing the
Comunion, not Doubting but that all Parents (46) Parents
and Masters of Families who Tender the Everlafting welfaire
of the Souls Committed to theire Charge would Readily Comply and allow Convenient Liberty to Theire Children and Servants to Repaire to Church at Such Times There to be In-
ftructed and prepaired for this Religious Duty This motion
was Then Thankfully and Cheerfully Entertained by the pʳsent
Veftry, and they Did unanimously Concurr wᵗʰ the Said mʳ
Pead theirein.

Att a Vestry held yᵉ 4ᵗʰ of Novemᵇʳ 1684 at the Houfe of
Mʳ Richard Robinson for Christ Church parish In Middlefex County

Mʳ Duell Pead Minister

The Honorᵇˡᵉ Ralph Wormeley Esqʳ

Collᵒ Chr Wormeley	Mʳ Matthew Kemp
Mʳ Richᵈ Perrott Senʳ	Mʳ John Man
Capᵗ Walter Whittaker	Mʳ Oswald Cary
Mʳ Robert Smith	Mʳ John Wortham
Mʳ Abrã. Weekes	Mʳ William Churchhill
Collᵒ Cuthbert Potter	Mʳ William Daniell
Mʳ Nicholas Cock	Mʳ Richᵈ Robinfon

It is ordered by this pʳsent Vestry that Duell Pead
Minister be paid for his Officiating as Minister in   lb. Tobo
This Pish this pʳsent Yeare the Sume of   16000

It is ordered by this Psent Vestry that Jos. Harvie
be paid   2500

It is Ordered that Mr William Churchhill Church
Warden for Reparations done to ye Lower Chappell Ac-
cording to his accompt be paid   2758

It is Ordered that Mr John Wortham Churchwarden
be paid for Posting of the Stable at ye Grt Church ac-
cording to his accot   250

It is Ordered that Mr Robert Price Ch. warden be paid
for Reparations done to the Uper Chapll according to
his accot   100

It is Ordered that Dor Stapleton be paid for his Physick Trouble and paines Taken about a poore Sick &
Diseased Man Termed Henry Fricston, of late Deseased   1000

(47)   Brought from the Other Side   22600

It is Ordered that Major Robert Beverley be paid for
Keeping of one Thomas Watson, a poore Decripped Man
a whole Yeare   1000

It is Ordered that Mr John Nicholls be paid for Richd
Watts a poore Aged Sick Weake Man being past his
Labor and now upon the parish   1000

It is Ordered That Jone Deverdale be pd for Keeping
a bastrd Child of Dorothy Suttons Servt to Collo Worme-
ley half a Yeare   500

It is Ordered that Tho Norman be pd for Keeping a
bastard Child of Mary Suttons Servt to Mrs Fra. Shep-
ard a whole yeare   1000

It is Ordered that Robert Guilliams be paid for Keeping a bastard Child of Eliz. Dowries Servt to mr James
Curtis ½ a yeare   500

It is ordered that mr Petty be pd for Keeping a poore
Sick woman   1000

It is ordered that Joseph Harvie Clerk hath an aug-
mentacon of his Sallery constantly for the prsent, and
for ye Future of 500lb ℔ annum, for the makeing his

Sallery 3000 ℔ ℥ anñ. for his officiating the Clerks place
to all yᵉ Thre Churches of this parish   500

    It is ordered yᵗ mʳ Richᵈ Robinson be pᵈ for Extra-
ordinary Charge   600

    (2

    $ lb   28700

    10   Cask at 8 ℥ Cent is   2296½

32554½ (51½ the parish

6344   47   the County   31004½

                          Sallery at 5 ℥ Cent is   1550

    63   98½ ℥ pole

           lb   28700   Totall lb   32554½

    It is ordered that Capᵗ Walter Whittaker High Sherriff Doe
Collect the parish Levey 51½ ℥ pole

    634 Tythables in all

    (48)   At a Vestry held the 5ᵗʰ of Janʳy 1685 at the houſe
of Mʳ Richᵈ Robinson for Christ Church Piſh Middlˣ County.

      Psent   Mʳ Duell Pead Minister

      Majoʳ Robert Beverly   Mʳ Oswald Cary

      Mʳ Robert Smith   Mʳ Richᵈ Robinson

      Mʳ Abrã. Weekes   Mʳ John Wortham

      Mʳ Chr Robinson   Mʳ William Daniell

      Coll°Cuthbert Potter   Mʳ Wᵐ Churchhill

      Mʳ Matthew Kemp   Mʳ Robert Price

    It is ordered by this pʳsent Vestry that mʳ Duell Pead
Minister be paid for his officiateing as Minister in   lb Tob°
This Piſh this pʳsent yeare the Suñe of   16000

    It is ordered by this pʳsent Vestry that Jos. Harvie Cl.
be paid   2500

    It is ordered that mʳ Duell Pead be allowed for to buy
him a Horse   2000

    It is ordered that mʳ Duell Pead be paid for Repaireing
the Houſen at yᵉ Gleab & makeing of them Tenantable   4000

    It is ordered that Richᵈ Watts a poore Decriped man be
paid   1000

    It is ordered that Jone Deverdale be paid for Keeping
of Thre baſtard Children 3000℔ of Tobacco & Caske,

wᶜʰ Suūe is by the Said Deverdale aſsigned to mʳ Willᵐ
Churchhill   3000

It is ordered that mʳ Wᵐ Churchhill be paid for
Cloaths Furnished Christoʳ Goulder in his Life Time   389

It is ordered that mʳ Wᵐ Poole be paid for Keeping
of Christoʳ Goulder Dureing his Sicknes & Lameneſs
1000ˡᵇ of Tobacco the wᶜʰ Suūe is aſsigned by the said
Poole to ye said mʳ Wᵐ Churchhill   1000

It is ordered that Daniell Trigg be paid for Keeping of
a baſtard Child of owen Foxes Servᵗ to mʳˢ Sheppard
for wᶜʰ Peter Richardson and Tho. obriſsell became
Security to yᵉ Court   750

It is ordered yᵗ Doʳ Robert Boodle be paid for Keeping
of wᵐ Stone   1000

It is ordered that Ann Roſs be paid for Keeping of a
baſtard Child begott by Edward Pearce Servᵗ to Majoʳ
Genʳˡˡ Robert Smith Esqʳ   100

It is ordered that Mary Norman be pᵈ for Keeping a
bastʳᵈ Child   1000

It is ordered that Tho. Norman be paid for takeing
Downe and putting up the Glaſs windows at yᵉ Great
Church   50

	lb.	
		32789
(49) Transported over		32789

It is ordered that mʳ Nicholas Cock be paid for Reparing
of the Uper Chappell   590

It is ordered yᵗ Joseph Harvie be paid for his Trouble
of Waſhing the Church Lynnen and Cleaning of the
Church Plate and Pewter   500

ʒ

ʒ0000 (60ˡᵇ ₱ pole is yᵉ parrish Levey   lb.   33879
                        Cask at 8 ₱ Cent   2710

6500 40½ ₱ pole is yᵉ County Levey   ————
  65   47   From Town   36589
  ————   Sallery at 5 ₱ Cent   1839
       147½ ₱ pole In all   ————
                                              lb   38418

To m^r Duell Pead for ye Discharge of his 2 Tythables at ye Gleabe, of Cuntry County and parish Leveys 147½ ⅌ p°	295
To m^r John Man for a Levey over Chargd last Yeare	84
To Mr Richard Robinson, &c	100
To the Under Sherriff ye overplus being	103

Totall is   lb   39000

It is ordered by this p^rsent Vestry y^t Thomas Wilſon a poore decriped Man be Entertained by Mrs Robinson for whose Entertainement and Cloathing Mrs Robinson is to *[have] be allowed 100^{lb} of Tobacco ⅌ month and if a Cure be Effected by her That then She is further to be Conſidered, and allowed as Shall Seeme meete and Fitting for such a Cure &c.

It is ordered that Mr William Churchill be Churchwarden (In the place of Mr Matthew Kemp) of the lower Chappell, in the Lower precinq this Enſueing yeare.

It is ordered that Mr John Wortham be Ch. Warden (In the place of m^r Richard Robinson,) of the great Church this Enſueing yeare.

Turn over

(50)   It is ordered that Mr Robert Price be Ch. warden (In ye place of m^r Nicholas Cock) of the Uper Chappell In ye Uper precinq And y^t he uſeing his best Discretion for ye Inlargeing of the uper Chappell, applying himſelfe to m^r Richard Perrott Senr and the other Gentlemen of the Vestry in those parts for advice There In.

It is ordered by this p^rsent Vestry that Mr Duell Pead Doe Continue our Miniſter this Enſueing yeare, and he to have Allowed him Sixteen Thouſand pounds of Tobacco & Caske will all perquiſits, and ye Benefitt of ye Gleab, as hath bin uſually allowed Formerly.

It is ordered by this p^rsent Veſtry y^t the 60^{lb} ⅌ pole, being the parish Levey be Collected by m^r Robert Smith High Sheriff of this County, and paid According to the orders of this p^rsent Vestry &c.

---

* Half erased.—C. G. C.

This p^rsent Vestry takeing into Theire Conſideration that There is a Certaine parcell of Land belonging to m^r John Cant Joyning upon the Gleab, being very Convenient to be added Thereto, It is Therefore ordered by this p^rsent Vestry that Mr Chr Robinson doe forthwith Treat with the Said m^r John Cant the owner thereof In the behalfe of this parish about ye buying of it for the use of the Said Gleab, and that upon the Said Treaty wth the Said m^r Cant There be Immediately a Veſtry Called for to give Theire opinnions about it &c.

This Vestry takeing Notice of Mary Hutſon Servant to Mrs Frances Sheppard, who hath brought Thre Severall baſtard Children which have been Nurſed at the Charge of this parriſh, and hath never yet been preſented for ye Same as the Law Directs, and there being further Information now made that Joseph Smith a Taylor, and Servt to the Said Mrs Sheppard peremptorily ownes himſelfe Father of the latter of the Said Thre Bastard Children, To the End the Same may be Duly Inquired into Doe order that Joseph Harvie doe Deliver a Coppie hereof to ye next Court held for this County that they may Call before them ye Said Mary and Joseph, and proceed againt them as the Law Directs &c.

                                                        This

(51)   This Vestry Doth also take Notice of one Elizabeth Dowrey Servant to m^r James Curtis who hath alſo brought a Baſtard Child, the which hath been Nurſed at ye Charge of this parrish, nor hath never yet been presented for ye Same, as ye Law directs, Therefore to the End ye Same may be Duly Inquired into, Doe ord^r that Joseph Harvie doe deliver a Coppie hereof to ye next Court held for this County that they may Call before them the Said Eliz. Dowrey and proceed againſt her as ye Law Directs &c.

This Veſtry doth likewiſe take notice of one Dorothy Sutton Servant to Coll^o Christo^r Wormeley which hath alſo brought a bast^rd Child which hath been Nurſed at ye Charge of this parrish, and hath never yet been p^rsented for the Same as ye Law directs Therefore to the End the same may be duly Inquired into, Doe ord^r that Joseph Harvie doe deliver a Coppie hereof to the next Court held for this County that they may Call before them yᵉ said Dorothy Sutton, and proceed agᵗ her as yᵉ Law directs &c.

It is ordered by this pʳsent Vestrey that mʳ Abraham Weekes be Church warden for the Uper Chappell in yᵉ upper precinq in the place of mʳ Robert Price.

It is ordered yᵗ mʳ Wᵐ Daniell be Ch. warden for the Great Church in yᵉ Middle precinq In yᵉ place of mᵒ Jnᵒ Wortham &c.

It is ordered that mʳ Robert Dudley be Church Warden for the Lower Chapˡˡ In yᵉ Lower precinq In yᵉ place of mʳ Wᵐ Churchhill.

It is ordered by this pʳsent Vestrey that mʳ William Daniell psent Church warden for yᵉ Middle precinq for this Enʃueing yeare Doe Immediately take into his poʃseʃsion the hundred Acres of Land left by the Laʃt Will and Testament of mʳ William Gordon Late Decᵈ for yᵉ use and bennifitt of a Free Schoole Together wᵗʰ Two Cows and their Encreaʃe, and that yᵉ said mʳ Wᵐ Daniell Ch. warden doe proceed according to the will of the Teʃtatoʳ &c.

It is Ordered by this pʳsent Veʃtry that mʳ Duell Pead Doe Continue our Minister (if he please) this Enʃueing yeare, and he to have the benifitt of yᵉ Gleabe and all perqᵗˢ and Sixteene Thousand poᵈˢ of Tobacco and Cask for the said Yeare &c.

(52)   (Blank.)

(53)   Att a Vestry held the 6ᵗʰ of Decembʳ 1686 Att the House of Mʳ Richard Robinson For Christ Church parrish In Middlesex County &c.

Present

Mʳ Duel Pead Minister

Mʳ Robert Smith	Mʳ Richard Robinson
Mʳ Abrā. Weekes	Mʳ John Wortham
Mʳ Matt Kemp	Mʳ William Daniell
Mʳ Oswald Cary	Mʳ William Churchhill
Mʳ Chr. Robinson	Mʳ Robert Dudley

It is ordered by this present Vestry that Mr Duell   lb Tobo
Pead minister be paid for his officiating as ministr this
present Yeare   16000
    It is ordered that Joseph Harvie Clerk be paid   3000
    It is ordered that Mr William Daniell Senr present
Church warden be paid for Railing in ye Comunion
Table and other Reparations at the Great Church according to his Accompt the Sume of   1400
    It is ordered that mr Robert Dudley present Church
Warden be paid for Reparations done at ye Lower
Chap11   180
    It is ordered that Richard Watts a poore Aged & Im-
potent Man be paid for mentainance 1000lb of Tobacco
and Caske which is Aſsigned to mr John Nicholls   1000
    It is ordered that Mary Norman be paid for keeping
a Baſtard Child of Mary Hutsons Servt to mrs Frances
Shepard a whole yeare Ending 13th of Janry next. And
yt then ye said Mary Norman is hereby ordered to deliver the Said Child up to the Church warden   1000
    It is ordered that Mary Thompson a poore Cripb be
paid   500
    It is ordered that mr Richard Robinson be paid   420

   (2   lb   23500
1$ Cask at 8 ₩ Cent   1880
2ø(o   _____
   (4   25380
26649(41   _____
ø4₿₿   Sallery at 5 ₩ Cent   1269
ø4   Totall lb   26649

        Add 441lb to this Fraction which will
    make ye parish Levy to be 42lb ₩ pole
    It is ordered that ye 441lb Tobo Above be Equally Divided
amongst These Thre poore men
                To Daniell Trig   147lb
                To Humpry Dudding   147
                To Jeffry Brookes   147
                                        lb   441

(54)   It is ordered by this psent Vestrey that m^r Oswald
Cary be Church warden for the Great Church In the Middle
precinq In the place of Mr William Daniell Senr

It is ordered that m^r Jn° Man be Churchwarden of the Lower
Chap^{ll} in the Lower precinq In the place of m^r Robert Dudly.

It is ordered that m^r Abraham Weekes doe Continue Ch.
warden for the uper Chap^{ll} In the uper precinq this Enſueing
year.

It is Ordered that the Two Cows Given and left to this
Pish ⅌ m^r William Gordon Dec^d being at p^rsent upon his said
plantation, That m^r Duel Pead takes them Into his Custody
and keeping and that ye said m^r Pead for the Future be Accomptable from Time to Time to the parish for them.

It is ordered that m^r Abraham Weekes p^rsent Churchwarden
Doe In Large the uper Chappell according to his Discretion and
as his Convenience will permitt him soe to doe, not Exceeding
Twenty Foot &c.

Whereas by the 79 Act of Aſsembly in the printed book
Intituled Surveyo^{rs} for ye highwayes It is amongst other Things
Enacted that the Vestrys of Every parish, are upon the deſire
of ye Surveyo^{rs} of ye Highwayes Injoyned and Impowered to
order the Prishon^{rs} Every one according to the Tythables he
hath in his Family to Send men upon the Dayes by the Sur-
veyo^{rs} Appointed, to help them in Clearing the wayes or makeing or Repaireing Bridges, And Whereas The Severall Sur-
veyo^{rs} of this County have Acquainted this Vestry that y^e
Roades and wayes in Theire Severall Pcints are much out of
Repare, and will require a great Deale of helpe to Cleare, and
make the Same paſsable, and they Desire this Vestry will
order the P^rishon^{rs} to Send Such helpe as may be Thought
neceſsary for performeing the Said worke, All which this
Vestry haveing taken into Theire Serious Conſiderations have
Thought fitt to order and Appoint That Every Master Miſtreſs
or overſeere In this parish Shall ſo often as the Surveyo^{rs}
Shall require not Exceeding once Every Quarter of a yeare,
send to theire Aſsiſtance In Clearing of the wayes aforesaid,
The one Third part of the Tythable p^rsons in his or Theire

Family or Charge, and where there are leſs than Thre Tythables in any Family That then yᵉ nearest Adjoyning Neighbour
Shall Contribute to Theire aſsistance &c.

It is ordered That mʳ Duell Pead Doe Continue our minister
(if he pleaſeth) this Enſueing yeare and he to have the Beniſitt
of the Gleab & all purquisits & 16000ˡᵇ of Tobacco & Cask
for the said yeare &c.

(55)   This Indenture Made the 6ᵗʰ Day of Septemᵇʳ one
Thouſand Six-hundred Seventy and Thre, And in yᵉ Twenty
Fifth Yeare of yᵉ Reign of our Soveraigne Lord King Charles
the Second Between Richard Robinson of the County of Mid-
dleſex in Virgᵃ Genᵗ & Ann his Wife on the one part, and the
Veſtry men and pʳishonʳˢ of Christ Church Piſh In the Said
County on the other part Witneſseth That yᵉ said Richard
Robinſon and Ann his Wife for and in Conſideration of yᵉ
Suᵐe of Ten Thouſand pounds of good and Merchantable
Tobacco and Cask to them yᵉ said Richard Robinſon and Ann
his Wife in hand paid at & before the Enſealing and De-
livery hereof by the said Veſtry men, and Pʳishonʳˢ of the parish
of Christ Church, the Receipt whereof they the said Richard
Robinson and Ann his Wife doe hereby Acknowledge and
themſelves Therewith fully Sattisfied and paid, and thereof
and of Every part and parcell Thereof Doth Clearly Acquit
Exonerate and Discharge yᵉ said Vestry men and Pʳishonʳˢ
of yᵉ parish of Christ Church and Theire Succeſsors for Ever.
—By Theſe pʳsents have Given Granted Bargained Alliened
and Sold Enfeoffed & Confirmed, And by Theſe pʳsents Doth
fully Clearly and Absolutely Give Graunt Bargaine Sell alien
Enfeoff and Confirme unto the said Veſtry men and Pʳishonʳˢ
of Christ Church Pʳish theire Succeſsoʳˢ and Aſsignes for
Ever one Certaine Tract or Devidend of Land Containeing
Foure hundred Acres or there abouts be yᵉ Same more or leſs,
Scituate Lying and being in Middleſex County in the pʳiſh
aforesaid, and upon Nimcock (Alias Roſe Gill) Creeke side,
and bounded as followeth Beginning at a White Oake Standing by Nimcock Creeke side, and Runing thence by an old
Line (Formerly mʳ Grimes Line) South-West one hundred

and Sixty pole to a White Oak by a Path Leading to yᵉ Kings
Road, Thence South East by South Thre hundred and Fifty
poles to Two Corner Spanish Oakes about Seventy poles from
Andrew Williams his Fence Side, Thence by a Marked Line
North North-Eaſt one hundred Sixty Eight poles to a Beach
by yᵉ side of a Branch, and Down yᵉ Branch to yᵉ Creek, And
by the Creeke side to yᵉ place first began at (Including the
plantation whereon mʳ John Sheppard Minister to yᵉ Said pʳish
now Liveth) With all and Singular Its Rights Members Juris-
dictions & Appurtenances Together with all Houſes Edifeſses
Buildings Barnes Stables orchards Gardens yards backsides
Eaſements lands Tenements Meaddowes paſtures Woods Under Woods Wayes Eaſements proffits Comodities Common of
Paſture Heriditaments priviliges and Appurtenances whatsoever to the same Tract of Land belonging and in yᵉ Bounds
thereof Contained. To have & To hold The said Tract or Devidend of Land wᵗʰ all and Singular other the pʳmises hereby
graunted Bargained and Sold, or Mentioned to be herein or
hereby granted bargained and Sold, with Theire and Every of
theire Rights Members and Appurtenances wᵗſoever unto the
said Vestry men and pʳishonʳˢ of the parish of Christ Church,
theire (56) Succeſsorˢ and Aſsignes for a Gleabe for the Said
pʳish for Ever, To the onely proper uſe and behoofe of them
the said Vestry men and pʳishonʳˢ of Christ Church Pʳish
Theire Succeſsorˢ & Aſsignes for Ever, Against them the
Said Richard Robinſon and Ann his Wife Theire Heires and
aſsignes and all and Every other Pson and pʳsons whatsoever
shall and will Warrent and for Ever Defend by theſe pʳsents,
And that yᵉ said Veſtry men and pʳishonʳˢ theire Succeſsorˢ
and aſsignes and Every of them Shall and may by Force and
vertue of Theſe pʳsents, from Time to Time and at all Times
for Ever hereafter Lawfully peaceably and quietly have hold
uſe occupie poſseſs and Enjoy the Said Meſsuage or Tene-
ment and all and Singular *[the Rights Members and Ap-
purtenances] The before granted pʳmiſes and Tract of Land,
with theire and Every of Theire Rights Members and Appurtenances, And have Receive and Take the Rents Isues

---

* Erased in MS. but still legible.—C. G. C.

and profits thereof to their own proper uſe and behoofe for
Ever, Without any Lawfull lett suite Trouble Denyall Inter-
uption Eviction or Disturbance of any pᵣson or pᵣ sons wᵗſoever,
(the Rents and Services which from henceforth Time to Time
for or in Respect of the pᵣmises Shall grow Due and payable
to the Kings Majestie his heires or Succeſsoᵣˢ onely Excepted
and Surprised) And further yᵉ Said Richard Robinſon and
Ann his Wife Doth hereby Covenant promiſe and Agree and
bind Themſelves to make Acknōledgmᵗ hereof In open Court
held for Middleſex whenſoever They shall be Required so
to doe, as also to make other and more Firme Aſsurance of
the said Land and premiſes to the Vestry men and Pᵣishonᵣˢ
aforesaid, any Time within Seven Yeares next Comeing as
Shall be thought needfull by the Learned of the Law, for the
Better Aſsurance Thereof to yᵉ Said Pᵣishonᵣˢ Theire Succeſsoᵣˢ and Aſsignes, provided it be at the Cost & Charge of
the ſaid pᵣishonᵣˢ and that They be not Conſtrained to Travell
beyond yᵉ Limits and bounds of Middleſex County to doe
The ſame, *In Witnesse* Whereof the said Richᵈ Robinson and
Ann his Wife have hereunto put Theire hands and Seales the
Day and Yeare first above Written.

Signed Sealed & Delivered   Richard Robinson (.)
In the Pᵣsence of us—   Ann A Robinson (.)
Christopᵣ Robinson
Thomas Wharton   Memᵒ That at a Court held
    Recordat. viii Die ejuſ ment.   for yᵉ County of Middleſex yᵉ
    Test Chr Robinson Clr   4ᵗʰ Day of Novembᵣ 1678
                         Pᵣsonally appeared Richard
                         Robinson and Ann his Wife
                         Pᵗies to this Indenture, and
                         did in open Court acknowledge
                         it Theire act and Deed, The
                         Said Ann being Examᵈ said
                         she did it Freely & Volluntary.

(57)   At a Vestry held the 3ᵗʰ of Octoᵣ 1687 at yᵉ houſe
of Mᵣ Richard Robinſon for Christ Church Pᵣish In Middleſex County &c.

Pʳsent	Mʳ Abraham Weekes	Mʳ Chr Robinson
Mʳ Duell	Mʳ Matthew Kemp	Mʳ Jnº Wortham
Pead	Mʳ Oſwald Cary	Mʳ William Daniell
Minister	Mʳ Richᵈ Robinſon	Mʳ Wᵐ Churchhill
	Mʳ Richᵈ Willis	Mʳ Robert Dudley

Vestrymen

1b Tobº

It is Ordered by this pʳsent Vestry that mʳ Duel Pead
Miniſter be paid for his officiateing as Minister In this
Pʳish this Pʳsent Yeare   16000

It is ordered by this pʳsent Vestry that Joseph Harvie
Clerke be paid   3000

It is ordered by this pʳſent Vestry yᵗ mʳ Oswald Cary
pʳsent Ch. warden be paid for Carpenters Worke done at
yᵉ Grẽt Church by mʳ John Stamper   100

_____

19100

It is ordered by this pʳsent Vestry that Richard Watts
a poore Aged and Impotent man be pᵈ for Maintenanᶜᵉ   1000

It is ordered by this pʳsent Vestry that Mary Norman
be paid for Keeping a bastard Child of Mary Hutſons
Servᵗ to mʳˢ Frances Sheppard one whole yeare Ending
yᵉ 13ᵗʰ of Janʳy next, and that then the Said Mary Norman is hereby Ordered to deliver the said Child up to yᵉ
Church Warden   1000

It is ordered by this pʳsent Veſtry that mʳ Duell Pead
Miniſter be paid for Repaireing the houſes at the Gleab
Land (on wᶜʰ he liveth) and making of yᵐ Tenantable   4000

It is ordered by this pʳsent Vestry That Mary Thompson a poore Woman (a very object of Charity) be allowed & paid toward her Maintenance 1500ˡᵇ of Tobº
& Cask   1500

It is Ordered by this pʳsent Vestry that 2000ˡᵇ of
Tobacco & Cask be depositted in yᵉ hands of yᵉ Churchwarden for this Enſueing Yeare namely mʳ Chr Robinson, the wᶜʰ Sume is towards yᵉ Defraying of yᵉ
Charges of the ornaments for the Severall Churches of

this P^{r}ish wch are comeing in by order of ye said m^r Robinson &c.   2000

                                                                   9500
                                             lb   28600
                                                        lb Tob^o

(58)   Brought from ye other Side the Sume of   28600
It is ordered by this p^{r}sent Vestry that m^r Oswald
Cary be paid for Glaſio^{rs} worke don at ye Gr^t Church
by Thomas Norman   100

It is ordered by this p^{r}sent Vestry That m^r Edwin
Thacker Surveyor be paid for Surveying the Gleab Land
and Kings Land adjoyning Thereunto and for Enter-
ing ye Kings Land by m^r Christop^r Robinſon in ye behalfe of the P^{r}ish and renuing the said Entry, with y^e
Charge of Carrying of ye Chaine, and other Charges Extraordinary, as ℔ his accompt   1235

1
7
52(8   lb   29935
842(5 lb   Cask at 8 ℔ Cent is   2400
33951(59 ℔ pole P^{r}ish Charge   ———
5744 23½ ℔ pole County Charge   32335
57——   Sallery at 5 ℔ Cent is   1616
    82½ ℔ pole In all   ———
                   The Totall Sume is   lb   33951
It is ordered by this p^{r}sent veſtry That m^r Matthew Kemp
High Sher. Doe Collect the P^{r}ish Levey being 59^{lb} ℔ pole &c.

It is Ordered by this p^{r}sent Vestry that m^r Francis Weekes
and m^r Richard Willis be added to this Vestry as members
Thereof &c.

It is Ordered by this p^{r}sent Veſtry that ye Uper Chappell
In ye uper precinq of this County be Inlarged Twenty Foot as
hereafter followeth Viz^t

    20 Foot in length to be added to ye West End There-
    of the Pulpit and ye Screan to be Removed, and the

Comunion Table to be Rayled in, All wch is to be done at ye Discretion of the Churchwardens, and to ye Intent that ſo neceſſary a Worke may be done wth great Care and Expedition   It is Further ordered by this Said Vestry that m^r Francis Weekes m^r Christop^r Robinſon and m^r Richard Willis do Treat and agree wth Some honest and able workman to p^rforme the Same in most Convenient order & Due Time.

It is ordered y^t m^r Edwin Thacker Survey the waſt Land Adjoyning upon the Gleabe, for wch with his former Survy of the Gleab Land, this Vestry will See ye said Edwin Thacker Sattisfied.

It is ordered by this p^rsent Veſtry that m^r Wm Churchhill be Ch. warden for ye lower Chap^{ll} in ye lower Pcinq In ye place of m^r Jno Cant Dec^d

It is ordered by this p^rsent Vestry that m^r Frã. Weekes be Church warden for ye uper Chap^{ll} In the Uper p^rcinq In the place of his Father m^r Abraham Weekes.

It is ordered that m^r Christop^r Robinſon be Ch. warden for the Great Church In the Middle precinq In the place of m^r Oswald Cary &c.

(59)   Att a Vestry held the 12th of Novem^{br} 1688 at the houſe of m^r Richard Robinſon for Christ Church P^rish In Middleſex County &c.

Present

m^r Duell	Mr Matthew Kemp	Mr Richd Robinson
Pead	Capt Oſwald Cary	Mr John Wortham
Minister	Mr Chr. Robinson	Mr Wm Churchhill
	Mr William Daniell	Mr Robert Dudley
	Mr Richard Willis	

1b Tob^o

Itt is Ordered by this p^rsent Vestry that m^r Duell Pead Minister be paid for his officiateing as Minister in this p^rish this p^t year   16000

Itt is Ordered by this p^rsent Vestry that Jos. Harvie Clerk be p^d for his officiateing at all ye 3 Churches this p^t yeare   3000

It is ordered that m^r Chr Robinson be paid ⅌ Rest
of his Disburʃtm^{ts} for Ornaments he furnished to all y^e
3 Churches being £10 : 16: 10 The wch Suṁe to be Re-
duced Into Sw^t Sented Tob° at 1^d ⅌ pound, to be paid
him at Soṁe Conven^t Landing wth Cask to Containe
ye same Ammounting to   2602

It is Ordered that m^r William Churchhill be paid for
the Charge of building the Stable below in ye Lower
P^{r}cinq the worke not being quite finished. It is further
ordered that ye Tobacco be Deposited in his said hands
until ye worke be finished, and he then to Discharge the
same being   1988

It is Ordered that Mary Thompson a very object
of Charity be allowed and paid towards her Maintain-
ance 1500^{lb} of Tob° & Cask   1500

It is Ordered that Richard Watts a poore Aged &
Impo^t man be paid for mentainance 1000^{lb} of Tob° and
Caske   1000

It is ordered that John Sutton be p^d for Maintenance
of Frances Worʃele a poore Lame Woman, who was
Entertained by ord^r of Court   1000

It is ordered that Jone Deverdale be paid for ½ a
yeares Nurʃing of a bastard Child belonging to a W°
Servt of Coll° Wormeleys   500

It is Ordered that Mich^a Musgrave be p^d for maintaining a W° Criple Named Bridgett Preʃs   500

It is Ordered That Tho. Norman be p^d for Twice
mending and putting up of ye Cap^{ll} Windows below, &
alʃo mending & putt. up the Wind^a at ye gr^t Chu.   500

It is Ordered that m^r Matthew Kemp be p^d for his Excellency for the Seale of ye Pattent for ye piece of Land
lately taken up and added to the Gleabe Land   200

More for m^r Secretarys Fees on Same accot   190

                                        Turn over   lb   28980
                                                        lb
(60)   Transported or Brought from the other Side   28980

It is Ordered by this p^rsent Veſtry That David Barwick be p^d for his Trouble and Releiveing of Elz Eddington Dureing her Sicknes at his houſe   300

It is Ordered that Robert Gilliam be paid for makeing
a horſe Block at y^e Great Church   200

$		29480
19$ lb	Cask at 8 ₩ Cent is	2350
33430 (53 ₩ pole P^rish Charge		
6311 53 ₩ pole County Charge		31838
63 —	Sallery at 5 ₩ Ct is	1592
106 ₩ pole In all		
	Totall lb	33430

It is Ordered by this p^rsent Vestry That m^r Matthew Kemp
High Sherriff doe Collect the P^rish Levey being 53^{lb} of Tob^o
& Cask ₩ pole.

It is ordered that m^r Matthew Kemp be Churchwarden for
The lower Chap^{ll} In ye Roome of m^r William Churchhill &c.

It is ordered that m^r Richard Willis be Ch. warden for the
Great Church In ye Middle P^rcinq. In ye Roome of m^r Xpher
Robinson.

It is ordered that m^r Francis Weekes Continue his place of
being Church warden for this p^rsent yeare Enſueing.

It is ordered by this p^rsent Veſtry That ye p^rsent Church-
Warden of ye Lower P^rcinq namely m^r Matthew Kemp Doe
Take into his Cuſtody and Care a poore Decripped & lame
Woman Named Bridgett Preſs Cauſeing her to be Conveyed
to Do^r Boodle and to have his Judgment about her lamenes
and that ye Said m^r Kemp and m^r Robert Dudley are by us
Directed to adviſe and agree wth ye Said Do^r Boodle or any
other able Doctor or Cirurgion about her Cure.

It is by this p^rsent Veſtry Requeſted of m^r Deuell Pead to
take The Trouble upon him to goe to Coll^o Christop^r Wormeley.

(61)   Att a Vestry held at Christ Church February the 5ta
1688

P^rsent   Ralph Wormeley Esqr   Mr Matthew Kemp
          Coll° Chr Wormeley   Mr Francis Weekes

It was then Confidered that a former Order Viz^t anno 1670
had Impowered foure or Five of the Veſtry to act in all affaires
of the said P^rish appertaineing to ye Veſtry, with full power
and authority,—In perſuance of ye said ord^r The foresaid
Gentlemen being mett upon a Lawfull Summons to Chuſe a
Clerk and finding that the Rest of ye Veſtry made not Theire
appearance, being Tender of giveing Diſtaste, Did Frely Referr
the said Ellection to a fuller Convention. But that ye P^rish
might not in the Intrim be unſupplyed, Did by Vertue of y^e
foresaid Ord^r appoint m^r Thomas Heyward to Supply the
place of a Clerke, promiſing to the Said Heyward Sattiſfacõn,
for ye Time So Employed.

(62)   Att a Vestry held Aprill the 2th 1689 at Chriſt Church
In Middleſex County &c.

          Ralph Wormeley Esqr   Mr William Daniell
P^rsent   Coll° Chr Wormeley   Mr John Wortham
          Mr Xphr Robinson   Mr Robert Dudley
          Mr Richd Robinson   Mr Richard Willis

It is Ordered by this p^rsent Veſtry that for the Future The
Veſtry be Summoned unto, and Sett in the Middle Church of
ye Pish And There and no where Elſe to Dispatch all P^rish
buſineſs.

It is alſo Ordered That for the Future the P^rish be Served
by Thre Clerks, Each Church haveing one Diſtinct, Who shall
Duely on ye Lords Day Read Divine Service, and a Homily
and alſo heare ye Children The Catechiſme of the Church of
England, Moreover Each Clerk shalbe a Man of good Sober
life and Converſation, and Carefully look after the Church
under his Charge Keeping of it Cleane & Decent Alſo Se-
cureing it from Danger by Due and Timely burning of the
Leaves about it.

It is alſo ordered That the Clerks of the upper and lower
parts doe keepe punctually an accompt of the Burialls Chriſt-
nings and Marriages In Theire Reſpective P^rcinq and make
a True and Timely Returne Thereof to the Clerke of the

Middle Church, Who Shall Insert Them into The publique Regiſter.

They must alſo Keepe the plate and the Linnen very Cleane and Decent.

It is further ordered by the pʳsent Veſtry That yᵉ Ch. wardens of yᵉ parish be for the future Choſen at a Veſtry held in Christ Church, which Shall alwayes be on Eaſter Tueſday, and the pʳsent Ch. wardens are here Deſired to continue in Theire places till yᵉ next Eaſter Tueſday in perſuance to yᵉ pʳsent order.

It is further Ordered by this pʳsent Veſtry That the Ministers Dues be according to Law gathered & paid by the Ch. wardens, for The Time being.

It is Further ordered That Thomas Heyward be Conſtituted Clerk of Christ Church, and do act as is above Directed &c.

(63)   August the 25ᵗʰ 1689

Then a Vestry held att Christ Church Pʳish In Middlesex County.

	Ralph Wormeley Esqʳ	Mʳ Richard Robinſon
Pʳsent	Mʳ Chr Robinson	Mʳ John Wortham
	Mʳ Matthew Kemp	Mʳ Oswald Cary
	Mʳ Robert Dudley	Mʳ Richard Willis
	Mʳ Robert Price	
	Veſtrymen	

It is Ordered by this Vestry That the Thre Churches are Forthwith To be Repaired.

Farther it is Ordered That all Pʳsons shall for yᵉ Future Submitt to the Direction of yᵉ Church wardens of Each Pʳcinq for Theire placeing & Sitting in the Church during the Time of Divine Service, till Such Time as a full Veſtry meeting a larger Order of this Nature be Iſsued forth and farther Care be Taken &c.

Further it is Ordered Thaᵗ mʳ Matthew Kemp as Ch. warden doe make Due pʳsentment to the next Court of Mʳˢ Jones, houſekeeper to the Honorᵇˡᵉ Collᵒ Xpher Wormeley for haveing bourn Two Children, wch are in this P^rish, and may put the P^rish to great Charge The Father Unknown.

Farther Whereas m^r Kemp hath given ye Ve∫try of this P^rish an acco^t that of Executeing his office as Churchwarden the 21th of July last past, In Peankatanke Church. That he hath Therefore received hard Words, and that this just and hone∫t Action of his in Displaceing of m^rs Jones Sitting above her Degree in ye Same Church, hath mett with a hard Con-∫truction, The P^ri∫h after Theire Thanks to the s^d m^r Kemp for his Dilligence in his Duty, have farther agreed and by this Theire Order do agree That they approve of what was Then and There done by the said m^r Kemp, and will Stand by him not onely in this but in all Actions of ye like Nature And that none in the lea∫t might be Incouraged in Disorder and Rudene∫ses, It is the De∫ire of the Ve∫try that this Theire Order be publi∫hed in Each Church of this P^rish.

Turn over

(64)   It is Ordered That on the Third Munday in Novem^br There is a full Ve∫try to meete According to ye former Order.

It is farther Ordered that Nicholas Love be Con∫tituted Clerk of Chri∫t Church P^rish In Middle∫ex &c.

(65)   Att a Ve∫try held at Christ Church In Middlesex County The 12th of Novemb^r 1689

Present

Mr Deuel	Ralph Wormeley Esqr	Capt William Daniell
Pead	Coll° Chr. Wormeley	Mr Francis Weekes
Mini∫ter	Mr Abrã. Weekes	Mr John Wortham
	Mr Matthew Kemp	Mr William Churchhill
	Mr Xpher Robinson	Mr Richd Perrott
	Ve∫trymen	

lb Tob°

It is Ordered by this p^rsent Vestry That Mr Deuell Pead Mini∫ter in this P^rish be paid for his officiateing as Minister This P^rsent Yeare The Sume of   16000

It is Ordered that m^rs Heyward be paid for her Hu∫-bands Officiateing as Clerk of the Middle Church   1000

Ordered that Nicholas Love be paid for ½ a Yeares
Officiateing as Clerk in yᵉ Middle Church   600

Ordered that John Nash be paid for ½ a Yeares Service in yᵉ Uper Chapˡˡ as Clerk   500

Ordered that Mich. Muſtgrave be paid for ½ a Yeares
Service in the Lower Chapˡˡ   500

Ordered that mʳ Deuel Pead be allowed as his Pde-
ceſsor Mʳ John Sheppard was in his Leveys and Tythable Vizᵗ Six Pʳish Levyes.

To Mary Norman for Nurſing a Pʳish Childe   1000
To Mʳ Maurice Cock for a Pʳish Child   1000

Ordered to mʳ Kemp as Ch. warden to pay The
Glaiſior, if he Se the work done Deſerve it, and hereof
mʳ Kemp is to give accoᵗ to yᵉ next Veſtry   900

Ordered that no accoᵗ [of worke]* be allowed for any
publique Worke but wᵗ Shalbe by Agreement wᵗʰ the
Church wardens.

To Richard Watts being Impotent   1000
To mʳ Robey for Entertaineing of Ann Winger   300

                                                       _____
                          Carried over   lb   22800
(66)   lb Tobᵒ
          Brought from the other Side   22800

To John Sandeford for Keeping a Pʳish Child   900

Mʳ Matthew Kemp is allowed for 25 Shillings layd
out upon Frances Wortley   300

To Mʳ Deul Pead an allowance for his being pᵈ Inconvenᵗ Tobᵒ   500

To John Sutton for Takeing Francis Wortley from being a farther Charge to the Pʳish, and that yᵉ Said John
Sutton give Bond to the Ch. warden of yᵉ lower Pʳcinq
for the same before a Juſtice of Peace   2000

It is Ordered That Doʳ Boodle be paid for Keeping
Bridgᵗ Preſs Twelve Months laſt past   1000

                                                       _____
                                                       27500

_____
* Half erased in the original, but still legible.—C. G. C.

To Mary Thompson at Thomas Cranks omitted above   1000

5(4
33(8   28500
446(1   28500 at 8 ℔ Cent for Caske   2280
31705(44   ℔ pole for Pᵣish Levey
7211 35½ ℔ County   30780
72 ——   Sallery at 5 ℔ Cent   1425
        79½ ℔ pole In all
                                    Totall is   32205
                                    Credit ℔ Willis   500

                                    Rest   31705

Ordered That Richard Willis pay Five hundred pounds of Tobᵒ being his Siſter Ellianor Alldin's fine laid Upon her by the Court for Coᵐitting Fornication for wᶜʰ he became Security, and upon his Refuſall mʳ Kemp is Deſired to Take out Execution as he is Ch. warden.

It is ordered That Richᵈ Willis bring an action agᵗ mʳ Edmund Chipsey for the Child born of his Servᵗ Abigall Redmond being a Pᵣish Charge, being at Nurse at Thomas Normans and if Willis Shall herein faile he Shall himſelfe pay The Charge.

It is farther ordered That Richᵈ Willis Ch. warden of yᵉ Middle Pᵣcinq do bring an Action Agᵗ mʳ Richᵈ Robinſon for bringing Bridget Preſs into this Pᵣish, who hath been a Charge to This Pᵣish, and a Copy of this ordʳ to be given to yᵉ Said Ch. warden by the Clerk.

This pʳsent Veſtry haveing Conſidered of Collecting yᵉ Leveys by the hands of the Ch. wardens In perſuance of a former order of Veſtry, and Deuel Pead the Pʳsent Minister finding the same Method Inconvenᵗ Deſired that the former Method of Collecting by the Sherif may be obſerved, To wᶜʰ motion they have Conſented, and accordingly mʳ Kemp high Sheriff is ordered to Collect yᵉ Pᵣish Levy being 28500 whereof 500 is Cut of by Credᵗ upon Richᵈ Willis.

(67)   Att a Vestry held for Christ Church Pᵣish In Middˣ County the first Day of June 1690

P^rsent	Capt William Daniell	Mr Richard Willis
m^r Deuel	Mr John Wortham	Mr Wm Churchhill
Pead	Mr Chr Robinson	Mr Richd Robinson
Miniſter	Mr William Dudley	Mr Allexander Smith

Vestrymen

Mr Randolph Seager m^r John Vause m^r Maurice Cock were This Day added and Sworne Veſtrymen.

Mr Randolph Seager was appointed Churchwarden for the Uper Chapell m^r John Vauſe for ye Middle Church, and m^r William Churchhill for the Lower Chappell &c.

Att a Vestry held the 22th of June Att Chriſt Church In Middleſex County Ann° 1690
P^rsent

The Majo^r part of ye Gentlemen of the Vestry For ye Said P^rish &c.

Edward Anne is Appointed by this P^rsent Veſtry to officiate as Clerk of the Great Church untill a full Veſtry shall meet to Determine of his longer Continuance &c.

(68)   (Blank.)

(69)   Att a Vestry held for Christ Church P^rish In Middle-ſex County Novemb^r the 11th 1690

Present

Mr Abraham Weekes	Mr William Churchhill
Mr William Daniell	Mr Robert Dudley
Mr John Wortham	Mr John Cant
Mr Chr. Robinſon	Mr Matthew Kemp

Mr Maurice Cock

lb Tob°

Ordered by this P^rsent Veſtry That m^r Deuel Pead be paid for Nine Months preaching the Suñe of Twelve Thous^d pounds of Tobacco and Caske   12000

Ordered That John Nash be paid for one yeares Service as Clerk of the Upper Chap¹¹ One Thousand pounds of Tob° and Cask. and for Two Months Service at the great Church 200^{1b} and Cask   1200

Ordered That Michaell Musgrave be paid for one years officiateing as Cl. of y⁹ Lower Chap¹¹ 1000¹ᵇ of Tob⁰ & Cask   1000

Ordered that mʳ Richard Perrott be paid 1000¹ᵇ of Tob⁰ & Cask for Timber for the New Addition of y⁹ Upper Chap¹¹ provided he do finde for the Finishing of the Same   1000

Ordered that Mʳ Randolph Seager as being Churchwarden for the Upper Pʳcinq of this Pʳish, Doe pay unto Samuell Matthews when he Shall have fully done and Finished the worke of the Upper Chap¹¹ Eight Thousand pounds of Tobacco and Caske   8000

Ordered that mʳ William Churchhill be paid 1000¹ᵇ of Tobacco and Caske for Disbursting Soe much last yeare to Bridgᵗ Preſs as being Ch. warden for the lower Pʳcinq of this Pʳish   1000

Ordered to mʳ Wᵐ Churchhill 335¹ᵇ of Tobo for Nailes & Worke Done to the lower Chap¹¹   335

                              Carried over   lb   24535
                                                      lb Tob⁰
(70) Brought from the Other Side   24535

Ordered to John Skeeres Executoʳ of Nicholas Love Six hundred pounds of Tob⁰ and Cask, for the said Love's being Cl. of the great Church Six Months   600

Ordered to Edward Anne 400¹ᵇ of Tobacco and Caske for being Foure Months Cl. of the great Church   400

Ordered to Richard Watts a poore Indigent Man one Thouſand pounds of Tobacco and Cask   1000

Ordered to Mary Thompson a poore Cripple one Thousand pounds of Tobacco and Cask   1000

Ordered That Thomas Marston be paid for Keeping a Baſtard Child   1000

Ordered that mʳ Robert Boodle be paid for Keeping of Bridᵗ Preſs 600¹ᵇ of Tobacco and Caske   600

Ordered to Thomas Norman 200¹ᵇ of Tob⁰ for Keeping a bastard Child, omitted last Yeare   200

Ordered to Thomas Norman 1000^{lb} of Tobacco and
Cask for Keeping a bastard Child this Yeare   1000

Ordered to m^r Maurice Cock 1000^{lb} of Tobacco &
Cask for Keeping of a Mulatto Bastard Named Ann
of ab^t Two Years old, and the Said Cock is to Discharg
this P^rish of all Trouble and Charge of the said Mulatto
for the Future   1000

Ordered to Mr John Vauſe 500^{lb} of Tobacco and Caske
to be by him p^rsented (as being Ch warden for the Mid-
dle P^rcqs of this P^rish) to m^r Clack with Kinde Thanks
for his Trouble and paines in Comeing to give us a Ser-
mon at the Great Church   500

                              lb Tob°
              Carried over   31835   lb.   31835
                                               lb Tob°
(71)   Brought or Transported over   31835

Ordered to m^r William Churchhill as being Ch warden for the Lower P^rcinq of this P^rish to be by him
p^rsented to m^r Booker (In like manner) for his Trouble
in Comeing to give us a Sermon at the lower Chap^{ll} &c   500

Ordered to m^r Randolph Seager as being Ch. warden
for the Upper P^rcinq of this P^rish 500^{lb} of Tob° and
Cask to be Disposed of as he and the other Gentlemen
of the Vestry In that P^rcinq Shall Se Convenient   500

                                      lb   32835
1(4   Cask at 8 ℔ Cent Comes to   2628
285(5
37105(53 lb ℔ pole the P^rish   lb   35463
7055 11½ ℔ pole County Sallery at 5 ℔ Cent is 1642
70
      64½ ℔ pole In all   Tottall   37105

Thomas Marston is Admitted by this P^rsent Vestry to be
Clerk of the Great Church for this Enſueing Yeare, and is
to Read Divine Service Every Sabbath day, and to Keepe
Cleane & Secure the Church from Fire.

Ordered that John Nash Doe Continue Clerke of the Upper Chap[ll] and Michaell Musgrave of the Lower, and to have According to theire last Yeares Allowance.

M[r] John Cant was This Day Admitted, and Sworne a Vestry Man for this P[r]ish.

(72)   Att a Vestry held for Christ Church P[r]ish In Midd[x] County the 22th of June 1691.

P[r]sent

	The Honor[ble] Ralph Wormeley Esq[r]	
	Coll° Chr Wormeley	M[r] Robert Dudley
	M[r] Matthew Kemp	M[r] Xpher Robinson
Vestrymen	Cap[t] William Daniell	M[r] John Cant
	M[r] John Wortham	M[r] Allexand[r] Smith
	M[r] W[m] Churchhill	M[r] Randolph Seager
	M[r] Maurice Cock	

The Honor[ble] Ralph Wormeley Esq[r] is Requested by the Gen[t]men of this Vestry to take the pa[ſ]sage of Elizabeth Thackston for England at his Discretion, and to be paid for the Same in the P[r]ish Levey next Lay'd.

Ordered by this p[r]sent Ve[ſ]try That M[r] William Daniell M[r] John Wortham and M[r] Allexand[r] Smith doe meete Sometime betweene this and the next Ve[ſ]try held for This P[r]ish, on the Gleabe of the Same, and View the Plantation and hou[ſ]eing to Se w[t] Repaireing they want and make Report to the next Ve[ſ]try according to the best of theire Judgments w[t] Reparation is wanting to the Said houseing belonging to the foresaid Gleab.

Ordered that Thomas Marston Doe Save the P[r]ish from a Bastard Child of one of m[r] Robin[ſ]ons Maids Named Ann.

(73)   I Deuel Pead Late of Middlesex In Virginia haveing lived in the Said County for at lest Seven Yeares pa[ſ]t, and Received Divers Kindne[ſ]ses from the P[r]ishon[rs] Thereof, And Almighty God [haveing]* In his great goodness haveing pre[ſ]erved me Through many Dangers in my Returne to England, and being most Kindly Received by my R[t] honorable, and R[t] Reverend Diocean Henry Lord Bp. of London.

---

* Half erased in the original, but still legible.—C. G. C.

Doe in point of Gratitude to Almighty God, and in honour
for the Church of England Freely Give and bestow for the
Uſe of my Succeſsoʳˢ in the Said Pʳish, Foure Milch Cows
& Calves Foure breeding Sows, a Mare and Colt, To be Delivered on The Gleab of the Said Pʳish to the next Incumbent,
he to Enjoy them and Theire Encreaſe for his Uuſe, and
leaveing the like Number and quallity on his Death or Re-
movell to his Succeſsoʳˢ Humbly Requesting my aforesaid Right
Reverend Dioceⁿ to give Charge to his Comiſsary there to Take
Due Care herein, and to Settle it in Such manner as to him
Shall Seeme Fitt according to the True Intent hereof, Witneſs
my hand in London this 12ᵗʰ Day of November In The Second
Yeare of the Reign of Our Soveraign Lᵈ & Lady King William and Q. Mary &c [Anny. Di]* 1690

Deuel Pead

This was done in
Pʳsence of us   Recorᵈ the 4ᵗʰ of March
    Micajah Perry   (From yᵉ Originall) In 1690/1
    William Sherwood   ℈ John Nash Cl. Vestry
(74)   (Blank.)
(75)   Att a Vestry held for Christ Church Pʳish In Middlesex County the 24ᵗʰ of Novembʳ 1691

Present

The Honʳᵇˡᵉ Ralph Wormeley Esqʳ

Mʳ Matthew Kemp   Mʳ John Cant
Mʳ Chr Robinson   Mʳ William Wormeley
Mʳ William Daniell   Mʳ Robert Dudley
Mʳ William Churchhill   Mʳ Richᵈ Robinson
Mʳ John Wortham   Mʳ Randolph Seager

It is Ordered by this pʳsent Vestry that Mʳ Xpher Robinſon
doe officiate as Church-warden for the Middle Pʳcinq of this
Pʳish Untill Easter next In the Roome of mʳ John Vause
Decᵈ

Ordered that the Church wardens doe Se and Enqʳ Into
what Reparations is wanting to the Gleab of this Pʳish, &

---

* These words may be incorrectly transcribed. They were difficult
to decipher. C. G. C.

Signifie the Same to the next Veſtry, and also that they Enqʳ
after Two Cows left for the uſe of the Free School by mʳ
William Gordon Decᵈ and Delivered to mʳ Deuel Pead our
late Miniſter, And alſo after Those Things Given by mʳ Pead
for the uſe of the Gleab &c.

Turn over to the Levy &c

lb Tobᵒ

(76) Ordered to Mʳ Matthew Lidford for Six
Months Preaching the Suñe of 8000ᵗᵇ of Tobacco &
Caske   8000
Ordered that one Thousand pounds of Tobacco &
Caske be preſented to Mʳ Samuell Gray Minister, by the
Ch. warden, for his Trouble in Comeing to preach in
This parrish   1000
Ordered to Thomas Marston for one yeares being
Clerk of the Great Church   1200
Ordered to Thomas Marston for Washing the Church
Lynen, and Cleaning the Church Yard   200
Ordered to John Nash for officiateing as Clerk of The
Uper Chapˡˡ last yeare   1000
Ordered to Michaell Musgrave Cl. of yᵉ lower Chapˡˡ   1000
Ordered to Mʳ John Gordon for one Sermon   500
Ordered to Claud Vallott for Worke done to yᵉ Free
School   250
Ordered to Henry Davis for Cleaning yᵉ Uper Capˡˡ
Yard   150
Ordered to mʳ Robinson for the Buriall of one Ruff
a poore Man   200
To Mary Thompson a poore Cripple   1000
Ordered to Bridget Woodard a poore Indigᵗ Woman   1000
Ordered to Mʳ Randolph Seager for Cloathing & put-
ting out a Bastard Child to Nurse, Two Months   200

lb   15700
lb Tobᵒ

(77)   Brought from the other Side   15700
Ordered to the Honorᵇˡᵉ Ralph Wormeley Esqʳ for
Takeing the paſsage of Elizabeth Thackston for England

Aſsigned by him to mᵣ William Churchhill, To be paid
him by the Sheriff in the Neck   1440

(2
$(0   lb   17140
565   Cask at 8 ℔ Cent is   1372
789(3
19439   28½ Pᵣish Charge   18512
6877   31½ County Charge   Sallery at 5 ℔ Cent is   927
68   20½ Charge from Town
─────   Totall Sum   19439
80½ In all

The Fraction being 344ˡᵇ of Tobacco is ordered to John
Nash for attending The Vestry.

This pᵣsent Vestry have Admitted Mᵣ Matthew Lidford to
be our Miniſter for this Enſueing Yeare, and ordered that
he have the uſe of The Gleabe, but if it happen that a Minister Should be Sent out of England to this Pᵣish, Then he to
have a Convenient Roome in yᵉ Gleab houſe, Dureing the Time
Agreed for wᵗʰ the Said mᵣ Lidford, and the said mᵣ Lidford
to have or give a quarters waning if he leave the Pᵣish at the
End of the Yeare &c.

It is Ordered that yᵉ Sherriff Doe Collect the Pᵣish Levey,
being 28½ ℔ pole, of 687 Tythables
&c

(78)   Att a Vestry held for Christ Church Pᵣish In Middˣ
County the 15th of Novembᵣ Annᵒ 1692

Present

Sᵣ William Skipwith, Baronᵗ

Capᵗ Matthew Kemp	Mᵣ John Cant
Capᵗ William Daniell	Mᵣ Maurice Cock
Capᵗ Robert Dudley	Mᵣ William Wormeley
Mᵣ Francis Weekes	Mᵣ Henry Thacker
Mᵣ Randolph Seager	Mᵣ Edwin Thacker

Sr William Skipwith K^t Mr William Wormeley Mr Henry
Thacker, and Mr Edwin Thacker were this Day Admitted, and
Sworne Vestrymen for this P^{r}ish.

Mr John Cant is Appointed Ch. warden for the Middle
P^{r}cinq Mr Maurice Cock for the Upper, and Mr William
Wormeley for the Lower P^{r}cinq of this P^{r}ish.   lb Tob°

It is ordered that Mr Matthew Lidford be paid for one
Yeares officiating as Mini∫ter in this P^{r}ish   16000

Ordered to Thomas Marston for officiating as Clerk
of The Great Church this last Yeare   1000

Ordered to John Nash Clerk of the Upper Chappell   1000

Ordered to Michaell Musgrave Clerk of the Lower
Chap^{11} 1000

Ordered that Anthony Slaughter be allowed Towards
Mentainance of him∫elfe and Family   1000

Ordered to Nicholas West for Keeping a ba∫tard
Child Ten Months   833

lb	20833
lb Tob°	

(79)   Brought from the other Side   20833

Ordered to Thomas Norman for Glaising the Middle and Lower Churches and finding Gla∫s and Lead   1000

Ordered to Bridg^t Woodard for Maintenance   500

Ordered to Mary Thompson a poore Cripple   1000

Ordered to William Thompson a Lame Man   150

lb	23483

Cred^t to Midd^x P^{r}ish by Mr Robert Dudley for Fines
by him Rec^d 1000

(2

5$4(2   Rest   lb   22483
700(5   Cask at 8 ⅌ Cent Comes to   1799
23496(37^{1b} ⅌rish Charge
0833 89 Publick & County Charge   lb   24282
08 ——   Sallery at 5 ⅌ Cent Comes to   1214
   126^{1b} ⅌ pole In all

Totall   25496

The Fraction (or overplus) being 225ᵗʰ of Tobacco is ordered to John Nash for Attending the Veſtry.

The Sherriff is ordered to Collect yᵉ Pʳish Levey being 37ᵗʰ of Tobacco ℔ pole of 683 Tythables.

It is ordered by this pʳsent Vestry that mʳ Matthew Lidford Doe Continue our Miniſter this Enſueing Yeare (if he please) and to have all Pʳquisitts that Shall become Due to him and the use of the Gleabe for the said Enſueing Yeare, and Sixteene Thousand pounds of Tobacco and Caske paid him at the Yeares End &c.

(80) (Blank.)

(81) Att a Vestry held for Christ Church Pʳish In Middlesex County, the 5ᵗʰ of Decemᵇʳ Annᵒ 1693

Present

mʳ Samuel Gray
   Miniſter

Sʳ William Skipwith Kᵗ	Capᵗ Richard Willis
Capᵗ Matthew Kemp	Mʳ Henry Thacker
Capᵗ William Daniell	Mʳ Edwin Thacker
Capᵗ Robert Dudley	Mʳ Richᵈ Perrott
Mʳ John Cant	Mʳ John Smith Senʳ
Mʳ William Wormeley	

Ordered by this pʳsent Vestry that Mʳˢ Lettice Lidford Reliq and Admˣ of mʳ Matthew Lidford Decᵈ be paid Foure Thousand Six hundred Sixty Six pounds of Tobacco and Cask, lying at yᵉ Severall places under Written and that the perſons in whoſe hands or in whose houſes the Tobacco is, Deliver the Same to her upon Sight of this Order &c.

	Gro		Ta
At Capᵗ William Daniells	690	—	81
At John Heads	610	—	98
At mʳ Henry Thackers	578	—	77
At Dittos on hhᵈ he made use of and is to pay	670	—	66
At Lᵗ John Smiths	766	—	86

At Dittos   660 — 80

                                                   3974   488

                                                              lb
                                                   Neet   3486
At m^r Maurice Cocks 2 hh^{ds} Weighing Neet   1010
In the Sheriffs hand to pay   170

                                                   Sum.   4666

Ordered that m^r [Thomas Stapleton]* Sam¹¹ Gray Minister be paid Seven Thousand Five hundred pounds of Tobacco and Cask for his preaching in this P^rish Since the Death
of m^r Lidford untill the Tenth of November last.

                                        Turn over

(82)   Ordered that m^r Thomas Stapleton pay unto m^r
Sam¹¹ Gray Minifter Three Thousand Eight hundred & Foure
pounds of Tobacco and Caske, part of the above order.

Ordered to m^r Sam¹¹ Gray In Mrs Seager's hands   lb
one hh^d of Tobacco, Grofs 640 Tare 75 Neat   565
   In Do^r Stapletons hands as afforesaid   3804

                                                   lb   4369

Ordered that Mrs Ann Seager pay and Deliver unto John
Nash or ord^r Two hh^{ds} of good Sw^t Sented Tobacco weighing
Neat one Thousand and Nineteen wth Cafk (lying in her
hands) upon Sight of This Order.

Ordered that m^{rs} Ann Seager pay and Deliver unto m^r
Thomas Marfton Five hundred and Fifty Thre pounds of Tobacco and Caske Lying in her hands.

Ordered that Mr Sam¹¹ Gray be paid Thre Thousand   lb
one hundred Thirty one pounds of Tobacco and Caske In
the P^rish Levey, part of the ord^r for Seven Thoufand
Five hundred   3131

* Half erased in the original, but still legible. C. G. C.

Ordered to m^r Thomas Marſton Six hundred Fourty
Seven pounds of Tobacco and Caske   647

   Ordered to Mary Clay a poore Indig^t Woman   500

   Ordered to Mary Freeſton a poore Woman   1000

   Ordered to Bridget Woodward   500

Transported over   lb.   5778

lb Tob°

(83) Brought from the other Side   5778

Ordered to Michaelſ Musgrave Clerk of the Lower
Chappell one Thouſand pounds of Tobacco and Caske
omitted above   1000

Ordered to m^r Maurice Cock Ch. warden of the upper
P^rcinq Five hundred pounds of Tobacco and Caske, to
be Disposed of by him for the Reliefe of Anthony
Slauter   500

Ordered to Nicholas Weſt for Keeping a baſtard Child
and the Said Weſt is to Save and Keepe this P^rish from
all Trouble and Charge of the Said Child for the Future
&c.   1500

lb   8778

(2   Cask at 8 ℔ Cent is   862

0̸(6

3̸1̸8̸(6   lb   9640

1̸0̸1̸2̸2̸ (14½ P^rish Charge   Sallery at 5 ℔ Cent is   482

7̸0̸4̸4̸ 68   Publique & County Charge

7̸0̸ ——   Totall lb.   10122

82½ ℔ pole In all

Ordered that ye Sher. Doe Collect the P^rish Levey being
Fourteene & a halfe pounds of Tobacco ℔ pole of Seven hun-
dred & Foure Tythables and make payment Thereof according
to the Tennor of the severall Orders before Mentioned.

Ordered that m^r Thomas Marſton be Clerk of the Great
Church and Lower Chap^{ll} and to have Seventeen hundred
pounds of Tob° and Caske for officiateing in the Two Said

Churches for this Enſuing Yeare, and is to Keepe yᵉ Churches and Church Linnen Decnt and Cleane Dureing yᵉ Said Yeare.

Ordered that John Nash Doe Continue Clerk of the Upper Chappell and to have the Yearely Rate or Sallery of one Thousand pounds of Tobacco and Caske paid him in the Pʳish Levey

Turn over

(84)   Ordered That mʳ John Cant mʳ William Wormeley and mʳ Maurice Cock Church wardens for Middlesex Pʳish or any Two of Them Doe at the Request of mʳ Samuell Gray Miniſter, Meete Upon, and View the Gleabe of this Pʳish, and Enquire wᵗ Reparation in Generall is Wanting Thereon, and alſo give the Said Mʳ Gray poſeſsion Thereof, and of all the Stock and Things wᵗſoever belonging to the Same, and make Report Thereof to the next Veſtry held for this Pʳish &c.

(85)   Att a Vestry held at Christ Church In Middlesex County Septemᵇʳ the 4ᵗʰ 1694

Present

mʳ Samˡˡ	Sʳ William Skipwith	Capᵗ Matthew Kemp
Gray	Knᵗ	Capᵗ Robᵗ Dudley
Miniſter	The Honorᵇˡᵉ Ralph	Mʳ Henry Thacker
	Wormeley Esqʳ	Capᵗ Richᵈ Willis

Ordered by this Veſtry that Capᵗ Richard Willis be Ch. warden for the Middle Pʳcinq. and that he wᵗʰ the other Ch. wardens or any Two of them View the Churches and Gleab, and See what Reparation they want, and agree with workmen for the Repaireing of them.

It is ordered by this Veſtry that mʳ John Grimes Lᵗ John Smith, and mʳ Robert Daniell be Veſtrymen, and to have Notice given them agᵗ the next Veſtry.

Ordered by this Veſtry that the Veſtry Booke be left at the Mother Church.

(86)   (Blank.)

(87)   Att a Vestry held at Christ Church In Middlesex County Novembʳ the 22ᵗʰ 1694

Present

	The Honor^ble Ralph	Mr William Wormely
Mr Sam^ll	Wormeley Esqr	Mr Henry Thacker
Gray	Capt Matthew Kemp	Mr John Smith
Minister	Capt William Daniell	Mr Edwin Thacker
	Capt Robert Dudley	Veſtrymen

Mr John Grimes haveing taken the Oath of a Veſtryman Is accordingly admitted.

Midd^x P^rish D^r	lb Tob°
To m^r Samuell Gray Miniſter	16000
To John Nash	1000
To Thomas Marſton	1700

Ordered that There be Levyed 1500^lb of Tobacco for the building a Stable at ye Middle Church, which Tobacco is to Remaine in the Ch. wardens hands 'till the Stable be Compleatly Finished ... 1500

To m^r William Wormeley Ch. warden for putting a Baſtard Child to Nurſs	550
To Thomas Dudley for a Horse-Block	150
To Ann Simpson a poore old Woman	600
To Bridg^t Woodard being afflicted wth Sickness	600
To Mary Clay	600

Carryed over	lb	22700
	lb Tob°	
(88) Brought from The other Side		22700
To Anthony Slauter		1000

Ordered that m^r Maurice Cock Doe dispose of it for The Said Slauters uſe &c.

To m^r John Grymes for Timber Boards, and the Carpent^rs Labour in getting Timber for ye Middle Church   730

To Richard Handson an old Man   80

| | lb. | 24510 |

~~633~~	Cask at 8 ℔ Cent is	1961
~~27697~~ (39ᵗᵇ ℔ pole		
~~7122~~		26471
~~71~~	Sallery at 5 ℔ Cᵗ is	1226

	Totall lb	27697

Ordered that yᵉ Sher. of Middleſex County Doe Collect The Pᵣish Levey being 39ᵗᵇ of Tobacco ℔ pole of Seven hundred and Twelve Tythables, and make payment Thereof according to the Tennor of the Severall orders before mentioned &c.

Ordered that Thomas Marſton Continue Clerk of the Two Lower Churches for this Enſueing Yeare.

(89)   Att a Vestry held at Christ Church In Middlesex County Novembʳ the 10ᵗʰ 1695
                         Psent
             The Honorᵇˡᵉ Ralph   Mʳ John Smith
Mʳ Samˡˡ   Wormeley Esqʳ   Mʳ Henry Thacker
Gray   Collᵒ Chr Wormeley Esqʳ Capᵗ Richᵈ Willis
Ministʳ   Capᵗ Matthew Kemp   Mʳ Edwin Thacker
             Mʳ William Churchhill   Mʳ John Grymes
             Capᵗ William Daniell
                      Vestrymen
        Christ Church Pᵣish, Middx. County Dʳ

	lb Tobᵒ
To mʳ Samˡˡ Gray Miniſter	16000
To John Nash	1000
To Thomas Marſton	1700
To Mary Clay a poore Woman	600
To Anthony Slauter a Lame Man	1000
To Bridget Woodard a Lame Woman	1000
To Ann Simpson an Old Woman	500

	lb	21800
(1	Cask at 8 ℔ Cent is	1744
~~2~~(5		
~~166~~	lb	23544

$\mathcal{BBB}$(4   lb   Sallery @ 5 ⑭ C^t is   1090
$\mathcal{24634}$(32½ ⑭ pole
$\mathcal{7655}$ Totall   lb   24634
$\mathcal{76}$
Turn over

(90) Ordered that Sr William Skipwith K^t High Sher. of this County Doe Collect and receive Thirty Two pounds & a halfe of Tobacco of Every Tythable in this County, for y^e Defraying of P^{r}i∫h Charge for this Yeare, and to make payment according to the Tenno^r of these Orders.

Ordered that Capt Richard Willis Doe pay this P^{r}ish when Demanded Fifteen hundred pounds of good Tobacco and Caske, for that wch was layd in his hands for building a Stable by a former Ve∫try, The Same to be paid by order of this Vestry.

Ordered that Capt Matthew Kemp be Ch. warden for the Lower precinq.

Ordered that m^r John Grimes be Ch. warden for the Middle precinq.

Ordered that m^r Edwin Thacker be Ch. warden for the Upper precinq.

Ordered that the Severall Su$\tilde{\text{m}}$es of Tobacco Levyed for the poore of this P^{r}ish be Lodged in the hands of the Churchwardens of the P^{r}cincts where they live, To be by them Disposed for Theire U∫e to the best advantage.

Ordered that Thomas Crisp be Clerk of the Upper Chap^{ll} In the Roome of John Nash.

Ordered that Thomas Marston Continue Clerke of the Tow Lower Churches.

(91) Att a Vestry held for the P^{r}ish of Christ Church In the County of Middlesex the 7th Day of Jan^{r}y 1695.

Present
m^r Sam^{ll} Gray Mini∫ter

The Honor^{ble} Ralph Wormeley Esqr	Capt Robert Dudley
Coll^o Xpher Wormeley Esqr	Mr Henry Thacker
Capt Matthew Kemp	Mr Maurice Cock
Mr William Churchhill	Capt Richard Willis
Capt William Daniell	Mr John Grimes

Mr Edwin Thacker

Ordered that the Church warden for the Middle Pcinct of This Prish Take Speedy Care to Repaire the Church in the Said Pcinct and to build a Stable of a Convenient Bigneſs, and to payle in a Church Yard, To be Done upon the best Termes for the Ease of the Prish &c.

(92)   (Blank.)

(93)   Att a Vestry held for Christ Church Prish In Middlesex County Novembr the 10th An. 1696

Present

Mr Samll Gray
    Miniſter

	Capt Matthew Kemp	Mr Henry Thacker
Vestrymen	Mr William Churchhill	Mr John Smith
	Capt Robert Dudley	Mr John Grimes
	Capt William Daniell	Capt Richard Willis
	Mr Edwin Thacker	

	Dr
Christ Church Prish In Middx County is	lb Tob°
To mr Samll Gray Miniſter	16000
To Thomas Marston Clerk	1700
To Thomas Chrisp Clerk	1000
To Capt Matthew Kemp Churchwarden for Repaireing The Lower Chappell	490
To Dor Tankerley for Administering Physick To a poore Man	800
To John Deverdale for Keeping a poore Sick Woman	400
To Ann Simpson a poore Woman	600
To Anthony Slauter	1000
To Henry Davis	600
Charity Williamson	600
To mr Henry Thacker for Keeping a Ladd of mr Stanards Troubled with Fitts	1000
To Widow Clay for last Yeare	400
To Ditto for this Yeare	600

Turn over	lb	25190
		lb Tob°

(94)   Brought From the other Side   25190

To Ellianor Slauter   1000

To m^r John Grimes Churchwarden for Carpenters
Worke and Materialls for Repaireing the Middle Church 14815

                                                                    ———
                                                                    41005

Ordered that Capt Richd Willis pay
Unto the P^{r}ish 1500^{lb} of good To-
bacco & Caske wch was putt in his   C^r ⅌ Willis   1500
hands for building a Stable

                                                          lb   39505
                            Cask at 8 ⅌ Cent   3160
                                                                 ———
                                                                 42665
                            Sallery at 5 ⅌ Cent   1975
                                                                 ———
                            Totall   lb   44640

Ordered that the Churchwardens of this P^{r}ish Take Speedy
Care for the building of a Dwelling house Upon the Gleab
For the Reception of the Minister, Forty foot long Twenty
Foot Wide, Two Inside Chimneys, wth a partition in ye Middle
of Nine foot pitch, and the Miniſter is to Keepe the said
houſe in good Repaire ——— and it is Farther ordered That
farther Care be taken abot the Repaireing Some of The other
houses, and when they are Repaired The Minister is to keepe
them in Repaire, as it may be Reasonably Thought the Said
Houſes may Stand.

It is ordered that m^r Wm Churchhill be Ch. warden for the
Lower Chap^{ll} m^r John Smith for the Middle Church, and m^r
Henry Thacker for the upper Chappell.

Ordered that Sr William Skipwith K^t High Sher. of this
County Doe Collect and Receive of Every Tythable in this
County 60½^{lb} of Tobacco, for the Defraying of the P^{r}ish
Charge, and make payment according to the Tennor of Theſe
Orders.

(95)   Att a Vestry held for the Prish of Christ Church In The County of Middlesex the 9ᵗʰ Day of Novembʳ 1697

Present

mʳ Samˡˡ Gray
    Minister

Sʳ William Skipwith Kᵗ   Mʳ Henry Thacker
Capᵗ Matthew Kemp   Mʳ John Smith   Veſtrymen
Mʳ Wᵐ Churchhill   Mʳ Edwin Thacker

Whereas by a Former order of Vestry There was a houſe to be built on the Gleab, It is farther ordered that yᵉ Said house be Compleatly Finished above and below, The Inside worke as well as the out Side, To be planked above and below, with Stairs and plaiſtering, with other Things needful as Glaſs &c.

Christ Church Prish In Middˣ County is Dʳ

	lb Tobᵒ
To mʳ Samˡˡ Gray Minister	16000
To Thomas Marſton Clerk	1900
To Thomas Chrisp	1000
To John Nash	100
To mʳ William Churchhill ℔ his accoᵗ	4285
To Doʳ William Oastler	600
To mʳ William Kilbee for Repairing yᵉ Lower Chapˡˡ	9600
To mʳ Edwin Thacker for Timber	1500
To Jone Deverdale	300
To mʳ Stapleton	200
To mʳ Edwin Thacker for Nailes	300
To mʳ Henry Thacker for Keeping a poore Ladd	1000
Carried over lb	36785

	lb Tobᵒ
(96) Brought over from the other Side	36785
To Ellianor Slauter	1000
To Mary Clay	1000
To Ann Dunkington for Keeping a baſtard Child	500
To John Ridgaway and his Wife	1000
To Thomas Norman for mending Windows	250

To Francis Dodson   300
To Charity Williamson   600
To Mr John Smith for Sending a poore Woman out
of the County   50
To James Smith Towards y^e Repaireing the Houses
at the Gleab   1000

                                                          _____

                                                          42485
                     Cask at 8 ⅌ Cent is   3568

                                                          _____

                                                          46053
                   Sallery 5 ⅌ Cent is   2124

                                                          _____

                              Totall   lb   48177
              C^r ⅌ Sr William Skipwith K^t   400

                                                          _____

                              Rest   lb   47777

Ordered by this Veſtry That m^r Francis Weekes High Sher.
of Middlesex Doe Collect of Every Tythable in This County
Sixty Foure pounds of Tobacco, to Defray the P^rish Charge
and to make payment according to The Tennor of these orders
&c.

(97)   Att a Vestry held for Christ Church P^rish In Midd^x
County the 15th of Novemb^r An. 1698

                         Present

Ralph Wormeley Esqr   Capt Robert Dudley
Sr Wm Skipwith Baro^t   Mr John Smith   Gent. of
Mr William Wormeley   Capt Richard Willis   the
Mr Frã. Weekes   Mr John Grimes   Vestry
Mr Henry Thacker   Mr Edwin Thacker

              Christ Church P^rish &c.   Dr.
                                                 lb Tob°

To m^r Thomas Stapleton for Keeping a baſtard Childe
borne of Ellianor Jaxson for ye Enſuing year   1000

Ordered that George Rhodes being the Reputed fath^r
of ye Said Child, Remaine in m^r Secretary Wormeleys
Service untill he be Committed into the Shers Cuſtody.

To mʳ Tho. Stapleton Adminiſtratoʳ of Richᵈ Fisher
for a horse block at yᵉ upper Chappell   300
   To Ditto a Fraction over Chargᵈ in yᵉ last Levey   186
   To mʳ John Smith ₱ the Gleab house, Workmens
wages Timbʳ and Nailes, and all other Things now done
to yᵉ Said houſe, Carting Dyatt, & all Things Incident   5000
                                                                    ─────────
                                                          lb   6486
   In Regard 1480ˡᵇ Tobacco was paid the last yeare to
the said Smith Toward Repaireing the house at the
Gleab, and the Same not being done, The said ſuᵐe of
1480ˡᵇ Tobacco was Deducted out of the ſuᵐe allowed
for the above Said worke, So that there Remaines only
the above sᵈ 5000ˡᵇ Tobacco &c.
                            Turn over   Whereas
   (98) Whereas Severall charges have been ᴴallowed for
building on yᵉ Gleab which now Seemes unreaſonable to the
Veſtry, It is Therefore ordered that noe other Tobacco Shalbe
Levyed upon yᵉ Pʳish for building on the said Gleab, But
that the houses on the Gleab be Kept in good repaire by the
Minister that shalbe Entertained in the parrish and that yᵉ
Said Minister shall leave the said houses in Repaire at leaveing
yᵉ Pʳish.
   Gawin Corbin Genᵗ Sworne and added to yᵉ Veſtry of this
Pʳish.
   Ordered That yᵉ Churchwarden forthwith cause the upper
Chappell in this Pʳish to be Glazed, or cauſe the old Windows
to be mended, The Tobacco to Remaine in the Churchwardens
hands untill the worke be Finished, and to find Glaſs for the
Said worke for wᶜʰ said worke There is Levyed   1000
   If it comes to more to be allowed next Levey.
   To mʳ William Churchhill for paying Edmund Saun-
ders for Nursing a baſtard Child   1000
   To Mary Clay a poore Woman   1000
   To be layd out by the Churchwarden
   To John Ridgaway & his Wife   1000
   To Dorothy Slaughter and her Daughter   1200

To Charity Williamson   600

To Thomas Marston   1900

To Thomas Chrisp   1000

To m^r Sam^{11} Gray his Clame for the last yeare, and upon the same Relinquishing all Clames he hath to the P^{r}ish for the said Consideration of his Induction or otherwise, It being the said m^r Sam^{11} Gray's one offer, and approved by the Vestry, They gave him his Sallery   16000

    Brought from the other Side   6486

	Carryed over	lb.	31186
			lb Tob°
(99)	Brought over		31186
	Sallery at 5 ⅌ Cent		1559
62	Cask at 8 ⅌ Cent		2619
75(8			
3536(4 49 ⅌ pole	Totall	lb	35364
7200			
72			

720 Tythables

Mr Gawin Corbin is appointed Church warden for the upper Prcincts of this P^{r}ish Capt Richd Willis for the Middle P^{r}cinq, m^r William Wormeley for the Lower P^{r}cinq &c.

Ordered that m^r Francis Weekes high Sherriff of this County Collect and Receive of Every Tythable Pson in this County 49^{lb} of Tobacco ⅌ pole, for Defraying the P^{r}ish Charge and make payment according to the Tennor of these orders.

Ordered by the Right honor^{ble} Ralph Wormeley Esqr and other Gen^{t}men of the Veſtry that m^r Robert Yates Minister be Entertained in this P^{r}ish beginning at May Day, till the Veſtry in November allowing him the Same Sallery as they have done to other Ministers.

    (100) (Blank.)

    (101) Att a Vestry held for the P^{r}ish of Christ Church In the County of Middlesex the 5th of June 1699

Present

Sʳ William Skipwith Kᵗ	Mʳ William Wormeley
Mʳ Matthew Kemp	Mʳ Robert Dudley Veſtrymen
Mʳ Wᵐ Churchhill	Mʳ Richard Willis

Ordered by this Veſtry that mʳ Robert Yates Minister be Entertained as Miniſter of this Pʳish from the first of May 'till the Veſtry in octobʳ Allowing him as the Law Directs.

Att a Vestry held at Christ Church
In Middlesex the 26ᵗʰ of July 1699

Pʳsent

Sʳ William Skipwith Kᵗ	Mʳ Robert Dudley
Capᵗ Matthew Kemp	Mʳ Richard Willis
Mʳ William Wormeley	Mʳ John Smith Vestrymen
Mʳ Gawin Corbin	Mʳ John Grimes

Ordered that mʳ Corbin mʳ Willis mʳ Edwin Thacker Doe View the upper Chappell and See what Repaireing She wanteth or any Two of them and returne word to the next Veſtry.

(102)   Att a Vestry held for the Pʳish of Christ Church In Middlesex County the 4ᵗʰ Day of Novembʳ 1699

Present

mʳ Robert Yates
   Miniſter

Sʳ William Skipwith Barroᵗ	Mʳ Henry Thacker
Mʳ Willᵐ Churchhill	Capᵗ Richard Willis
Capᵗ Robert Dudley	Mʳ John Grimes
Capᵗ John Smith	Mʳ Edwin Thacker

The Pʳish of Chriſt Church In the County of

Middleſex is	Dʳ	lb Tob°
To Mʳ Robert Yates Minister		8000
To the said mʳ Yates a Gift		2000
To Thomas Marston Clerk		1900
To Thomas Crisp Clerk		1000
To John Nash		1000
To Dorothy Manell an old Woman		300
To Margery Ridgaway a poore old Woman		600
To Henry Baskett a Cripple		400
To Mary Clay a Lame Woman		1000

To the Clerk of the Aſsembly omitted in yᵉ County
Levey   350
To Henry Towser a Levey over Chargd laſt yeare
Omitted in the County Levey   69
To Capᵗ Richard Willis ℔ his accoᵗ   455
                                                                          ————
                              Transported over   lb   17074
                                                                 lb Tobᵒ
(103)   Brought from the other Side   17074
To Dorothy Slauter an old Woman   300
To Doʳ Robert Deputy for the Cure of Ellianor
Slauter To be paid him when he gives good Security
at this County Court for her Cure, and for Ever Keep-
ing her the Said Ellianor from being a parrish Charge,
and if Such Security be not given the Said Tobacco to
Remaine in the Sherriffs hands   2000
To Edmund Sanders aſsigned to mʳ William Church-
hill   1000
To the Sexton at yᵉ Lower Chappell   200
                                                                          ————
                                                                          20575
(2   Sallery at 5 ℔ Cent   2057
3(9   ————
100   lb   22631
337(2   Cask at 8 ℔ Cent   1810
24441(31ˡᵇ ℔ pole   ————
7799   Totall   lb   24441
77

Ordered that the Severall Churchwardens in this Pʳish Ren-
der an accoᵗ to the next Court held for this County how the
Tobaccoes putt into Theire hands for the Reliefe of the poore,
was Disposed of, how Layd out, wᵗ Sold for and wᵗ Rates was
putt upon the Goods.

Ordered that the Sherriff of this County Collect & Receive
of Every Tythable Pʳson in this County, Thirty one & a halfe
pounds of Tobacco, for the Defraying the Pʳish Levey for this
Pʳsent yeare.

                              William Churchhill

(104)   Att a Vestry held for the Pᵣish of Christ Church In
the County of Middlesex Novembᵣ 18ᵗʰ 1700

Present

Mᵣ Robert Yates
  Minister

Sᵣ William Skipwith Barroᵗ	Mᵣ Henry Thacker
Collᵒ Matthew Kemp	Mᵣ Richard Willis
Mᵣ Gawin Corbin	Mᵣ John Grimes
Mᵣ John Smith	Mᵣ Edwin Thacker

	Dᵣ	lb Tobᵒ
Christ Church Pᵣish is		
To Mᵣ Robert Yates Minister		16000
To Thomas Marston Clerk of Two Churches		1900
To Thomas Chrisp Clerk		1000
To mᵣ Henry Thacker aſsigned by Edward Ball ℔ ordᵣ of Court		1000
To Ezekias Rhodes for mending the Pulpits		100
To Dorothy Slauter a poore Woman		300
To Mary Clay a Cripple		1000
To Margery Ridgaway and old Woman		600
To mᵣ Stapleton for his Trouble wᵗʰ Mumpus		600
To William Brooks for Keeping the said Man &c.		400
To Edward Ball for Keeping Charity Williamson the Enſueing Yeare		600
	Carried over lb	23500

		lb Tobᵒ
(105) Brought over		23500
Pᵣ Contra Credᵣ		
By William Mountague ℔ yᵉ Fine of Ann Watkyns		500
By Wᵐ Wise ℔ the Fine of Jane Floyd		500
		1000
	Rest lb	22500
∮	Sallery at 5 ℔ Cent	1125
117		
23425 (32ˡᵇ ℔ pole		23625

$155   Cask at 8 ℔ Cent   1800
$1
                              Totall   lb.   25425
Ordered that the Sherriff of This County Collect and Receive of Every Tythable In this County 32ᵗᵇ of Tobacco a head
for Defraying The Pᵣish Charges this yeare. Tythables 815.

Ordered that mᵣ Robert Yates Minister Continue an other
yeare which is from the First of Novembᵣ allowing him the
uſuall Sallery.

Ordered that a Veſtry be held at the upper Chappell the
First of Decembᵣ In order to the Repaireing, or otherwise.

Lᵗ Collᵒ Kemp Ch. warden of the Lower precinq. Capᵗ
John Grimes of the Middle. mᵣ Edwin Thacker of the Upper.

Ordered that Jane Floyd Serve Lᵗ Collᵒ Kemp one yeare
for her offence in haveing a baſtard begotten by her Maſter
and the Said Lᵗ Collᵒ Kemp doth promise And oblidge him-
selfe to pay the Pᵣish Five hundred pounds of Tobacco this
Enſuing yeare, In Consideration of the said yeares Service.

Ordered that Thomas Marſton Continue Cl. of Two
Churches.

Ordered that Thomas Chrisp Continue Clk. at the upper
Chappell.

                              Robert Yates

    (106) Att a Vestry held for the Pᵣish of Christ Church
In the County of Middlesex the 20ᵗʰ Day of Novembᵣ 1701

                        Present

Mᵣ Robert Yates
   Minister
Sᵣ William Skipwith Barroᵗ   Collᵒ Gawin Corbin
Lᵗ Collᵒ Matthew Kemp   Mᵣ Henry Thacker
Mᵣ William Churchhill   Capᵗ John Smith
               Mᵣ Edwin Thacker
        The above Pᵣish is   Dᵣ   lb Tobᵒ
    To Mᵣ Robert Yates Minister   16000
    To Thomas Marston Clerk   2000
    To Thomas Chrisp Clerk aſsigned to Gawin Corbin
Genᵗ   830

To Richard Stephens Sub, Sher. ℔ acco^t   70
To William Churchhill Gen^t aſsignee of Richd Ran-
ſtead for Sarah Poole   900
To Richard Ranſtead for Sarah Poole   100
To Coll° Matthew Kemp by acco^t   90
To John Chedle Sexton for Two Yeares   500
To Richard Ranſtead ℔ Ditto one Yeare   500
To Do^r Lomax for his Care about Charles Branshaw   800
To Charity Williamson   600

                              Carried over   lb   22390
                                                             lb Tob°
(107) Brought over   22390
To Mary Clay a poore Lame Woman   1000
To Edward Siddon for Nursing a Child Two Months   200
To Mr John Smith Aſsignee of Charity Williamson   400
To Hugh Watts for Nursing a baſtard Child Six
Months   500
To Elizabeth Blewford a poore old Woman   1000
To Henry Baskett a poore Lame Ladd   400
To William Churchhill Gen^t ℔ acco^t   459
To Andrew Folke an old Man   80

                                             lb   26429
               Deducted for Thre Fines   1500

                     Rest   lb   24929
For Buying Two Books for the P^rish   250

                     Totall   lb   25179
          To Sallery at 5 ℔ Cent   1258

                                                26437
          To Caske at 8 ℔ Cent   2114

                     Total Charge   28551

Ordered that Lt Coll° Matthew Kemp Sher. of the County of Midd^x Collect and Receive of Every Tythable p^{r}son in the P^{r}ish of Christ Church in the Said County The Sume of Thirty Five pounds of Tobacco for the Defraying of the P^{r}ish Levey for this P^{r}sent Yeare.

(108)   Ordered that Mr Robert Yates Miniſter of this P^{r}ish be Continued in the Said P^{r}ish according to Law.

Ordered that the Inhabitance of this P^{r}ish in the Severall precinq of the Same proſseſion Theire Lands according to Law.

*Ordered that John Nash fairely Transcribe the whole Veſtry booke of this P^{r}ish, and that he be paid for the Same at the Laying the next P^{r}ish Levey.

William Churchhill Gen^t is appointed Churchwarden for the Lower precinq of this P^{r}ish the Ensueing yeare.

Capt Tobias Mickleburrough is appointed Ch. warden for the Middle precinq. of this P^{r}ish ye Ensuing yeare.

Capt Robert Daniell is appointed Ch. warden for the upper precinq. of this P^{r}ish the Ensueing yeare.

Ordered that Christopher Robinson and Wm Kilbee be Summoned to the next Veſtry to be added to the Vestry.

Ordered that the Churchwardens buy Two books for the P^{r}ish Viz^t a Veſtry booke and a Regiſter book There being Tobacco Levied for the Same.

Ordered that the Ch. wardens be Impowered to Imploy a Doctor to take Care of Sarah Poole, and Endeavo^r to Cure her if poſsible.

M^d †Ordered That William Churchhill Gen^t be allowed one hundred pounds of Tobacco in the next P^{r}ish Levey, being for So much paid Richd Ranſtead by order of the Veſtry.

Ordered

(109)   Ordered that the Clerks of this P^{r}ish bring the Lists of the Marriages Chriſtenings and Burialls to the Miniſter of this P^{r}ish Every Quarter of a year.

---

* It may be noted here that up to this point all the entries in this book are in one and the same handwriting.—C. G. C.

† This word is half erased in the MS. but is still legible.—C. G. C.

Ordered that John Bristow be Clerk of the Upper Chappell The Ensueing yeare, and that he be allowed for the Same as uſuall.

Ordered that Collº Gawin Corbin Rayle the Coṁunion Table in the Upper Chappell in, and finde an new Table, and that he be allowed Six hundred pounds of Tobacco in the next Pᵣish Levey for the Same.

Transcribed out of the Old Vestry Book, by Order of Vestry held 20ᵗʰ of Novemb. Annº 1701 ℔ Jnº Nash.

Att a Vestry held for the Parish of Christ church in Middˣ County 4ᵗʰ of May 1702

Pᵣsent

Sʳ William Skipwith Barᵗ	Capᵗ John Grimes
Lᵗ Collº Matthew Kemp	Capᵗ John Smith
Mʳ William Churchhill	Mʳ Edwin Thacker
Collº Gawin Corbin	Capᵗ Robert Daniell
Mʳ Henry Thacker	

Upon the Motion of mʳ Robert Yates Minister of yᵉ above Named Pish Who Deſires for England, It is Ordered that he be paid According to Law for this present yeare, from the laying yᵉ last parish Levyes, And that he be Continued in his place, Or an Account be given of his Incapacity of Returning.

	William Skipwith	John Grimes
Entered ℔ J. N.	Matthew Kemp	John Smith
	Gawin Corbin	William Churchhill
	Henry Thacker	Edwin Thacker

(110)   Att a Vestry held for the Parish of Christ Church In the County of Middlesex the 7ᵗʰ Day of Novembʳ 1702

Present

Lieuᵗ Collº Matthew Kemp	Capᵗ John Smith
Capᵗ John Grimes	Capᵗ Robert Daniell
Mʳ William Churchhill	Mʳ Henry Thacker
	Mʳ Edwin Thacker

Mʳ Harry Beverley, Mʳ William Kilbee and Mʳ Richard Kemp Was Sworne Vestry Men and according Admitted.

Christ Church Parish is D^r	
To Mr Robert Yates Minister	16000
To Thomas Marston Clerk	1900
To John Bristow Clerk	1000
To The said Bristow for Former Service	168
To John Marston for Work done to the lower Chappell	150
To Coll° Gawin Corbin for Worke done to y° Upper Chap^{ll} as by Acco^t After the Same was Regulated	1100
To Lieu^t Coll° Matthew Kemp for Sallary and Caske ⅌ Receiveing Three Fines ommitted	195
To Mr William Churchhill ⅌ Acco^t	2019
To Ditto for Peter Chilton	40
To John Nash for Transcribeing the Register And Vestry Books	1500
To Edward Ball for Charity Williamson to the Time of her Death	600
To Mary Clay for the Ensueing yeare	1000
Transported over	25672
(111) Brought Over	25672
To Alice Silvester a poore Woman	250
To Hugh Watts for Keeping a Bastard Child one Yeare	1000
To Richard Ranstead Sexton	500
To Ditto for Extraordinary Service	100
To John Chedle Sexton	250
To Elizabeth Blewford as Usuall	1000
To Thomas Brooks a lame Ladd	1000
To Mr Edwin Thacker ⅌ Acco^t Clerks Fees	178
Totall	29950
To Cask Att 8 ⅌ Cent is	2396
	32346
To Sallary Att 5 ⅌ Cent is	1617
	33963

Deducted For Edward Gotts Judgment   606

                                                     33357
Deducted For Judgment Against Jonathan Harrin   156

                                    Remaines   33201

1
3320|1 (40ᴸᵇ ℔ Pole   Parrish Charge
3330
$

Money in the hands of Severall Pʳsons for yᵉ use of the Parish
                                               s   d
Mʳ William Churchhill ℔ Ditto   5   0
Mʳ Beverley Ditto   10   0
Mʳ Paul Thilman ℔ Ditto   5   0
Capᵗ John Grimes ℔ Ditto   5   0
John Sandeford   10   0

                                    £1   15   0
Ordered the Said Money to be paid to mʳ Paul Thilman
for Service done for the Pʳish.

                        Turn over

(112)   Whereas Mʳ Robert Yates Minister hath Drawn a
Note on The Vestry for the Suñe of Foure Thousand pounds
of Tobacco And Caske, payable to Mʳ William Churchhill
Genᵗ Which Said Note is by the Vestry Accepted, and Ordered
that the Said Suñe be paid by the Collecter to the said Mʳ
Churchhill Or Order, out of the Sixteene Thousand Leavied
for him.

    Edward Docker is Appointed Sexton of the Upper Chappell.

    Mʳ William Churchhill is Appointed Church-Warden for
the lower Pʳcincts of this parish.

    Capᵗ John Grimes is Appointed Church-warden for the
Middle Precincts of this Parish.

    Mʳ Richard Kemp is Appointed Church-Warden for The
Upper Precincts of This Parish.

Ordered that Sr William Skipwith Baron{t} doe Collect and Receive The Suḿe of Fourty pounds of Tobacco & Cask of Every Tythable person in this Parish, for ye Defraying The parish Charge for this P{r}sent Yeare — And that he make payment of the Same to whome it is proportioned by this P{r}sent Vestry.

Matt. Kemp*

(113) Att a Vestry held for the P{r}iſh of Christ Church In the County of Middlesex the 6th Day of November 1703

Present

Sr William Skipwith Barron{tt}

Collo Matthew Kemp	Mr Harry Beaverly	
Mr William Churchhill	Mr Edwin Thacker	
Mr Henry Thacker	Mr Richard Kemp	Vestry Men
Cap{tt} John Smith	Mr William Killbee	
Mr Frances Weekes		

The above said Parriſh is   Dr

To the Reverend Mr Bartholomew Yates Miniſter for his Preaching	†1200
To Thomas Marston Clerk	1900
To John Briſtow Clerk	1000
To Mr John Grimes Gen{t} ℔{r} Account	430
To Mr William Churchhill Gen{t} ℔{r} Acct Conſerning Charles Branshaw	569
To Collo Matthew Kemp Gen{t} for the S{d} Branshaw Rent	600
To Mr John Sandiford for Keeping Charles Branſhaw and Mary his Wife and to be allowed one Thousand Next Leavy for his Keeping them till that time	1000
To Mr Richard Kemp Church warden for Alice Silvester ye Laſt Yeare	1000
To Edward Docker Sexton	260

18759

---

* Up to this point (112 pages) all the writing in the MS. volume is in one and the same hand.—C. G. C.

† Evidently an error. Should have been 12,000.—C. G. C.

To John Webster a poore old man   1000
To Thomas Brookes a Cripple   1000
To Alice Cannady a poore Woman   1000
To Mary Clay a Lame Woman   1000
To Mr John Nafh ℘r Entering the Last order of
Vestry and Keeping the Regefter   500
To Elizabeth Bewford an old woman   1000
   (114)   To Richard Ranfford saxton att two Churches
Afsigned over to Mr William Churchhill   500
To Alice Silvester for the Enfewing Yeare   1000
To Hugh Watts for Keeping a Bafterd Child   833

                                                        ─────
                                                         7833
                                                        26592
                                                        ─────

To Hugh Watts for Keeping a Baftard Child untill
the Last Day of May   367

                                                        ─────
                                                        26959
To Patrick Miller a Lame man   500

                                                        ─────
                                                        27459
To sallery att 5 pr Cent   1377

                                                        ─────
                                                        28836
To Cafke att 8 pr Cent   2313

                                                        ─────
                                                        31149
To Patrick Miller a Fraction   185

                                                        ─────
                            The Sum   31334
806 Tythables

                      ──────────────

Order that Henry Thacker Gent High Sherriffe of the said
County doe Collect and Receave of Every tythable person in
the Aforefaid Parrifh the Sume of Thirty nine pounds of
Tobacco of the Prifh Grofe for the payment of the said

pareiſh Levey and in Caſe any person or persons Refuſe to Make Speedy payment to Make Diſtreſs.

Order that Harry Beaverley Gent Surveyor of the high Ways in the Lower Percintes of this County doe forthwith Cleare the Roads in his said percints and to take what Helpe he Thinks Neceſsary for the Doeing the same.

ordered that the Like be Done by all other surveyors of the High Ways in this County.

Matt Kemp

(115)

on Consideration of the Lawes of Virginia provision being maide by the act Entituled Church to be Built or Chappell of Eaſe for the Building a Church in Each pariſh and by the act Entituled Mineſters to be Inducted that miniſters of each pariſh and shall be Inducted on the presentation of the parishioners and the Church wardens being by the act Entituled Churchwardens to Keep the Church in Repare and Provide Ornaments to Collect yᵉ Miniſters Dues and by the act for the better support and Maintanance of the Clergy provision being maide for the Miniſters of the Pariſhes and by the said act for Inducting Miniſters the Governour being to Induct the Miniſters to be preſented and thereby he He being Constituted ordinary and as Bishop of the Plantation and with a Power to punish Ministers Preaching Contrary to that Law I am of opinion the Advewson and right of presentation to the Churches is subject to the Lawes of England there being no Expreſs Law of that Plantation made further Conſerning the same therefore when the Parishioners present their Clerk and he is inducted by the Governour who is to and muſt induct on the Preſsentation of the parishioners the Incumbent is in for his life and Cannot be Diſplaced by the parishioners If the Parishioners do not present a Miniſster to the Governour within six months after any Church shall be void the Governour as ordinary shall and may Collate a Clark to such Church by laps and his Collatee shall hold the Church for his life If the Parishioners have never presented they have a reasonable time to present a Miniſter but if they will not present being required so to doe the Governour may also in their Default Collate a Minister In inducting Ministers by the Governour on the Presentation of the parishes or on his owne Collation he is to see the Ministers be qualifyed according as that act for Inducting Miniſters requires In Case of the avoidance of any Church the Governour as ordinary of the plantation is according to yᵉ statute of 28 H 8 Cap 11ᵗʰ Sect 5ᵗʰ to appoint a Minister to officiate till the parish shall present one or the Six months be lapsed and such person appointed to officiate in the Vacancy is to be paid for his service out of the Profitts theireof from the time the Church becomes voyd By the Law above stated in this Case noe Minister is to officiate as such till he hath shewed to the Governour he is qualifyed according as the said act for Induction Directs if the Vestry do not levy the Tobaeco for the Minister the Courts their must Decree the same to be Levyed.

Edw Northey
July 29ᵗʰ 1703

(116)   (Blank.)

(117)   Att a Council held at Williams Burgh the 3ᵈ Day of March 1703

Upon reading at this Board Sir Edward Northey Knᵗ her Matys attorney Genˡˡ his opinion upon the act of Aſsembly of this Colony relating to the Church and particularly Concerning Induction of Miniſʳ[ ] his Excellency in Councel is pleased to order that a Copy of the Said Sʳ Edw Northey his opinion be sent to the Churchwardens of each parish within this Colony Requiring them upon recept theirof forthwith to Call a Vestry and theirto Cauſe the same be read and Entered in the vestry books to the intent the said vestery may offer to his Exelley what they think proper their upon

Fr. Nicholson   Wil Robertson Cll Con

At a Vestry held February yᵉ 15ᵗʰ 170¾
Present

Sʳ William Skipwith	Mʳ Harry Beverly
Mʳ William Churchill	Mʳ Richard Kemp
Mʳ John Smith	Mʳ William Kilbee
Mʳ John Grymes	

Itt is Ordered that the presentation following be fairly drawn
And Sent to the Governor that Mr Bartholomew Yates may be
Inducted Into this Parrish now being Vacant.

William Skipwith

To his Excellency Francis Nicholson &c.

We the Subscribers the Vestry for the parrish of Christ
church In Middlesex County humbly acquaint Your Excellency
that this Parrish is now destitute of A Minister to Supply which
Vacancy we prefent Mr Bartholomew Yates whom If Your
Excellency is pleased to Admit we desire may be Instituted and
Inducted Into our Parrish; And we Shall be moft thankfull
who are Your Excellencies moft dutifull and humble Servants.

William Skipwith   S c

(118)   (Blank.)

(119)   Att a Vestry Held for the Parrish of Christ Church
In the In the County of Middlesex the 18th Day of November,
Anno Dom 1704.

Present

Sr Will Skipwith Barronet
Coll^nl Matthew Kemp   Mr Barth. Yates Minist^r
Mr William Churchill   Captn Harry Beverly
Coll^nl Gowen Corban   Mr Richard Kemp
Coll^nl John Grymes   Mr WILLIAM KILBEE
Maj^r John Smith

To Mr Barth: Yates Minist^r	16000
To Mr Maston Clark 1300 being Afsigned to Mr Churchill	01900
To Mr Bristow Clark	01000
To Richard Ransford Sexton of two Churches Afsigned to M^r Ch:	00500
To Mr William Churchill Churchwarden	00258
To Coll^nl John Grymes	00280
To Edmund Ryan for Patrick Millars Board 5 Months	00500
To Edward Docker Sexton	00260
To Mr William Stannard	00226
To Mr Edwin Thacker	00050

To Mr. Harry Beverly for going to the Govern^r   01000
To Mr Nathaniel Juice for curing of William New-
berry And Patrick Millar   04600
  To Thomas Kid for Maintaining A Bastard Child   00500
  To Evan Jones   00080

To 200¹ to be divided Between the 2 Sextons   27354
            ℔ sall 5 ℔^r C^t   1368

                                        28722
        Cask 8 ℔ C^t   2297¾

                                        31019¾
                                         2000
                                        29019¾

                                Vide Dividend
Divided By 883 Tithables Amounts to 35½ ℔^r Poll.
Sr William Skipwith Barronett Sherriff Shall Receive the
35½ ℔^r Poll to discharge The Above Parrish Charges.
  Order Nathan: Underwood Being Made Clark of   1
Christ Church and of the Vestry Shall have   1400
  Mr Bristow being Clark of the Upper Chappel Shall
have   1000
  Robert Biggs being Clark of the Lower Chappel
Shall have   1000
  The above Clarks to Officiate the places of Readers
by reading divine Service And Homilies When there
is No Sermon.
                        Coll^nl Matthew Kemp
  (120) Att a Vestry held for Christ Church Parrish March
Y^e 5th Anno Dom 1704-5
                    Then P^rsent
Mr Bartholomew Yates Minist^r   Coll^nl Gowen Corbin
Mr William Churchhill   Mr John Smith
Mr Henry Thacker   Mr Richard Kemp
Mr John Grymes   Mr Harry Beverley
                                  Mr Robert Daniel
            Vestry Men

Upon Consideration of his Excellency ℗ʳ Order In Council and proclamation Relateing to Yᵉ Opinion of Sʳ Edward Northey about the Induction of Ministers In Answer to which we humbly Say that we had Inducted Mʳ Barth: Yates before Order of Council the proclamation came to our hands And yᵗ Mʳ Yates our Pʳsent Minister hath In his poſſeſsion Yᵉ Bible Sent by Sʳ Jeoffery Jeffreys And that the Glebe for this Parrish doth Contain four hundred twenty Eight Acres; by Estimation worth Two hundred pounds.

William Churchhill

(121)   Att a Vestry held for the Parrish of Christ Church In the County of Middlesex Yᵉ 26 day of November Anno Domi 1705

Present

Mʳ Bartholomew Yates Minister	Colloⁿˡˡ John Grymes
William Churchhill Eſqʳ	Captⁿ John Smith
Collonˡˡ Matthew Kemp	Mʳ Richard Kemp
Mʳ Henry Thacker	Mʳ William Kilbee

Gentle Men

Ordered by Yᵉ Aforesd Gentlemen of the Vestry as followeth

lb Tobᵒ

To Mʳ Bartholomew Yates Minister	16000
To Nathan Underwood Clark	01400
To John Bristow Clark	01000
To Robert Biggs Clark	01000
To Richard Ranstead Sexton Aſsigned to Esqʳ Churchhill	00500
To Edward Docker Sexton	00260
To Collⁿˡˡ John Grymes Churchwarden for Cureing John Fomett	01000
To Thomas Townsend an 100 And for the future to be levy free	00100
To Richard Reynald an 100 And for the future to be levy free	00100
To William Provert for keeping Elizabeth Beuford	01000
To Hannah Watt for keeping a Bastard Child	01000

To Richard Winn for keeping Alice Silvester   01000
To Henry Lane for burying of Anne Sherman &c.   00250
To William Stannard for Clarks fees ℔ᵣ fines &c.   00635
To Mʳ Richard Kemp Churchwarden for keeping of
John Webster   01000
To Mary Clay Aſsigned to Mʳ Richard Kemp Church-
warden   01000
To Michael Curliſs Aſsigned to Mʳ Richard Kemp
Churchwarden   00600
To William Churchhill Esq for Sending a Meſsenger
about Yᵉ Gleab Land
To Thomas Kidd for keeping a Bastard Child   01000

The first total   28905
The total deduction of fines   02159

The Remainder   26746
To Cask att 8 ℔ᵣ Cent   02140

The Addition   28886
To Sallery at 5 ℔ᵣ Cent   01444

The Addition and last total   30330

Which last total Sum̃ Namely 30330 being divided by 864
which is the Number of Tithables the product will Amount
to 35 ℔ᵣ Poll with a fraction of 90 which Is to be divided
between The two Sextons.

(122) Captᵃ John Smith for Yᵉ Middle precincts Mʳ
Richard Kemp Churchwarden for Yᵉ Upper Precincts And
Mʳ William Kilbee for the Lower precincts Are hereby Im-
powered and Authorized to Collect and Receive Yᵉ Parrish
Dues for this Pʳsent Year 1705 being 35 pounds of Tobaccoes
℔ᵣ poll And it is further Ordered that they Account for the
Same in due time, to the Severall persons to whom it is pro-
portioned; by the Aforesd Gentlemen of the Vestry.

Itt is Ordered that the Severall Clarks of yᵉ three Churches
in this Parrish Continue In their Several places and Stations

And to have their Usual Allowance Only Nathan Underwood his Sallery is to be but Twelve hundred pounds of Tobaccoes In Casque Richard Ranstead and Edward Docker yᵉ Sextons are Continued In their Stations And to have their Usual Sallery.

Itt is also Ordered that a Vestry be held for this Parrish at the Mother Church; On the Muñday In Easter Week; to Elect New Churchwardens for the Said Parrish; And that The Clarks of the Respective Churches Make publication of this Order.

Itt is likewise Ordered by way of Complyance of an Order of Court dated the 2ᵈ of April 1705 That Yᵉ Churchwardens Cause the Several precincts within this Parriſh to be proceſsioned According to Law; to begin the first day of March If fair If not the next fair day.

Signed ꝑʳ William: Churchhill Esqʳ

(123)   Att a Vestry held for Yᵉ Parrish of Christ Church in the County of Middleſex Yᵉ 18th Day of Novembʳ Anno Domi 1706

Present

Mʳ Barth: Yates Ministʳ	Mʳ Harry Beverley
Collⁿˡ William Churchhill Esqʳ	Mʳ Richard Kemp
Collⁿˡ Gowen Corbin	Mⁿ Robert Daniel
Mʳ Henry Thacker	Mʳ John Robinson
Captⁿ John Smith	Gentlemen

Ordered by Yᵉ AforeSaid Gentlemen Of Yᵉ Vestry as followeth

	lb Tob
To Mʳ Bartholomew Yates Minister	16000
To Nathan Underwood Clark; 685 of Yᵉ same Aſsigned to Esqʳ Churchhill	01200
To John Bristow Clark	01000
To Robert Biggs Clark	01000
To Richard Ranstead Sexton: Aſsigned to Esqʳ Churchhill	00500
To Edward Docker Sexton	00260
To Michal Curlis	00800
To Nathaniel Dodson	00800

To Sarah Brooks for Keeping of Mary Clay   01000

To Richard Warrick for Keeping of a Baſtard Child   01000

To Mr Richard Kemp for Keeping of John Webster   01000

To a Case for Keeping Ye Church Linen   00030

To Mending a Lock for Ye Church   00018

To William Probart for Keeping Elizabeth Buford   00500

To Ye Clark for Burying of Ye AforeSaid Woman   00025

To Henry Lane for Keeping of Alice Silveſter four Months   00333

The half of Ye Same to Ye Churchwarden for her Cloathing Namely 166½   00000

To John Bird for Keeping of Alice Silvester Seven Months   00583

The halfe of Ye Same to Ye Churchwarden for her Cloathing Namely 291½   00000

To Hannah Watts for Keeping of a Baſtard Child   01000

To Mr Nathaniel Juice for Curing of James Bendal   00298

To Collnl John Grymes for Repairing of Ye Church & Mending & Makeing of benches   00600

To Nathan Underwood for Extraordinary Service   00050

This laſt total (Namely) 31149 being divided by 985 Ye Number of Tithables for this Prſent Year to wit 1706 the Quotient Amounts to 31¾ of pounds of Tobaccoes ℔r Poll And there Remains 124¾ pounds of Tobaccoes Overplus by Reason of Ye fraction.

The first total	27997
To Casque at 8 ℔r Cent	02240
Addition	30237
To Sallery at 5 pr Cent	01512
Addition	31749
Deduction of fines	00600
The last total	31149

It is Ordered Yt Mr John Robinson be one of Ye Gentlemen of Ye Vestry for this Parrish This day he took his Oath Accordingly.

Mary Shepherds fine	500
Hugh Macktyres	050
Dudly Jollyes	050
In all	600

(124)   It is Ordered that Y⁰ Churchwardens Collect Y⁰ publick Dues for this Prſent year 1706 Being 31¾ˡᵇ pounds of
Tobaccoes ℔ʳ Poll; And it is further Ordered that they Account for the Same in due time to Y⁰ Severall Persons to
whom it is proportioned By Y⁰ AforeSaid Gentlemen of Y⁰
Vestry; All Y⁰ AboveSaid Tobaccoes to be made In Y⁰ Above-
Said Parrish of Christ Church; and County of Middlesex.

It is Ordered that Nathan Underwood Serve as Clark for
Y⁰ Middle Church & For Y⁰ Lower Chãpel; And that he Shall
have Y⁰ Same Allowance As Mʳ Marſton formerly had, And
Yᵗ Mʳ Bristow Continue as he was, And likewise the Sextons;
And to Have their Usual Salleries;

It is Ordered that Y⁰ Gentlemen of Y⁰ Vestry Meet Y⁰
9th day of December Next To consider of the Building of a
Church in Y⁰ Upper Pʳcincts.

Signed ℔ʳ Collⁿˡ William: Churchhill Esqʳ

(125)   Att a Veſtry held for Y⁰ Parriſh of Chriſt Church
In Y⁰ County of Middlesex Y⁰ 2ᵈ of July Anno; Domi 1707

Present

Mʳ Bartholomew: Yates: Ministʳ   Mʳ Harry: Beverley
Collonˡ Matthew Kemp   Mʳ Richard: Kemp
Colloⁿˡ John: Grymes   Captⁿ: Robert Daniel
Mʳ Henry: Thacker   Mʳ: John Robinson
Captⁿ John. Smith:

Gentlm̃e

Mʳ Christopher: Robinson: was this day sworn a Veſtry
Man.

Present Mʳ Christopher Robinson

Ordered by Y⁰ Above Sᵈ Gentlemen of Y⁰ Vestry as followeth

Ordered Yᵗ Mʳ Henry Thacker: be Y⁰ Churchwarden for
Y⁰ Middle pʳcincts; Coll Matthew Kemp for Y⁰ Lower; &
Mʳ Richard Kemp: for Y⁰ Upper Precincts.

Ordered Yᵗ the Collectʳˢ Of Y⁰ Parish Levy: in Y⁰ Year
1705 Bring to Y⁰ Next Veſtry their Accompts; of their Collection to be Examined.

Ordered Yᵗ a new Church be Built; As soon as conveniently
may be in Y⁰ Upper Pʳcincts; in Stead of Y⁰ Chappel now

gone to Ruine & Y^t it be placed in Y^e moſt convenient place
near Pipers Spring; in Mr Richard Kemps plantation;

Ordered: that Y^e Veſtry Meet at Y^e Mother Church Y^e
24 of July Inſtant if fair; If not Y^e next fair day; to consult
& consider upon Y^e dimensions & Method of Building a
Church in Y^e Upper Precincts at Y^e place Appointed;

Ordered that Mr John Smith & Mr Christopher Robinson
between this & Y^e next Veſtry goe upon Y^e Glebe & make
Inquiry into Y^e State of Y^e Buildings there; and Report their
Opinions thereon to Y^e Next Veſtry.

Matt: Kemp

(126) At a Veſtry held for the pariſh of Christchurch in
the County of Middleſex the 24th day of July 1707

Bartholomew Yates Minister

	William Churchhill Esqr	Richd Kemp
Preſent	Henry Thacker	Robert Daniel
	John Smith	Christop^r Robinſon
	John Grymes	& John Robinſon

Gentlemen

Purſuant to an Order of Veſtry held for this parish y^e
Second day of July 1707 this Veſtry takeing into their Serious
conſideration the demenſions of ye Church appointed to be
built by the Said order for the upper precinct of this parish
in Mr Kemps plantation in ye moſt Convenient place Near
pipers Spring a Scheme of the Said Church being this day
laid before the Vestry and the Said Veſtry after mature de-
liberation are of Opinion & Accordingly order that ye said
Church be fifty Six foot long and forty eight foot wide and
that ye poſts be twelve foot pitch and the pillars twenty four
foot long, the Rafters over y^e ſingle pews and for the body
of ye Church to be according to Architect and from the poſt
of Each Side to ye pillar Eight foot ye body of ye Church to
be thirty two foot wide the Pulpit Chancell & pews to be Laid
of at ye diſcretion of ye Veſtry.

Ordered that ye dwelling houſe upon the Gleab be forthwith framed & removed out of ye place where it now ſtands
and ſet upon blocks in the Moſt Com̃odious place that may be

upon the ſaid plantation and that it be well ſhingled with Cypreſs ſhingles and weather boarded with feather edged plank and that an Entry be made through the Said houſe Eight foot wide with Stair's windows and dormant windows and all partitions and diviſions neceſsary both above ſtaires and below with double out Side brick Chimneys with fyer places above ſtaires at Each end and that yᵉ ſame be glazed lathed filled plastered and white waſhed with all doors hinges lockes and keys Neceſsary and that yᵉ ſame be in all Respects Compleatly finiſhed.

Ordered that a Kitchin be built upon the Said Gleabe twenty four foot long & Sixteen foot wide with a brick Chimney and that yᵉ ſame be lathed filled plastered and white washed with all neceſsary windows doors and partitions neceſsary and that yᵉ ſame be Compleatly finiſhed.

Ordered that a Dairy be built upon the Said Gleab fifteen foot Square and that the ſame be lathed filled plaſtered and white waſhed with all windows and doors Neceſsary & that yᵉ ſame be Compleatly finiſhed.

(127)   Ordered that Edward Sherman and Thomas Griffin be bound to William Churchhill Esqʳ According to Law.

Capᵗⁿ John Smith in behalfe of the parish is hereby impowered to undertake and overſee the buildings appointed this day to be built upon yᵉ Gleab and it is ordered that he find and provide all things Neceſsary towards the Accomplishment of the ſaid buildings and that he cauſe them forthwith to be Compleatly finished and it is further ordered that he bring an Account of the Charges to the Veſtry who are to allow him yᵉ ſame and alſo that he be allowed his reaſonable account for his trouble therein.

Ordered that yᵉ Gentlemen of yᵉ Veſtry meet at yᵉ Court houſe next Court day about Ten a Clock in yᵉ morning.

W : Churchhill

At a Vestry held for Yᵉ Parriſh of Chriſt Church In Yᵉ County of Middlesex Novembʳ Yᵉ 13th Anno Domi 1707

Mr Barth: Yates Minist^r Present   Mr Harry Beverley
Coll^{al} Matthew Kemp   Mr Richard Kemp
Collo^{nl} Gowen Corbin   Gentlemen   Cap^{tn} Robert Daniel
Mr Henry Thacker   Mr Chriſtopher Robinson
Cap^{tn} John Smith   Mr John Robinson

Ordered by Y^e AforeSd Gentlemen of Y^e Veſtry as followeth

To Mr Bartholomew Yates Miniſter	16000
To Nathan Underwood Clark	01900
To John Bristow Clark	01000
To Richard Ranſtead Sexton	00500
To Edward Docker	00260
To Mr John Smith towards carrying on Y^e work of Y^e Glebe	18000
To Dorothy Manel for Cloathing	00300
To Richard Warwick for Keeping of Mary Hudles Baſtard Child	00500
To Thomas Kidd for Keeping and Burying of Chriſtopher Barnet	00400
To Michal Curlis	00800
To John Webſter	01000

Carryed Over

(128) To Mary Clay	01000
To Alice Silveſter	00500
To John Briſtow for Mending Y^e Upper Chappel doors pews & benches	00150
To Collo^{nl} Kemp for work done at Y^e Lower Chappel	00110
To Hannah Watts for Keeping of a Baſtard Child	01000
To pay to Mr Armiſtead two Levies being Overcharged	00063½
To Mr Richard Kemp for Absenters	00290½

The firſt total   43774

Being Multiplied by 14$^{pr\ cent}$ for Casque & Sallery   14

$$\begin{array}{r} 1748 \\ 438 \end{array}$$

	Tacit	6128
	Addition	43774

The laſt total   49902

This last total Namely 49902 being Divided by 1032 Yᵉ Number of Tithables for this present Year to wit 1707 the Quotient Amounts to 48 and a ½ pounds of Tobaccoes ℔ poll; And there Remains 150 pounds of Tobaccoes Overplus by reason of the fraction.

Ordered that Mᵣ John Smith Build and Erect or cause to be Erected On Yᵉ Glebe a dwelling House to be Set on blocks to Contain fourty foot Long; twenty foot broad two Rooms and an Entry below Stairs at Yᵉ direction of Mᵣ Bartholomew Yates to be weather boarded with feather Edg plank; and Shingled Roof Stairs Windows dormor Windows Doors and All partitions and divisions Neceſsary to Compleat Yᵉ Same with two Double out Side brick Chimneys to be Glaſed filled plaiſtered white Waſhed hinges Caſements Locks and Keys; the Same in all Respects to be Compleatly finished.

Ordered Yᵗ Mᵣ Harry Beverley Mᵣ Christopher Robinson and Mᵣ John Robinson or any two or One of them take Bond with good Security of Mᵣ Richard Kemp for his true performance In Receiving and diſcharging the parriſh Credit this Pᵣſent Year.

Matt Kemp

Ordered that Yᵉ Clarks of Yᵉ Churches be Continued In their places for the Uſual Sallery.

Ordered Yᵗ Edward Docker Sexton of yᵉ Upper Chappel be Continued in his place for Yᵉ Uſual Allowance And that Collⁿˡ Matthew Kemp is hereby Impowered to Appoint a New Sexton in Yᵉ Room of Richard Ranstead Late Sexton of Yᵉ Middle and Lower Church.

Matt: Kemp

(129)   At a Vestry held for Y⁰ Parriſh of Chriſt Church
In Y⁰ County of Middleſex Decembʳ 30th A: D: 1707
                        Present
Mʳ Barth: Yates Ministʳ   Mʳ Richard: Kemp
Mʳ Henry: Thacker   Captⁿ Robert: Daniel
Captⁿ John: Smith   Gentlemen Mʳ Chriſtopher Robinson
Mʳ Harry: Beverley   Mʳ John: Robinson

Ordered that Mʳ Richard Kemp Collect and Receive of every
Tithable person in this Parrish the Summ of fourty eight
pounds & a half of Tobaccoes of the growth of Y⁰ Parrish
for Y⁰ Payment & Defraying the parrish Levy, for this Year,
And it is further Ordered that he Accompt for & pay the
Same to the Several Persons to whom it is proportioned;
by the 7th of May: 1708 And In Case of any perſons refusal
of payment to make diſtreſs.

Mʳ Richard Kemp Acknowledged his Bond for the Collection of the Parriſh Levy in Y⁰ Veſtry; which Bond was
admitted to Record.

Ordered that Mʳ Richard Kemp be Allowed In Y⁰ next
Parriſh Levy the Suṁ of twelve hundred & Sixty four pounds
of Tobaccoes.

                        Henry: Thacker

                             1707

(130)   Know all Men by these pʳsents that I Richard Kemp
of the County of Middleſex & Parriſh of Chriſt Church do
Stand Indebted & am firmly Bound to Henry Thacker & John
Smith for & in behalf of Y⁰ Parriſh of Chriſt Church In Y⁰
Suṁ of One hundred thousand pounds of good Sweetsenteḍ
Tobaccoe and Caſk; which Suṁ well & truely to be paid I
doe hereby bind my Self my heirs Executʳˢ & Adminiſtratʳˢ
to Y⁰ AforeSd Henry Thacker & John Smith Jointly & Sev-
erally To them & their Heirs Executʳˢ & Adminiſtratʳˢ to Y⁰
Use and behoof of Y⁰ Parriſh AforeSd Witneſs my hand &
Seal this 30th Day of Decembʳ 1707.

The Condition of Y⁰ Above Bond Is such that If Y⁰ Above
Bound Richard Kemp Shall well & truely Collect & pay away;
before Y⁰ Seventh day of May; Next Enſueing Y⁰ Date hereof,

to the Several Creditors all Yᵉ Tobaccoe levied by the Veſtry
this present Year 1707 as it is Aſsigned by an Order of Vestry
held Yᵉ 13th Day of Novembʳ 1707 to each Creditor In hogs-
heads to Contain Eight hundred Neat Tobaccoe One With
another & Convenient to a Landing, Then Yᵉ Above Bond to
be Void & of none Effect otherwise to Remain in full force
& Virtue.

Richard Kemp

Signed Sealed and delivered
In Yᵉ presence of Us
  Wil: Stanard
  Nathan Underwood
  (131)   At a Veſtry held for Chriſt Church Pariſh in Mid-
dleſex County Novembʳ Yᵉ 2d Anno Domi 1708

Present

Mʳ Bartholomew Yates Miniſter Captⁿ John Smith
Collⁿˡ Matthew Kemp   Mʳ Harry Beverley
Sʳ William Skipwith   Captⁿ Robert Daniel
Mʳ Henry Thacker   Mʳ Chriſtopher Robinson
Collⁿˡ John Grymes   Mʳ John Robinson

(bracketed, sideways:) Gentlemen

Ordered by Yᵉ AboveSd Gentlemen of Y⋅ Veſtry as followeth

	1 Tobb
To Mʳ Bartholomew Yates Miniſter	16000
To Nathan Underwood Clerk	01900
To John Briſtow Clerk	01000
To Edmund Sanders Sexton	00500
To Edward Docker Sexton	00260
To Collⁿˡ John Grymes for Curing & Cloathing of Georg Wade	01360
To Thomas Kidd for Keeping Catherine five Weeks and Burying her	00375
To Mʳ John Robinson for keeping of Sarah Walker & tending on her In her Sickniſs	01100
To Edmund Mickleborough for keeping of Dorothy Manell	01000
To Mercy Curliſs for her Husband Michael Curliſs Deceased	00800

To Robert James   01000
To Richard Ran∫tead   00600
To Mr Richard Kemp for a Cu∫hin in Y^e upper
Chappel   00050
Ditto for keeping of John Web∫ter   01000
To Richard Winn for keeping of Alice Silve∫ter   01000
To Sarah Brooks for Mary Clay   01000
To John Gibbs on Account of Chri∫topher Kelshaw
by Y^e C: W: Agree^{mt} 01000
To Ralph Baker for curing of Anne Ingram   02000
Itt for his Attendance on Sarah Walker   00500
To James Jordan for Keeping of Catherine   00100
To Henry Rose for Catherine Brooks   01000
To John Row for John Hoyls his Keeping   00400
Towards Carrying on Y^e Glebe Work to be p^d to
Cap^{tn} John Smith   24000
To Mr Richard Kemp by a former Order of Ve∫try   01264

This last total (Namely)	The fir∫t Total	59209
67142 being divided by 1048	To Cask at 8 ℔ ^{r} C^t	04736
the Number of Tithables		
for this P^{r}sent Year to wit	Addition	63945
1708 the Quotient Amounts	To Sallery at 5 ℔ ^{r} C^t	03197
to 64^{lb} of Tobaccoes ℔ ^{r} poll		

Y^e Addition & la∫t total 67142

(132) Ordered that John Gibbs be Allowed Y^e next Levy
Seven hundred pounds of Tobaccoes provided he make a per-
fect Cure of Chri∫topher Kelshaws Legg If no Cure to be
Allowed nothing;

Ordered that William Wallis be Bound unto Hugh Watts;
by Y^e Church Warden of Y^e Middle Precinct;

Ordered that Mr Richard Kemp pay Elizabeth Whites fine;
to Mr Chri∫topher Robinson Church Warden of Y^e Upper
Precinct;

Ordered that William Stanard Receive all Y^e fines due to Y^e
Pari∫h; and that he Account for what he Receives of the Same
at Y^e laying Y^e next Levie; being above his fees; & Sallery;
out of Y^e Same;

Ordered that Sr William Skipwith be Church Warden for Y^e Lower Precincts; And Mr Chriſtopher Robinson for Y^e Upper; & Mr John Robinson for the Middle Precincts;

Ordered that Y^e Several Clarks of ye three Churches In the Pariſh; Continue in their places; And be Allowed as Usual; The Sextons to be Continued And Allowed as formerly;

Ordered that Y^e Church Wardens Collect Y^e Tobaccoe due to Y^e Pariſh in their Several Precincts; and Account for Y^e Same In due time to the Several Creditors; being at 64 pounds of Tobaccoe ℔^r poll;

Mr James Walker is Chosen a Veſtry Man this day; in the Room of Collⁿⁱ Grymes; who hath this Day Refused to Continue any longer; And Ordered that the Clerk give him Notice to give his Attendance at Y^e next Veſtry;

Henry Thacker

(133)   Att a Vestry held for Christ Church parish In Middx County November ye 8th 1709.

Preſent

Mr Bartholomew Yates Min^r   Captⁿ John Smith
Sir Wm Skipwith   Mr Richard Kemp
Coll^o Matthew Kemp   Mr Chriſtopher Robinſon
Mr Henry Thacker   Mr John Robinſon
Mr Harry Beverley

Gentlemen

Ordered by the Gentlemen of the Vestry abovenamed as followeth (vizt)

To Mr Bartholomew Yates Miniſter	16000
To Nathan Underwood Clerke	01900
To Jno Briſtow Clerke	01000
To Edmund Sanders Sexton	00600
To Edward Docker	00500
To Robert James	01000
To Richd Ranſtead	00600
To Edmund Mickleborough for keeping Dorothy Manell	01200
To Thomas Lee for keeping Alice Silveſter	01000
To Mary Clay	01000

To Doctor Baker for curing Dorothy Minor, Alice
Silvester & Thos White   04000
   To Jno Bristow for worke done att ye Upper Chappell 00100
   To Jno Webster   01000
The Vestry have agreed to bind Tho: Griffin to Samll
Loe as an Appretice according to Law That ye Church
Wardens or either of them bind him
   To Mr Jno Robinson for A Dyell post & 3 bottles of
wine   00220
   To Sr Wm Skipwith for 2 bottles of wine   00100
   To Doctor Crannavett   02500
   To Jno Gibbs   00700
                                                          ———
                                                          33420
              Wm Skipwith

(134)   Att a Vestry held for Christ Church parish in
Middlesex County November ye 18th Anno Domini 1709.
              Present
Mr Bartholomew Yates Minister   Coll° Gawin Corbin
Sr Wm Skipwith   Mr Christopher Robinson
Mr Henery Thacker   Mr John Robinson
Capt Jno Smith
Mr Richd Kemp   Gentlemen

              Gentlemen

Ordered by the abovenamed Gentlēn of the Vestry as followes
(vizt)
   To Brought over   33420
   To James Browne for Keeping Alice Silvester   00166
   To Dorothy Manell for Cloathing allowd to be paid
to Ye Church Warden   00400
   To Captn Jno Smith for goeing on with the Glebe   18000
   To the Church Warden of the lower Precincts one
tythable run away   00064
   To the Church Warden of the Upper Precincts one
tythable run away   00064
   To Credit to the parish for 3 Supernumeryes   00192
   To the parish use   00202
                                                          ———
                                                          52508

Ordered That Mr Xtopher Robinſon be Churchwarden for ye Upper Precincts. Capt Jno Smith for the Middle p^{r}cincts and Coll^o Matthew Kemp for the Lower Precincts.

Ordered That Jno Wacomb, Dorothy Needles, & Richd Reynalds Equally receive ye fines y^t are in the hands of Mr Jno Robinſon being 350^{lb} of Tob^{cco} & in ye hands of Jno Curtis being 250^{lb} of Tob^{cco}

Ordered That Jno Owen be Clerke of the Mother Church with ye conſent of Mr Bartholomew Yates Miniſter.

Ordered That the Gentlemen of the Veſtry of the lower parts with the approbation of ye Miniſter chuſe A Clerke for the lower Chappell.

Ordered That Jno Briſtow continue Clke of the Upper Chappell.

Ordered That the Church Wardens Collect 57^{lb} of Tob^{cco} of each Tythable in their reſpective Precincts & pay to the Piſh Credito^{rs}.

Ordered That the Sextons continue in their Offices.

Ordered That Nathan Underwood the late Clke Deliver all the Bookes & papers belonging to the Veſtry to Jno Owen p^{r}ſent Clke.

Cask & Sallery att 13 ₱ Cent amounts to

52508
6825
―――――
59333

Wᵐ Skipwith
1709

(135) Att a Veſtry held for Chriſt Church piſh in middleſex County the 29th day of December 1710.

Present

Mr Bartho: Yates Miniſter	Mr Harry Beverley
Sr William Skipwith Kn^t	Mr Richard Kemp
Coll^o Matthew Kemp	Mr Jno Robinſon
Captn Jno Smyth	Mr Chriſtopher Robinſon
Captn Robert Daniell	
Coll^t Gawin Corbin	Gentlemen

Mʳ James Walker and Captⁿ Geo: Wortham were this day
Sworne Veſtry Men.

Preſent

Ordered by the abovenamed Gentlemen of the Veſtry as
followeth (Vizᵗ)

To Mr. Bartholomew Yates Miniſter	16000
John Briſtow Clerke	01000
Nathan Underwood Clerke	01000
Edmond Saunders Sexton	00600
Edward Docker Sexton	00500
Margarett Symonds ℔ keeping Avarilla Baker 9 months & an halfe	00864
Richard Ranſtead	01000
Coll° Matthew Kemp ℔ Communion wine	00200
Sam¹¹ Loe ℔ keeping A pish woman named Ann Furrell	00400
Richard Daniell ℔ keeping Ditto 2 months & 12 dayes & one ℔e of Shoes	00300
Doctor Baker ℔ Thomas Syms	01400
Captⁿ Smyth his Accoᵗ allowed	00575
Edmᵈ Mickleborough for Keeping Honour Baſkett 7 Months	00700
Robert James	01000
Doctor Baker for Medicines for Old John	01800
Ditto ℔ Ditto for Alice King	00600
Mʳ Richard Kemp for keeping John Webster 13 Months	01300
Ditto for keeping Alice King 6 Months	00600
Mary Clay	01000
Henry Ball ℔ keeping Dorothy Manuell One yeare	00600

Tranſferred to the Other Side	31439

Ordered That John Briſtow Nathan Underwood & the two
Sextons continue in their places.

Ordered That John Furnett be free of the pish Levy.

Ordered That Henery Barnes be free of the pish Levy.

Ordered That Wᵐ Hern be free of the pish Levy.

Ordered That Churchwardens agree with A Doctor for cure of Francis Horne.

Ordered That the Church warden bind Eliz^a Canida to Wm Marcum & his wife.

Ordered That John Owen continue Clerke of the Mother Church & Clerke of the Veſtry.

Ordered That Capt Robert Daniell be Churchwarden for the Upper Precincts Mr Harry Beverly for the Middle Precincts & Coll° Matthew Kemp for the Lower Precincts.

Ordered That the Veſtry meete att the Mother Church on Thurſday the 4th day of January next if faire, if not the next faire day.

Corbin

(136) Att A Veſtry held for Chriſt Church piſh in Mid-dleſex County the 4th day of January 1710/11.

Present

Mr Bartho: Yates Minister
Sr Willm Skipwith Kn^t
Coll° Matthew Kemp
Captn John Smyth
Coll° Gawin Corbin
Captn Robert Daniell

Mr Harry Beverly
Mr Richard Kemp
M^r Jn° Robinſon
Mr Chriſtopher Robinſon
Mr James Walker
Captn Geo: Wortham

Gentlemen

Mr Ralph Wormley was this day Sworne Veſtryman Preſent Ordered by the abovenamed Gentlemen of the Veſtry as followeth (Viz^t).

Upon Settling the Collectors Accounts with Captn Geo: Wortham there appeares Due to the piſh 4487^lb of Tob^cco

Brought from the other Side   31439

To John Owen as Clerke of the Mother Church & Clerke of the Veſtry   01700

Captn John Smyth for Tar & Tarring the Glebe houſe   01600

Ordered That Three Churches be built in ye piſh of Chriſst Church.

Ordered That A new Church be built, as Soone as conveniently may be, in the upper Precincts, inſtead of the Chappell, now gone to ruine: And that it be placed neare Mr Marvell Mofelyes Plantation, on the Maine Roade.

Ordered That the above Church be Sixty foot long, & five & twenty foot wide.

Ordered That One hundred Thoufand pounds of Tob^cco be Levyed this yeare towards building the Upper Church &c^a   100000

Ordered That the Churchwardens Collect One hundred Sixty nine pounds of Tob^cco ꝑ Pole of Eight hundred ninety nine Tythables & make payment thereof according to the Tenour of the Severall Orders abovementioned.

	133739
To Cafk att 8 ꝑ C^t	10696
	144435
To Sallery att 5 ꝑ Cent	7221
	151656

To an Addition of 275^lb of Tob^cco to make the Levy even Due to Collectors   275

                                                           151931

```
899) 151931 (169
     899
     ___
     6203
     5394
     ___
      8091
      8091
      ___
```

                                                     Corbin

(137) Att a Vestry held for Christ Church Parish in Middx County the 23 Day of January 1710.

Present

Mr Bartholomew Yates Minister	Mr John Robinson
Captn John Smyth	Mr James Walker
Coll^o Gawin Corbin	Captn George Wortham
Mr Harry Beverly	Mr Ralph Wormley
Mr Richard Kemp	Gentlemen

Ordered by the abovenamed Gentlemen of Vestry as followeth (vizt). In purſuance of an Order of Vestry made the
4th day of January Instant That A New Church be built as
Soone as conveniently may be in the Upper Precincts inſtead of
the Upper Chappell now gone to ruine.

It is Ordered That the above Church be Sixty foot long and
five and twenty foot wide. That the Ground frame (vizt:) the
Sills of the said Church the Suṁers and Girders be of the best
White Oake to be of quartered Stuff and A foot Square att
least. That there be Seven Girders and Six Suṁers. That
the Sleepers be of the same Sort of Oake sawed, five and seven
inches Square.

Item That the Poſts of the s^d Church be sawed of the s^d
White Oake to be fourteene foot from the Sill to the Plate to
be twelve and Six inches Square. That the Braces be eight and
Six inches Square That the Plates of the S^d Church be Sawed
of good Oake to be nine and Six inches Square That there be
four Girders nine and Eleven inches Square.

Item That the principall Rafters of the s^d Church be Sawed
of good white Oake to be six and nine inches Square att the
foot and six and four inches att the Top That the Small Rafters
be of three and four inches Square That the principall wind
beams be five and Seven inches Square. That the Purloins be
Six and Seven inches Square That the Braces be three and four
inches Square.

Item That the Shingling Laths be of Sawed white Oake one
inch thick and four inches broad. That the Shingles be of the
Heart of Cypreſs three quarters of an inch att least att the
thickest end to be Sixteene inches long and to Shew when laid
five inches out.

Item That there be Seven windows. Three of each Side of
eight foot long and four foot wide The End Window to be
from the Arch within Six foot of the Sill, Ten foot wide, The
side windows to be saſhes.

Item That there be two doors one att the Weſt end to be nine
foot high and Six foot wide, folding doores, The Doore in the

Chancell to be Six foot four inches high and three foot wide to be of Oake Plank.

Item That the Chancell be from the East end to the Screene twelve foot That the Railes and Banifters about the Comunion Table be fourteene foot one way and Seven foot the other way to be of White Oake.

Item That there be five high framed Pewes, three of the South Side and two of the North Side The reft of the Church to be Devided into pewes five foot wide to be Seated round.

Item That there be A comendable Screene to Divide the Church from the Chancell.

Item That the Pulpitt and two Defks Stand on the North Side of the Church below the high pewes.

Item That the floore be laid with white Oake plank, one inch and quarter thick when wrought.

Item That the s^d Church be ceiled with three quarters inch plank either popler or Cyprefs to be laid in with oyle and white lead, And Arch fashion.

Item That the pewes be of poplar plank.

Item That the Church windows be well glazed with long Square glafs.

Item that the Comunion Table be made of Black Wallnutt or White Oake.

Item That the Window frames be of good white Oake.

Item That the s^d Church be cornifhed all round. That the window frames the Doors and Cornifhes be all Laid in Oyle and Colours.

Item That the s^d Church be hipped above the wind beams.

Item That the s^d Church be weatherboarded with feather edged inch Cyprefs Plank to be nailed with double tens.

Item That the s^d Church floore be tongued.

Turne Over

(138)   Item That the s^d Church Stand upon Stone Pillars one under each Poft and two att each End That Steps into the Church be made of Mulberry Blocks.

Ordered That Coll^o Corbin Mr Harry Beverly and Mr James Walker or any two of them agree with the Owner of the Land on which the s^d Church muft Stand for two Acres of Land.

Ordered That the Veſtry meete att Urbanna the firſt Monday in February to Auditt & Settle all Accounts belonging to the Pish. And to Agree with workmen for building the aboveſaid Church.

Corbin

Att A Vestry held for Christ Church parish in Middleſex County the 5ᵗʰ day of February 1710

Present

Mʳ Bartholomew Yates Minister	Mʳ Richard Kemp
Captⁿ John Smyth	Mʳ John Robinson
Collᵒ Gawen Corbin	Mʳ James Walker
Captⁿ Robert Daniell	Captⁿ Geo: Wortham
Mʳ Harry Beverly	Gentlemen

Ordered by the abovenamed Gentlemen of the Veſtry as followeth (Vizᵗ)

Ordered That Mʳ Harry Beverly Mʳ John Robinson & Mʳ James Walker Examine and Settle the Parish Accounts with yᵉ Severall Churchwardens & Collectors of this Parish for yᵉ three years last past, And Report their proceedings to the next Vestry.

Itt appearing to this Vestry That the Sills of yᵉ aforesaid Church, which were Ordered to be of quartered Stuff being too difficult to be gott, Itt is now Ordered That the said peices be of yᵉ best Ring Oake Squared with yᵉ Saw of the Same Demencons Collᵒ Gawin Corbin Mʳ Harry Beverly and Mʳ James Walker Having bin appointed by Order of Vestry to agree with yᵉ Owner of yᵉ Land (On which yᵉ abovesaid Church must Stand) for two Acres of Land, Having retorn'd A Deed & Platt for two Acres purchased of Mʳ Marvell Moſely for the said purpose, The Same is approv'd off.

Order'd That the Chancell be rais'd one Step (of Six inches) higher than yᵉ said Church floore. And the Comunion Table, to be rais'd two Steps (of Six inches each) higher then yᵉ floore of yᵉ Chancell.

Mʳ John Clark having offer'd to Undertake yᵉ building & finishing yᵉ abovesaid Church purſuant to yᵉ tenour of yᵉ former Orders for One hundred & ten thousand pounds of

Tob^{cco} And offering Coll° Gawen Corbin Security for the
Pforming ye said Building Itt is hereby Ordered That y^e
said John Clark (Bond being first given for the building y^e
said Church) be paid Ninety thousand pounds of Tob^{cco} by
ye Church wardens & Collectors of the Parish Dues this yeare.

Ordered That Mr Harry Beverly & Mr James Walker take
Bond of the s^d John Clark for ye performance of ye s^d worke
And finishing it by ye last day of Aprill One thousand seven
hundred & twelve.

Ordered That Captⁿ John Smith Captⁿ Robert Daniell &
Mr John Robinson be appointed Overseers of ye s^d Building
to Oversee & direct the s^d worke.

Ordered That if ye Gentlemen appointed to examine the
Parish accounts find anything due from ye Parish That they
have power to draw upon ye Severall Churchwardens & Collectors for ye same Whoe are hereby impower'd to pay y^e
same soe far as they have in their hands.

John Smith

(139) Att a Veſtry held for X^t Church Pariſh in Middx
County ye 7th Jan^{ry} 1711

Present

Mr Bartho: Yates Minister	Mr Harry Beverley
Sr Wm Skipwith	M^r Jn° Robinſon
Coll° Matthew Kemp	Captⁿ Geo: Wortham
Captⁿ Jn° Smyth	Mr Ralph Wormeley
Captⁿ Robert Daniell	Gentlemen

M^r Jn° Grymes was this day Sworne Veſtryman   Preſent

Order'd by the above named Gentlemen of ye Veſtry as
followeth (Viz^t)

To Mr Bartho: Yates Minister	16000
Jn° Owen Clerke of ye Mother Church & Veſtry	01700
Jn° Briſtoll Cl: of ye Upper Chappell	01000
Nathan Underwood Cl: of ye Lower Chappell	01000
Edm^d Saunders Sexton	00600
Ralph Mazy for Serving as Sexton 3 months	00125
Marg^{tt} Symonds for keeping Avarilla Baker 3 weekes & buriall	00222

Richd Ranſtead   01000

                                                                   21647
Mich^ll Smyth for keeping Mary Clay A twelve month 01000
Robt James   00800
Hen: Ball for keeping Dorothy Mannell one yeare   01000
Edm^d Mickleborough for keeping Hono^r Baſkett one
yeare   01200
Mr Harry Beverley for waſhing Linen & Scouring
Comunion plate   00100
Jno W^ms for Edwd Dockers Serving as Sexton 9
months   00375
Jno Lawrence for keeping Alice Knig one year &
buriall   01165
Doctor Thornton for Phyſick to Eli: Molloughon   01000
Jno Day   00600

                                                    07240
Thos Kid for keeping Jno Webſter one fortnight &
buriall   00350
Doctor Baker for a viſitt to Fran: Horne   00100
Mad^m Churchill for two bottles of Comunion wine   00100
James Meecham for A Coffin for Fran: Horne   00200
Coll^o Matthew Kemp for Comunion wine   00300
Mr Xtopher Robinſon for keeping Eli: Molloughon
two months   01000
Jno Clarke for ye Church due by former Order   20000
Ordered That Thirty Thouſand be levyed towards
building another Church   30000

                                                    52050

                                                    80937
                      Caſk at 8 ℔ Cent   6475

                                                    87412
                      Sallary att 5 ℔ Cent   4370

                      Sume Totall   91782

Order'd That 18ᵗᵇ be added to yᵉ Suṁe Totall *[& yᵗ
it remaine in Church Wardens hands due to yᵉ Pariſh]
due to Church Wardens   18

                          Laſt Totall   91800
Which sᵈ Laſt Totall Devided by 900 the number of Tythables It amounts to 102 per Pole.

Order'd That the Clerks & Sextons continue in their Offices

Order'd That Mʳ Roger Jones be deſired to take yᵉ Oath
of A Veſtryman of this Pariſh.

Order'd That Mʳ Jnᵒ Robinſon be Church Warden of yᵉ
Upper Precincts Captⁿ George Wortham of yᵉ Middle & Collᵒ
Matthew Kemp of yᵉ Lower Precincts.

Order'd That yᵉ Church Wardens collect 102ᵗᵇ of Tobᶜᶜᵒ of
each Tythable pſon in their reſpective Precincts, And pay to
yᵉ Pariſh Creditoʳˢ

Orderd That Mʳ Jnᵒ Robinſon Mʳ Ralph Wormley Mʳ
Jnᵒ Grymes or any two of them be impowerd to meete at
Urbanna on Monday yᵉ 14ᵗʰ Inſtant to Auditt & Settle Laſt
yeares Accoᵗˢ

Order'd That a Veſtry meete on Satturnday yᵉ 19ᵗʰ Inſtant at the Mother Church.

                          Wᵐ Skipwith

(140) Att a Veſtry held for Chriſt Church Pariſh in
Middleſex County yᵉ 7ᵗʰ day of Apʳˡˡ 1712
                          Present

†[Mʳ Bar]tha Yates Miniſter Mʳ Harry Beverley
†[Sʳ Wᵐ] Skipwith Knᵗ   Mʳ Jnᵒ Robinſon
†[Collᵒ] Matt: Kemp   Captⁿ Geo: Wortham
†[Ca]pᵗⁿ Jnᵒ Smith   Mʳ Ralph Wormley
Captⁿ Robᵗ Daniell   Mʳ Jnᵒ Grymes
                                   Gentlemen

Mʳ Roger Jones Gentleman was this day Sworne Veſtryman.
Preſent.

Ordered by yᵉ abovenamed Gentlemen of yᵉ Veſtry as followeth.

---

* Half erased in original, but still legible.—C. G. C.
† Half illegible.—C. G. C.

Ordered That A New Church be built as Soon as conveniently may be in y⁰ Middle Precincts in y⁰ same place where
y⁰ old one now stands.

Ordered That y⁰ above Church be sixty foot long & thirty
foot wide.

Ordered That y⁰ walls of y⁰ sᵈ Church be built with brick
well temperd & well burnt, That y⁰ water Table be three foot
from y⁰ ground. three bricks thick. From y⁰ water Table to y⁰
Roofe two bricks & an halfe thick, The gable end from y⁰
Square to y⁰ roofe one brick & an halfe thick. to be plaiſterd
with lime & haire and white waſhd, The bricks to be laid
with two thirds Lime & one third sand. That y⁰ Sᵈ brick wall
be fourteene foot high from y⁰ Surface of y⁰ Earth to the
Plate.

Ordered That there be Seven windows. three of each side
of eight foot long & four foot wide. The End window to be
from y⁰ Arch within six foot of y⁰ Sill ten foot wide, the
side windows Saſhes.

Ordered That there be two doors. One at y⁰ weſt end
Eight foot & an halfe high and five foot and an halfe wide,
folding doores, the doore in y⁰ Chancell to be Six foot four
inches high & three foot wide. the sᵈ Doores to be of Oake
plank, well fix'd with locks & bolts That the sills of y⁰ sᵈ
doors be made of Cedar.

That Mʳ Alexander Graves doe y⁰ above brick worke provided he give good Security for y⁰ finiſhing thereof by y⁰
laſt of October 1713. And that he be then paid Sixty Thouſand
pounds of Tobᶜᶜᵒ for his Said worke.

That y⁰ Principall Rafters of y⁰ sᵈ Church be sawd of good
white Oake, 8 & 12 inches Square at y⁰ foot & 7 & 5 inches
Square at y⁰ Top, That y⁰ small Rafters be of 3 & 4 inches
Square. That the principall wind beams be 5 & 7 inches
Square, That y⁰ purloins be 6 & 7 inches Square That y⁰
braces be 3 & 4 inches Square. That the Shingling Laths
be of sawd white Oake one inch thick & 4 inches broad, That
y⁰ Shingles be of y⁰ heart of Cypreſs 3 quarters of an inch
at leaſt at y⁰ thickeſt end, to be 16 inches long & to show when

laid 5 inches out. That yᵉ Doores & windows be of yᵉ demencons as above, That yᵉ Chancell be from yᵉ East end to
yᵉ Screene twelve foot That yᵉ Railes & baniſters about yᵉ
Coṁunion Table be 14 foot one way & 7 foot the other way
That yᵉ pews be four foot & an halfe high, That four of yᵒ
sᵈ pewes be raiſed higher then yᵉ reſt according to yᵉ direccons
of yᵉ Gentlemen appointed to be Overſeers, That there be a
comendable Screene to divide the Church from yᵉ Chancell,
That yᵉ Pullpitt & two Deſks stand on yᵉ North side of yᵉ
Church below yᵉ high Pewes That yᵉ floore be laid with white
Oake plank one inch & quarter when wrought, on Sleepers
nine inches deepe, three inches from yᵉ Ground to be laid on
three Cedar Sills.

That the sᵈ Church be ceiled with 3 quarters inch Plank
either popler or Cypreſs to be laid in with oyle & white lead,
and Arch faſhion, That yᵉ pewes be of popler plank, That yᵉ
Church windowes be well glazed with long Sqare glaſs, That
yᵉ comunion Table be made of black wallnutt or white Oake;
That yᵉ window frames, yᵉ doores & corniſhes be all laid in
oyle & colours, That yᵉ Church be hipp'd above yᵉ wind beams,
That yᵉ sᵈ Church floore be tongued.

That yᵉ Chancell be raiſed one step (of six inches) higher
then yᵉ sᵈ Church floore, & yᵉ Coṁunion Table to be raiſed
two steps (of six inches each) higher then the floore of yᵉ
chancell.

Orderd That Jnᵒ Clark doe the Carpenter's worke above
menconed according to yᵉ above demencons & other directions
of yᵉ Overseer's hereinafter named, Provided he give good
Security for yᵉ finishing of yᵉ same by yᵉ laſt of December
1713. He failing therein The Overseer's are impower'd to
employ any other workmen as they shall think fitt upon giving
yᵉ like good Security.

Ordered That fifty thouſand pounds of Tobᶜᶜᵒ be paid to yᵉ
Undertaker of yᵉ sᵈ Carpenters worke.

Ordered That yᵉ Thirty thouſand pounds of Tobᶜᶜᵒ now
in yᵉ Church Warden's hands be paid to the Undertakers of

yᵉ sᵈ Church fifteene thouſand to each in part of yᵉ Sumes above Specified upon giving good security.

Ordered That Captⁿ Jnᵒ Smyth Mʳ Jnᵒ Robinſon & Mʳ Ralph Wormley be appointed Overſeer's of yᵉ sᵈ building to Overſee & direct yᵉ sᵈ worke for the benefit of yᵉ said Building.

Turne Over   Ordered

(141) Ordered That Captⁿ Jnᵒ Smyth Mʳ Jnᵒ Robinſon & Captⁿ Geo: Wortham or any two of *[them meet] at Ur- banna on yᵉ 14ᵗʰ of this Instant Aprill or any other day to take Bonds of *[yᵉ] sᵈ Undertakers.

Ordered That Captⁿ Jnᵒ Smith Mʳ Jnᵒ Robinſon Captⁿ Geo: Wortham & Mʳ Ralph Wormley or any two of them be im- power'd to Settle & auditt all Pariſh Accounts & report yᵉ same to yᵉ next Veſtry.

Matt Kemp

Att a Veſtry held for Chriſt Church Pariſh in Middleſex County yᵉ 9ᵗʰ day of June 17*[12]

Present

Mʳ Bartho: Yates Minister	Capⁿ Geo: Wortham
Collᵒ Matt Kemp	Mʳ Ralph Wormley
Capⁿ Jnᵒ Smyth	Mʳ Jnᵒ Grymes
Mʳ Harry Beverley	Mʳ Roger Jones
Mʳ Jnᵒ Robinſon	Gentlemen

Ordered by yᵉ abovenamed Gentlemen of yᵉ Veſtry as fol- loweth (that is to Say)

Ordered That the Demencons of yᵉ New Church Ordered to be built by yᵉ laſt Veſtry be conſtrued to be Sixty foot long in yᵉ cleare & thirty foot wide in the cleare.

Ordered That (Upon Jnᵒ Clarks failing to give Security) Jnᵒ Hipkins Senʳ doe the Carpent*[er's] worke of yᵉ afore- ſaid Church of yᵉ above demencons purſuant to former Orders.

Ordered That Sixty Thouſand pounds of Tobᶜᶜᵒ be paid him upon finishing of his said worke.

Ordered That he finiſh his sᵈ worke by yᵉ tenth day of June 1714.

---

* Supplied by me.—C. G. C.

Ordered That Mr Alexander Graves build Jetts & Peers of brick for ye Sleepers to be laid on according to the direccons of ye Overſeer's meñconed in theſe & former Orders.

Ordered That M^r Jn° Grymes be added to ye Overſeers of ye Said building.

Ordered That Captn Jn° Smyth M^r Jn° Robinſon Mr Ralph Wormeley and M^r Jn° Grymes, the aforementioned Overſeers they or any three of them be impowered to take Bonds of the s^d Alexander Graves & Jn° Hipkins Senr att Such tyme as they shall think fitt.

Ordered That fifteene thouſand pounds of Tob^cco in Church Warden's hands be paid *[to] Jn° Hipkins Senr in part of ye above Sixty thouſand upon giving Bond as above.

Ordered That ye remaining part of ye Tob^cco be paid the above Undertakers as they *[get] on with their worke.

Ordered That two thouſand pounds of Tob^cco be paid Mr Alexander Graves for building ye above Jetts & Peers as above.

Ordered That ye above Bonds when taken be entered in ye Veſtry Booke.

Matt Kemp

(142)   Know All men by theſe p^rſents that I John Hipkins of ye Piſh of Chriſt Church in ye County of Middx Carpenter doe Stand and am firmly bounden and Obliedged to Coll° Matthew Kemp Mr John Robinſon & Capt George Wortham (Church Wardens of Chriſt Church pariſh) in the full and Juſt ſuñe of One hundred and twenty Thouſand pounds of merchantable Sw^t Scented Tob^cco and Cask to be paid to the said Matthew Kemp John Robinſon and George Wortham or their Succeſſo^rs To which paym^t well faithfully and truly to be made I doe bind my Selfe my Heires Exec^rs and Adm^rs firmly by theſe p^rſents Sealed with my Seale dated this 14th day of June A° Dom: 1712.

The Condition of ye above Obligation is Such That whereas ye abovementioned John Hipkins has agreed with ye Veſtry

---

* Supplied by me.—C. G. C.

of Chriſt Church Pariſh and Undertaken for and in conſideration of 60000ᶦᵇ of Swᵗ Scented Tobᶜᶜᵒ to do all yᵉ Carpenters
Pluṁers and Glaſiers work of A new Church appointed by
yᵉ sᵈ Veſtry to be built where yᵉ Mother Church now Stands
by two Orders of Veſtry dated yᵉ 7ᵗʰ of Aprill & yᵉ 9ᵗʰ of
June Instant   Now if yᵉ sᵈ John Hipkins his heires Execʳˢ
or Admʳˢ &cᵃ Shall well and truly within yᵉ tyme Limitted by yᵉ
aforeſaid Orders at his & theire owne proper coſts & charges
well workmenlike & Sufficiently make build Erect Sett up &
fully finiſh or cauſe to be made built erected Set up & fully
finiſhed in all things belonging to yᵉ Trades of Carpenter
Plumer and Glaſier in & upon yᵉ ground where yᵉ old Mother
Church now Standeth A new Church according to yᵉ demencons & directions of yᵉ aforeſaid Orders of Veſtry &
yᵉ directions of yᵉ Overſeer's appointed by yᵉ sᵈ Orders to
overſee yᵉ sᵈ building and shall find & provide all neceſsaryes
for yᵉ carrying on & finiſhing yᵉ sᵈ Church as is directed by
yᵉ sᵈ Orders Then this prſent Obligation to be void otherwiſe
to remaine in full force and vertue.

Signed Sealed and Delivered   John Hipkins Sʳ Loco Sigilli
In yᵉ preſence of . . . . .

 Alexander Graves
 Richard Paffatt
 William Lawſon
 John Owen

 Know All men by theſe prſents That I Alexʳ Graves of yᵉ
pariſh of Christ Church in yᵉ County of Middx Bricklayer
doe Stand and am firmly bounden & obliedged to Collᵒ Matth:
Kemp Mʳ John Robinſon & Capⁿ Geo: Wortham (Church
wardens of Xᵗ Church pariſh) in yᵉ full & Just suṁe of one
hundred and twenty four thouſand pounds of merchantable
Swᵗ Scented Tobᶜᶜᵒ & Cask to be paid unto yᵉ sᵈ Matt: Kemp
Jnᵒ Robinſon & Geo: Wortham or their Succeſsʳˢ To yᵉ
which paymᵗ well truly & faithfully to be made I doe bind my
Selfe my heires Execʳˢ & Admʳˢ firmly by theſe prſents Sealed
with my Seale Dat this 14ᵗʰ day of June Aᵒ Dom: 1712.

The Condition of this Obligation is Such That whereas yᵉ abovementioned Alexander Graves has agreed with yᵉ Veſtry of Xᵗ Church Pariſh (for yᵉ Suñe of 62000ˡᵇ of Swᵗ Scented Tobᶜᶜᵒ) to doe all yᵉ Brick worke of A new Church appointed by yᵉ sᵈ Veſtry to be built where yᵉ Mother Church now stands by two Orders of Veſtry dated yᵉ 7ᵗʰ of Aprill & yᵉ 9ᵗʰ of June Instant Now if yᵉ sᵈ Alexʳ Graves his heires Execʳˢ Admʳˢ &cᵃ shall well & truly within yᵉ tyme Limitted by yᵉ aforeſaid Orders att his or their owne proper coſts & charges well workmenlike & sufficiently make build erect Sett up & fully finiſh or cauſe to be made built erected Sett up & fully finiſhed in all things belonging to yᵉ Arts or Trades of Brick-maker bricklayer & Plaiſterer in & upon yᵉ ground where yᵉ old mother Church now Standeth yᵉ walls of A new Church according to the dimenſions & directions of yᵉ aforeſaid Orders of Veſtry & yᵉ directions of yᵉ Overſeers mentioned in yᵉ sᵈ Orders And shall find & provide all neceſsaryes at his owne proper coſts & charges for yᵉ carrying on & finiſhing all yᵉ Brick worke about ye sᵈ Church & Plaister & white waſh yᵉ inſide as is directed by yᵉ sᵈ Orders Then this pᵣſent Obligation to be void otherwiſe to remaine in full force & vertue.

Signed Sealed and Delivered
  In the pᵣſence of
John Hipkings   Alexander Graves Loco Sigilli
Richard Paffatt
William Lawſon
John Owen
(143) Middx County ſst   Att a Veſtry held for Chriſt Church
          Virgᵃ   Pariſh in Middx County yᵉ 21 *[ˢᵗ]
                             day of July Aᵒ Dom: 1712.

                         Present

Mʳ Bartho: Yates Minister   Capⁿ Geo: Wortham
Captⁿ Jnᵒ Smyth   Mʳ Ralph Wormley
Mʳ Harry Beverley   Mʳ Jnᵒ Grymes
Mʳ Jnᵒ Robinſon   Gentlemen

* Supplied by me.—C. G. C.

Ordered by the abovenamed Gentlemen of yᵉ Veſtry as followeth (Vizᵗ)

Ordered That this Veſtry doth hereby acknowledge this day to have Reced of Mādm Elizabeth Churchill & Mʳ Ralph Wormley two of yᵉ Execʳˢ of yᵉ Laſt Will of Collᵒ William Churchill deced the suñe of one hundred & twenty five pounds sterling which was given by the said Will to this Veſtry for certaine uſes therein mentioned And that the sᵈ Execʳˢ be for the same hereby fully diſcharged.

Mʳ Jnᵒ Loemax having taken the aboveſaid one hundred & twenty five pounds att six ℈ Cent Intereſt & given Bond and Security for yᵉ payment of the same, Ordered That the sᵈ Bond be entered in the Veſtry Booke.

John Smith

Virgᵃ Middx ⎫
County   ⎬ ſst
           ⎭

Know all men by theſe preſents That wee John Loemax of Eſsex County & Ralph Wormley of Middx County in Virgᵃ gentlemen are Joyntly & Severally holden & firmly bounden unto Collᵒ Matthew Kemp Mʳ John Robinſon & Mʳ George Wortham (Church wardens of Chriſt Church pariſh in the County of Middx in Virgᵃ) in the full & Juſt suñe of Two hundred & fifty pounds Sterling to be paid to the said Matthew Kemp John Robinſon & George Wortham or their Succeſors Joyntly & Severally To which payment well truly & faithfully to be made We bind ourselves our heires Execʳˢ & Admʳˢ Joyntly & Severally firmly by theſe pʳſents Sealed with our Seales Dated this 21ᵗʰ day of July Aᵒ Dom: 1712.

The Condition of this Obligation is Such That whereas Madam Elizabeth Churchill Widow & the above bounden Ralph Wormley (Execʳˢ of Collᵒ Wᵐ Churchill deced) have this day paid unto the Veſtry of Chriſt Church pariſh One hundred & twenty five pounds Sterling (purſuant to two Clauſes contained in the Laſt Will & Teſtamᵗ of the sᵈ Deceadant) And whereas the sᵈ Veſtry hath now put the same to Intereſt (purſuant to the sᵈ Will) to the above bounden

John Loemax att Six ℔ Cent ℔ Annum   NOW if the above
bounden John Loemax his heires Exec^{rs} or Adm^{rs} shall well
truly & faithfully pay or caufe to be paid Att a Veftry in the
abovefaid Parifh during ye Sitting of ye Veftry *[purfuant to
the abovefaid Will the] unto the abovenamed Matthew Kemp
John Robinfon & George Wortham or either of them or their
Succefso^{rs} to & for the ufe of the Veftry purfuant to the abovefaid Will the full Juft Sume of one hundred & twenty five
pounds Sterling with Intereft for the same att Six pounds ℔
Cent as aforefaid on the one & twentieth day of July next following the date here of Then this p^{r}fent Obligation to be null
& void Otherwise to remaine in full force & vertue.

Jno Loemax   Loco Sigilli

Sealed & Delivered
    In the prefence of   Ralph Wormeley   Loco Sigilli
John Smith
Harry Beverley
John Grymes
John Owen

   (144) Att A Veftry held for Chrift Church parifh in Middx
County ye 22^d day of Septr A^o Dom.   1712.

Present

Mr Bartho: Yates Minister	Mr Jno Robinfon
Sr Wm Skipwith Kn^t	Captn Geo: Wortham
Coll^o Matt. Kemp	Mr Ralph Wormley
Captn Jno Smyth	Mr Roger Jones
Cap^n Robt Daniell	Gentlemen

   Ordered by ye abovenamed Gentlemen of ye Veftry As followeth (Viz^t)

   Ordered to Mr Bartho: Yates (Cafk & sallary added
to ye 16000)   18156

   Ordered That Mr Bartho: Yates as his Order collect
of each Tytheable perfon one & twenty pounds of
Tob^{cco} ℔ pole.

   To Jno Owen as Cl. of ye Mo: Church 1200, as Cl. of
ye Veftry 8000   02000

---

   * Half erased in the original. C. G. C.

Jn° Briſtoll Cl. of yᵉ Upper chappell	01000	
Nath: Underwood Cl. of yᵉ Lower Chappell	01000	
Edmᵈ Saunders Sexton	00600	
Ralph Mazy Sexton	00500	
Michⁱⁱ Smyth for keeping Mary Clay one year	01000	
Richᵈ Ranſtead	01000	
		07100
Hen: Ball for keeping Doro: Mannell one yeare	01000	
Hen: Baſkett for keeping Honour Baſkett one yeare	01000	
Jn° Birk allowed him	00200	
Robᵗ James	00800	
James Smyths Accoᵗ of work att yᵉ Mo. Ch: allowed	00500	
Mʳ Jn° Robinſon for waſhing Linen & Scouring Coм. plate	00100	
Geo: Berwick's Accoᵗ of worke att yᵉ Lower Chappell allowed	00390	
Robᵗ Humfreys allowed	00102	
		04092
Mʳ Jn° Robinſon on Ballance of his Accoᵗ	00142	
Coll° Matt: Kemps Accoᵗ allowed	00546	
Captⁿ Geo: Wortham's Accoᵗ allowed	00254	

Ordered That Seven & twenty thouſand pounds
of Tobᶜᶜᵒ be paid Mʳ Graves towards building yᵉ
new Church upon his Giving Bond and Security to
yᵉ Ch: Wardens for the same   27000

Ordered That fifteen thouſand pounds of Tobᶜᶜᵒ
be paid Mʳ Jn° Hipkins towards building yᵉ New
Church upon his giving Bond and Security to yᵉ
Ch. Wardens for yᵉ same   15000
                                      ───── 42942

Number of Tythables 878	54134
Caſk @ 8 ﴾ Cent	4332
	58466
Sallary @ 5 ﴾ Cent	2933
Laſt Totall	61399

Ordered That yᵉ Clerks & Sextons continue in their Offices.

Ordered That Mʳ Xtopher Robinſon, Mʳ Jnᵒ Vivion, Wᵐ Stannard & Joſeph Gore or any three of them be impowered to meete at yᵉ Court houſe on the 9ᵗʰ day of October next or any other tyme that they shall appoint to Auditt & Settle all Pish Accoᵗˢ & Report their proceedings to yᵉ Chu: wardens whoe are hereby impowered to draw the Tobᶜᶜᵒ out of yᵉ Severall collectors hands & pay the same to yᵉ pariſh Creditors.

Ordered That yᵉ Clerke of yᵉ Veſtry attend yᵉ above Auditors with yᵉ Veſtry Booke.

Ordered That Mʳ Ralph Wormley be Ch: warden of yᵉ Upper Precincts. Capⁿ Geo: Wortham of yᵉ Middle & Mʳ Roger Jones Church Warden of yᵉ Lower Precincts.

Ordered That yᵉ Church Wardens Collect of every Tythable pſon within their Reſpective Precincts Seventy one pounds of Tobᶜᶜᵒ ℔ Pole & pay yᵉ same to yᵉ pariſh Creditors as above.

(145) Middx County	ſsᵗ	Wᵐ Skipwith Att a Vestry held for Christ Church Pariſh in Middx County the 21ᵗʰ day of July Aᵒ Dom: 1713

Present

Mʳ Bartho: Yates Minister	Mʳ Harry Beverley
Sʳ Wᵐ Skipwith Knᵗ	Mʳ James Walker
Collᵒ Matt. Kemp	Capᵗ Geo: Wortham
Capᵗ Jnᵒ Smyth	Mʳ Roger Jones
Capᵗ Robᵗ Daniell	

Gentlemen

Ordered by the abovenamed Gentlemen of the Vestry As followeth. (Vizᵗ)

Ordered That the one hundred and twenty five pounds Sterling Which was given by the last Will of Collᵒ Wᵐ Churchill to this Vestry continue in the hands of Mʳ John Loemax att Six pounds Sterling per Cent ℔ Annum Interest for this enſueing yeare pursuant to A former Order.

Ordered That the quarterly Sermons uſually preached upon wensdays be preached upon the first fridays in the respective months.

Ordered That the Churchwarden bind *[   ] Moxom daughter of Thoˢ and Elizᵃ Moxom to John Murrey and his wife only 'till she attaine the Age of eighteen years.

Ordered That Joseph Jacobus of the Age of fifteen yeares May last be bound by the Churchwarden to Matthew Hunt 'till shall attaine the Age of one and twenty yeares.

Ordered That Mʳ Harry Beverley Capᵗ George Wortham and Mʳ James Walker be added to the Overſeers of the building the new Church in the Middle Precinct.

Ordered That Alexander Graves build the Church walls five courses of bricks higher all round then allready Ordered. And that he be paid four thousand pounds of Tobᶜᶜᵒ for the doeing thereof.

Wᵐ Skipwith

Chriſt Church   ſsᵗ   Att a Vestry held for Christ
Pariſh   Church Pariſh in Middx County
                 the 8ᵗʰ of October 1713.

Present

Mʳ Bartho: Yates Minister	Capᵗ Geo: Wortham
Sʳ Wᵐ Skipwith Knᵗ	Mʳ Ralph Wormley
Capᵗ Jnᵒ Smyth	Mʳ Roger Jones
Capᵗ Robᵗ Daniell	Gentlemen
Mʳ Harry Beverley	

Ordered by the abovenamed gentl of yᵉ Vestry As followeth (That is to say)

To Mʳ Bartho Yates (Cask and Salary added to yᵉ 16000) is   18380

Ordered that Mʳ Bartho. Yates or his Order collect of each Tytheable person 20ˡᵇ Tobᶜᶜᵒ ℔ pole.

To Jnᵒ Owen Clke of the Vestry and Mother Church for the last yeare   02000

Jnᵒ Owen for keeping Hannah Cheedle   00300

Jnᵒ Briſtow Clke of yᵉ Upper Chappell   01000

---

* Blank in the original here. C. G. C.

Jnᵒ Briſtow for washing Lien & Scouring comunion
plate   00100
  Nathan Underwood Clke of yᵉ Lower Chappell   01000
  Edmᵈ Saunders Sexton   00600
  Edmᵈ Saunders Sexton for building an Arboʳ & waſh-
ing comunion Linen &cᵃ   00130
  Ralph Mazy Sexton   00500
  Michaell Smyth for Keeping Mary Clay one yeare 01000
  Richᵈ Ranstead   01000
  Hen: Ball for keeping Doro: Mannell one yeare   01000
  Hen: Baſkett for keeping Honora Baſkett one yeare 01000
  Robᵗ James   00800
  James Meecham's Accoᵗ allowd   01500
                         ———

                  Carried Over   11930
(146)   Brought Over   11930
To Capᵗ Robᵗ Daniells Accoᵗ   00100
Capᵗ Harry Beverleys Accoᵗ allow'd   02093
Mʳ Oliver Seagar's Accoᵗ allowd   00800
Madam Elizᵃ Churchill for the new Version of the
Psalms   00100
  Madᵐ Churchill for 2 botles comunion wine   00100
  Mʳ Roger Jones two botles comunion wine   00100
  Capᵗ Geo: Wortham's Accoᵗ allow'd   00142
  Mʳ Ralph Wormley two botles comunion wine   00100
  Mʳ Yates allowd for 4 levys wanting @ 21ˡᵇ ℔ pole 00084
  Mʳ Oliver Seagar for 2 Delinquent Tythables 71ˡᵇ ℔
pole   00142
  Mʳ Yates allow'd for his extraordinary Trouble   02000
  Jnᵒ Lawrence for keeping Sarah Ingram 6½ months 00540
  Richᵈ Daniell for keeping Easton Moxum & Jnᵒ
Wakum   00883
  James Risq for keeping Jeffery Hundle 1 month   00083
  Abraᵐ Trigg for Cloathing Sarah Ingram   00400
  Mʳ Jnᵒ Hipkins towards building the New Church   15000

Mr Alex^r Graves towards building ye New Church   10000

		44597
	Cask @ 8 ℔ Cent	3567

Number of   (82

Tytheables 918)50572(55   48164

℔ pole with A fraction of   Salary @ 5 ℔ Cent   2408

82 due to Ch: Wardens

upon ballance   Sume Totall   50572

Ordered That Francis Dodson be free of the pari∫h Levy.

Ordered That Eliz^a Jenings remaine wth Jno Curtis 'till next Court where ye matter is referr'd.

Ordered That Jno Okill be appointed Clke of ye lower Chappell for ye en∫ueing yeare instead of Nathan Underwood.

Ordered That Jno Owen be appointed Clke of the Upper chappell and Clke of the Vestry for the ensueing yeare.

Ordered That the Clke of ye Vestry Attend the Severall *[Collectors] Churchwardens for ye yeares 1710 & 1711 and Settle Parish Accounts And report ye Same to ye next Vestry.

Ordered That ye Sextons continue in their Offices.

Ordered That the Ch: Wardens collect 55^{lb} Tob^{cco} ℔ pole of each Tytheable Pson within their Precincts And pay to the Pari∫h Credito^{rs}

Ordered That Capt Edmond Berkley and Mr Oliver Seager be de∫ired to take ye Oaths of Vestry men next Vestry.

Ordered That Mr Harry Beverley be appointed Ch: Warden of ye Upper Precincts and Mr Roger Jones Ch: Warden of ye Lower Precincts.

Ordered That the Pari∫h be devided into two Precincts, from Prettymans Quarter to the Dragon Bridge by the Roade.

Errors Excepted ℔   Wm Skipwith

(147)   Att A Ve∫try held for Chri∫t Church Pari∫h in Middle∫ex County this 7th day of June 1714

Present

Mr Bartholomew Yates Minister   Mr James Walker

Sr Wm Skipwith Kn^t Cap^n Geo: Wortham

* Half erased in the original.—C. G. C.

Coll° Matt: Kemp   Mʳ John Grymes
Captⁿ John Smith   Mʳ Roger Jones
                        Gentlemen
Mʳ John Wormley was this Day Sworne Vestryman. Preſent.
Ordered by the abovenamed Gentlemen of the Veſtry as
followeth (Vizᵗ)
Ordered That the Clarke of the Veſtry waite on Capⁿ Robert
Daniell to know whether *[he] will Act as A Veſtryman and
Report his Answere to the next Veſtry.
Ordered That A New Church be built as Soone as con-
veniently may be in the Lower Precincts, on the North Side
of the Old Church.
Ordered That the above Church be fifty foot Long in the
cleare and five and twenty foot wide in the cleare.
Ordered That the Walls of the Said Church be built with
Brick well tempered and well burnt, That the Water Table
be three foot from the Ground, three bricks thick, from the
*[water] table to the Roofe two bricks and an halfe thick, The
gable End from the Square to the *[Roof] one brick and an
halfe thick, To be plaiſtered with Lime and haire & white
waſhed, The Bricks to be laid with two thirds Lime and one
third Sand, That there be Jetts and Peers built *[of] Brick
for the Sleepers to be laid on, That the said Brick wall be
Sixteene foote high *[from] the Surface of the Earth to the
Plate, The foundation of the said Wall Jetts and Peers to be
two foot within the Ground.
Ordered That there be Seven Windows, Three of each Side,
of Eight foot long & four foot wide each. The End window
to be from the Arch within Six foot of the Sill Ten foot wide
the Side windows and the End window to be Saſh'd.
Ordered That there be two doores, One at yᵉ Weſt end,
Eight foot and an halfe high, and five foot and an halfe wide,
folding Doores; The Doore in the chancell to be Six foot foure
inches high, and three foot wide, the said Doores to be of
Oake plank, well fixed *[with] Locks and bolts; That the
Sills of the Said Doores be made of Cedar.

───────────────────────────

* Supplied for illegible word.—C. G. C.

Ordered That the Principall Rafters of the said Church be Saw'd of good white Oake 8 & 12 inches Square, att the foot, & 7 & 5 inches Square at the Top, That the Small Rafters be 3 & 4 inches Square, That the principall wind beams be 5 & 7 inches Square, That the braces be 3 & 4 inches Square, That the Shingling Laths be of Saw'd white Oake, an inch thick & four inches broad, That the Shingles be of the heart of Cyprefs, three quarters of an Inch att leaft at the thickest end, to be 16 inches long, and to Shew when laid 5 inches out. That there be 5 Girders of poplar, 12 inches Square, That the Roofe of the sᵈ Church be hipp'd above the wind beams, That the Doores and windows be of the Dementions above, That the Chancell be from the East end to the Screene, twelve foot, That the Railes and Banifters about the Cõmunion Table be 14 foot one way and 7 foot the other way, That the Pews be 4 foot and an halfe high, That four of the said Pews be raifed higher then the Reft according to the Directions of the Gentlemen appointed to *[be] Overfeers, That there be A comendable Screene to divide the Church from the Chancell; That the Pulpitt and two Defks Stand on the North Side of the Church below the high Pews, That the floore be laid with white Oake Plank one inch and quarter when wrought, Sleepers nine Inches deepe, three inches from the ground, to be laid on the abovemenconed Jetts & Peers.

That the said church be ceiled with three quarter Inch plank either Poplar or Cyprefs, to be laid in with Oyle and white Lead and Arch fafhion, That the Pews be of Poplar plank That the Church windows be well glazed with Long Square glafs, That the Cõmunion Table be made of Black wallnutt or white Oake. That the window frames Doores and Cornifhes be all laid in Oyle and Colours, That the said Church floore be tongued. That the Chancell be raifed one Step (of Six Inches) higher then the Church floore, The Comunion Table to be raifed, two Steps (of Six Inches each) higher then the floore of the Chancell.

* Supplied for illegible word.—C. G. C.

Ordered That Mr John Wormley be added to the Overfeers of the building the New Church in the Middle Precincts
in the Stead of Mr Ralph Wormley deceafed.

Turn Over

(148)   Ordered That the Gentlemen of the Veftry meete
againe att the Mother Church In Order to Agree with Undertakers for building the abovemenconed Church Purfuant to
the abovemenconed Orders on the first Monday in July next
enfueing.

Ordered That Mr Wm Blackbourne continue Clark of the
Lower Church the Remainder of this yeare having fifty pounds
of Tobcco more then the Ufuall Sallary allow'd him.

Ordered That the Severall Church Wardens for the Yeares
1710, 1711, 1712 & 1713 have notice to attend the next Veftry
to Settle their Parifh Accounts.

Wm Skipwith

Att a Vestry held for Christ Church parish in Middlesex
County the 12th day of October 1714

Present

Mr Bartho: Yates Minister	Capt Robert Daniell	
Sr Wm Skipwith Knt	Mr James Walker	
Collo Matt: Kemp	Capt Geo: Wortham	Gentlemen
Capt John Smith	Mr Roger Jones	
Mr Harry Beverley	Mr John Wormley	

Mr. Oliver Seager was this day Sworne Vestryman. Present.

Ordered by ye abovenamed Gentlemen of the Vestry as followeth (that is to Say)

To Mr Bartho: Yates Minister	16,720
John Owen Clerke of ye Upper Church & Clerke of ye Vestry	1,800
John Owen for attending Church Wardens, and cleaning Church Linen & plate	0300
Wm Blackbourne Clke of ye Lower Church	1050
Ralph Mazy Sexton of ye Upper Church	500
Mr Yates three Levies unpaid last Collection att 20lb Tobcco ℔ pole	060

Edm^d Saunders Sexton of ye Lower Chappell, & washing Church Linen	350	
James Smith allowed for burying Jno Okill	415	
Coll^o Kemps Acco^t allowed	500	
Madam Churchill, for 2 botles of Communion wine	080	
Jno Degge's Acco^t allowed	200	
		21975

That Mrs Perrotts Negro Dick be added to ye List of Tythables.

Abra^m Trigg for keeping Sarah Ingram	600	
Hen: Baskett for keeping Honour Baskett	1000	
Robt James	500	
John Lawrence for keeping Hannah Cheedle	1000	
Wm Gardiner for keeping Alice Silvester 6 months	500	

That Ch: Lee keepe Alice Silvester for ye ensueing yeare.

Michaell Smith for keeping Mary Clay one yeare	1000	
Hen: Ball for keeping Dorothy Mannell	1000	
John Smith for keeping John Wakum 8 months	1200	
Mr Jno Vivion 3 delinquent Tytheables last Levy @ 55 ℔ pole	165	
Mr Jno Vivion due to him on ballance of last Levy	82	7047
		29022

Ordered That Mr Wm Blackbourne have ye preference of Serving as Clarke of ye Lower Chappell att ye usuall Sallary. If he refuse to officiate as clarke in all respects Church Warden have liberty to appoint A Clarke for ye Lower Chappell.

Ordered That John Owen continue Clarke of ye Vestry.

Ordered That John Owen Officiate as Clarke of the Upper Church till ye Mother Church be finished, And then that he Officiate as Clarke of that Church And that John Bristow then Officiate as Clke of ye Upper Chappell att ye usuall Sallarys.

Ordered That Ralph Mazy be Sexton of ye Upper Church, Edwd Ball Sexton of ye Midle. & John Roe Sexton of ye Lower Chappell.

John Smith

(149)   Att a Vestry held for Christ Church parish in Middlesex County ye 13th day of October 1714

Present

Mr Bartho: Yates Minister	Mr James Walker
Capt John Smith	Capt Geo: Wortham
Mr Harry Beverly	Mr John Wormley
Capt Robt Daniell	Mr Oliver Seagar

Gentlemen

Ordered by ye abovenamed Gentlemen of ye Vestry as followeth (that is to Say)

Tob^cco Ordered to parish Creditors last Vestry   29022

Ordered That fifteene Thousand pounds of Tob^cco be paid John Hipkings upon finishing ye New Church now building in the Middle Precincts of this Parish   15000

Ordered That fourteene Thousand pounds of Tob^cco be paid Alexander Graves upon finishing ye New Church now building in ye Middle precincts of this parish   14000

To Doctor Thorton for attending Eliz^a Molloughon, John Curtis to produce Doctor Thorntons Acco^t next Vestry   400

To Alexander Graves for worke done att ye Glebe   80

Ordered That Mr Oliver Seagar be appointed Church warden of the Upper precincts Mr James Walker of ye Midle precincts & Sr Wm Skipwith Churchwarden of the Lower precincts of this parish.

Ordered That Mr Yates have Liberty of Keeping ye Register Booke of this Parish att his owne house 'till ye Vestry shall think fitt to Order it otherwise.

Ordered That ye Church Warden of the Midle precincts See John Wacum cloathed out of ye 1200^lb Tob^cco Ordered to Mr John Smith for keeping ye Said Wacum by this Vestry.

Ordered That Six hundred pounds of Tob^{cco} be paid each Church Warden for three days attendance each to receive ye parish Levyes pursuant to the New Law   1800

60302

Ordered That the Clarke of the Vestry attend ye Severall Church Wardens & take Bonds pursuant to ye new Law.

Ordered That ye Church Wardens collect of each Tytheable person within their precincts 65^{lb} of Tob^{cco} ℔ pole & pay ye same to ye Parish Creditors pursuant to Orders of Vestry.

Ordered That the Charges which Mr Hipkings & Mr Graves Shall expend in Recovering Tob^{cco} formerly Ordered them by this Vestry, be Reimbursed them by this Vestry.

1714   Christ Church Parish is D^r   Pr Contra   C^r
To the Severall parish Creditors 60,302

By 927 Tytheables @ 65 p pole   60255
Ballance due to ye Ch. Wardens   47

60302

John Smith

(150)   Att A Vestry held for Christ Church Parish in Middlesex County the 11th day of November 1714

Present

Mr Bartho: Yates Minister   Mr Jno Robinson
Coll^o Matt: Kemp   Capt Geo: Wortham
Sr Wm Skipwith Kn^t   Mr Jno Grymes
Capt Jno Smyth   Mr Roger Jones
Capt Robt Daniell   Gentlemen

Ordered by ye abovenamed gentlemen of ye Vestry as followeth (That is to Say)

This Vestry Taking in consideration That the Demensions in A former Order of Vestry about building ye Lower Chappell being too Short by Ten foot, It's Ordered That the s^d Chappell is to be built Ten foot Longer, That is, Sixty foot

Long in the Cleare and five and Twenty foot wide in yᵉ cleare, In all other matters Referrence to be had to the former Order.

It's Ordered That A Vestry meete att yᵉ Mother Church the first monday in December next to agree with Workmen towards building of the Sᵈ Chappell.

Wᵐ Skipwith

Att A Vestry held for Christ Church parish in Middleſex County the 6ᵗʰ day of December 1714

Present

Mʳ Bartho: Yates Minister	Mʳ Jnᵒ Robinson
Sʳ Wᵐ Skipwith	Mʳ James Walker
Collᵒ Matt: Kemp	Mʳ Jnᵒ Grymes
Capᵗ Jnᵒ Smith	Mʳ Roger Jones
Capᵗ Robert Daniell	Mʳ Jnᵒ Wormley
Mʳ Harry Beverley	Mʳ Oliver Seager

Gentlemen

Ordered by yᵉ abovenamed Gentlemen of the Vestry as followeth (that is to Say)

This Vestry taking into Consideration the Dimensions of the Lower Chappell mentioned in former Orders of Vestry not being Uniforme It is therefore Ordered That the said Chappell be built two and fifty long in the cleare and Thirty foot wide in the cleare.

Ordered That there be two double pews below yᵉ Screene, one of each side, Eight foot wide each the Rest to be single pews three foot & an halfe wide each

Ordered That yᵉ Walls of yᵉ above Chappell be built Seventeene foot high from the Surface of the Earth to yᵉ plate.

Ordered That yᵉ pulpitt and two Desks Stand in yᵉ Ally of yᵉ said Chappell betweene yᵉ two double pews That there be two Single pews of three foot and an halfe wide each one of each side of yᵉ Comunion Table.

Ordered That the side windows of yᵉ sᵈ Chappell be 10 foot high and 5 foot wide to be Arched A top. That there be A Round window of 5 foot Diameter over yᵉ west doore, That yᵉ Railes of yᵉ Comunion Table be 16. foot long & 10 foot

wide. That y⁰ sᵈ Chancell be from y⁰ East end to y⁰ Screene
16. foot.

Ordered that the floore of y⁰ Said Chappell be laid with
pine plank one Inch & quarter when wrought.

Ordered That y⁰ sᵈ Chappell be built in the same place
where y⁰ Old one now Stands.

Ordered That y⁰ window frames & Doore cases be made
of Cedar Locust or Mulberry.

Ordered That A Vestry meete att y⁰ Mother Church y⁰
first monday in January next to Agree with Undertakers for
building y⁰ Lower Chappell in this Parish.

Wᵐ Skipwith

(151) Ordered That Mʳ John Hipkings build the Chancell
Pulpitt and pews of y⁰ Mother Church pursuant to y⁰ above
Orders of the Lower Chappell and that he be paid for building
y⁰ Pulpitt What two Gentlemen (one to be appointed by Mʳ
Hipkings & one by y⁰ Vestry) shall value it to be worth.

John Smith

Att A Vestry held for Christ Church parish in Middlesex
County y⁰ 3ᵈ day of Janʳʸ 1714

Present

Mʳ Bar : Yates Minister	Capⁿ Geo : Wortham
Sʳ Wᵐ Skipwith Knᵗ	Mʳ John Grymes
Captⁿ John Smith	Mʳ Roger Jones
Mʳ John Robinson	Mʳ John Wormley
Mʳ James Walker	Gentlemen

Ordered by y⁰ abovenamed Gentlemen of y⁰ Vestry as followeth (that is to Say)

Ordered That John Roe be allowed one thousand pounds
of Tobaccoe A yeare for keeping John Purton & finding him
Sufficient cloaths, Dyett washing & Lodging, and that he be
allowed what the Vestry Shall think fitt for his wives dreſsing
his Sores.

Ordered That the Chancell of y⁰ Lower Chappell be from
y⁰ East end to y⁰ Screene 12 foot, That y⁰ railes & banisters
about y⁰ Comunion Table be 14 foot long and 7 foot wide,
That y⁰ two pews in y⁰ Chancell be 5 foot wide each. That

yᵉ South doore be made in yᵉ body of yᵉ Chappell below yᵉ Screene, That yᵉ pulpitt & two deſks Stand on yᵉ North Side oppoſite to yᵉ South doore, That the two double pews mentioned in yᵉ last Orders of Vestry be but 7 foot wide each, That yᵉ *[   ] be open pursuant to the directions of yᵉ Overseers of yᵉ worke. That yᵉ Church floore be laid *[   ] Sleepers to be of white Oake one foot from yᵉ ground.

Ordered That Captⁿ Henry Armstead and Major Edmond Berkley Undertake yᵉ Building the Lower Chappell pursuant to Orders of Vestry relating thereto. And that they be paid Ninety Thousand pounds of lawfull Swᵗ Scented Tobaccoe for yᵉ building of yᵉ Said Chappell.

Ordered That they finish the Building of yᵉ said Chappell by yᵉ 3ᵈ day of January 1716.

Ordered That Mʳ John Robinson Mʳ James Walker and Mʳ John Grymes or any two of them be impowered to take Bond for the Building the said Chappell, And that they be appointed Overseers of yᵉ said Building.

Ordered That the said Undertakers be paid forty thousand pounds of Tobᶜᶜᵒ in part of the said *[   ] thousand this ensueing fall, And the remaining fifty thousand pounds of Tobᶜᶜᵒ upon finishing the said Chappell.

Ordered That yᵉ Clarke of yᵉ Vestry draw off two faire Abstracts of yᵉ dimensions of yᵉ *[   ] Chappell and likewise one Copy of all yᵉ rough Orders of Vestry relating to yᵉ building *[   ] said Chappell.

Wᵐ Skipwith

(152)   Att A Vestry held for Christ Church Parish in Middx County the 8ᵗʰ day of July 1715.

Present

Mʳ Bartho: Yates Minister	Mʳ James Walker
Sʳ Wᵐ Skipwith Knight	Captⁿ Geo: Wortham
Capⁿ Jnᵒ Smith	Mʳ Roger Jones
Mʳ Jnᵒ Robinson	Mʳ Oliver Seagar

Gentlemen

* Word illegible in original MS.—C. G. C.

Ordered by the abovenamed Gentlemen of the Vestry as followeth (that is to Say)

Ordered That David Morgan be allowed five hundred pounds of Tob^cco for keeping Thomas White one yeare and finding him Sufficient Cloathing Dyett and Lodging.

This Vestry being of Opinion That the Order Of Court relating to proceſsioning, is not pursuant to the new Law, have Referred their proceedings 'till A fuller Order.

Wm Skipwith

Att A Vestry held for Christ Church parish in Middx County the 12th day of September 1715

Present

Mr Bartho: Yates Minister	Mr John Robinson
S^r W^m: Skipwith Knight	Captn Geo: Wortham
Coll^o: Matt: Kemp	Mr Roger Jones
Cap^n John Smith	Mr Jno Wormley
Mr Harry Beverly	Mr Oliver Seagar

Gentlemen

Ordered by the above named Gentlemen of the Vestry as followeth (Viz^t)

In pursuance of an Order of Middx County Court dated the 2^d day of August 1715—

This Vestry have divided this parish into Severall Precincts, And have appointed two Intelligent honest Freeholders of every Severall Precinct to See all the Lands within the said Severall Precincts proceſsioned as followeth (Viz^t)

Ordered That Wm Barbee and Geo: Hardin Sometime between the Second Tuesday in October and the last of March next proceſsion every particular mans land between the Lower end of this County and Coll^o Kemp's Mill croſs the Neck to Coll^o Churchill's Creeke.

Ordered That Joseph Gore and Wm Blackbourne Proceſsion every particular man's land between Coll^o Kemp's Mill and the Piping Tree on the South side of the maine Roade Sometime betweene the last Tuesday in October and the last day of March next.

Ordered That Captn Jno Diggs and Geo: Berrick Sometime betweene the Second Tuesday in November and the last day of March next proce∫sion every particular mans land from Coll^o Kemp's Mill to the Piping Tree along Coll^o Wormleys bounds to the River side on the North side of the maine Roade.

(153)   Ordered that James Smith and James Daniell Sometime between the Last Tuesday in November and the last day of March next Proce∫sion every particular mans land betweene the piping Tree and Prittiman's Rolling Road from the River to the Dragon.

Ordered That James Curtis Junr and John Davies Sometime between the Second Tuesday in December and the last day of March next proce∫sion every particular mans land betweene Prittiman's Rolling roade and Robert Williamsons land from the maine Roade to the Hea*[d] of Mr Christopher Robinsons Mill Dam on the North side of the maine Roade.

Ordered That John Smith Junr & Henry Tuggle Sometime betweene the Second Tuesd*[ay] in October and the last day of March next proce∫sion every particular man's Land betweene Prittiman's Rolling Roade and Robt Williamsons land, Running from the maine Roade to the Dragon on the South Side of the maine Roade.

Ordered That James Meecham & John Alldin Sometime betweene the last Tuesday in October and the last day of March next proce∫sion every particular mans land betweene Robt Williamson's land (including Williamsons land) and the Briary Swamp to the Millstone Valley running from the maine Roade to the Dragon on the South side of the maine Roade.

Ordered That Humphrey Jones & Hobbs Weekes, Sometimes betweene the Second Tuesday in November and the last day of March next proce∫sion every particular mans land betweene ye head of Mr Christopher Robinsons Mill Dam and the Head of Perrotts Creeke to the Millstone Vally on the North side of the maine Roade from the Roade to the River.

* Supplied by me.—C. G. C.

Ordered That Jn° Seagar and Hen: Goodloe Sometime betweene the last Tuesday in November and yᵉ last day of March next Proceſsion every particular mans Land betweene the Bryary Swamp (from the Millstone Vally to the Dragon Swamp) and the Upper End of the Country from the maine Roade to the Dragon Swamp on the South side of the maine Roade.

Ordered That Wᵐ Seagar & Thomas Mountague Sometime betweene the Second Tuesday in December and the last day of March next Proceſsion every particular mans land betweene the Head of Perrotts Creeke (from the Millstone Vally to yᵉ River) and the Upper end of the County from the maine Roade to the River on the North side of the maine Roade.

Ordered That the abovenamed Freeholders Proceſsion every particular mans land pursuant to the above Orders of Veſtry, And that they Take & Returne an Account of every persons land they Shall See proceſsion, of the Time when, & of the persons present att the same, And of *[whose] Lands in their Respective Precincts they shall faile to proceſsion, and of the particular reasons of Such failure to the next Vestry which shall happen after yᵉ last day of March next coming.

Wᵐ Skipwith

(154) Att A Vestry held for Christ Church Parish in Middx County the 5ᵗʰ day of October 1715.

Present

Mʳ Bartho: Yates Minister

Capⁿ John Smith	Capⁿ Geo. Wortham
Capⁿ Robᵗ Daniell	Mʳ John Grymes
Mʳ Harry Beverley	Mʳ Roger Jones
Mʳ John Robinson	Mʳ John Wormley
Mʳ James Walker	Mʳ Oliver Seager

Gentlemen

Ordered by the abovenamed Gentlemen of the Vestry as followeth (that is to Say)

To Mʳ Bartho Yates Minister   16,720

---

* Supplied by me. Word was illegible in MS.—C. G. C.

Jnᵒ Owen Clarke of the Midle Church &
Clke of yᵉ Vestry   2,000.
Jnᵒ Bristow Clke of the Upper Chappell for
half A yeares Service aſsigned to Madam Elizᵃ
Churchill   500.
Jnᵒ Hicks Clke of the Lower Chappell   666.
Ralph Mazy Sexton of Upper Chappell (Aſ-
signed to Madᵐ Churchill)   500
Edward Ball Sexton of the Midle Church
for Six months Service   250.
John Roe Sexton of the Lower Chappell for
8 months Service (Aſsigned to Mʳ Harry
Beverly)   333.
Charles Lee for keeping Alice Silvester 4
months and buriall   700.
Robert Humfrys for keeping Daniell Roſs
7 months   700.
Doctor Tomkins for Salivating Daniell Roſs 1000.
Robert James   200.   23569

John Roe for keeping Jnᵒ Purton one yeare
1000ˡᵇ and for his wives dreſsing his Sores
300ˡᵇ (Aſsigned to Mʳ Harry Beverly)   1300.
John Ingram for keeping Sarah Ingram one
yeare   600.
Henry Smith for burying John White 346
and keeping Hannah Cheedle one yeare 1000ˡᵇ
(Aſsigned to Madᵐ Elizᵃ Churchill)   1346
Richard Daniell for burying Jnᵒ Wakum
(Aſsigned to Mᵐ Churchill   200
Valentine Mayo for keeping Dorothy Main-
well one yeare   1000
Edmond Cambridge burying John Davies   285.
Michaell Smith for keeping Mary Clay one
yeare   1000.
Augustin Owen for keeping John Burk 8
dayes   150
John Hipkings for A Coffin for John Burk   100.

Henry Baskett for keeping Honour Baskett one yeare	1000.	
Jn⁰ Owen washing and cleaning Church Linen & plate, and two Copys of Law to prevent burning Warehouses	75.	7056

Mr James Walker charges for burying John Burk	120.	
Mr James Walker 4 botles of Comunion wine @ 30ᵇ ℔ botle	120.	
Mr Oliver Seager's Account allowed	427.	
Capⁿ Geo: Wortham's Account allowed	200.	
Mr John Hipkings Account allowed (2280ᵇ of it aſsigned to Mr John Robinson)	3600.	
Mr James Walker 7 delinquent Tytheables @ 65ᵇ ℔ pole	455.	
Mr James Walker 3 Tytheables insolvent @ 65ᵇ ℔ pole	195.	
Mr Oliver Seager 7 Delinquents @ 65 ℔ pole	455.	
Capⁿ Henry Armstead and Major Edmond Berkley 40,000ᵇ in part of 90,000ᵇ Tobᶜᶜᵒ for building yᵉ Lower Chappell	40000.	
Mr John Bevan 1 delinquent @ 55	55.	
Church Wardens for two dayes attendance each to receive parish Levyes	1200.	
Mr Harry Beverly	200.	47027

77652

Ordered That one Levy belonging to Major Edmond Berkley be added to the List of Tytheables this yeare.

Ordered That Capⁿ Geo: Wortham be Church Warden for the Upper Precincts, Mr James Walker for the Midle, And Mr John Robinson Church Warden for the Lower Precincts this yeare.

Ordered That the Church Wardens Collect of every Tytheable person within their Reſpective Precincts 82 pounds of Tobᶜᶜᵒ ¾ per Pole and pay the same to the Parish Creditors.

Ordered That every Pensioner be allowed but 800^{1b} of Tob^{cco} for every 1000^{1b} of Tob^{cco} and Soe in proportion att the laying of the next Levy.

Ordered That the two Sextons continue in their Offices.

(155) Ordered That John Owen be appointed Clarke of the Upper Chappell and Clarke of the Vestry this Ensueing yeare.

Ordered That John Hicks be appointed Clarke of the Midle Church this ensueing yeare In case of failure Church warden have Liberty to appoint another.

John Smith

1715 Christ Church Parish is D^r
To Parish Creditors   77652
Ballance due to the Parish   144¾
                                                       ———
                                                       77796¾
Pr Contra   C^r
By 937 Tytheables @ 82¾ ₱ pole   77536¾
By 4 Levies of James Risq due since last yeare @
65 ₱ pole   260
                                                       ———
                                                       77796¾

Att A Vestry held for Christ Church Parish in Middlesex County ye 8th day of May 1716

Present

Mr Bartho: Yates Minister, Capt Jno Smith, Mr John Robinson, Mr James Walker, Capt Geo: Wortham, Mr John Grymes, Mr Roger Jones, Mr John Wormley, Mr Oliver Seager
Gentlemen

Ordered by ye abovenamed Gentl: of ye Vestry as followeth (that is to Say)

Ordered That the Church wardens Accounts Stated by this Vestry be entered on ye vestry Booke.

Jo^n Smith

1715 Capt Geo: Wortham Ch:
Warden of the Upper Precincts   D^r
To 316 Tytheables @ 82¾ 26,148   Pr Contra   C^r
                                   By paid Parish Creditors 16437

| | Bad debts | 09510 |
| | Due to Balance | 00201 |

26148

1715 Mr James Walker Ch:

Ward. Mid Prec. D^r   Pr Contra   C^r

To 394 Tytheables @ 82¾	32,603	By paid Credito^rs	28050½
" 4 Levyes of Jam.		Bad Debts	29113¾
Rifque @ 65	260	Due to Ball^a	1901¼

32,863   32863

1715 M^r Jn° Robinson Ch:

Ward: Lo: Prec. D^r   Pr Contra   C^r

To 228 Tytheables @ 82¾	18,867	By paid Cred^rs	10218
		Bad Debts	8223
		Due to Ballance	⁄26

18867

(156) Att A Vestry held for Christ Church Parish in Midlesex County ye 10th day of October 1716.

Present

Mr Barth° Yates. Minister Sr Wm Skipwith Knight. Capt *[Geo Wortham] John Smith. Mr John Robinson. Mr James Walker. Capt Geo: Wortham. Mr Roger Jones. Mr John Wormley. Mr Oliver Seagar   Gentlemen

Ordered by the abovenamed Gentlemen of ye Vestry as followeth (that is to Say)

To Mr. Barth° Yates Minister	16720
To John Hicks Clarke of ye Mother Church	01200
John Owen clke of ye Upper Church, and Vestry	01800
Alice Mazy Relict of Ralph Mazy Sexton deceased	500
Edward Ball Sexton of ye Midle Church	715
John Hipkins on Account of charges allow'd	475
Mr Yates 3 delinquents allow'd	210

* Half erased in original MS, but still legible. C. G. C.

Alex^r Graves 3 delinquents @ 65 ₱ pole
allowd   195
John Hipkins 4 delinquents @ 65 ₱ pole
& 1 @ 22 allowd   282
                                                        ———————   22097
Capt Geo: Wortham 6 delinquents & 1 insol-
vent @ 82¾   496
Capt Geo: Wortham 4 botles of comunion
wine @ 30   120
Richd Hill one Levy @ 65 in ye yeare 1714
overcharged   65
Sr Wm Skipwith 4 botles of comunion wine
@ 30 ₱ botle   120
Jno Ingram   700
Alice Mazy   500
John Price for two barrells of corne @ 80
₱ barrell allowd   160
Powell Stamper for keeping Honora Baskett   800
Hugh M^{eck}tyre for keeping Eliz^a Sumers   800
Doctor Tomkins for meanes administred to
Sarah Haines   2500
Ann Mayo for keeping Dorothy Mainwell 3
months & buriall   400   6661

Mr John Robinson for keeping Sarah Haines
6 weekes   280
Mr Wm Stannard for 4 Copyes of Laws   300
Capt Geo: Wortham for copy of Mr Shep-
herd's Will   35
Mr Oliver Seagers Account paid Mr Stannard   176
Wm Herne for mainteinance of Selfe & wife   1000
Ralph Loyall for keeping Geo: Jennings 10
months   670
Mich^{ll} Smith for keeping Mary Clay 2
months & buriall   230
Mr James Walker 7 botles of com. wine &
goods for Ma. Purvis   410

Mary Purvis	600	
Robt Holmes for keeping Hannah Cheedle one year	800	
John Roe for Keeping John Purton	800	
Mr James Walker allow'd Edward Peirce as a delinquent	82¾	
Mr John Robinson allowed Rowl^d Jones, Wm Dos & Peter Norton as 3 delinquents @ 82¾	248¼	
Robt James	400	
Coll^o Edm^d Berkley & Capt Henry Armstead	50000	
Church Wardens for 2 days Attendance each @ 200 ℔ day	1,200	57232

85990

1716 Christ Church Parish is	D^r	P^r	Contra	C^r
To Parish Creditors	85,990	By 909 Tythables @ 95		
Ballance due to ye Parish	365	℔ pole		86355
		By an Error of 500 al-		
	86355	lowd Alice Mazy		
An Error as ℔ Contra	500	twice		500

86,855	86855

Ordered That Mr Oliver Seagar be Churchwarden of ye Upper Precincts Mr James Walker of ye Midle & Mr Roger Jones of ye Lower Precincts this ensueing yeare.

Ordered That ye Ch: Wardens collect of 909 Tythables 95^{lb} of Tob^o ℔ pole and pay ye Same to Parish Creditors.

Ordered That Alice Mazy have ye benefitt of ye Sexton's place of ye Upper Church, and Edward Ball continue Sexton of ye Midle Church.

Ordered That John Owen continue Clarke of ye Upper church & Clark of the Vestry.

Ordered That Jonathan Gayre be appointed Clarke of ye Midle Church.

(157) Ordered That Mr John Wormley sue Charles Haines for 2780^{lb} Tob^o levyed on Account of Sarah Haines his daughter.

Ordered That Mr John Robinson take Bond of Mr James Walker for the one hundred and twenty five pounds and Interest left to ye Parish by ye last Will of Coll^o Wm Churchill deceased.

Memd^m That in ye yeare 1715 Mr Barth^o Yates reced of Mr James Walker 6978¼^{lb} of Mr John Robinson 3,000^{lb} of Mr Geo: Wortham 3087½^{lb}.

Memd^m That in ye yeare 1715 Mr John Robinson & Mr James Walker paid Coll^o Edmond Berkley 8902¼^{lb} Capt Geo: Wortham paid him 514^{lb}.

Wm Skipwith

Att a Vestry held for Christ Church Parish in Midle∫ex County the 5th day of August 1717.

Present

Mr Barth^o Yates Minister	Mr James Walker
Capt John Smith	Mr John Grymes
Mr Harry Beverly	Mr Roger Jones
Mr John Robinson	Mr Oliver Seagar

Gentlemen

Ordered by the abovenamed gentlemen of the Vestry (as followeth) Viz^t.

Ordered That the Clarke of the Vestry prepare A Booke to enter Chruch Warden Accounts yearly.

Ordered That the Severall Church-warden's Accounts this day Stated & Setled by the Vestry be entered in the said Booke of Accounts.

Upon Setling Mr James Walkers Accounts for the yeare 1715 there remaines due to Ballance Eight hundred twenty Seven pounds and an halfe of Tob^o.

Ordered That the Severall Churchwardens for the yeares 1715 & 1716 have notice to prepare faire Lists of Delinquents & returne the Same to the Sheriff of this County in Some convenient time betweene this & the first day of October next.

Ordered That the Sheriff of this County Collect the Tob^o due from the abovesaid Delinquents And Account for the Same to the Vestry.

Mr John Grymes Accounts for two fines for
breach of ye Sabbath   £ 00 ‖ 10 ‖ 0

Mr Oliver Seagar Accounts for one fine for
Swearing   00 || 05 || 0
Mr James Walker Accounts for two fines for
Swearing   00 || 10 || 0
Mr Harry Beverly Accounts for one fine
Recd of Thos Smith for A Bastard Child   02 || 10 || 0

                                                            3 || 15|| 0
Mr Walker for one more for Swearing   5|| 0

Ordered That the above fines be distributed amongst ye Poore
of this Parish at the laying ye next Levy.

This Vestry being Acquainted That the Builders of the
Lower Chappell are putting up Inconvenient Pews contrary to
Agreement and former Orders of Vestry.

It is therefore Ordered That the Gentlemen appointed by
the Vestry Overseers of the Building of the said Chappell
Acquaint the Undertakers of the said Building That they pur-
sue the Orders of Vestry made relating to the Pews in the said
Chappell.

Ordered That Mr John Robinson & Mr John Grymes Auditt
& Setle the Severall Collectors Accounts for the yeares 1710 &
1711 . . September Court next at the Court-house And that
the said Collectors have notice to Attend the said Auditors wth:
their Vo*[uchers].

                                        Jon Smith

(158)   Att A Vestry for Christ Church in Middx County
ye 18th day of October 1717.

                                        Present

Mr Bartho Yates Minister   Capt Geo: Wortham
Sr Wm Skipwith   Mr John Grymes
Capt Jno Smith   Mr Roger Jones
Capt Robt Daniell   Mr John Wormley
Mr Harry Beverly   Mr Oliver Seager
Mr Jno Robinson   Collo Edmond Berkley
Mr James Walker   Gentleman

---

* Illegible in MS, and supplied by me.—C. G. C.

Coll° Edmond Berkley was this day Elected & Sworne
Vestryman.

Ordered by the abovenamed Gentlemen of the Vestry as followeth (that is to Say).

To Mr Barth° Yates Minister	16,000
Jonathan Gayre Clke of the Midle Church	1,200
John Owen Clke of the Upper Church & Vestry	1,800
Alice Mazy for Serving as Sexton of the Upper Church	500
Ditto for cleaning Comūnion plate & Linen two yeares	100
Edward Ball Sexton of the Midle Church	600
Hugh M^cktyre for Keeping Eliz^a Suñers	700
Robt Holmes for Keeping Hannah Cheedle 4 months & Buriall	500
Wm Hill for keeping Mary Ranstead 5 months & an ½	333
Ann Mayo for keeping Sarah Adcock 1 weeke & Buriall, & for keeping the said Adcocks Child 11 months	700
Wm Brookes for keeping Wm Robeson 1 month & fastning Com^dts in the Upper Church	92
Eliz^a Morgan for curing Sarah Ingram of A Sore leg	200

                                                              22725

David Morgan for keeping Geo: Jenings & Sarah Ingram 16 months and Burialls	960
Henry Baskett for keeping Honora Baskett 7 months & ½	467
Jonathan Brookes for keeping Ditto 2 weeks	33
Powell Stamper for keeping Ditto 4 months	267
Richd Perrott for keeping Sarah Ingram 2 months & ½	125
Mabell Dodson for keeping Cha: M^ck Carty 2 weekes, 1 quart of Rum, one dose of Physick	100

Mary Ingram for keeping Sarah Ingram 3 months	133	
Mary Purvis	600	
John Roe for keeping John Purton	800	
Ralph Loyall for keeping Geo: Jenings 5 weekes	85	
Wᵐ Herne & Isabell his wife	1000	
Mʳ James Walker for cloths for Sarah Ingram	67	
		4637
Edward Sittern	400	
Mʳ Roger Jones allow'd 5 delinquents @ 95 ⅌ pole	475	
Jnᵒ Gibbs for keeping Cha: MᶜᵏCarty 6 months	1,200	
Doctor Tomkins for Physick Administered to Cha: MᶜᵏCarty	2000	
Jnᵒ Hipkins's Account allowd	175	
Ditto allowd 2 delinquents @ 65 ⅌ pole	130	
Ditto allowd Richard Wait's Widow's 2 delinquents @ 65 ⅌ pole	130	
Doctor Wallford for Physick administered to Mary Ranstead	500	
Ditto for Physick administered to Ann Gardner	600	
Mʳ Oliver Seagers Account allowd	30	
Mʳ Jnᵒ Robeson for two Botles of comunion wine	60	
Mʳ James Walker for 8 botles of Ditto and his Account allowd	440	
An Addition made, due to the Parish on Balance	246	
		6386
		33748

Number of Tytheables	890	Caske @ 8 ₩ Cent	2699
Levy ₩ pole	43		
	———		36447
	2670	Sallary @ 5 ₩ Cent	1823
	3560		———
	———		38270
	38270		

(159) Ordered That the Severall Church Wardens take care to have Church Linen & plate cleaned yearly.

Ordered That Jnᵒ Roe be appointed Sexton of the Lower Church.

Ordered That Jonathan Gayre be appointed Clke of the Lower Church & John Hicks Clarke of the Midle Church.

Ordered That John Owen continue Clarke of the Upper Church & Clke of the Vestry.

Ordered That the Sextons continue in their Offices.

Ordered That Mʳ John Robinson be appointed Church Warden of the Upper Precincts, Mʳ John Grymes of the Midle & Mʳ Roger Jones of the Lower Precincts this ensueing yeare.

Ordered That the Severall Church Wardens Collectors for the yeares 1710 & 1711 make up their Accounts of their parish Collections before Mʳ John Grymes, and the said Mʳ Grymes is hereby desired & impowered to comence Suit in any Court within this Collony, against all or any of the said Churchwardens as shall appe*[ar] to him to be delinquent, in behalfe of the Vestry of Christ Church Parish.

Ordered That the Severall Churchwardens collect 43ᵗʰ of Tobᵒ ₩ pole of every Tytheable person within their respective precincts & pay the same to the parish Creditors.

Ordered That Mʳ Yates begin to preach in the Lower Church this Ensueing Sabbath Day.

Ordered That the Churchwardens be impowered to agree with workmen to pale in the Severall Church-Yards in their respective precincts with pales four foot & an halfe high of Saw'd white Oake.

Wᵐ Skipwith

* Supplied be me.—C. G. C.

Att A Vestry held for Christ Church Parrish in Midd^x County the 31th day of March 1718.

Present

Mr Barth^o Yates Minister   Mr James Walker
Sr Wm Skipwith   Capt Geo: Wortham
Captn John Smith   Mr Roger Jones
Mr Harry Beverly   Coll^o Edmond Berkly
Mr John Robinson   Gentlemen

Ordered by the above named Gentlemen of ye Vestry as followeth (vizt).

Ordered That Mr James Walker Pay the Tob^o (Received by him for Delinquents putt into his hands by the Church wardens for the Severall yeares 1715 and 1716) to the Severall parish Creditors as followeth (vizt).

To Mr Bartho. Yates   1616 pounds of Tob^o
" Coll^o Edm^d Berkly   7763 pounds of Tob^o
" Capt Henry Armstead   6211 pounds of Tob^o
" Doctor Lewis Tomkins   510 pounds of Tob^o

Ordered That one of the Churchwardens take care of the two youngest children of John Purvis, born att one Birth.

This Vestry being Informed by Mr John Robinson That the Bishop of London had Sent A Bell for the use of this parish—

Ordered That Mr Barth^o Yates & Mr John Robinson draw up A Letter of Thanks to his Lordshipp for the Same, And that it be Signed by all the members of this Vestry & Sent by them to his Lordshipp.

Ordered That A convenient Cupulo be forthwith built at the West end of the Mother Church, to hang the said Bell in, And that the Church Warden of ye Middle precincts agree with workmen to doe ye Same.

Ordered that Mr James Walker is Desired to Send for two Setts of Comunion Plate & that Tob^o be levied to pay for the Same att ye laying the next Levy att the rate of ten Shillings ℔ hundred (with Cask) for the first cost of the said plate, And that Mr Walker have the old Church plate, and give the parish creditt for the Same.

Verte.

(160)   Ordered That the said two Setts of Comunion Plate consist off four Flagons two chalices and five Plates.

Wm Skipwith

Att A Vestry held for Christ Church Parish in Middlesex County the 16th day of June 1718.

Present

Mr Barth^o Yates Minister	Capt George Wortham
Capt John Smith	Mr John Grymes
Capt Robt Daniell	Mr Roger Jones
Mr Harry Beverley	Mr John Wormley
Mr John Robinson	Mr Oliver Seager
Mr James Walker	Coll^o Edmond Berkley

Gentlemen

Ordered by the above named Gentlemen of the Vestry As followeth (That is to Say) Mr John Grymes having Acquainted this Vestry That he hath in his hands five and Twenty pounds towards buying Ornaments for the Midle Church, The Executo^{rs} of Madam Elizabeth Churchill deceased are defired to pay unto the said Mr John Grymes the money left by the said Madam Elizabeth Churchill for the same use.

Whereas by A former Order of Vestry Two Setts of Comunion Plate were to be Sent for, Mr John Grymes undertaking to provide A new Sett of Comunion plate for the Lower Church, And Mr John Robinson (upon consideration of having the Old Comunion Plate belonging to the Upper Church & Midle Church) Undertaking to provide A New Sett of Comunion Plate for the Upepr Church It is Ordered That the said former Order of Vestry be made void, And that the said old Comunion plate belonging to the Midle Church & Upper Church be delivered to the said Mr John Robinson, Mr James Walker being desired to See the said Old Comunion Plate first weighed and give an Account thereof to the Vestry.

Ordered That David Morgan keepe Arthur Johnson And that he be allow'd for the Same at the laying the next Levy.

(161)   At A Vestry held for Christ Church Parish in Middlefex County the 13th day of October 1718.

Present

Mr Barth° Yates Minister	Mr John Grymes
Sr Wm Skipwith Kn^t	Mr Roger Jones
Capt John Smith	Mr John Wormley
Mr Harry Beverly	Mr Oliver Seager
Mr John Robinson	Gentlemen
Mr James Walker	

Ordered by the abovenamed Gentlemen of the Vestry as followeth (vizt)

	Tob°	
To Mr Barth° Yates Minister	16,000	
John Owen Clarke of the Upper Church and Vestry	1,800	
Thos Field for 7 months & an halfe Service as Clarke of the Midle Church	750	
Jonathan Gayre Clarke of the Lower Chappell	1,000	
Alice Mazy for Officiating as Sexton of the Upper Church	500	
Edward Ball Sexton of the Middle Church	600	
Jn° Roe Sexton of the Lower Church	500	
Ditto for keeping John Purton one yeare	800	
David Morgan for keeping Arthur Johnson *[one yeare] four months	267	
Ann Mayo for keeping Adcocks Orphan one yeare	500	22717

Ordered That She be paid noe longer for keeping the said Orphan without an Agreem^t with A Church warden.

Mr Roger Jones 4 botles of comunion wine	120	
William Hill for keeping Mary Ranstead one yeare	800	
James Lewis for keeping William Anderson 3 months & 2 weekes	500	
Doctor Tomkins for meanes Administered to Arthur Johnson	500	

* Scratched over in MS., but still legible.—C. G. C.

Ditto for curing William Anderson	800	
Ditto for Salivating Cha: M^{cc}Carty	800	
Jn° Gibbs for keeping Cha: M^{cc}Carty 8 months	1600	5120

Ordered That Cha: M^{cc}Carty be allowed ye usuall pension from the date of these Orders.

Edward Sitterne	400	
Wm Herne & Isabell his wife	1000	
Mary Purvis	600	
Mich¹¹ Smith for burying Mary Middleton	200	
Sam¹¹ Batcheller for keeping Honora Baskett 1 yeare	800	
Wm Brookes for keeping Wm Robeson 3 months & two weekes	234	
Hugh M^{cc}tyre for keeping Eliz^a Suñers 1 yeare	700	

Ordered That the Churchwarden Enquire as to Wm Bakers circumstances.

Mr James Walkers Acco^t allow'd	351	
Ditto allow'd 4 delinquents @ 43^{1b}	172	
Mr John Robinson's Acco^t allow'd	1008	5465

33302

Mr Roger Jones for palling in ye Lower Church yard &c^a	5,500	8 ₱ c^t	
Stokely Toles for palling in ye Midle Church yard	5,250	for cask	2664

Mr John Robinson for paleing in y^e upper Church yard	5,000	35966
Mr John Grymes for Tarring y^e Midle Church & Ladder	1,000	
Mr John Hipkings's Acco^t allow'd	622	

17,372	17372
	53338

Sallary @ 5 ⅌ Cent   2666

Number of
Tythables   918)56004(61¹ᵇ ⅌ pole
                                   _____
                            Parish Charge   56004

Mr James Walker is appointed Churchwarden for y^e upper
precincts, Mr John Grymes for the Midle, & Coll^o Edm^d Berkley
for the Lower precincts.

Ordered That Churchwardens collect 61¹ᵇ Tob^o ⅌ pole of
every Tythable person within their respective precincts & pay
ye Same to the parish Credito^{rs}

Ordered That noe parish charge be allow'd for the future
but what is Ordered by the Vestry or Some Churchwarden.

                                   Wm Skipwith.

(162)   Att A Vestry held for Christ Church Parish in Middlesex County the 16th day of September 1719

                            Present

Mr Barth^o Yates Minister, Capt John Smith, Capt Robert
Daniell, Mr Harry Beverley, Mr James Walker, Mr Roger
Jones, Mr John Wormley, Mr Oliver Seager — Gentlemen

Ordered by the abovenamed Gentlemen of the Vestry as
followeth (that is to say)

In pursuance of an Order of Midd^x County Court dated the
first day of September Instant This Vestry have Divided this
Parish into Severall Precincts And have appointed two Intelligent Free-holders of every Severall Precinct to See all
the Lands within the said Severall Precincts Proceſsioned, as
followeth (that is to Say)

Ordered That Wm Barbee and George Hardin Proceſsion
every particular mans land, betweene the Lower End of this
County & Coll^o Kemps Mill croſs the neck, to Coll^o Churchill's
Creeke, Beginning to proceſsion the Second Tuesday in October next, and finish the Same by the last day of March next.

Ordered That Jos: Gore & Wm Blackbourne proceſsion every
particular mans land, between Coll^o Kemps Mill & the Piping
Tree on the South Side of the maine Road begining to proceſsion the last Tuesday in October next, and finish the Same
by the last day of March next.

Ordered That Geo: Berrick and John Rhodes proceſsion every particular mans land, from Collᵒ Kemps Mill to the Piping Tree, along Collᵒ Wormleys bounds to the River Side on the North Side of the main Road Begining to proceſsion the last Tuesday in November next and finish the Same by the last day of March next.

Ordered That James Smith and James Daniell proceſsion every particular mans land between the Piping Tree, and Prittymans Rolling roade from Rappᵃ River to Piank A Tank begining to proceſsion the Second Tuesday in November next, And finish the Same by the last day of March next.

Ordered That Robert Gailbraith and Stokely Toles Proceſsion every particular mans land betweene Prittymans Rolling Roade & Robert Williamson's land from the maine Roade to the Head of Mʳ Xtopher Robinsons Mill Dam on the North side of the maine Roade begining to proceſsion, the Second Tuesday in December next, And finish the Same by the last day of March next.

Ordered That John Smith Junʳ and Henry Tugle proceſsion every particular mans land, betweene Prittymans Rolling Roade and Robert Wᵐson's runing from the maine Roade to the Dragon on the South Side of the maine road Begining to proceſsion the Second Tuesday in October next, And finish the Same by the last day of March next.

Ordered That James Meecham and John Aldin Proceſsion every particular mans land, betweene Robᵗ Wᵐsons Land (including WᵐSon's Land) and the Bryary Swamp to the Millstone Valley, Runing from the maine Roade to the Dragon on the South Side of the maine Roade.—begining to proceſsion yᵉ last Tuesday in 8ᵇᵉʳ next &ᶜᵃ

Ordered That Hum: Jones & Richᵈ Perrott Proceſsion every particular mans land, betweene the Head of Mʳ Xtopher Robinsons Mill Dam & the Head of Perrotts Creeke to the Millstone Valley on the North Side of the maine Roade from the Roade to the River. Begining to Proceſsion the Second Tuesday in November next And finish the Same by the last day of March next.

Ordered That John Seager & Henry Goodloe Procefsion every particular man's Land betweene the Bryary Swamp (from the Millstone Valley to the Dragon Swamp) and the Upper End of the County, from the maine Roade to the Dragon Swamp on the South Side of

(163) South Side of the maine Road. Begining to procefsion the last Tuesday in November next, And finish the same by the last day of March next.

Ordered That William Seager and Thomas Mountague Senr Procefsion every particular mans land Betweene the Head of Perrotts Creeke (from the Millstone Vally to the River, to Henry Robinsons Mill dam to the Slash from the Maine Roade to the River on the North Side of the maine Roade Begining to procefsion the Second Tuesday in Decembe[r] next, And finish the Same by the last day of March next.

Ordered That Robert W^{m}fon Junr and Henry Bewford Procefsion every particular mans land betweene Henry Robinsons Mill dam and the Slash to the upper End of the County from the maine Roade to the River on the North Side of the maine Roade Beginning to procefsion the last Tuesday in Xber next, And finish the Same by the last day of March next.

Ordered That the abovenamed Free-holders Procefsion every particu^r mans land pursuant to the above Ord^{rs} of Vestry, And that they take and returne an Account of every persons land they Shall See procefsion of the time when, and of the persons p^{r}sent at the Same, And of what lands in their respective Precincts they Shall faile to procefsion, and of the particular reasons of Such failure to the next Vestry wch Shall happen after the last day of March next coming.

Ordered that Mr James Walker Provide A Folio Booke to Record the Returns of the Procefsioners, And that he be paid for the Same by the Vestry.

John Smith

(164) Att A Vestry held for Christ Church Parish in Midd^x County the 7th day of October 1719

Present

Mr Barth^o Yates Minister, Sr Wm Skipwith Kn^t Capt John Smith, Capt Robert Daniell, Mr Harry Beverly, Mr John Robinson, Mr James Walker Capt Geo: Wortham, Mr John Grymes, Mr Roger Jones, Mr John Wormley, Mr Oliver Seager — Gentlemen

Ordered by the abovenamed Gentlemen of the Vestry as followeth (Viz^t)

	lb Tob^o
To Mr Barth^o Yates Minister	16000
John Owen Clke of the Upper Chappell and Vestry	1800
Wm Batcheller Clke of the Mother Church	1200
Jonathan Gayre Clke of the Lower Chappell	1000
Alice Mazy Serving as Sexton of the Upper Chappell 5 months	208
John Bird Serving as Sexton of the Upper Chappell 7 months	292
Edward Ball Sexton of the Middle Church	600
John Roe Sexton of the Lower Chappell	500
Ditto for keeping John Purton	800
Mary Purvis	600
Wm Herne and Isabell his wife	1000
David Morgan for keeping & burying Arthur Johnson	400
Ditto for A Coffin	100
Sam^{11} Batcheller for keeping Honora Baskett	800
Geo: Freestone for keeping Eliz^a Curlis	300
Ordered that Eliz^a Curlis be allow'd 500^{1b} Tobacco A yeare for mainteinance	
Hugh M^{ck}Tyre for keeping Eliz^a Suñers	500
Cha: Cooper for keeping John Purvis's child	500
Wm Hill for keeping Mary Ranstead	800
Mr John Robinsons Account for worke done at the Upper Chapp^{11}	1570
Angelo Cuñins for keeping Cha. M^{ck}carty	800
Mr Barth^o Yates for 3 Books for the use of the Church	234

Mr Ja: Walker 4 delinqts @ 61lb (vizt) Jno Jervis,
Geo: Purvis, Edwd Pendergest and James Jemson
allow'd   244

Andrew Hipkings's Accot for painting the Midle
Church   500

Doctor Wallford for meanes to Adcocks Orphan   500

Allow'd Mr John Grymes the Balla of his Accot
for Ch: Ornamts   2068

Upon reading A former Order of Vestry dated the
31th of March 1718 Directing A Convenient Cupilo to
be forthwith built at the west end of the Midle Church
to hang A Bell in And that the Ch: Warden of the
Midle precincts agree wth workmen to doe the Same,
The said Church Warden failing to comply with the   2068
Said Order And Mr John Robinson undertaking to
Comply therewith It is Ordered That he be paid 2068lb
of Tobo for the Same, Giving Security to Mr Matt:
Kemp and Mr Oliver Seager to finish the worke by
the laying of the next Parish Levy

Mr Jam: Walker Sundry Delinquents as ℞ List
allow'd   7669¼

Ordered That Mr James Walker pay the said Tobo
to parish Credrs for the years 1715 & 1716 whoe have
not reced their dues.

Transferred to the other Side	43053¼
	lb Tobo
(165) Brought over	43053¼
Allowd Mr Jno Grymes for Fees paid by him in the parish Cause and for Clothes for A parish Child	1174½
	44227¾
Cask @ 8 ℞ Ct	3538
	47765¾
Salla @ 5 ℞ Ct	2388
	50153¾

The Parish of Christ Church Dr Pr Contra   C^r
    To Sundry Credit^{rs} 50,153¾   By 1006 Tythables
        Due to Ball^a 146¼   @ 50 ₩ pole 50300

                        50,300

Ordered That Mr John Robinson be appointed Ch: Warden for the Midle precincts, Mr Oliver Seager for the Upper p^{r}cincts and Mr Matthew Kemp for the Lower p^{r}cincts.

Ordered That Chu: Wardens Collect 50^{lb} Tob° ₩ pole of every Tythable per∫on within their respective Precincts and pay the same to parish Cred^{rs}

Ordered That Mr John Robinson make Such Alterations in the Glebe Chimneys as Mr Yates and he Shall think fitt, And that he be paid for the Same at the Laying of the next Levy.

Ordered That Mr John Robinson be Impowerd to send for 3 Surplices for the use of this Parish.

Ordered That the Clke of the V^{r}y prepare Copys of the Lists of Delinquents Given into this V^{r}y for each Ch: Warden Whoe are hereby Impowered to receive the Same And Account for the Same to the Vestry.

Ordered That Mr John Grymes be Impowered to Divide the Altar Piece and Sett up the Same Each Side of the East Window, He offering to doe the Same at his owne charge.

                            Wm Skipwith

(166) At A Vestry held for Christ Church Parish in Midd^x County the 22^d day of Jan^{ry} 1719.

                        Present

Mr Bartho: Yates, Minister, Sr William Skipwith, Knight, Capt John Smith, Mr John Robinson, Capt Geo: Wortham, Mr John Grymes, Mr Roger Jones, Mr Oliver Seager, Mr Matt. Kemp   Gentlemen

Ordered by the abovenamed Gentlemen of the Vestry as followeth (that is to Say)

Upon Reading A Decree of the Gen^{rll} Court Dated ye 31th of October 1719 And made in A Suit in Chancery brought by John Grymes E∫q^r in behalfe of the Vestry and Parishioners of this Parish Complain^t and Matt Kemp Adm^r with the will

annexed of Matt Kemp Gentleman deced, Robert Daniell
Harry Beverly John Robinson Geo: Wortham and Oliver
Seager Gent Refpond^{ts} This Vestry in pursuance of A Clause
in the s^d Decree doe Impower the said Harry Beverly to Sue
the Adm^{rx} of Jno Clark deced for the Suñe of four thousand
nine hundred and ninety pounds of Tob^o to his owne use.
Which Suñe is by the s^d Decree Adjudged to have bin overpaid to the Said Clark more than his due from this Parish.

Ordered That Mr Harry Beverly pursuant to the abovementioned Decree pay John Hipkings five Thousand two hundred
& nine pounds of Tob^o on Demand, And that he also pay
Alexander Graves Two thousand eight hundred ninety nine
pounds of Tob^o on demand.

Ordered That Mr Matt. Kemp pay Alexander Graves Two
hundred & forty pounds of Tob^o on demand.

Ordered That Mr Harry Beverly pay Mr John Robinson
One Thousand and Six hundred pounds of Tob^o towards
making Alterations in the Glebe Chimneys as directed by an
Order of Vestry dated the 7th of October.

Sr William Skipwith absent

Jno Smith

Ordered That Capt Robt Daniell's Account of Charges in
the parish cause be referred 'till the Laying of the next Levy.

(167)   At A Vestry held for Christ Church Parish in
Midd^x County the 7th day of March 1719

Present

Mr Bartho: Yates, Capt John Smith, Capt Robt Daniell, M^r
John Robinson, Mr James Walker, Capt George Wortham, M^r
John Grymes, Mr John Wormley, Mr Oliver Seager, M^r
Matt Kemp.   Gentlemen

Mr John Robinson Church Warden of the Midle Precincts
Acquainted this Vestry That the Occasion of calling this meeting this day, was upon Complaint made to him by John Hipkings & Alexander Graves That Mr Harry Beverley refused
to pay them So much Tob^o as he was by an Order of Vestry
made the 22^d day of January 1719. Ordered to pay them Which
the Said Harry Beverley told the Said Church Warden he

could not doe for Several Reasons, Which he would Acquaint the Vestry with by A Letter when they mett.

A Letter from Mr Harry Beverley to the Vestry was this day read upon consideration whereof This Vestry is of Opinion They have allready Impowerd the S^d Harry Beverley by former Order of Vestry to Sue the Adm^rx of John Clark deced So far as they are Enjoyned by the Decree of the Gener^ll Court.

Where as in A Suit in Chancery brought to the Gen^rll Co^rt by John Grymes Eſq^r in behalfe of the Vestry & parishioners of this Parish against Matt. Kemp Adm^r with the Will annexed of Matt Kemp gentl deced, Robt Daniell, Harry Beverley, John Robinson, Geo: Wortham, Oliver Seager gentl. Reſpond^ts It was on the 31th day of October last Decreed by the S^d Court That the Said Beverley Should pay unto the Vestry, Nine thousand Seven hundred & eight pounds of Tob^o to be dispoſed off by them for the use of the Parish, Pursuant to which Decree A Vestry being legally met together on the 22^d day of January last did think fit to Order five thousand two hundred & nine pounds of the Said Tob^o to John Hipkings and two thousand eight hundred ninety nine pounds thereof to Alexander Graves to discharg[e] So much remaining due to them from this parish for the building of the Midle Church and to Mr John Robinson one thousand Six hundred pounds of Tob^o towards making alterations in the Glebe Chimneys, And althô that Vestr[y] did cause an Entry to be made in the Register of their proceedings That the S^d Harry Beverley Should pay the Said respective Sumes of Tob^o to those persons And allthô also the Said Harry Beverley hath had Sufficient knowledge of the S^d Entry & bin likewise requested by the S^d Hipkings & Graves to pay them their parts of the S^d Tob^o accordingly Yet it manifestly appeares that he hath hitherto refused the payment thereof. Wherefore this present Vestry having taken th[e] premises in consideration Do think fit to Impower, As accordingly Mr John Grymes is hereby Impowered & deſired in behalfe of the V^ry of this parish to use all Lawfull meanes to Enforce the said Beverley's complyance with the Said Decree, And when the said John Grymes Shall obtaine the pay-

ment of the S⁴ Tob° Decreed against the S⁴ Beverly as aforesaid Then he is further defired to pay the s⁴ Hipkings Graves
& Robinson Such refpective Sumes thereof as the S⁴ Beverley
was directed by the afores⁴ Order of Vestry to pay them: But
the said John Grymes is not to take out Execution on the S⁴
Decree against the S⁴ Beverley 'till the 20ᵗʰ day of March Instant; And in case the S⁴ Mʳ Grymes Shall disburse any money
for Lawyers advice in Levying the s⁴ Execution, He is to be
allowed the Same by this Parish.

Jn° Smith

(168)   At A Vestry held for Christ Church Parish in Middlefex County the 10ᵗʰ day of October 1720

Present

Mʳ Barth° Yates Minister, Sʳ William Skipwith, Capᵗ Robert
Daniell, Mʳ Harry Beverley, Mʳ John Robinson, Capᵗ Geo:
Wortham, Mʳ John Grymes, Mʳ Roger Jones, Mʳ John Worm-
ley, Mʳ Oliver Seager, Mʳ Matt. Kemp.   Gentlemen

Ordered	lb Tob°
To Mʳ Barth° Yates Minister	16000
John Owen Clke of the Upper Church & Veſtry	1800
Wᵐ Batchelder Clke of the Midle Church	1200
John Maſton Serving as Clke of the Lower Chappell 4 months	333
Richᵈ Stevens Serving as Clke of the Lower Chappell 8 months	667
John Bird Sexton of the Upper Church	500
Edwᵈ Ball Sexton of the Midle Church	600
John Roe Sexton of the Lower Church	500
Mary Purvis	600
Isabell Herne Widow	500
Robert Holdernefs for keeping John Purton	800
Wᵐ Guttry for keeping Honora Baſkett	800
Geo: Freeſtone for keeping Elizᵃ Curlis	500
Hugh Mᶜᵏtyre for keeping Elizᵃ Sumers	400
Angelo Comings for keeping Cha: MᶜᵏCarty 3 months at 200ˡᵇ of Tob° ⅌ month & nine months at the usuall Sallary	1200

OLD TOMBS AT CHRIST CHURCH

Eliz^a Morgan for keeping Susannah Midleton 3
months & curing her of A Sore legg   300

Ann Hill for keeping Mary Ranstead 11 months &
Buriall   800

Ann Hill widow   800

Doctor Lewis Tomkins for meanes Administrd to
Cha: M^{ck}Carty   800

John Digg for making A Stand for the Church   100

Mr Matt Kemp for glaſs lead Sodder & nailes—
5/3^d at 2^d ꝑ lb is   31½

Geo: Walker for glazing work at the lower Church
15^s at 2^d ꝑ^{1b} is   90

Ann Winger widow   600

Geo: Berrick for work done at the lower Church   250

Sam^{ll} Batchelder one parish levy last yeare overcharged allowed   50

Mr John Grymes for Secr^{tys} & Sheriffs fees in the
parish cause   362

Mr John Robinsons Account of worke about the
Glebe Chimneys allowd   3859

Capt Robt Daniell his charges in the parish Cause
allowd 5^{1b} 11^s 666

Mr Oliver Seager's account of comunion wine &
fees in ye pish cause   272

Capt Geo: Wortham for Sec^{rys} fees in ye parish
cause allow'd   40

Mr Barth^o Yates for arreares due by his Account for
the yeares 1715 & 1716   1644

Sum	37064
Caſk at 8 ꝑ Cent	2965
Sall^a of the whole at 5 ꝑ Cent	2001
Sum	42030

(169) 1720 The Parish of

Christ Church	D^r	lb Tob°	P^r	Contra	C^r
To Sundry Cr^ts		42030		By 1057 Tytheables	lb Tob°
Due to Ballance		250		at 40^lb ℔ pole	42280

42280

Ordered That John Purton be allow'd 600^lb Tob° for next yeares mainteniance.

Ordered That Edm^d Mickleborough Junr is allowd one parish Levy for negro Sara appearing not a Tytheable

Ordered That Mr John Vivion be allowd 50^lb Tob° for Cha: Oneell A Delinquent out of the Tob° in his hands.

Ordered That Mr John Vivion pay Mr Barth° Yates 284^lb Tob° due to the parish in his hands.

Ordered That Mr James Walker Account with Mr John Robinson for the 7669¼ of Tob° put into his hands last yeare to make good the Collection for the yeares 1715 & 1716 — and that Mr John Robinson report the Same to the next Veſtry

It is the Opinion of this Veſtry That the priviledge of choosing Clarks wholly lyes in the Minister of this parish.

Mr John Robinson, Mr Oliver Seager & Mr Matt Kemp are hereby appointed Churchwarden[s] of this parish.

Ordered That the abovenamed Church Wardens are hereby Impowered to receive the Delinquents put in their hands last yeare yet unpaid & Account for the Same to the Veſtry.

Ordered That Mr Oliver Seager one of the Church wardens of this parish Collect 40^lb Tob° per pole of every Tythable person within the upper Precincts & pay the Same to parish Cred^rs

Ordered That Mr John Robinson one of the Church wardens of this parish Collect 40^lb Tob° per pole of every Tytheable person within the Midle precincts & pay the Same to parish Cred^rs

Ordered That Mr Matt Kemp one of the Church wardens of this parish Collect 40^lb of Tob° per pole of every Tytheable person within the lower p^rcincts & pay the Same to parish Cr^rs

Ordered That the Severall Returns of the procefsioners to this Vʳy be Recorded &cᵃ according to Law.

Wᵐ Skipwith

(170)   Att A Vestry held for Christ Church Parish in Middˣ County the 6ᵗʰ day of January 1720

Present

Mʳ Barthᵒ Yates Minister

Capᵗ John Smith, Mʳ John Robinson, Mʳ James Walker, Capᵗ Geo: Wortham, Mʳ John Grymes, Mʳ John Wormley, Mʳ Matt Kemp   Gentlemen

Mʳ John Robinfon one of the Church Wardens of this parish Acquainted the Gentlemen of the Veftry, That he was Informed That our Minister Mʳ Barthᵒ Yates had received an Invitation from York Hampton parish to come to that parifh. The Veftry this day met and Defired to know of Mʳ Yates Whether he had any thoughts of accepting of it; Whoe was pleased to tell us That as there was greater Encouragement in that parish he thought to embrace it. It is therefore Re-folved by this Veftry, In consideration of the Extraordinary Satiffaction he has given to this parish for Seventeene yeares to give him the Additionall Sũme of four thousand pounds of Tobᵒ and Cask per annum for the future.

John Smith

(171)   Att A Veftry Held for Chrift Church Parifh in Middlefex County the 9ᵗʰ Day of October 1721

Present

Mʳ Barthᵒ Yates minifter, Sʳ Wᵐ Skipwith Coll: John Rob-infon, Capᵗ John Smith, mʳ Harry Beverley Capᵗ George Wortham John Grymes Efqʳ mʳ Roger Jones mʳ John Worm-ley mʳ Oliver Segar mʳ Matt. Kemp   Gentlemen

Ordered that John Vivion be Clark of the Veftry.

Ordered that mʳ Chriftopher Robinfon & mʳ John Price be aded to this Veftrey As Veftrymen for this Parifh.

Mʳ Chriftopher Robinfon Came in And Takeing yᵉ Oath of a Veftryman Satt accordingl[y].

Ordered that mʳ Matt Kemp Accoᵗˢ for the laft year as Churchwarden be entered And Recorded in the Other Book.

Mr Richard Walker haveing the Money in his hands that was left to this Parifh by Wm Churchhill Efqr deced It is Hereby Ordered that mr Bartho: Yates putt the Said Money Out to Ufe takeing good Bond & Security for the Same.

The Order made by the Veftrey for makeing An Addition to the Minifters Sallerey the 6th day of January 1720 is hereby this Veftry Confirmed.

Ordered to mr Barthᵒ Yates Minifter	20000
To Wm Batchelder Clark of the middle Church	1200
Richard Moulfon Clark of the uper Chapell 9 months	750
Richd Steevens Clark of the Lower Chapell	1000
John Owen Executors for being Clark of yᵉ uper Chapell 3 month	250
Ditto for being Clark of yᵉ Veftry 3 month	200
Wm Wood Sexton of yᵉ uper Chapell	374
Edward Ball Sexton of the Middle Church	600
Jnᵒ Row Sexton of the lower Chapell	500
Jnᵒ Bird as Sexton of the Uper Chapell 3 month	126
Elizabeth Humphreys	500
Jn° Smith for keeping Honour Bafket 1 month	200
Sarah Murry for one levey Over paid the laft year	40
Jnᵒ Williams for Keeping Elizabeth Curlis	500
Angelo Cumings for Keeping & Buriing Charles Maccartey	700
Jnᵒ Gibs for Buring Alice Davis	200
Nichᵒ Briftow for Keeping a Girle of George Freftons	250
Ann Hill	800
Hugh Mactyer for Keeping Elizᵃ Sumors	300
Coll Jnᵒ Robinfon for mending yᵉ Old Horfe block & makeing 1 new one	200
Jnᵒ Purton	600
Robert Daniell for his accoᵗ mending yᵉ Horfe Block at yᵉ Uper Chapell	70
Wm Wood for makeing Benches at the Uper Chapell	400
Jnᵒ Gutterey for Keeping Grace Southworth 8 months	560
Jnᵒ Alden for Keeping of Ditto 13 days	33
Henry Ingwel for Buriing Honor Bafket	350

Samuell Loe his acco^t again$\int$t the Gleab   400
To Oliver Seger   180
Coll John Robin$\int$on for three Surplices £18 || 6 || 0^d
at 10 / ₴ C^t 3660

                                                                            34943
Credited by m^r Matt Kemp Acco^t in the Other Book   259

                                                Carried Over   34684
                                                Brought Over   34684
(172)
            To Ca$\int$k at 8 ₴ C^t 2774

                                                                            37458
            Salerey 5 ₴ C^t 1873

                                                                            39331
The Pari$\int$h of Chri$\int$t Church Dr   ₴   Contra   C^r
To Sundry Claimes   39331   By 1045 Tithables
Due from Contra   379   at 38 ₴^{r} pole   39710

                        39710

The Question being putt Whether there Should be Three
Church wardens or Two in this Pari$\int$h It was Carried for
Three.

Orderd that Sr Wm Skipwith m^r John Wormley and Capt
John Smith be Churchwardens for this Pari$\int$h this In$\int$ueing
Year.

Ordered that Sr Wm Skipwith one of the Church wardens
of this Pari$\int$h Collect 38^{1b} Tobacco ₴^{r} pole of each Tithable
in the lower precints And pay the Same to the pari$\int$h Creditors.

Ordered that m^r John Wormley one of the Church wardens
for this pari$\int$h Collect 38^{1b} Tobacco ₴^{r} pole of each Tithable
per$\int$on in the Middle precints And pay the Same to the pari$\int$h
Creditors.

Ordered that Capt John Smith one of the Churchwardens
for this pari$\int$h Collect 38^{1b} Tobacco ₴^{r} pole of each Tithable
per$\int$on in the Uper precints And pay the Same to the pari$\int$h
Creditors.

Ordered that Edward Ball Continnue Sexton of the Middle Church.

Ordered that Wm Wood Continue Sexton of the Uper Chapell.

Ordered that John Row Continue Sexton of the lower Chapell.

Ordered that the Churchwarden Bind Mary Preſton to Nicholas Briſtow As the Law Derects.

John Smith

(173) Att a Veſtry Held for Chriſt Church Pariſh in Midd^x County the Seventh day of May 1722

Preſent

Mr Barth^o Yates Minister, Coll John Robinson Capt John Smith Mr Harry Beverley Capt George Wortham Mr Rog^r Jones Jno Grimes Eſq Mr Jno Wormeley Mr Matt: Kemp Mr Chriſtopher Robinson   Gentlemen

Churchhill Jones is appointed Clark of this Veſtry and is sworn accordingly.

Orderd that the preſent clark of the Veſtry take the Reccords into his Coſtody.

Orderd that the Collector receive one hundred pounds of Tob^o of Each Veſtry man preſent Except Mr Kemp to make up the delinquents laſt levy being by Conſent to pay the Miniſter.

Ordered that the Petition this day agree'd on and Sign'd, be preſented to the Honourable Gen^ll aſsembly.

To the Honble the Gen^ll Aſsembly

The humble Petition of the Veſtry, held for Chriſt Church pariſh the Seventh day of May 1722

Sheweth.

That this Veſtry taking into Conſideration the great Satisfaction given to this Pariſh, for about Eighteen years, and the General Good Charecter of our Minister Mr Barth^o Yates, wch we are Apprehenſive has induce'd Some other Pariſhes, to Entertain thoughts of Endeavouring to prevaile wth him to quit this pariſh for some of thoſe more Convenient

Humbly pray they may be enabled to make uſe of Such
Meaſures, as may be proper and reaſonable, to Secure So great
a good, to the pariſh

And they Shall pray.

John Robinſon

(174)   At a Veſtry held for Chriſt Church Pariſh in Midd^x
County the 11th Day of October 1722

Preſent

Mr Bartho: Yates, Sr William Skipwith, John Robinſon
Esqr, Mr John Smith, Mr John Grymes, Mr Rog^r Jones, M^r
John Wormeley, Mr Matt: Kemp, Mr Chriſtopher Robinſon

Gentlemen

Order'd	lb Tob^o
To Mr Bartho: Yates Minister	16000
Churchhill Jones Clerk of the Veſtry five months	420
Wm Batchelder Clerk of the Middle Church	1200
Richd Stevens Clerk of the Lower D^o	1000
Richd Molson Clerk of the upper Church	1000
Edward Bawl Sexton of the Middle Church	600
Jno Roe Sexton of the Lower Church	500
Wm Woods Sexton of the upper Church	500
Jno Guttery for keeping Grace Southworth Six Months at 70 per month	420
Richd Allin's Acco^t	1150
Doc^t Lewis Tomkies allow'd for meanes & attendance to Edward & Kathrine Cannedy	1600
Jno Sanders for Burying Jno Purtin	285
Wm Woods for waſhing the Church Linnin	100
Ann Hill Widdow	800
D^o towards paying the Doc^t	600
Eliz: Humphris	500
Isable Herne Widdow	500
Ann Wingar Widdow	800
Jno Hipkins for Setting up the Ornements in the upper Chapple	130
Eliz: Vivion	400
Jno Williams for keeping Eliz: Curlis	500

Cap Jnº Smith for keeping Mary Freestone 8 months
1½ Ell linnin   415
Mʳ Jnº Grymes's accoᵗ againſt the Pariſh   620
Mʳ Bartho: Yates, for Isable Herne & Ann Wingar's
last years Pention   1300
Mʳ Bartho: Yates for work done to the Gleb   1500
Mʳ Jnº Wormeley one of the Church-Wardens, to Tar
the Gleb-houſes   1000
Sʳ Wᵐ Skipwith for two Delinquints   76

                        Carred Over   33916
(175)   Brought Over   33916
        Caſk at 8 ℔ C   2713
        Salary at 5 ℔ C   1831

                                    38460

The Pariſh of Chriſt Church Dʳ   Pʳ   Con   Cʳ
  To Sundry Claimes   38460 By 1120 Titheables
Due from Contra   180   at 34½ ℔ʳ pole 38640

            38640

Order'd that the Church-Wardens Collect 34½ Pᵈˢ of Tobº
pʳ pole of every Titheable in the pariſh, & pay the Same
to the Pariſh Creditors, and a fraction Remainding of 180 pᵈˢ
Tobº is Order'd to be Accounted for by the Church-wardens
Next year.

Order'd that Sʳ Wᵐ Skipwith, Mʳ Jnº Wormeley, & Mʳ
Chriſtopher Robinſon, be Churchwardens of this pariſh this
inſueing year.

Order'd that the Said Church Wardens receive four pounds
of Tobº ℔ʳ pole of the Severall Titheables within this Pariſh,
that are willing to pay the Same, for the Uſe of Mʳ Yates
Miniſter. And this Veſtry undertake to make good, in their
private Capacity any Defficiency that Shall happen therein, in
proportion to their reſpective Titheables.

Order'd that the Church Wardens have the appointment of
the Sextons.

                             Jnº Smith

(176)   Att a Vestry held for Chrijt Church Parijh in Middˢˣ County the 16ᵗʰ Day of Aprill 1723
Prejent

Mʳ Bartho: Yates Minister, Coll John Robinson, Capᵗ John Smith, Capᵗ Geo: Wortham, Mʳ John Grymes, Mʳ Rogʳ Jones, Mʳ John Wormely, Mʳ Chrijtopher Robinjon   Gentlemen

Coll John Robinjon Accoᵗˢ to this Vestry for 500 pᵈˢ of Tobᵒ Recd of Mʳ Jonathan Hyde for Elizᵃ Davis, being a fine for a Bastard Child and Thirty five Shillings Recd of Severall perjons for Swaring and 500 pᵈˢ of Tobᵒ for a judgment Obtain'd againjt Elizᵃ Nickcolls.

Mʳ Jnᵒ Grymes Accounts for fifteen Shillings.

Order'd That Mʳ Chrijtopher Robinson one of the Churchwardens receive the Sᵈ fines and Dijtribute them as followeth

To Chʳ Kilsha	333 pᵈˢ Tobᵒ		
To Jnᵒ South	333 pᵈˢ Tobᵒ		
To Jnᵒ Jones	333 pᵈˢ Tobᵒ		
To Ann Freeman Cajh	£	12 ǁ 6	
To Mary Yarro Dᵒ		12 ǁ 6	
To Mary Finlee Dᵒ		12 ǁ 6	
To Ann Cooper Dᵒ		12 ǁ 6	

Order'd That Mʳ Chrijtopher Robinjon Accoᵗ with Mʳ William Stanard Mʳ Harry Beverley, & Jnᵒ Curtis, for the fines Due to the poor of this Parijh in their hands and reporte his proceedings to yᵉ next Vejtry.

Jnᵒ Smith

(177)
Att a Vestry held for Chrijt Church Parijh in Middˢˣ County the 16ᵗʰ Day of July 1723
Prejent

Mʳ Bartho: Yates, Sʳ William Skipwith, Coll: John Robinjon, Capᵗ John Smith, Mʳ John Wormeley Mʳ Matt: Kemp Mʳ Rogʳ Jones Mʳ Chʳ Robinjon   Gentlemen

In Purjuance of an Order of Middˢˣ County Court Dated the Second day of July 1723. this Vestry have divided this Parijh into Several Preci[ncts] and have appointed two Intelligent Freeholders of Every Several Precinct to See all the

Lands within the Said Several Precinct Proceſsioned as followeth.

Ordered That Geo: Hardin & Chʳ Sutton Proceſsion Every Particular Perſons Land between the Lower End of this County & Mʳ Kemps Mill, Croſs the Neck to Coll: Churchills Creek Beginning to proceſsion the Second Tuesday in October next & finiſh the Same by the 21ˢᵗ Day of March next.

Ordered That Jos: Gore, & Wᵐ Blackburn, Proceſsion Every particular perſons Land between Mʳ Kemps Mill & the Piping-Tree on the South Side of the Main Road Beginning to Proceſsion yᵉ Laſt Tuesday in October next & finiſh the Same by the 22ᵈ Day of March next.

Order'd That Geo: Barrick, & Jnᵒ Roads, Proceſsion Every particular perſons Land from Mʳ Kemps Mill to the Pipeing-Tree along Coll Wormeley's Bounds to the river Side on the North Side of the Main Road Beginning to Proceſsion the Laſt Tuesday in November next & finiſh the Same by the 23ᵈ Day of March next.

Order'd That James Smith & James Daniel Proceſsion Every particular perſons Land Between the Pipeing-Tree & Prittymans roleing road from Rappᵃ River to Piankatank, Beginning to Proceſsion the 2ᵈ Tuesday in November & finiſh the Same by the 24ᵗʰ Day of March next.

Ordered That John Aldin, & Stockle Toles Proceſsion Every particular perſon's Land Between Prittymans roleing Road & Robᵗ Wᵐson's Land from the main Road to the head of Mʳ Chʳ Robinſon's Mill-Dam on the North Side of the main Road Beginning to Proceſsion the Second Tuesday in December next & finiſh the Same by the 25ᵗʰ Day of March next.

Order'd That Jnᵒ Smith junʳ, & Hen: Tugle Proceſsion Every particular perſon's Land, Between Prittymans Roleing Road & Robᵗ Wᵐson's running from the Main Road to the Dragon on the South Side of the Main Road Beginning to Proceſsion the 2ᵈ Tuesday in October nex & finiſh the Same by the 26ᵗʰ Day of March next.

Order'd That James Macham & Robᵗ Daniel Proceſsion Every particular perſon's Land Between Robᵗ Wᵐson's Land (including Wᵐson's Land) and t[he] (178) And the Bryary Swamp, to the Millstone Valley running from the Main Road to the Dragon, on the South Side of the Main Road Beginning to Proceſsion the Last Tuesday in October next & finish the Same by the 27ᵗʰ Day of March next.

Order'd That Hum: Jones, & Richᵈ Parrott, Proceſsion Every particular peſon's Land Between the head of Mʳ Chʳ Robinſon's Mill-Dam & the head of Parrots Creek, to the Millston Valley on the North Side of the Main Road from the Road to the river beginning to Proceſsion the Second Tuesday in November Next & finiſh the Same by the 28ᵗʰ Day of March next.

Ordered That Jnᵒ Segar, & Jos: Hardee Proceſsion Every particular perſon's Land Between the Bryary Swamp (from the Millstone Valley to the Dragon Swamp) and the upper End of the County from the Main Road to the Dragon Swamp on the South Side of the Main Road Beginning to proceſsion the Last Tuesday in November next & finiſh the Same by the 29ᵗʰ Day of March next.

Order'd That Wᵐ Segar, & Thoˢ Mountague, Proceſsion Every particular perſon's Land Between the head of Parrots Creek, from the Mill-stone Valley to the river, to Hen: Robinſon Mill-Dam, to the Slaſh, from the Main Road to the river on the north Side of the Main Road Beginning to proceſsion the 2ᵈ Tuesday in December next & finiſh the Same by the 30ᵗʰ Day of March next.

Ordered That Robᵗ Wᵐson junʳ & Rice Curtis Proceſsion Every particular perſon's Land Between Hen: Robinſon Mill-Dam & the Shaſh to the upper End of the County from the Main Road to the river one the North side of the Main road Beginning to Proceſsion to Laſt Tuesday December next & finiſh the Same by the Laſt Day of March next.

Order'd That the aboveſᵈ Freeholders Proceſsion Every particular person['s] Land purſuant to the above Orders of Vestry, and that they take & return an accoᵗ of Every perſon's Land they Shall See proceſsion of the time wⁿ & of the perſon's preſent att the Same and of wᵗ Lands in their reſpective pre-

cinct they Shall faile to procefsion, and of the particular rea-
fons of Such failure to the next Vestry wᶜʰ Shall happen after
the Laft Day of March next coming and it is further Order'd
that all the Freeholders of the Severall precincts above mention'd, attend the above Said procefsioners in their refpective
precincts to perform the Procefsioning above Directed. And
the Said procefsioners are to take Notice that if the Owner
of Any Land in their refpective precinct Shall refufe to Suffer
his or her Land to be procefsion'd the Law requires that within
ten Days after Such refufal they Certify the Same under their
hands to the Church-wardens of the Parifh.

Wᵐ Skipwith

(179)   Att a Vestry held for Chrift Church Parifh in
Middˢˣ County the tenth Day of October 1723

Prefent

Mʳ Bartho: Yates Minifter Sʳ William Skipwith Coll:
John Robinfon Capᵗ John Smith Mʳ John Grymes Mʳ
Rogʳ Jones Mʳ George Wortham Mʳ John Wormeley Mʳ
Oliver Seager Mʳ Matt: Kemp Mʳ Chrʳ Robin[fon]

Gentlemen

	lb Tobᵒ
Ordered	
To Mʳ Bartho: Yates Minifter	16000
Churchhill Jones Clke of the Vestry	600
William Batchelder Clke of the Middle Church	1200
Richᵈ Steevens Clke of the Lower Chappel	1000
Richᵈ Moulson Clke of the Upper Chappel	1000
Edward Bawl Sexton of the Middle Church	600
John Row Sexton of the Lower Chappel three Months	125
Williams Woods Sexton of the Upper Chappel	500
Chʳ: Kilshaw Sexton of the Lower Chappel Nine Months	375
Mʳ John Price having taken the Oath of a Vestry Man, Satt Accordingly.	
Isabell Herne	600
Ann Wingar	800
Elizabeth Humphres	500

Ann Hill	800
Henry Thacker's Acco⁺ Allowed	100
John Williams Acco⁺ Allowed	150
William Davis's Acco⁺ Allowed	100
Charles Cooper allow'd for keeping & burying Grace Southworth	400
Majʳ Chriſtopher Robinſon's Acco⁺ allow'd	110
James Fiſher for releaſe in his ſickneſs	400
John Degge for a Horſe block	200
Mʳ Matt: Kemp the Omition of Isabell Herne's allowance in 1722	100
John Southworth for keeping Grace Southworth	400
Hugh Macktire for keeping Six Months & burying Elizᵃ Summers	600
Robᵗ Daniel allow'd one pariſh Levy la	34½
Lewis Tomkies	50
Jacob Stiff allow'd one pariſh Levy	34½

Sum̃	26779
Caſk @ 8 ℔ʳ Cᵗ	2142
Salary @ 5 ℔ʳ Cᵗ	1446
	30367

To Coll John Robinſon Chwarden his Coſt of Suit agᵗ Jnᵒ Segar	4984
Capᵗ John Smith	212

Carred over	35563 Tobᵒ
Brought Over	35563 Tobᵒ

(180)

Chriſt Church Pariſh	Dr	Pʳ	Con	Cʳ
	Tobᵒ			
To Sundry Claimes	35563	By 1129 Titheables		Tobᵒ
		at 31½ ℔ʳ pole		35563

Mʳ Edwin Thacker Choſe Vestry Man in the room of Mʳ
Harry Beverley.

Ordered That Mr John Wormeley, Mr Chriſtopher Robinson, & Mr Matt Kemp be Churchwardens of this Pariſh this En-ſueing year.

Order'd that the Said Churchwardens Collect Thirty one an a half pounds of Tob^o ℔^r pole of Every titheable in the pariſh & pay the Same to the pariſ Creditors.   Mr John Wormeley to Collect in the Middle precincts Mr Ch^r Rob-inſon in the Upper precincts and Mr Matt: Kemp in the Lower precincts.

Order'd That the Said Churchwardens receive four P^{ds} of Tob^o ℔^r pole of the Severall Titheables within this Pariſh, that are willing to pay the Same for the Use of Mr Yates Miniſter.

Att the Request of Mr Yates the Vestry do unanimously Certify that he hath been Miniſter of this Pariſh aboute Twenty years & Dureing wch time hath truly & deligently Ex-ercis'd his Function without any Blemiſh in his life & con-versation but has always like a good Miniſter Set us Pious Examples by Living a righteous, Sober, & Godly, Life.

Wm Skipwith

(181)   Att a Vestry held for Chriſt Church Pariſh in Midd^sx County the Seventh day of Aprill 1724

Preſent

Mr Bartho. Yates, Coll John Robinſon, Mr Jno Smith, Mr George Wortham, Mr Rog^r Jones, Mr John Wormeley, Mr Ch^r Robinſon, Mr Matt. Kemp, Mr John Price

Gentlemen

Mr Matt Kemp acco^{ts} for five Shillings which he recd for prophane Swaring.

Mr Edwin Thacker was this Day Sworn Vestry Man & Satt accordingly.

Order'd That Mr Kemp pay the above Said fine to Mary Yarro.

Mr James Smith & James Daniell return'd their proceedings of their Proceſsioning.

Mr Jno Segar & Mr Jos: Hardee return'd their proceedings of their Proceſsioning.

Mr Richd Parrot & Mr Humphrey Jones return'd their proceedings of their Proceſsioning.

John Smith

(182)   An Act directing the Tryall of Slaves committing Capitol crimes and for the more Effectual puniſhing conspiracies and Inſurrections of them and for the better Government of Negros Mullato's and Indians Bond or free.

Whereas the laws now in force for the better Ordering and Governing of Slaves and for the Spedy Tryall of Such of them as Committ Capital crymes are found inſufficient to Restrain their Tumultuouse & unlawfull meetings or to puniſh the Secrett plotts and Conspiraces carryed on amongst them and known only to Such as by the Laws now Establiſhed are not Accounted Legal Evidence And it being found neceſsary that some further proviſion be made for detecting & puniſhing all Such Dangerous Combination for the Futer.   Be it Enacted by the Lieut Govenr Councill and Burgeſses of this present Genl Aſsembly it is hereby Enacted by the Authority of the Same, That if any numbr of Negros or Other Slaves exceeding five Shall at any time here after conſult adviſe or Conſpire to Rebell or make inſurrection or Shall plott or conſpire the Murther of any perſon or perſons whatſoever ever Such Conſulting plotting or Conſpireing Shall be adjudged and deemed felony, and the Slave or Slaves Convicted thereof in Manner hereinafter directed Shall Suffer death and be Utterly excluded the benefit of the Clergy & of all laws made concerning the Same.   And be it further Enacted by the Authority aforeſaid that every Slave committing Such Offence as by the Laws Ought to be puniſhd by death or loſs of Membr Shall be forthwith Committed to the Common Goal of the County within which Such Offence Shall be Commited there to be Safley keept and that the Sheirf of such County upon Such Committment Shall forthwith Certifie the Same with the cauſe thereof to the Governr or Commander in Chief of this his Majtis Colony & Dominion for the time Being who is thereupon Deſired and Impowered to iſsue a Comiſion of Oyer & Terminer to Such perſons as he Shall think fitt wch perſons

forthwith after the receipt of Such Comiſsion are Impowered
& required to cauſe the offender to be publickly arraigned and
tryed at the Court houſe of the Sᵈ County And to take for
Evidence the Cofeſsion of the Offender the oath of one or
more credible wittneſses or Such Teſtimony of Negroes Mulatto's or Indians bond or free with pregnant circumſtances
as to them Shall Seem Convincing without the Solemnity of a
jury and the Offender being by them found guilty to paſs
Such judment upon Such Offender as the law Directs for
the like Crymes on Such judment to award Execution And to
the end Such Negros Mollattos or Indians not being Chriſtians
as Shall hereafter be produced as Evidence on the tryal of
any Slave for Capital Crymes may be under the greater obligation to declare the truth Be it Enacted that where any
Such Negro Molatto or Indian Shall upon due proofe made or
pregnant circumstances appearing before any County Court
within this Colony be found to have given a false Testimony
Every Such Offender Shall wᵗʰout further Tryal be ordered
by the Said Court to have one (183) One Ear Naild to the
Pillory and there to Stand for the Space of one hour and yⁿ
the Said Ear to be Cutt of and there after the Other Ear
Nailed in like man[ner] and cut off at the Expiration of one
other hour, and More Over to order ever[y] Such Offender
thirtynine laſhes well laid on, on his or her bare Back at the
Common Whipping Post and Be it further Enacted that at
Every Such Try[al] of Slave Committing Capitall offences
the perſon who shall be firſt named in the Commiſson Sitting
on Such tryal shall Before the examination of every Negro
Mollatto or Indian Evidence not being a Chriſtian charge Such
Evidence to declare the truth which charge Shall be in the
words following Viz—you are brought hether as a wittneſs
and by the direction of the Law I am to tell you before you
give your Evidence that you must tell the truth the whole
truth & nothing but the truth and that if it be found her[e]-
after that you tell a lie and give false Testimony in this matter
you must for so doing have boath your Ears nailed to the
Pillory and cut off and receive thirtynine Laſhes on your

bare back well laid on at the Common Whipping poſt. Provided always and it is hereby intended that the Master or
Owner of Any Slave to be arraign'd by virtue of this Act
may appear at the try[al] and make what just defence he
can for Such Slave so as Such defence do not relate to any
formality in the proceedings on the Tryal And be it further
Enacted by the Authority aforſd and it is hereby Enacted that
when any Slave Shall be Convicted by virtue of this act the
Comiſsioners that Shal[l] sit on triall Shall put a valuation in
money upon Such Slave So Convicted & certyfie such valuation
to the next Aſsembly that the ſd Aſsembly may be Enabled to
make a Suitable Allowance thereupon to the Maſter or Owner
of Suc[h] Slave And whereas many Inconveniancys have ariſen
by the Meeting of great Numbers of Negros and Other Slaves
for prevention hereof be it Enacted by the authority aforeſd
and it is hereby Enacted that from henceforth no meeting
of negro's or other Slaves be allowed on any pretence whatsoever Except as is hereafter Excepted And that Every Maſter
Owner or Overſeer of any plantatio[n] who shall knowingly
or willingly permit any Such meeting or Suffer more then five
Negros or Slaves other then the negroes or Slaves belonging
to his her or their plantation or Quarters to be or remain upon
any plantation or Quarter at any one time Shall forfeit and
pay the Sum of five Shillings or fifty pounds of Tobᵒ for
Each Negro or Slave over and above Such number that Shall
at any time hereafter So unlawfully meet or aſsemble on his
her or their plantation to the Informer to be recovered with
coſts before any Justice of the Peace of the County where
Such offence Shall be comited. Provided always that nothing
herein conta[ ] Shall be conſtrued to Restrain the negro's or
other Slaves belonging to one & the Sam[e] Owner and Seated
at Distinct Quarters or plantations to meet by the licence of
Such Owner or his or her Overſeer at any of the Quarters
or plantation to Such Owner belonging nor to reſtrain the Meeting of any number of Slaves on their Owner or Overſeers busi-
neſs at any public Mill So as Such Meeting be not in the night
or on Sunday nor to reſtrain their meetings on any Other Law-

full Occaſion by the lycence in writing of their Master Mistreſs or Overſeer nor to prohibit an[y] Slav[es] (184) Slaves repairing to & meeting at Church to attend Devine Service on the Lords Day or at any other time Sett apart by Lawfull authority for public Worship but that all & Every Such Meetings Shall be Counted lawfull meetings any thing in this act contained to the Contrary thereof notwithstanding. And Be it further Enacted by the Aurthority aforeſᵈ that if any white perſon free negro Mulatto or Indian Shall at any time here after be found in Company with any Such Slaves att any Such unlawfull meetings as aforeſaid or harbour or Entertain any negro or other Slave what ſoever without the Consent of their Owners he She or they so Offending upon being thereof lawfully Convicted Shall forfeit & pay the Sum̃ of fifteen Shillings or on hundred & fifty pounds of Tobᵒ to the informer to be recovered with Coſts before any Justice of the peace and upon failure to make preſent payment Shall have and receive on his her or their Bare Back for Every Such offence twenty laſhes well laid on and Every Negro Mullatto or Indian Slave who Shall come or aſsemble to Such unlawfull meetings Shall upon Information thereof made to any Justice of the peace of the County where Such Offence Shall be Committed for Every Such Offence have & receive on his her or there bare backs any number of Laſhes not exceeding thirty nine An Be it further Enacted by the Aurthority aforeſᵈ and it is hereby Enacted that every Justice of the peace of any County wherein any Such unlawfull Meetings Shall happen upon his own Knowledge or upon information thereof to him made within Ten days after Such Offence Committed Shall forthwith Iſsue his Warrant to Apprehend all Such perſons who So Mett or Aſsembled & Cauſe Such Offenders to be brought before him or Some other Justice of the peace of the Said County and that every Such Justice Who Shall faile in his Duty hearein Shall forfeit and pay the Sum̃ of fifty Shillings or five hundred pounds of Tobᵒ for Every offence by him Committed And be it farther Enacted by the Authority aforeſᵈ that Every Sheriff or under Sheriff or Conſtable Who Upon his or their

own Knowledge or upon information thereof to him or them
made of any Such unlawfull meetings as aforeſᵈ Shall fail
forthwith to Endeavour to Supprefs and Disperse the Same
and to Carry the Offenders before Some Justice of the peace
in order for the Said Offenders to receive due puniſhment. The
Sheriff for Every offence by him committed Shall forfeit and
pay the Sum̃ of fifty Shillings or five hundred pounds of Tobᵒ
both which Sevrall finens of fifty Shillings or five hundred
pounds of Tobᵒ herein before mentioned Shall be to the informer and be recovered with Coſt in any Court or Courts of
Record wᵗʰin this Colony and Dominion by action of debt, bill,
plaint, or Information, wherein no Eſsoin protection or Wager
of Law Shall be allowed or any more then one Imparlance And
the Under Sheriff or Constable failing to perform his or their
Duty herein Shall for Every Offence by him or them Committed forfeit & pay Twenty Shillings or two hundred pounds
of Tobᵒ to the Informer to be recovered with Coſts before any
Justice of the peace of the County wherein Such offence Shall
be Committed And be it further Enacted by the Authority
aforeſᵈ that if any Negro Mulatto or Indian Slave Shall att
any time here after preſume to come and be upon the plantation
of any perſon or perſons whatsoever without the Leave or
Conſent in writing of his or her Maſter Owner or Overſeer
and without the conſent and (185) and approbation of the
Owner or Overſeer of Such Plantation it Shall & may be
Lawfull to and for the Maſter Owner or Overſeer of any
Such plantation or Quarter to Correct and give Such Slave or
Slaves ten laſhes well laid on on his or her bare back for every
Such Offence And Be it further Enacted by the authority
aforeſaid that no neg[ro] mulattoor Indian whatſoever Except
as is hereafter Excepted Shall hereafter preſume to keep or
carry Gun powder Shott or any Club or other weapon Whatsoever Offensive or Defensive but that Every Gun and all
powder & Shott and every Such Club Weapon as as afore-
ſ[aid] found or taken in the hands Custody or poſseſsion of
any Such Negro Mulatto or Indian Shall be taken away and
upon Due proofe thereof Made before any Justice of the peaſe

of the County where such offence Shall be Committed be for-
feited to the Seizer and Informer And Moreover every Such
Negro Mulatto or Indian in whoſe hands Custody or poſseſsion
the Same Shall be found Shall by Order of the Said Justice
have & recei[ve] any number of Laſhes not Exceeding Thirty
nine Well laid on on his or her bare back for every Such
offence Provided Nevertheleſs that Every free Negro Mulatto
or Indian being a Houſekeeper or Listed in the Militia may be
permitted to Keep one Gun powder & Shott and that thoſe
who are not houſe Keepers nor Listed in the Militia aforeſ[aid]
Who are now poſseſsed of any Gun powder Shott or any
Weapons offensive & Defensive May Sell & diſpose thereof att
any time before the laſt day of October Next Enſueing and
that all Negros Mullattos or Indian's bond or free living at
any Frontier Plantation be permitted to Keep & uſe Guns
powder and Shott and Other Weapons Offenſive or defensive
haveing first Obtained a Lycence for the Same from Some
Justice of the peace of the County Wherein Such plantations
lye the Said Licence to be had & Obtained upon the Application
of Such free Negro's Mullotto's or Indian's or of the Owner
or Owners of Such as are Slaves any thing herein contained
to the Contrary thereof in any Wiſe notwithſtanding And Be
it further Enacted by the Authority aforeſᵈ that in the Dis-
perseing of any unlawfull aſsembleis perſuit of Rebells or Con-
spirators or Seiſing the armes or amunition of Such Slaves
as are prohibited by this Act to Keep the Same any Slave
Shall happen to be killed or Distroyed the Court of the County
Where Such Slave Shall be killed upon the Application of the
Owner of Such Slave & due proof there of Made Shall put
a Valueation in Money upon Such Slave so kill[ed] and Certifie Such Valueation to the next Seſsion of Aſsembly that the
Said Aſsembley may be Enabled to Make a Suitable Allowance
thereupon to the Maſter or Owner of Such Slave And Be it
further Enacted by the Authority aforeſᵈ that No Negro Mulatto or Indian Slaves Shall be Sett free upon any pretence
whatsoever Except for Some Meritorious Services to be ajudged
& allowed on by the Governer and Council for the time being

And a licence thereupon first had and obtain'd and that Wher[e] any Slave Shall be Sett free by his Mafter or Owner Otherwise then is herein before directed it shall and may be Lawfull for the Churchwardens of the parifh wher[e]in Such Negro Mullatto or Indian Shall refide for the Space of one Month next after his or her being sett free And they are hereby Authorifed and required to take up and Sell the Said Negro Mulatto or Indian as Slaves att the next Court held for the Said County by publick Outcry and that the Monys arifeing by Such Saile Shall be appli'd to the ufe of the Said parifh by the Vestry thereof And forasmuch as the Act pafsed in the forth year of the Reign of her Late Maj[ty] Queen Ann Intituled an Act Concerning Servants & Slaves Whereby power is given to the County (186) County Courts to Order the Dismembering of Incorrigable Runaways and Other Slaves hath not had the Intended Effect by reason of Some Misconftructions of the powers thereby Granted Be it Enacted that where any Slave Shall hereafter be found notoriously guilty of going abroad in the night or runing away and lying out and cannot be reclaimed from Such Disorderly Courfes by the Common Methods of punifhment It Shall & may be Lawfull to & for the Court of the County upon complaint and proof thereof to them made by the Owner of Such Slave to Order & Direct Every Such Slave to be punifhed by Dismembring Or any Other Way not touching life as the Said County Court shall think fitt and for preventing all Doubts which may arife upon the Conftruction of this or any other Act of Afsembly of this Colony touching the Death of Slaves Under Correction or Lawfull punifhment. Be it Enacted by the Authority aforef[d] that if any Slave happen to die by meanes of Such dismembring by order of the County Court or for or by reafon of any Stroak or blow given dureing his or her Correction by his or her owner for any Offence by Such Slave Committed or for or by reafon of any Accidental blow whatsoever given by Such owner no perfon concerned in Such Dismembring Correction or Accidental Homicide Shall undergo any profecution or punifhment for the Same unlefs upon Examination

befor the County Court It Shall be proved by the Oath of one
Lawfull and Credible Witneſs at the leaſt that Such Slave
was Killed Willfully Maliciously or deſignedly neither Shall
any perſon Whatsoever Who Shall be Indited for the Murder
of any Slave and upon Tryall shall be found guilty of Man-
Slaughter Incure any forfeiture or puniſhment for Such Offence or Misfortune Provided always that nothing herein be
Contained Shall be Conſtrued Deemed or taken to defeat or
barr the action of any perſon or perſons Whoſe Slave or Slaves
Shall happen to be Killed by any Other perſon Whatsoever
or Whoſe Slaves shall happen to Die thrô the negligence of
any Surgeon or other perſon under takeing the Dismembring
or Cure of Such Slave liable to Such puniſhment by the Act
but all and Every Owner and Owners of Such Slave or Slaves
Shall & may bring his or her action for recovery of Damages
for Such Slave or Slaves So Killed or dying as if this act had
never been made. And Be it further Enacted by the Authority
aforeſaid That all Free Negros Mulattos or Indians Except
Tributary Indian to this Goverment Male or female above the
Age of Sixteen Years and all wives of Such negros Mulattos
or Indians (Except as before Excepted) Shall be Deemed and
Accounted Tythables any law uſage or Cuſtom to the Contrary
in any wiſe notwithstanding. And be it further Enacted by
the͞ Authority aforeſᵈ that whare any female Mulatto or Indian
by Law Obliged to Serve till the Age of thirty one years Shall
dureing the Term of her Servitude have any Child born of her
Body Every Such Child Shall Serve the Maſter or Miſtreſs
of Such Mulatto or Indian untill it Shall attain the Same Age
the Mother of Such Child was Oblige by Law to Serve unto.
And be it further Enacted by the Authority afore Said And
it is hereby Enacted and Declared that no free Negro Mulatto
or Indian Whatſoever Shall hereafter have any Vote at the
Ellection of Burgeſses or any Other Ellection Whatſoever
And be it further Enacted that the Church wardens of Each
Pariſh within this his Majᵗʸˢ Colony and (187) and Dominion
at the Charge of their pariſh Shall provid a true Copy of this
Actt and cauſe Entry thereof to be Made in the Register Book

of Each parifh Respectively And the Minifter or Reader of
Each parifh Shall on Some Sunday in the Months of Aprill
and October yearly after Divine Service Ended at the door of
Every Church and Chapple in their parifh publickly Read the
Same and th[e] Sheirff of Each County Shall at the Court held
for the County in the Months of June or July yearly publifh
this act at the doore of the Court house of the Said County.
And Every Churchwarden & Sherif Making Default herein
Shall for Each time So Offending forfeit and pay five hundred
pounds of Tob° to the Informer to be recovered wᵗʰ Cofts by
Action of Debt in any Court or Courts of Record within this
Colony & Dominion and the Minister or Reader making Default herein Shall for Each time So Offending forfeit & pay
two hundred Pounds of Tob° to the Informer to be recovered
with Cofts before any Justice of the peace of the County
Wherein Such Defaults Shall happen And be it further Enacted
by the Authority aforefᵈ and it is hereby Enacted that the act
of Afsembly made in the fourth year of the Reign of Our
late Sovereign Lady Queen Ann Entituled an Act for the
Speedy and Easie Profecution of Slaves Committing Capital
Crimes be from henceforth repealed and made Void to all In-
tents Conftructions and purpofes.

(188)   Att a Vestry held for Chrift Church Parifh in
Middˢˣ County the Sixteenth Day of June 1724

Prefent

Mʳ Bartho: Yates Sʳ William Skipwith, Coll John Robin-
fon, Capᵗ John Smith, Mʳ George Wortham John Grymes
Esqʳ Mʳ Rogʳ Jones Mʳ Chriftopher Robinfon Mʳ Matthew
Kemp Mʳ John Price & Major Edwin Thacker.

Purfuant to an Act of the laft Sefsion of Afsembly Entitled an Act for the better and more effectual Improveing the
Staple of Tobacco

This Vestry doe lay out the Parifh into precincts and appoint two perfons in Each precinct to Examine and Enquire
of the names & number of yᵉ perfons Allow'd by the Said Act
to tend Tob° and the Crops of the Several planters within the
fᵈ precinct refpectively and the numbʳ of plants growing or

Shall have been tended on any plantation or plantations Some time in July next.

From the Lower End of yᵉ County to Mʳ Kemp's Mill Croſs the neck to Churchhill's Creek. George Hardin & Churchhill Jones are appointed to Examin &c: in yᵉ ſᵈ precinct.

From Mʳ Kemp's Mill & Churchhill's Creek (on yᵉ North Side of the Main Road) up to Brandon (including brandon plantation) Thomas Machen & Jonathan Johnſon are appointed to Examin &c in the Said precinct.

From Kemp's Mill on the South Side of the Main Road up to Brandon-Road down the Sᵈ road to my Lady's Bridg & down that Swamp to the river. Capᵗ William Blackburn & John Berry are appointed to Examin &c: in the ſᵈ precinct.

From the upper Bounds of the two Laſt mention'd precincts up the County to yᵉ Road leading from Prittymans to the Dragon Bridg James Smith & James Daniell are appointed to Examine &c: in the Sᵈ precinct.

From the laſt Mention'd Road to Major Thacker's Mill Thence a Croſs the County to the new Bridg including yᵉ widdow Cheedle's plantation. Capᵗ Henry Thacker and John Smith junʳ are appointed to Examine &c: in the Sᵈ precinct.

From the new Bridg road up the County on yᵉ South Side of the Main road to the Mill-Stone Valley and Soe down the Bryery to the Dragon Swamp John Segar & John Mosly are apointed to Examin &c: in the Said precinct.

From Majʳ Thackers Mill on the North Side of the Main Road up to parrotts Creek and up the ſᵈ Creek & Gardner's Swamp to the Millſtone Valley, George Chowning and Richᵈ Parrott are appointed to Examin &c: in the ſaid precinct.

From the upper Bounds of the two Laſt Mentioned precincts to the head of the County on both Sides of the Main Road Thomas Mountague & Willᵐ Seger are appointed to Examin &c in the Said precinct.

Order'd that if the bounds of any precinct Shall Strike through any plantation or plantations, the Crops on Such plantation or plantations Shall fall under yᵉ View & numbering of the Viewers &c appointed for that precinct wherein the house Stands (189) Stands that the people Tending Such Crop Shall live in.

Order'd That Mʳ Chriſtopher Robinſone of yᵉ Ch wardens repair the Gleab houſe.

Mʳ Matt: Kemp one of yᵉ Ch wardens put in his Accoᵗ of the Pariſh Collection it is refer'd till next Vestry to be Consider'd on.

Order'd that the petition of Capᵗ Willᵐ Blackburn &c: be refer'd till the next Vestry to be Consider'd on.

Order'd that the Clark of this Vestry do diſtribute the above appointments to John Price Edwin Thacker & Matthew Kemp Gent: or any other Justice Convenient who are deſir'd to Cauſe the Examiners &c to appear and take the Oath appointed by Law to qualify them for the truſt aforeſᵈ.

William Skipwith

July the 13: 1724 At a Called Vestry for appointing an Examiner and Counter of Tobᵒ plants in room of Capᵗ Henry Thacker appointed by Order of Vestry Dated the 16ᵗʰ day of June laſt, Who refuſes to comply with the Said Order.

Preſent

Mʳ Bartho: Yates Minister, Sʳ William Skipwith, Coll John Robinſon, Capᵗ John Smith, Mʳ George Wortham, Mʳ Rogʳ Jones, John Grymes Esqʳ Mʳ Mʳ John Wormeley, Mʳ Chriſtopher Robinſon, Mʳ Matthew Kemp, Mʳ John Price, Major Edwin Thacker.

Mʳ Andrew Hipkins is appointed Examiner in the room of the Said Capᵗ Henry Thacker.

This day all the returns made by yᵉ proceſsioners Were Examined. Mʳ Matthew Kemp did this day proteſt againſt the Return of George Barrick & John Roads of their laſt proceſsioning So far as relates to the Said Kemps Land adjoining on Sʳ William Skipwith the ſᵈ proceſsioners having taken upon them in the Abaſence of the Said Kemp & without his knowledge to make a new boundary between the Sᵈ Skipwith & him & to return an old Line tree as of their own knowledge Which the sᵈ Kemp avers not to be the true bounds.

Mʳ John Wormeley one of the Churchwardens Objected to all the returns made by the proceſsioners So far relating to the bounds of his Lands they being in diſpute.

William Skipwith

(190) Att a Vestry held for Chriſt Church Pariſh in Middˢˣ County the Eight Day of October 1724

Preſent

Mʳ Bartho: Yates, Coll. John Robinſon, Capᵗ John Smith, Mʳ George Wortham, John Grymes Esqʳ, Mʳ Rogʳ Jones, Mʳ Oliver Segar, Mʳ Matt. Kemp & Mʳ Chriſtopher Robinſon

Genᵗⁱmen

Order'd	Tobᵒ
To Mʳ Bartho Yates Miniſter	16000
Churchhill Jones Clk of yᵉ Vestry	800
William Batchelder Clk of yᵉ Middle Church	1200
Richᵈ Steevens Clk of yᵉ Lower Church	1000
Richᵈ Moulson Clk of yᵉ Upper Church	1000
Edward Bawl Sexton of yᵉ Middle Church	600
William Woods Sexton of yᵉ Upper Church	500
Mary Kilshaw Sexton of yᵉ Lower Church	500
Churchhill Jones's Omition laſt year	200
Docᵗ Mark Bannerman alow'd for Serviſses done for yᵉ Pariſh for Mary Coſley 2000 Tobᵒ for Mary Robinſon's Girle 1000	3000
Richᵈ Daniel's Accoᵗ allow'd	1400
Charles Cooper allow'd for keeping of Mary Robinſon's Girle	1200
Mʳ Chriſtopher Robinſon for 5 yᵈˢ Canves	30
George Walker for worke done to yᵉ Gleeb	222
Chriſtopher Kilbee for keeping James Fiſher 4 months & burying him	300
Thoˢ Clarke for Richᵈ Warren's pariſh Levy & burying him	181½
Isabel Herne	600
Ann Wingar	800
Elizabeth Humphres	500
Ann Hill	800

Mr Matt. Kemp's acco^t allow'd   104½
Jn° Curtis for Salary of 3783^{lb} Tob° Omited la$\int$t
year & one pari$\int$h levy   219½

                                                                        31157½
                                    Ca$\int$k at 8 p^r C^t 2492
                                    Salay at 5 p^r C^t 1682

                                                                        35331
A fraction Which is Order'd to be laid out by the
Church Wardens for the reliefe of Margaret Bowman   369

                                                                        35700

Christ Church Pari$\int$h   Dr Pr Con.   C^r
                            Tob°

To Sundry Claimes 35,700   By 1190 Tithables
                           at 30 p^{ds} Tob° p^r pole   35700

(191)   Order'd That Mr Roger Jones, John Grymes Esqr
& Mr Oliver Segar be Churchwarden[s] of this Pari$\int$h this
En$\int$ueing year.

Order'd That Mr Rog^r Jones Collect 30 p^{ds} of Tob° p^r pole
in the Lower Precinct.

Order'd That John Grymes Esqr Collect 30 p^{ds} of Tob°
p^r pole in the Middle precinct.

Orderd That Mr Oliver Segar Collect 30 p^{ds} of Tob° p^r
pole in the Upper precinct.

Order'd That S^d Church Wardens pay the Same to the
Pari$\int$h Creditors.

Order'd That the S^d Church Wardens receive four p^{ds} of
Tob° p^r pole of the Several Tithables Within this Pari$\int$h that
are Willing to pay the Same for the u$\int$e of Mr Bartho: Yates
Mini$\int$ter.

                                                    John Smith

At a Vestry held for Chri$\int$t Church Pari$\int$h in Midd^{sx} County
the 29th Day of June 1725

Prefent

Mr Bartho: Yates, Capt John Smith, Capt Geo: Wortham, John Grymes Esqr, Mr Rogr Jones, Mr Oliver Segar, Mr Matt. Kemp Mr Chriftopher Robinfon Mr John Price

Gentl Men

Purfuant to an Act of the laft Sefsion of Afsembly Entitled an Act for the Better and more Effectual Improveing the Staple of Tobacco.

This Vestry doe lay out the Parifh into precincts and appoint two perfons in Each precinct to Examin & Enquire of the names & numbr of the perfons Allow'd by the Said Act to Tend Tobo—and the Crops of the Several planters within the Sd precinct Respectively, and the number of Plants growing or Shall have been tended on any Plantation or plantations Some time in July next.

Mr Geo: Hardin & Churchhill Jones are appointed to Examin &c from the Lower End of this County to Mr Kemps mill, Crofs the neck to Churchhill's Creek.

Capt William Blackburn & Mr Thos Machen, are appointed to Examin &c from Kemps Mill & Churchhill's Creek to the Lower bounds of Mr Grymes's Land a Crofs from Rappa to Piankatank.

Mr James Smith, & Mr James Daniel, are appointed to Examin &c. from the Lower Bounds of mr Grymes's Land up the County to the Road leading from Prittymans to the Dragon Bridg.

mr John Smith, & Mr Hen: Tugle, are appointed to Examin &c: from the affore Sd Road to majr Thackers Mill, thence a Crofs ye County to the new Bridg including the Widdow Cheedle's plantation.

mr John Segar, & mr Joseph Hardee are appointed to Examin &c: from the new Bridg Road up the County, on the South Side of the Main Road to ye upper End of the County.

Mr Willm Segar, & mr Richd Perrott, are appointed to Examin &c: from majr Thacker[s] Mill on the north Side of ye Main Road up to the head of the County.

Order'd that if the Bounds of any precinct Shall Strik through any plantation or plantations the Crops on Such plantation or plantations Shall fall under the View and numbering of the Viewers &c: appointed for that precinct Wherein the Houſe Stands yᵗ the people Tending Such Crop Shall live in.

Mʳ Matt. Kemp Accoᵗˢ to the Vestry for 50 Shillings recd of Dorothy Row for a Baſtard Child.

Order'd That he pay the Same to Ann Cooper.

turn over

(192)   Order'd that the Clark of the Vestry do distribute the above appointments to John Grymes & mʳ Oliver Segar Genᵗ'men, or any Other Juſtice Convenient Who are desire'd to Cauſe the Examiners &c: to appear and take the Oath appointed by Law to Quallifie them for the truſt aforeſᵈ

Jnᵒ Smith

At a Vestry held for Chriſt Church Parish in Middˢˣ County the Seventh Day of October 1725

Preſent

Mʳ Bartho Yates, Coll. John Robinſon, Capᵗ John Smith, Mʳ Geo: Wortham, John Grimes Esqʳ, Mʳ Rogʳ Jones, Coll John Wormeley, Mʳ Oliver Segar, Mʳ Matt. Kemp, Majʳ Edwin Thacker

Order'd	Tobᵒ
To Mʳ Bartho: Yates Minister	16000
Churchhill Jones Clk of the Vestry	800
Willᵐ Batchelder Clk of the Middle Church	1200
Richᵈ Steevens Clk of the Lower Church	1000
Richᵈ Moulson Clk of the upper Church	1000
Edward Bawl Sexton of the Middle Church	600
Willᵐ Woods Sexton of the upper Ch.	500
Mary Kilshaw Sexton of the lower Ch.	500
Isabel Hern	600
Ann Wingar	800
Ann Hill	800
Elizᵃ Humphres	500
Mʳ John Grymes's Expences on Mary Coffley	200
Richᵈ Daniel's Accoᵗ for keeping Mary Coffley	2000

Doc^t Lewis Tomkis for means & attendance on Mary Coffley	500
Charles Cooper for keeping Mary Finick 3 months	300
Agnis Newberry for keeping Mary Finick	600
John Curtis for keeping Margaret Bowman	185
Agnis Newberry for keeping Mary Coffley 2 Weeks in 1723	50
John Hipkins Acco^t	50
Sam^ll Loe for Work done at ye Gleab	40
Mary Kilshaw towards Maintaining her Children	100
To the Ch warden of ye upper precinct for repairing the Ch. & yard	200
To the Ch warden of the Middle precinct for Taring the Middle Church	700
Will Woods Acco^t	30
Mr Oliver Segar Acco^t of Delinquints & Wine	310
Mr Rog^r Jones for 5 bottles of wine	85
Geo: Walker	40

	29690
	Tob[°]
(193) Brought over	29690
Ca∫k at 8 p^r C^t	2375
Salary at 5 p^r C^t	1603
To Ann Hackey	320
	33988

Christ Church Pari∫h D^r	P^r	Con	C^r
Tob°	By 1172 Tithables at		Tob°
To Sundry Clames 33988	29 p^r pole		33988

Order'd That Rog^r Jones John Grymes Esqr & Oliver Segar Continue Ch: wardens of this Pari∫h.

Order'd That Mr Rog^r Jones Collect 29^lb Tob° p^r pole in the lower precinct & pay the Same to the Pari∫h Cred^rs

Order'd That John Grymes Esqr Collect 29^lb Tob° p^r pole in the Middle precinct and pay the Same to the Pari∫h Cred^rs

Order'd That Mr Oliver Segar Collect 29^lb Tob° p^r pole in the upper precinct & pay the Same to the Pari∫h Cred^rs

Order'd That the Ch: wardens receive four p^{ds} of Tob^o p^r pole of the Several Tithables within this Parifh that are willing to pay the Same for the ufe of Mr Bartho: Yates Minister.

John Smith

(194)   At a Vestry held for Chrift Church Parifh in Midd^{sx} County the 12th Day of Aprill 1726

Prefent

Mr Bartho: Yates, Sr William Skipwith, Coll John Robinfon Ctp^t John Smith, Mr George Wortham, Mr Rog^r Jones, Coll. John Wormeley Mr Matt. Kemp Mr Chriftopher Robinfon & Maj^r Edwin Thacker

Coll: John Wormley Acco^{ts} to this Vestry for a fine of five Shillings which he is Order'd to pay Mary Finley.

The Vestry being inform'd that Zebulon Shilton paid a fine of five hundred pounds of Tob^o to John Curtis for the ufe of the parifh: It is Order'd that Mr Rog^r Jones Ch: warden receive the Same of the Said Curtis & Acco^t for it to the Vestry.

Order'd that John Curtis keep Margaret Bowman no longer on the Acco^t of the Parifh.

Mr John Grymes one of the Ch: wardens is defir'd to agree wth Workmen to Pale in a Garden at the Gleab.

The Reverend Mr Yates our Minister acquainting this Vestry that he had Occations that call him to England and that he had taken care to have the parifh Supply'd in his absince, the Vestry return him their thanks for the Same.

William Skipwith

(195)   At a Vestry held for Chrift Church Parifh in Midd^{sx} County the 28th Day of June 1726

Prefent

Coll: John Robinfon, Capt John Smith, Mr George Wortham, John Grymes Esqr, Mr Rog^r Jones, Mr Matt: Kemp, Maj^r Edwin Thacker, & Mr Chriftopher Robinfon

Pursuant to an Act of Afsembly Entitled an Act for the better and more Effectual Improving the Staple of Tob^o

This Vestry doe lay out the parifh into precincts, and appoint two perfons in Each precinct to Examin & Enquire of the names and number of the perſons allow'd to Tend Tobᵒ and the Crops of the Several planters within the Said precinct respectively and the plants growing or that have been Tended or any plantation or plantations Some time in July next.

Mʳ George Harding & Churchhill Jones are appointed to Examin &c: from the lower End of this County to Mʳ Kemps Mill Croſs the Neck to Churchhill's Creek.

Mʳ Joſeph Goar & Mʳ George Barrick are appointed to Examin &c: from the laſt mention'd bounds to the lower bounds of Mʳ Grymes's Land a Croſs from Rappᵃ to Piank-atank.

Mʳ James Smith, & Mʳ James Daniel, are appointed to Examin [&c:] from the lower bounds of Mʳ Grymes's Land, up the County to the Road leading from Prittymans to the Dragon Bridg.

Mʳ John Smith, & Mʳ Hen: Tugle, are appointed to Examin &c: from the affore Sᵈ Road, to Major Thacker's Mill, thence a Croſs the County to the new-Bridg, Including the Widdow Cheddles plantation.

Mʳ John Segar, & Mʳ Joſeph Hardee are appointed to Examin &c: from the new bridg Road up the County on the South Side of the Main Road to the Upper End of the County.

Mʳ Willᵐ Segar, & Mʳ Richᵈ Parrott, are appointed to Examin &c: from Major Thacker's Mill, on the North Side of the Main Road up to yᵉ head of the County.

Order'd That if the Bounds of any Precinct Shall Strike through any plantation or plantations the Crops on Such plantation or plantations Shall fall under the View & numbering of the Viewers &c: appointed for that Precinct wherein the Houſe Stands that the people tending Such Crop Shall live in.

John Robinſon

(196) At a Vestry held for Chriſt Church Pariſh in Middˢˣ County the 13ᵗʰ Day of October 1726

Preſent

Capᵗ John Smith, Mʳ George Wortham, John Grymes Esqʳ Mʳ Roger Jones, Coll John Wormeley, Mʳ Oliver Segar, Mʳ

Matthew Kemp, Major Edwin Thacker, & Mʳ Chriſtopher Robinſon

	lb Tobᵒ
Ordered	
To Mʳ Bartho: Yates Minister	16000
Churchhill Jones Clk of the Vestry	800
Willᵐ Bachelder Clk of the Middle Ch:	1200
Richᵈ Steevens Clk of the Lower Ch:	1000
Richᵈ Moulson Clk of the Upper Ch:	1000
Edward Bawl Sexton of the Middle Ch:	600
Willᵐ Woods Sexton of the Upper Ch:	500
Mary Kilshaw Sexton of the Lower Ch:	500
Isabel Hearn	600
Anne Hill	1200
Rachel Dodſon for keeping Ann Wingar Nine Months & burying her	800
Elizᵃ Humphres	500
Richᵈ Daniel for keeping Mary Coffle	2000
To Dᵒ for Phisick for Dᵒ	50
Willᵐ Woods Accoᵗ	50
Agnis Newbery for keeping Mary Finnick	600
Richᵈ Daniel for keeping a Pariſh Child ½ year	400
John Southern for keeping a pariſh Child ½ year	400
Docter Lewis Tomkis Accoᵗ	300
Mʳ John Hipkins's Accoᵗ	300
Docᵗ Mark Banerman's Accoᵗ	300
Capᵗ Willᵐ Blackburn for Taring the Lower Ch:	600
Docᵗ Lewis Tomkis for his Attendance on Ann Hill	500
Major Edwin Thacker	288
John Curtis for keeping Margaret Bowman	325
Mʳ Oliver Segar's Accoᵗ	593
John Lewis	150

	31556
(197)	lb T[obᵒ]
Brought Over	31556
To Mary Gibbs	50

Isaack Burtin   400

                                                            32006
                        Caſk at 8 pʳ Cᵗ   2560

                                                            34566
To John Grymes Esqʳ for repairs to the Glebe Houſe   2000
To the Sᵈ Grymes for paling in a Garden for the Glebe   5250

                                                            41816
                        Salary at 5 ℔ Cᵗ   2090

                                                            43906
To Willᵐ Stanard for Clk fees   500

                                                            44406
                        A Depoſ: 358

                                                            44764

Christ Church Pariſh	Dʳ	Contra	Cʳ
	Tobᵒ	By 1178 Tithables	Tobᵒ
To Sundry Clames	44,764	at 38 ℔ pole	44,764

Ordered That Coll: John Wormeley, Mʳ Matthew Kemp
& Major Edwin Thacker be Ch: wardens this Inſuing year.

Order'd That Coll: John Wormeley Collect 38ˡᵇ Tobᵒ ℔
pole in the Middle precincts and pay the Same to the Pariſh
Credʳˢ

Order'd That Mʳ Matt: Kemp Collect 38ˡᵇ Tobᵒ ℔ pole
in the Lower precincts and pay the Same to the Pariſh Credʳˢ

Order'd That Majʳ Edwin Thacker Collect 38ˡᵇ Tobᵒ ℔
pole in the Upper precinct and pay the Same to the Pariſh
Credʳˢ

Order'd That the Ch: wardens Receive four pᵈˢ of Tobᵒ ℔
pole of the Several Tithables within this parish that are willing to pay the Same for the Uſe of Mʳ Bartho: Yates Minister.

                                                    John Smith

(198)   At a Vestry held for Chriſt Church Pariſh in Middˢˣ
County the 8ᵗʰ Day of June 1727

Pre∫ent

Mʳ Bartho: Yates, Capᵗ John Smith, John Grymes Esqʳ, Mʳ Rogʳ Jones Mʳ George Wortham, Mʳ Oliver Segar, Mʳ Matt: Kemp & Majʳ Edwin Thacker   Gentlemen

Mʳ William Stannard, & Mʳ Armistead Churchhill are cho∫en Vestry Men and Sworn accordingly.

Pursuant to an Act of A∫sembly Entitled an Act for the better & more Effectual Improving the Staple of Tobᵒ.

This Vestry doe lay out the Pari∫h into precincts and appoint two per∫ons in each precinct to Examin and Enquire of the names and number of the per∫ons allow'd to tend Tobᵒ And the Crops of the Several planters within the Sᵈ precinct respectively, and the plants growing or that have been tended on any plantation or plantations Some time in July Next.

Mʳ George Hardin, & Churchhill Jones, are appointed to Examin &c: from the lower end of this County, to Mʳ Kemp's Mill, Cro∫s the Neck to Mʳ Churchhill's Creek.

Mʳ George Barrick & Mʳ John Curtis, are appointed to Examin &c: from the last mention'd bounds to the lower bounds of Mʳ Gryms's Land, a Cro∫s from Rappᵃ to Piank-atank.

Mʳ James Smith, & Mʳ James Daniel, are appointed to Examin &c: from the lower bounds of Mʳ Grymes's Land, up the County to the Road leading from Prittyman's to the Dragon Bridg.

Mʳ John Smith, & Mʳ Henry Tugle, are appointed to Examin &c: from the affore Sᵈ Road, to Majʳ Thacker's Mill, thence a Cro∫s the County to the new Bridg, including the Widdow Cheedle's Plantation.

Mʳ John Segar & Mʳ James Macham are appointed to Examin &c: from the new Bridg road (on the South side of the Main road) to the upper end of the County.

Mʳ William Segar & Mʳ Richᵈ Parrot are appointed to Examin &c: from Majʳ Thacker's Mill (on the North Side of the Main road) up to the head of the County.

Order'd That if the bounds of any Precinct Shall Strike through any plantation or plantations, the Crops on Such plantation or plantations, Shall fall under the View & numbering of the Viewers &c appointed for that precinct where the house Stands that the people tending Such Crop Shall live in.

In Purʃuance of an Order of Midd⁽ˣ⁾ County Court dated the 6ᵗʰ day of June 1727 this Vestry have divided this pariʃh into Several precincts, and have appointed two freeholders of Every Several precinct to Se all the Lands within the Several precincts proceʃsion'd as followeth.

Order'd that Mʳ Rogʳ Jones & Mʳ George Hardin proceʃsion Every perʃons Land Between*

(199)   At a Vestry held for Chriʃt Church Pariʃh in Midd⁽ˣ⁾ County the 10ᵗʰ Day of October 1727

Preʃent

Mʳ Bartho: Yates, Sʳ William Skipwith, Capᵗ George Wortham, John Grymes Esqʳ, Mʳ Rogʳ Jones, Mʳ Oliver Segar, Mʳ Matt. Kemp, Majʳ Edwin Thacker, & Mʳ Willia[m] Stanard   Genᵗ

Order'd		lb Tobᵒ
To Mʳ Bartho: Yates Minister		16000
Churchhill Jones Clk. of the Vestry	800	
Willᵐ Batchelder's Excutʳˢ	667	
Richᵈ Steevens Clk. of the lower Ch:	1000	
Richᵈ Moulson Clk of the upper Ch:	1000	
Keziah Bawl Sexton of the Middle Ch:	600	
William Woods Sexton of the upper Ch:	500	
Mary Kilshaw Sexton of the lower Ch.	500	
Isabel Hearn	600	
Elizᵃ Humphreys	500	6176

Edward Smith for Serving as Clk of the Middle Ch: 2 months   200
John Lark for Serving as Clk of the Middle Ch: 3 months & od days   333

* Note! This book has evidently been rebound. When the rebinding was being done one leaf (which should have been pages 199 and 200) was put in *after* the sheet which was properly pages 201 and 202; hence the discrepancy, which will easily be noted by the careful reader.— C. G. C.

Joſeph Humphreys for keeping Ann Hill 15
days & burying her   300
George Walker for work done att the upper Ch:
& Gleab   350   1183
_____

Capᵗ Henry Thacker came in and took the Oath
of Vestryman and Sat accordingly
Caleb Brooks for keeping Mary Coffley 5 months
& od days & burying her   1100
 Willᵐ Daniel for keeping Mary Coffley 2 months   334
 John Lewis for a Coffin for Mary Coffley   100
 John Lewis for keeping a Pariſh Child one year   750
 Jnᵒ Jones for keeping a Pariſh Child 9 months   565
 William Daniel for keeping the Sᵈ Child 3
months   185   3034
_____

 Alexander Graves for plank of the upper Church 40
 John Marſtin junʳ for keeping Robᵗ Mahaffey's
Child till yᵉ 19ᵗʰ day of this month   800
 John Hipkins for mending the middle Church
yard   30
 John Curtis allow'd for 2 delinquints, Thoˢ Bor-
den & Jnᵒ Quorles   76
 Willᵐ Crutchfield allow'd one Levey laſt year
he being Conſtable   38
 Willᵐ Gray allow'd one Levey over Charg'd
laſt year   38   1022
_____

Capᵗ Henry Thacker for 2 Horſeblocks made for
the upper Ch: 600
 John Hearn for 2 Dᵒ the frames made of Seder   650
 Mʳ Williaf Stanard's Accoᵗ Allow'd   316   1566
_____

                                                                                28972
                    Caſk at 8 pʳ Cᵗ   2318
                                                                                _____

                                                                                31290

Salary at 5 pr Ct   1564
                                     ——
                                     32854
A Depoʃ: to be accounted for   477
                                     ——
                                     33331
(200)   turn over
Chriʃt Church Pariʃh   Dr   Pr   Con   Cr
To Sundry Clames   33331 By a Depoʃ: in the
                               Ch: Wardens hands
                               last year   358
                               By 1137 Tithables at
                               29ˡᵇ pr pole   32973
                                                      ——
                                                      33331

Order'd That Mr Matt. Kemp, Majr Edwin Thacker, &
Mr Willm Stanard be Ch: Wardens this Inʃuing year.

Order'd That Mr Matt. Kemp Collect 29ˡᵇ of Tobᵒ pr pole
in the lower precinct and pay the Same to the Pariʃh Credrs

Order'd That Major Edwin Thacker Collect 29ˡᵇ Tobᵒ pr
pole in the Middle precinct and pay the Same to the Pariʃh
Credrs

Order'r That Mr William Stanard, Collect 29ˡᵇ Tobᵒ pr
pole in the upper Precinct and pay the Same to the Pariʃh
Credrs

Order'd that the Church Wardens recieve four pounds of
Tobᵒ pr pole of the Several tithables within this Pariʃh that
are willing to pay the Same for the uʃe of Mr Bartho. Yates
Minister.

Majr Edwin Thacker Church Warden this Day accounted
to the Vestry for 50 ʃ a fine red. of Mary Mullins for having
a baʃtard Child.

John Curtis accounted for two fines of 50 ʃhill each, the
one recd of Joseph Hardee on accot of Mary Mullins, and the
Other of Jane Taylor for having a baʃtard Child..

Order'd That the Sd Curtis, & Thacker, pay the Sd fines
to Mary Kilshaw; a poor woman in Conʃidration of the loʃs
She has lately Suʃtain'd by fire.

Order'd That the Church Wardens procure Copies of the
Will of Mr Willm Gordon relating to Land given to this pariʃh

for a free ſchool, and alſo of the Will of Mr John Shepherd relating to Land given to the Church of this Pariſh and that they adviſe with Councel learn'd in the Law with reſpect to the titles of thoſe Lands; & bring Suits for recovery of the Same; if they find it adviſeable and that the Charge thereof be defray'd by the Pariſh.

William Skipwith

(201)   Between the lower End of this County, and Mr Kemp's Mill, Croſs the [MS. torn, and at least two words missing here.—C. G. C.] Mr Churchhill's Creek, beginning to proceſsion the 2d Tuesday in October & finish [   ] Same by the 21st Day of March next.

Order'd that Mr William Owin, & Mr James Dudley proceſsion Ever particul[ar] perſon's Land between Mr Kemp's Mill & the Pipeing Tree on the South Sid[e of] the main road, beginning to proceſsion the last Tuesday in October & to finis[h the] Same by the 22d Day of March next.

Order'd that Mr John Rhoads, & Mr John Fearn, proceſsion Every particu[lar] perſon's Land from Mr Kemp's Mill to the pipeing-Tree, along Coll. Wor[   ] bounds, to the river Side on the north Side of the main road. begining to proc[eſsion] the laſt Tueſday in November & finiſh the Same by the 23d Day of March n[ext].

Order'd that Mr James Daniel, & Mr Edward Smith proceſsion Every particular p[erſon's] Land between the pipeing-Tree & prittymans roleing road, from Rappa R[iver] to piankatank. begining to proceſsion the 2d Tuesday in Novembr & finiſh the [Same] by the 24th Day of March next.

Order'd that Mr Stokley Towles, & Samll Batchelder proceſsion Ever particu[lar] perſon's Land between prittyman's roleing road, and Robt Williamson's La[nd] from the main road to the head of Mr Christopher Robinſons Mill-dam [on the] North Side of the main road begining to proceſsion the 2d in December & f[iniſh] the Same by the 25th Day of March next.

Order'd that Mr John Smith junr & Mr Henry Tugle proceſsion Every particu[lar] perſon's Land between Prittyman's

roleing road and Rob᠂ Williamson's run from the main road to
the Dragon on the South Side of the main road begining
[to] procefsion the 2ᵈ Tuesday in Octobʳ & finifh the Same
by the 26ᵗʰ Day of March [next].

Order'd that 'John Segar & James Macham, procefsion
Every particular perf[on's] Land between Rob᠂ Williamsons
Land (including Williamsons Land) and the Bryary Swamp,
thence to the Millstone Valley, runing from the main road
to [the] Dragon on the South Side of the main road begining
to procefsion the last Tu[esday] in October & finish the Same
by the 27ᵗʰ day of March next.

Order'd that Mʳ Richᵈ Parrot, & Humphrey Jones, procefsion Every particular p[erfon's] Land between the head of
Mʳ Chriftopher Robinfons Mill-dam & the head of [Mʳ]
Parrots Creek, thence to the Millstone Valley, on the North
Side of the main r[oad] and from the Said Road to the river
begining to procefsion the 2ᵈ Tuesd[ay] in November & finifh
the Same by the 28ᵗʰ Day of March Next.

Order'd that Mʳ Garrot Daniel, & Mʳ Ralph Shelton, procefsion Every particular perfon's Land between the Briery
Swamp, (from the Millstone Valley to the Dragon Swamp)
and the upper End of the County, and from the main road
to the Dragon Swamp, on the South Side of the main road
beginning to p[rocefsion] (202) the Last Tuesday in November & finifh the Same by the 29ᵗʰ Day of March Next.

Order'd that William Segar, & Thoˢ Mountague, procefsion Every particular perfons Land, between the head of Parrots Creek (from the Millstone Valley) and Mʳ Rice Curtice's
Milldam, thence to the Slafh, and from the Slafh to the main
Road, & from thence to the River, on the North Side of the
Main road, begining to procefsion the 2ᵈ Tuesday in December & finish the same by the 30ᵗʰ Day of March Next.

Order'd that Mʳ Rice Curtis & Mʳ Thoˢ Blewford procefsion Every particular perfon['s] Land between Mʳ Rice Curtis's Milldam & the Slafh, and the Upper End of the coun[ty]
and from the main road to the river, on the North Side of

the main road begining to procefsion the Last tues-Day in December & finifh the Same by the laft Day of March next.

Order'd that the above S^d freeholders procefsion Every particular perfons Land Pursuant to the above Orders of Vestry, and that they take & return an Acco^t of Every perfons Land they Shall So procefsion, of the time when & of the perfons prefent at the Same, and of what Lands in their refpective precin[cts] they Shall fail to procefsion, & of the reafon of Such failure to the next Vestry which Shall happen after the last Day of March next coming and it is further Order'd that all the Freeholders of the Several precincts above mention'd attend the above Said procefsioners in their refpective precinct[s] to perform the procefsioning above directed. And the Said procefsioners are to ta[ke] notice that if the Owner of any Land in their refpective precinct Shall refus[e] to Suffer his or her land to be procefsion'd the Law requires that within te[n] days after Such refusal they Certifie the Same under their hands to the Church Warden of the Parifh.

John Grymes Esqr late Church Warden Acco^{ts} to this Vestry for a fine of 500^{lb} Tob^o and Cask laid on Mary Mullen together with 240^{lb} Tob^o the Cost of that profecution it is order'd to be distrebuted between Robt Baker & Mary Yarrow.

Mr Edmun Barkley, & Mr Henry Thacker, are Chofen Vestrymen for this Parifh.

John Smith

(203)   At a Vestry held for Chrift Church Parifh in Midd^{sx} County the 15th day of June 172[8]

Prefent

Mr Bartho: Yates, Sr William Skipwith, Capt George Wortham, Coll John Grymes, Mr Rog^r Jones, Mr Matthew Kemp, Maj^r Edwin Thacker, Mr William Stanard, Capt Henry Thacker & Mr Armistead Churchhill.

Order'd That Mr Richd Hill & Mr John Marfton, in the beginning of the next Month do Examine & Enq^r of the names & number of the perfons allow'd by Law to tend Tob^o and the Crops of the Several Planters & number of Plants growing on any & Every Plantation or Plantations from the Lower end of this Parifh to M[r] Kemp's Mill and So acrofs to M[r] Churchhill's Creek w[ch] is alotted for their precinct. And that they cut up or cause to be cut up & distroy'd all Stalks Slips & Suckers w[th]in the S[d] P[r]cinct and perform & Execute the Several duties & powers given & enjoin'd them by the Act of affembly for the better & more Effectual improving the Staple of Tob[o]

M[r] John Rhodes, & M[r] John Curtis, to do the Same from M[r] Kemps Mill a crofs to M[r] Churchhill's Creek up the Parifh to the Lower bounds of Col[o] Grymes's Land crofs from Rapp[a] to Pianketank.

M[r] James Smith & M[r] James Daniel to do the Same from the lower bounds of Col[o] Grymes's Land up the Parifh to the road leading from Prittymans to the Dragon Bridge.

M[r] Henry Tugle, & M[r] John Smith jun[r], to do the Same from the upper Side of the Road leading from Prittyman's Landing to the Dragon Bridge up the Parifh to Maj[r] Thacker's Mill, thence acrofs the Parifh to the new Dragon Bridge including the Widdow Cheedles Plantation.

M[r] William Segar, & M[r] Rich[d] Parrott, to do the Same from Maj[r] Thacker's Mill on the North Side of the Main Road to the upper end of the Parifh.

M[r] Garrot Daniel, & M[r] Ralph Shelton, to do the Same from the new Drago[n] Bridge road on the South side the main road to the upper End of the Parifh.

M[r] John Segar, & m[r] James, Macham return'd the proceedings of their Procefsioning.

M[r] Rich[d] Parrott, & m[r] Hum: Jones, return'd the proceedings of their Procefsioning.

M[r] Rog[r] Jones & M[r] Georg Hardin return'd y[e] proceedings of their Procefsioning.

M[r] Jn[o] Smith & M[r] Henry Tugle return'd the proceedings of their Procefsioning.

M[r] James Daniel & m[r] Edward Smith, return'd the procedings of their Procefsioning.

M[r] Garrott Daniel & M[r] Ralph Shelton, return'd the proceedings of their Procefsioning.

Mr Jno Rhods & Mr Jno Fearn, return'd the proceedings of their Proceſsioning.

Mr Rice Curtis & Mr Thos Bluford, return'd the proceedings of their Proceſsioning.

Mr Willm Segar & Thos Mountague return'd the proceedings of their Proceſsioning.

Order'd That the Clk of the Vestry register the returns of the Proceſsioners against the next Vestry.

Willm Skipwith

(204)   At a Vestry held for Chriſt Church Pariſh in Midd^sx County the 4th Day of October 1728

Mr Bartho: Yates Capt George Wortham, Col John Grymes Capt Oliver Seager Maj^r Matt: Kemp, Col Edwin Thacker, Mr William Stanard Col Armistead Churchhill

Maj^r Edmun Bearkley was this day Sworn Vestryman for this Pariſh.

Mr Chr. Robinſon was this day Elected and Sworn Vestryman for this Pariſh.

Order'd		lb Tob^o
To Mr Bartho: Yates Minister		16000
Churchhill Jones Clk of the Vestry	800	
John Lark Clk of the Middle Church	1200	
Richd Steevens Clk of the Lower Church	1000	
Richd Moulson Clk of the Upper Ch	1000	
Keziah Bawl Sexton of the Middle Ch	600	
William Woods Sexton of the Upper Ch	500	
Mary Kilshaw Sexton of the lower Ch	500	
Eliz^a Humphres	500	6100
John Curtis allow'd for 3 delinquents at 29	87	
John Marſton jun^r for keeping Robt Mahaffey's Child till ye 19th of this month	750	
John Lewis for keeping a Pariſh Child one year	750	
John Jones for keeping a Pariſh Child one year	750	
To the Estate of Mark Bannerman	600	
Ann Cooper	500	

Mr William Stanard   144   3581

	25681
Caſk at 8 p^r C^t	2055
	27736
Salary at 10 p^r C^t	2773
	30509

Chriſt Church Pariſh	D^r	Con:	C^r
	lb Tob^o	By a Depoſ in the	
To Sundry Clames	30509	Collecters hands	477
a Depoſ to be Account-		By 1169 Tithables at	
ed for	362	26^{lb} Tob^o p^r pole	30394
	30871		30871

Order'd That Coll Armistead Churchhill & Mr William Stanard be Ch: wardens this inſuing year.

Order'd That the Ch: wardens Receive four p^{ds} of Tob^o p^r pole of the Several tithables within this pariſh that are willing to pay the Same for the Uſe of Mr Bartho: Yates Minister.

(205)   Order'd That Capt Oliver Segar Collect 26 pounds of Tob^o ℔^{r} Pole and Pay the Same to the Pariſh Cred^{rs}

This day Capt Oliver Segar gave bond and Security for the pariſh Collection.

Coll. Armistead Churchhill Acco^{ts} to this Vestry for a fine of five Shill.

Maj^r Edmun Bearkley Acco^{ts} to this Vestry for a fine of fifteen Shill.

Order'd That the above S^d fines of five Shill & fifteen Shill together wth Francis Porter & his Wife's fine & Coſt and a fine of 750 pounds of Tob^o recover'd againſt the Widdow Daniel and the Depoſ in the Collecters hands be Equaly divided by the Ch: wardens between Elenor Bromel, Mary Kilshaw Ann Callahan & Lettis Pateman.

Mr Yates inform'd the Vestry that the Mansion houſe and other Building upon his Glebe are in so ruinous a Condition

that rather than undertake to put & keep them in Such repair
as the Law requires He muſt quit his Incumbency   The Vestry
being very Sensible that in caſe Mr Yates Should reſign the
Living no other Minister would receive the Buildings in the
condition they are at preſent And very ardently deſiring his
continuance doe unanimouſly Agree and According Order that
the Pariſh Buildings on the Glebe be repaired at the Charge of
the Pariſh Untill new ones are erected.

Order'd That the Ch: Wardens make Such repairs on the
Glebe as is neceſsary.

Geo: Wortham

(206)   At a Vestry held for Chriſt Church Pariſh in Middˢˣ
County the 16ᵗʰ day of June 1729

Preſent

Mr Bartho: Yates, Sr William Skipwith Capt George Wortham Colᵒ John Grymes, Mr Rogr Jones, Capt Oliver Segar
Majr Matt Kemp, Colᵒ Edwin Thacker Colᵒ Armistead Churchhill Mr Willᵐ Stanard Capt Henry Thacker & Majr Edmun
Bearkley

Order'd That Mr George Hardin & Churchhill Jones in the
beginning of the next Month do Examine & Enquire of the
names and number of the perſons allow'd by Law to tend
Tobᵒ and the Crops of the Several planters and numbr of
plants Growing on any and every plantation or plantations
from the lower end of this pariſh to Majr Kemps Mill and So
acroſs to Colᵒ Churchhill's Creek which is alotted for their
precinct And that they cut up or cauſe to be cut up & de-
ſroy'd all Stalk Slips & Suckers within the Said precinct and
perform & Execute the Several duties & powers given and en-
joing'd them by the Act of Aſsembly for the better & more
Effectual improving the Staple of Tobᵒ

Mr John Curtis & Mr John Rhodes to do the Same Majr
Kemp's Mill and Colᵒ Churchhill's Creek up the Pariſh to
the Lower bounds of Colᵒ Grymes Land and So a Croſs from
Rappᵃ to Piankatank.

Mr James Daniel & Mr Edward Smith to do the Same from
the lower bounds of Colᵒ Grymes's Land up the Pariſh to the
Road leading from Prettymans Landing to the Dragon Bridge.

Mʳ Henry Tugle & Mʳ John Smith junʳ to do the Same
from the upper Side of the road leading from Prettymans
Landing to the Dragon Bridge up the pariſh to Colᵒ Thacker's
Mill, thence acroſs the pariſh to the new Dragon Bridge including the Widdow Cheedle's plantation.

Mʳ William Segar & Mʳ Humphrey Jones, to do the Same
from Colᵒ Thacker['s] Mill on the North Side of the Main
road to the upper End of the Pariſh.

Mʳ James Macham & Mʳ John Segar to do the Same from
the new Dragon-Bridge road, on the South Side of the main
road to the upper end of the Pariſh.

The Proceſsioners returns were this Day Examined by the
Church Wardens in preſence of the Vestry.

Willᵐ Skipwith

(207)   At a Vestry held for Christ Church Pariſh in Middˢˣ
County the 9ᵗʰ day of October 1729
Preſent

Mʳ Bartho: Yates, George Wortham, John Grymes Esqʳ,
Oliver Segar, Matt: Kemp, Edwin Thacker, William Stanard,
Armistead Churchhill, Henry Thacker, Edmund Bearkley,
Gent.

Order'd To

Mʳ Bartho: Yates Minister		16000
Churchill Jones Clk of the Vestry	800	
John Lark Clk of the Middle Church	1200	
Richᵈ Steevens Clk of the Lower Church	1000	
Robᵗ Perry Clk of the Upper Church	1000	
Keziah Bawl Sexton of the Middle Church	600	
William Woods Sexton of the Upper Church	500	
Mary Kelshaw Sexton of the Lower Church	500	
Elizabeth Humphreys	500	
Ann Cooper	500	6600

John Marston for keeping Robᵗ Mahaffey's Child
& Burying him   750

Ann Cambridg fo two days attendance in a Suit
of the Ch: Wardens against Joſep Hardee and Cost 104

Mary Bristow for one days attendance for Dᵒ	50	
George Walker's Accoᵗ allow'd	150	
Elenor Bromel allow'd	600	1654

John Lewis for keeping Joshua Jones a pariſh Child	600	
John Lewis in consideration that he takes the Sᵈ Child Joshua off of the Pariſh	500	
John Jones's keeping a Pariſh Child	600	
William Stapleton allow'd for Repairing the Glebe	5000	
Capᵗ Henry Thacker allow'd	1125	
Mʳ William Stanard his accoᵗ	589	
the Sᵈ Stanard Ch: warden for 32 days labour about repairing the Glebe at 10ˡᵇ Tobᵒ ℔ʳ day	320	
Archible McᶜCurdy	600	9334

	33588
Cask at 8 ℔ʳ Cᵗ	2687
Salary at 10 ℔ʳ Cᵗ	3627
To a Deposition in the Collectors hands	482

	40384

(208) Christ Church Pariſh	Dʳ	Pʳ	Con	Cʳ
To Sundry Clames	40,384	By 1,262 Tithables		
		at 32 pʳ pole		40,384

Order'd That Col. Armistead Churchhill & Capᵗ Henry Thacker be Ch: wardens this inſuing year.

Capᵗ Oliver Segar paſs'd his Accoᵗˢ for the pariſh Collection and perduc'd his Vouchers Order'd that his Bond be deliver'd him.

Majʳ Matt Kemp this Day gave Bond & Security for the Pariſh Collection.

Order'd That Majʳ Matt Kemp Shrieff Collect of the Titheable perſons in this pariſh thirty two pounds of Tobᵒ pʳ pole and pay the Same to the Pariſh Credʳˢ

And that the Sᵈ Shrieff receive four pounds of Tobᵒ pʳ pole of the Several Titheables Within this Pariſh that are willing to pay the Same for the Use of Mr Bartho. Yates Minister.

Order'd that the S^d Collect^r distribute the following fines to Wit.

	£	S	d
Reb^a Gillets fine of	2 || 10 || 0
Alex^r Graves's fine of		15 || 0
The fine of a Stranger recd p^r Mr Stanard	2 || 10 || 0
Robt Knight's fine of		5 || 0
Mich^{ll} Roane's fine of		5 || 0
John Bohannah's fine of		5 || 0

	lb Tob^o
James Batchelder fine of	500
and Avarila Hardee fine of	500

as followeth

	£	S	d
To Mary Finley	2 || 0 || 0

and the refidue of the S^d fines to John Guthrey Margaret Bowman & the Widow of Jofep Hardee in Equal parts, after his Salary deducted.

And that the depofitum be likewife distributed between the S^d Guthrey and Hardee, for relief of their Children.

Geo: Wortham

(209) At at Vestry held for Chrift Church Parifh in Midd^{sx} County ye 9th Day of October 1730

Prefent

Mr Bartho: Yates, John Grymes, George Wortham, Roger Jones, Oliver Segar, Matt: Kemp, Edwin Thacker Armistead Churchhill, Willm Stanard, Henry Thacker   Gent.

Gent.

Order'd	lb Tob^o
To Mr Bartho: Yates Minister	16,000
Churchhill Jones Clk. of the Vestry	800
John Lark Clk. of the Middle Church	1,200
Richd Steevens Clk. of the Lower Church	1,000
Robt Perry Clk. of the Upper Church	1,000
Keziah Bawl Sexton of the Middle Church	600

Willm Woods Sexton of the upper Church	500	
Archible M^{cc}Curdy Sexton of the lower Church	334	
Elizabeth Humphreys	500	
Ann Cooper	500	
Elenor Bromel	600	
To the Administ^{rs} of Mary Kilshaw	166	23200

To Capt Hen: Thacker to Enable him to comply with his agreement for Pla∫tering the Glebe Hou∫e	2,300	
To D^o for 100 heart Cypress Boards & 800 Shingles	150	
Rachel Baker	800	
Margaret Bowman	300	
George Walker for keeping Margaret Bowman	500	4050

John Humphryes	800	
Joseph Humphryes for making a Hor∫eblock	100	
Henry Bawl for keeping a pari∫h Child	450	
John Jones for keeping a Pari∫h Child	500	
Coll Churchhill allow'd as p^r acco^t	2360	
George Walker allow'd as p^r acco^t	72	
Docter James Boyd allow'd as p^r acco^t	1280	
John Williams for keeping Richd Parrot	500	
Thomas Falkner	25	
To the Church Wardens for the use of Wm Stapleton when he has perform his agreement	100	
To Mr Yates for dieting the workmen at the Glebe	1200	
To Mr Stanard for Clk^s fees	209	
William Stapleton	750	
To Coll Churchhill for three Common prayer Books	756	9102

Caried over	36352
	lb Tob^o
(210) Brought over	36352

Caſk at 8 pʳ Cᵗ   2908
                                                  ───────
                                                         39260
Sallary at 10 pʳ Cᵗ   3926
                                                  ───────
                                                         43186
a Depoſitum in the Collectors hands   338
                                                  ───────
                                                         43524

Chriſt Church Pariſh   Dʳ   Con   Cʳ   lb Tobᵒ
  To Sundry Clames   43,524   By 1194 Tithables at
                                    36 pʳ pole   43,524

Order'd That Henry Thacker & Edmund Berkley Gent. be
Church Wardens this Year.

John Curtis this Day gave Bond & Security for the Pariſh
Collection Order'd that the Sᵈ Curtis Collect 36ˡᵇ Tobᵒ pʳ
pole of the Titheable perſons in this pariſh & pay the Same
to the Pariſh Credʳˢ and that the Sᵈ Collector receive four
pᵈˢ of Tobᵒ pʳ pole of the Several Titheables within this Pariſh
that are willing to pay the Same for the use of Mʳ Bartho
Yates Minister.

Order'd that the Shrieff Distribute the fines & the Depoſitum between Lettis Pateman, Mary Stamper, Mary Finly,
Ann Callaham, Elizᵃ Pinnill and Occaney Palto.

                                          George Wortham

(211) At a Vestry held for Chriſt Church Pariſh in
Middˢˣ County the 11ᵗʰ Day of Augˢᵗ 1731

                          Preſent

Mʳ Bartho. Yates, John Grymes, Esqʳ, Edwin Thacker,
Oliver Segar, Armistead Churchhill, Willᵐ Stanard, Edmund
Bearkley, Henry Thacker, Gent.

In pursuance of an Order of Middˢˣ County Court dated
the 3ᵈ day of Augˢᵗ 1731 This Vestry have Divided this Pariſh
into Several Precincts And have appointed two Freeholds of
Every Several Precinct to Se all the Lands Proceſsion'd within the Said Precincts as followeth.

Order'd that m^r Chriftopher Sutton, & Churchhill Jones, Procefsion Every perfons Land between the lower end of this County & Maj^r Kemp's Mill crofs the neck to Coll Churchhill's Creek beginning to Procefsion the Second Tuesday in Octob^r & finifh the Same by the 21st Day of March next.

Order'd that Mr Willm Owin, & Mr John Davis, Procefsion Every perfons Land between Maj^r Kemp's Mill & ye Pipeing Tree on the South Side of the main road, begining to Procefsion the last Tuesday in October & finifh the Same by the 22^d Day of March next.

Order'd that Mr John Fearn & Mr Jacob Stiff Procefsion Every perfons Land from Maj[^{r}] Kemp's Mill to the Pipeing Tree along Coll. Wormeley's bounds to the river Side on the North Side of the main road begining to procefsion the last Tuesday in November and finifh the Same by the 23^d Day of March next.

Order'd that Mr Edward Smith & Mr Edward Clark, Procefsion Every perfons Land betwee[n] the Pipeing Tree & Prittymans roleing road from Rapp^a River to Piankatank begining to Procefsion the 2^d Tuesday in November & finifh the Same by the 24th day of March next.

Order'd that Mr John Smith jur. & Mr Sam^{ll} Batchelder, Procefsion Every perfons Land between Prittymans roleing road & the main Branch of Mickleborrough Swamp including the Widdow Cheedles plantation on the North Side of the main road begining to Procefsion the 2^d Tuesday in Decemb^r & finifh ye Same by ye 25th day of March next.

Order'd that Mr John Smith & Mr Larrance Orrill, Procefsion Every perfons Land betwee Prittymans roleing road & ye new Dragon bridg road runing from the main road to the Dragon on the South Side of ye main road. begining to Procefsion the 2^d Tuesday in Octob[^{r}] and finifh the Same by the 26th Day of March next.

Order'd that m^r John Mosley & m^r James Daniel, Procefsion Every perfons Land between ye lowe[r] end of the new Dragon bridg road & ye Bryary Swamp thence to ye Millstone Valley runing from the main road to ye Dragon on the South Side of y⁰ main road begining to Procefsion the Laſt Tuesday in October & finiſh the Same by the 27 Day of March next.

Order'd that Mʳ George Chewning & Mʳ Humphrey Jones Procefsion Every perſons Land between the head of Coll Thackers Mill Dam & the head of Parrots Creek thence to y⁰ Millston[e] Valley on the North Side of y⁰ Main road & from the Sᵈ road to y⁰ river begining to Procefsion the 2ᵈ Tueſday in Novembʳ & finiſh y⁰ Same by y⁰ 28ᵗʰ Day of March next.

(212)   Order'd that Mʳ John Briant & Mʳ Garrot Daniel Procefsion Every perſons Land between the Bryary Swamp (from the Millstone Valley to the Dragon Swamp) and the upper End of the County on the South Side of the main road begining to Procefsion y⁰ laſt Tuesday in Novembʳ & finiſh y⁰ Same by y⁰ 29ᵗʰ day of March next.

Order'd that Mʳ Thomas Mountague & Mʳ Willᵐ Mountague Procefsion Every perſons Land between the head of Parrots Creek from the Millstone Valley to y⁰ upper End of the County on the north Side of y⁰ Main road begining to Procefsion the Second Tuesday in December & finiſh the Same by the last Day of March next.

Ordered that the above Sᵈ Freeholders Procefsion Every perſons Land purſuant to the above Orders of Vestry And that they take & return and account of Every perſons Land they Shall So Procefsion of the time when & of the Perſons preſent at the Same and of what Lands in their reſpective Precinct they Shall fail to Procefsion & the reaſon of Such failure to the next Vestry which Shall happen after the laſt Day of March next coming. And it is further Order'd that all the Freeholders of the Several Precincts above mention'd attend the above Sᵈ Procefsioners in their reſpective precinct to perform the Procefsioning above directed. And the Said Procefsioners are to take notice that if the Owner of any Land Shall refuse to Suffer his or her Land to be procefsion'd the Law requires that within ten Days after Such refuſal they Certifie the Same under their hands to the Church Wardens of the Pariſh.

John Grymes

(213)   At a Vestry held for Chriſt Church Pariſh in Middˢˣ County the 11ᵗʰ Day of Octobʳ 1731

Preſent

Mʳ Bartho: Yates, Sʳ William Skipwith, George Wortham, John Grymes Esqʳ Roger Jones, Oliver Segar, Edwin Thacker, Armistead Churchhill, Henry Thacke[r] and Edmund Beark-ley   Genᵗ

Order'd	lb Tobᵒ
To Mʳ Bartho: Yates Minister	16000
Churchhill Jones Clk of the Vestry	800
John Lark Clk of the Middle Church	1200
Richard Steevens Clk of the lower Church	1000
John Baldin Clk of the Upper Church	1000
Keziah Bawl Sexton of the Middle Church	600
William Woods Sexton of the Upper Church	500
Archible MᶜᶜCurdy Sexton of the Lower Church	500
Elizᵃ Humphres	500
Ann Cooper	500
Elenor Bromel	600
Rachel Baker	800
Majʳ Edmund Bearkley's accoᵗ allow'd	1400
Lettis Pateman	250
Coll Edwin Thacker accoᵗ allow'd	712
William Crocker	500
Occany Palto	300
Capᵗ Henry Thacker accoᵗ allow'd	79
George Walker for keeping Margaret Bowman	300
Margaret Bowman	300
John Curtis for keeping Willᵐ Owen	200
Wᵐ Owen	400
John Jones for keeping a Pariſh Child three Months	125
Henry Ball for keeping a Pariſh Child four Months	150

To the Church Wardens for the use of the Pariſh to lay the Iles of the three Churchs with Stone & make

an Addition to the Upper Church	11284
	40000
Caſk at 4 ℔ʳ Cᵗ	1600
Salary at 4 ℔ʳ Cᵗ	1654
To 10℔ʳ Cᵗ allow'd to all perſons that will pay their Pariſh Dues in Inſpectors Notes	4325
	47579

Mʳ Thomas Price was this Day Choſen Vestry Man in the room of Majʳ Kemp the Sᵈ Kemp being removed out of the Pariſh.

Wᵐ Skipwith

(214)   At a Vestry held for Chriſt Church Pariſh in Middˢˣ County the 6ᵗʰ day of Nevember 1731

Preſent

Mʳ Bartho: Yates, Rogʳ Jones, Oliver Segar, Edwin Thacker, William Stanard Armistead Churchhill, Henry Thacker, & Thomas Price Genᵗ

Capᵗ Thoˢ Price was this Day Sworn Vestryman for this Pariſh.

Chriſt Church Pariſh	Dʳ	Con	Cʳ
To Sundry Claimes as			lb Tobᵒ
appears by a former Vestry	47579	By 1219 Tithables	
To Mʳ Stanard for fees	246	at 39½ᵗᵇ Tobᵒ	
To 10 ℔ʳ Cᵗ on Dᵒ	24	℔ʳ pole	48150
To 4 ℔ʳ Cᵗ on 270 is	11		
	47860		
a Fraction	290		
	48150		

Order'd That Edmund Bearkley & Thomas Price Genᵗ be Church Wardens this year.

Order'd that the Church Wardens Collect 39½ᵗᵇ Tobᵒ ℔ʳ pole of the Several Tithables in this Pariſh and pay the Same

to the Parifh Cret^{rs} And that the S^d Ch: Wardens receive
four pounds of Tob^o p^r pole of the Several Tithables within
this Parifh that are Willing to pay the Same for the Ufe of
Mr Bartho: Yates Minister.

Rog^r Jones

(215)   At a Vestry held for Chrift Church Parifh in Midd^{sx}
County the 11th Day of Octob^r 1732

Prefent

Mr Bartho: Yates, George Wortham, John Grymes Esqr
Edwin Thacker Wm Stanard Henry Thacker Edmund Berkeley & Thomas Price Gen^t

	lb Tob^o
Order'd	
To Mr Bartho Yates Minister	16000
Churchhill Jones Clk of the Vestry	800
John Lark Clk of the Middle Church 9 months	900
Henry Towls Clk of D^o 3 months	300
Richd Steevens Clk of the Lower Church	1000
John Baldin Clk of the Upper Church	1000
Keziah Bawl Sexton of the Middle Church	600
William Woods Sexton of the Upper Church	500
Archible M^{cc}Curdy Sexton of the lower Church	500
Eliz^a Humphreys	500
Ann Cooper	500
Elenor Bromel	600
Rachel Baker	800
William Crocker	500
Mr James Reid for two Levys	79
William Owen	400
William Cain's Acco^t against the Said Owen	150
John Curtis for keeping the Said Owen 9 months	450
Occany Palto	300
George Walker for keeping Margaret Bowman	300
Margaret Bowman	300
Lettis Pateman	250
Robt Davidson his acco^t against Willm Owen	200
Maj^r Berkeley his Acco^t	2000
Capt Thomas Price his acco^t	650

To the Ch: Wardens for repairing the Midd Church	400
To the Ch: Wardens for the use of the Parifh	10000
	39979
Cafk at 4 pr Ct	1599
Salary at 4 pr Ct	1663
10 pr Ct allow'd to all perfons that will pay their Parifh Dues in Inspectors Notes	4324
	47565

Chrift Church Parifh Dr	Con	Cr
lb Tob°	By a Fraction in the Collec-	
To Sundry Claims 47,565	tors hands	290
	By 1208 Tithables at 39lb	
	Tob° pr pole	47112
	By Tob° paid John Southward	163
		47565

(216)   Order'd That Edmund Berkeley & Thomas Price Gent be Church wardens this year   Orderd that the Church wardens Collect 30lb of Tob° pr pole of the Several Tithables in this Parifh and pay the Same to the Parifh Creditors.   And that the Said Ch: wardens receive four pds of Tob° pr pole of the Several Tithables within this Parifh that are willing to pay the Same for the Use of Mr Bartho: Yates Minister.

The accots of the Last years Levy were this Day Examin'd and Majr Edmund Berkeley reported that he had Sold 11284lb of Tob° at 13/2 pr Ct in Current Money.

Churchhill Jones & Mr Christopher Sutton this Day return'd the proceedings of their Procefsioning.

Mr John Bryant & mr Garrit Daniel did the Same.

Mr Edwd Smith & Mr Edwd Clark return'd the Same.

Mr John Fearn & Mr Jacob Stiff return'd the Same.

Mr John Smith & Mr Law: Orrill return'd the Same.

Mr Thomas Mountague & Mr William Mountague return'd the Same.

Mr John Smith & Mr Samll Batchelder return'd the Same.

Mr William Owin & Mr John Davis return'd the Same.

Order'd That the Clerk of the Vestry register the returns of the Procefsioners against the next Vestry.

George Wortham

(217)   At a Vestry held for Chrift Church Parifh in Midd^{sx} County the 9th Day of Octob^r 1733

Prefent

Mr Bartho: Yates, Sr William Skipwith, George Wortham, John Grymes Esqr, Rog^r Jones, Edwin Thacker, Armist^d Churchhill Henry Thacker Edmund Berkeley Chriftopher Robinfon & Tho: Price   Gen^t

Order'd	lb Tob^o
To Mr Bartho: Yates Minister	16000
Churchhill Jones Clk of the Vestry	800
Henry Towls Clk of the Middle Church	1200
Richard Steevens Clk of the lower Chapple	1000
John Baldwin Clk of the upper Chapple	1000
Keziah Bawl Sexton of the Middle Church	600
William Woods Sexton of the upper Chapple	500
Archible McCurdy Sexton of the lower Chapple	500
Eliz^a Humphries	500
Ann Cooper	500
Elenor Bromel	600
Rachel Baker	800
William Crocker	500
Occany Palto	300
Lettis Pateman	250
Margaret Bowman	200
George Walker for keeping the S^d Bowman	200
Rice Jones one Levy over charg'd last year	39
Mr James Reid allow'd Eleven delinquents	387
Occany Palto further allow'd	200
Her: Rhods for keeping & burying Susanna Shelton	400
William Cain for keeping Willm Owin	600
William Owin	400
George Walker his acco^t allow'd	110
Doc^t John Symmer his acco^t allow'd	860
Maj^r Edm^d Berkeley his acco^t allow'd	84

Capt Thomas Price his acco^t allow'd   533
The Churchwardens for the use of the Parifh   10000

                                                     39063
Cafk at 4 p^r C^t   1566
Salary at 4 p^r C^t   1665

                                                     42294
10 ℔ C^t allow'd all perfons that will pay their Parifh
Dues in Inspect^{rs} Notes   4229

                                                     46523
a mistake in Maj^r Berkeley's acco^t above   216

                                                     46739
                                                     lb Tob°
(218)   Brought over   46739
Christ Church Parish   D^r   Con   C^r
         lb Tob°   lb Tob°
To Sundry Clames   46739   By 1178 Tithables at 39
                             p^r pole   45942
                       Ball. due to the Collect^r   797

                                                     46739

It appearing to a Vestry held the 15th Day of Novemb^r following that there was an Error in laying the Levy, (not having the true numb^r of Tithables) and they made an Ord^r that the Ch: wardens Collect 40^{lb} Tob° p^r pole, then the Levy is as followeth

Chrift Church Parifh   D^r   Con   C^r
         lb Tob°   lb Tob°
To Sundry Clames   46,739   By 1184 Tithables
a Depofitum in the   at 40 p^r pole   47360
   Collect^{rs} hands   621

                 47,360

Order'd That Armist⁴ Churchhill & Ch⁻ Robinson Genᵗ be Ch: wardens this year and it is Order'd that the S⁴ Church Wardens Collect 39ᵗʰ of Tobᵒ pʳ pole of the Several Tithables in this Pariʃh and pay the Same to the Pariʃh Creditʳˢ and they are to receive four pᵈˢ of Tobᵒ pʳ pole of the Several tithables within the Pariʃh that are willing to pay the Same for the use of Mʳ Bartho Yates Minister

The Accoᵗˢ of the Laʃt years Levy were this Day Examin'd and Capᵗ Thoˢ Price reported that he had Sould 10,000 pounds of Tobᵒ at 16 Shillings & ten pence pʳ Cᵗ amounting in the whole to Eighty four pounds three Shill & four pence Current Money.

Order'd That an addition of Forty foot in length & Twenty five foot in breadth be aded to the upper Chapple as Soon as conveniently may be, and that the Said Building be made of Wood.

Order'd That the three Churchs be inclosed with Brick walls

Order'd That the wall round the Middle Church be first Built.

Order'd That the Church Wardens give Publick notice that there is a Building of Forty foot in length & twenty five foot wide to be let, and like wise a Brick Wall round the Middle Church.

Orderd That a Vestry meet on Thursday the 15ᵗʰ of Novembʳ if fair if not the next fair Day.

Order'd That the fines in the hands of the Collectʳˢ be accounted for the next Vestry.

Wᵐ Skipwith

(219)   At a Vestry held for Christ Church Pariʃh in Middˢˣ County the 15ᵗʰ Day of Novembʳ 1733

Preʃent

Bartho: Yates, Sʳ William Skipwith, George Wortham, John Grymes Esqʳ. Rogʳ Jones, Edwin Thacker, Armist⁴ Churchhill, Henry Thacker, Edm⁴ Berkeley, Christopher Robinson, & Thomas Price Genᵗ

It appearing there was an Error in Laying of the Levy the last Vestry it is Order'd that the Church Wardens Collect

40^{lb} of Tob° p^r pole of the Several Tithables in this Parifh and pay the Same to the Parifh Creditors.

The Vestry having agreed with Mr Henry Gains to Build the addition to the Upper Chapple for one hundred forty Eight pounds Current money, the Dementions of the Said Building are to be according to the Order of the laft Vestry and the Frame & other meterials be of the Same Propotion of the p^rfent Building. It is Order'd that he give Bond & Security to the Church Wardens. And the Church Wardens to give him an Order for the Money in Col. Grymes's hands which is Eighty four pounds Three Shill and four pence in part of pay.

The Vestry likwife having agreed with Mr John Moor to Build a Brick wall round the Middle Church, one hundred & Thirty four foot Long, and one hundred & ten, foot Wide, four & a half foot High, Eighteen Inches thick, from the foundation to the Water Table, and fourteen Inches afterwards, for one Hundred & fourteen Pounds. Order'd that the S^d Moor give Bond & Security to the Church Wardens to Perform the Same by the firft Day of next October in a well & workmanlike Manner and the Church Wardens are Order'd to pay him Seventy four pounds five Shill^s & Eight pence. And he further agrees to Build Walls round the two Chappels, of the Same Dementions as above and for the Same Sum of Money, and to finifh that round the Lower Chapple by the first Day of Octob next, and the Other the year following. on Confideration of the Produce of Twelve Thoufand Pounds, of Tob° to be Levy'd by the Vestry yearly till the S^d Sums be paid.

Leave is given by this Vestry to Col John Grymes in behalf of himself Mr Wormely's Col Churchhill's & Maj^r Berkeley's families to Build an Addition of Twenty foot Squar. to the Middle Church, and they are to have a property in the Same keeping it in repair at their Own Charge. provided they do no Damage to the prefent Building.

And likwise leave is given to Col Armist^d Churchhill & Maj^r Edm^d Berkeley in behalf of themselves, Col Grymes's

& Mr Wormely's families to build an Addition to the Lower Chapple of Twenty foot Squar and they are to have a property in the Same keeping it in repair at their own Charge provided they do no Damage to the preſent Building.

The Suṁ of nine pounds and three Barrills of Corn, fines Accounted for to this Vestry it is Order'd that the money be Equally Devided between the following Perſons

(220) Eliz^a Terry, Wm Crocker, Widdow Stamper, Mary Finly, Eberson's Children and John Southworth. Arthur Thomas to have the three Barrils of Corn.

Wm Skipwith

At a Vestry held for Christ Church Pariſh in Midd^{sx} County the 5th Day of June 1734

Preſent

Bartho : Yates, John Grymes, Rog^r Jones, Edwin Thacker Armist^d Churchhill Hen : Thacker, Edm^d Berkeley, & Chriſtopher Robinſon Gen^t

It appearing to this Vestry that Mr Henry Gains the Person who undertook to Build the Addition to the upper Chapple is Since dead and Mr Robt Gains who was his Security is Willing to perform the Same provided he has more time allow'd him it is Order'd that he have till the laſt of next June to finiſh the Same.

Order'd that the Church Wardens pay Mr Robt Gayns Twenty five Shill^s for work done to the upper Chapple.

Order'd That John Walker John Robinson & George Hardin be Added to this Vestry as Vestrymen for this Pariſh.

John Grymes

(221) At a Vestry held for Chriſt Church Pariſh in Midd^{sx} County the 14th Day of Octob^r 1734

m^r John Robinſon, and Mr George Hardin was this day Sworn Vestry Men.   Preſent

John Grymes Esqr Rog^r Jones, Armistead Churchhill, Edmund Berkeley, Chriſtopher Robinſon, Tho : Price, John Robinſon, & George Hardin, Gentlemen

	lb Tob⁰
Order'd	
To the Execut^{rs} or Administ^{rs} of Mr Bartho: Yates, Decd	16000
Churchhill Jones Clk. of the Vestry	800
Henry Towls Clk. of the Middle Church	1200
Richd Steevens Clk. of the Lower Chapple	1000
John Balwin Clk of the upper Chapple	1000
Keziah Bawl Sexton of the Middle Church	600
Katharin Woods Sexton of the Upper Chapple	500
Archible McCurdy Sexton of the lower Chapple Six months	250
George Barrick Sexton of D⁰ Six months	250
Eliz^a Humphries	500
Ann Cooper	500
Rachel Baker	800
William Crocker	500
Ocany Palto	500
Lettis Pateman	250
Margaret Bowman	200
Lettis Pateman further alow'd	250
Nicokolas Mealer for making Wm Owin's Coffin	100
John Curtis for a Sheet &c: for D⁰	50
William Cain for the S^d Owin's Levy laſt year	40
Doct^r John Symmer as p^r acco^t	721
Mr Ch^r Robinſon as p^r acco^t	168
Col. Churchhill one delinquen^t	40
To the Ch: wardens for the use of the Pariſh	12000
	38219
Caſk at 4 p^r C^t	1528
Salary at 4 p^r C^t	1589
To 10 p^r C^t for Inspectors notes	4133
	45469

Order'd — lb Tob⁰

To the Execut[rs] or Administ[rs] of M[r] Bartho: Yates, Decd — 16000

Churchhill Jones Clk. of the Vestry — 800
Henry Towls Clk. of the Middle Church — 1200
Rich[d] Steevens Clk. of the Lower Chapple — 1000
John Balwin Clk of the upper Chapple — 1000
Keziah Bawl Sexton of the Middle Church — 600
Katharin Woods Sexton of the Upper Chapple — 500
Archible M[c]Curdy Sexton of the lower Chapple Six months — 250
George Barrick Sexton of D⁰ Six months — 250
Eliz[a] Humphries — 500
Ann Cooper — 500
Rachel Baker — 800
William Crocker — 500
Ocany Palto — 500
Lettis Pateman — 250
Margaret Bowman — 200
Lettis Pateman further alow'd — 250
Nicokolas Mealer for making W[m] Owin's Coffin — 100
John Curtis for a Sheet &c: for D⁰ — 50
William Cain for the S[d] Owin's Levy laſt year — 40
Doct[r] John Symmer as p[r] acco[t] — 721
M[r] Ch[r] Robinſon as p[r] acco[t] — 168
Col. Churchhill one delinquen[t] — 40
To the Ch: wardens for the use of the Pariſh — 12000

38219

Caſk at 4 p[r] C[t] — 1528
Salary at 4 p[r] C[t] — 1589
To 10 p[r] C[t] for Inspectors notes — 4133

45469

Chriſt Church Pariſh	Dr	Con	Cr
	lb Tob°		
To Sundry Clames	45,469	By 1182 Tithables	
To a Depoſ: in the		at 39 pr pole	46098
Collectrs hands	629		

46,098

Order'd That

(222)   Order'd That Armistd Churchhill & Chr Robinſon Gent be Ch: Wardens this year.

Order'd That the Sd Ch: Wardens Collect 39 pds of Tob° pr pole of the Several Tithable in this Pariſh and pay the Same to the Pariſh Creditrs And that they receive four pds of Tob° pr pole of the Several Tithables in this Pariſh that are willing to pay the Same and that the Sd Ch: Wardens pay the Sd Tob° to the Executrs or Administrs of Mr Bar: Yates Decd.

The Accots of the laſt years Levy was this Day Examined, and Col. Armistd Churchhill reported that he has Sould 10,-000 pds of Tob° at 15 Shills & 8 pence pr Ct amounting in the Whole to £78-6-8 Current Money.

Mr Robr Gaines moving to the Vestry to know Who he Should apply himself too in caſe of any Difficalty in carrying on the Building of the upper Chapple; it is Order'd that he apply himself to Mr Chr Robinſon Ch: Warden.

Order'd That the Sextons cut down all the Weeds & Bryers in the Church Yards and keep the Said Yards Clean.

Order'd That the Ch: Wardens provide Cuſhians to lay round the Communion Tables in the Church & each Chapple.

John Grymes

(223)   At a Vestry held for Christ Church Pariſh in Middsx County the 11th Day of Novembr 1734

Preſent

John Grymes Esqr, Rogr Jones, Edwin Thacker, Armistead Churchhill, Henry Thacker, Edmund Berkeley, Christopher Robinson Thomas Price and John Robinson Gent

M[r] John Walker was this Day Sworn Vestryman for this Parijh and took his place accordingly.

The Reverend M[r] John Reade offering to officiate as Minister of this Parijh until the arival of one of the Sons of our late worthy Minister M[r] Bartho Yates for the Legal Salary and usual Perquesits, And then to quit the Same upon the Request of the then Vestry, And also disclaiming all right to the use or benifits Accruing from the Glebe dureing the life of M[rs] Yates Relict of Our Said late Minister, This Vestry do agree to receive him upon the terms afore S[d] And accordingly Order that he be admitted as Minister of this Parijh from this Day to the end of the term aforesaid Provided he can obtain the Governor's leave to remove himself into the Parijh.

Order'd That 800 pd[s] of Tob[o] be paid by the Collect[r] to Eliz[a] Porter out of the Depoj: of last year & this present year. And the remainder 450 p[ds] of Tob[o] to be divided between Mary Finley, & Mary Guttery.

John Grymes   John Reade

(224)   At a Vestry held for Christ Church Parish in Midd[sx] County the 8th Day of Octob[r] 1735

Present

M[r] John Reade, John Grymes Esq[r] Rog[r] Jones, Armistead Churchhill, Edm[d] Berkeley, Henry Thacker, Christopher Robinson, & Thomas Price, Gen[t]

In Pursuance of an Order of Midd[sx] County Court dated the 5th Day of Aug[st] 1735 This Vestry have Divided this Parijh into Several Precincts and have appointed two Freeholders of Every Several Precinct to Se all the Lands Procejsion'd within the Said Precincts as followeth

Order'd That M[r] James Dudley & Churchhill Jones Procejsion Every persons Land between the lower End of this County and Maj[r] Kemp's Mill, crojs the Neck to Col: Churchhill's Creek. beginning to Procejsion the Second Tuesday in Octob[r] & finish the Same by the 21st Day of March next.

Order'd that M[r] William Owin, & M[r] Patrick Purcel, Procejsion Every person Land between Maj[r] Kemp's Mill, &

the Pipeing Tree on the South Side of the Main Road beginning to Proceſsion the last Tuesday in Octobʳ & finish the Same by the 22ᵈ Day of March next.

Order'd that Mʳ Jacob Stiff & Mʳ Thomas Brumel Proceſsion Every persons Land from Majʳ Kemp's Mill to the Pipeing Tree along Mʳ Christopher Robinson's bounds to the River Side, on the North Side of the Main Road. beginning to Proceſsion the last Tuesday in Novembʳ and finish the same by the 23ᵈ Day of March next.

Order'd that Mʳ Edward Clark, & Mʳ Gregory Smith, Proceſsion Every perſons Land between the Pipeing-Tree & Pritty-Mans Roleing Road from Rappᵃ River to Piankatank beginning to Proceſsion the 2ᵈ Tuesday in Novembʳ & finish the Same by the 24ᵗʰ of March next.

Order'd that Mʳ John Smith & Mʳ Edward Dillard Proceſsion Every persons Land between Pritty-mans Roleing-Road and the Main branch of Mickleberroughs Swamp including the Widdow Cheedles Plantation on the North Side of the Main Road beginning to Proceſsion the Second Tuesday in Decembʳ and finish the same by the 25ᵗʰ Day of March next.

Order'd that Mʳ Larrance Orrill, & Mʳ Willᵐ Daniel, Proceſsion Every persons Land between Pritty-mans Roleing Rode and the new Dragon bridg Road, running from the Main Road to the Dragon on the South Side of the Main Road, beginnin to Proceſsion the 3ᵈ Tuesday in Octobʳ and finish the same by the 26ᵗʰ Day of March next.

Order'd that Mʳ John Segar, & Mʳ John Meacham, Proceſsion Every perſons Land between the lower end of the new Dragon bridg road and the Bryary Swamp thence to the Millstone Valley running from the Main Road to the Dragon, on the South Side of the Main Road beginning to Proceſsion the laſt Tuesday in Octobʳ & finish the Same by the 27ᵗʰ Day of March next.

(225) Order'd that Mʳ Humphrey Jones, & Mʳ Richᵈ George, Proceſsion Every persons Land between the head of Col Thacker's Mill-dam and the head of Parrotts Creek then to the Millstone Valley on the North Side of the Main

Road, and from the S^d Road to the river, beginning to Proce∫sion the 2^d Tuesday in Novemb^r & finish the Same by the 28th Day of March next.

Order'd that m^r Garrot Daniel, & Mr John Jones, Proce∫sion Every persons Land between the Bryary Swamp, from the Millstone Valley to the Dragon Swamp, and the upper End of the County on the South Side of the Main Road beginning to Proce∫sion the last Tuesday in Novemb^r & finish the same by the 29th Day of March next.

Order'd that m^r Thomas Mountague & Mr George Goodwin, Proce∫sion Every persons Land between the head of Parrotts Creek from the Mill Stone Valley to the upper End of the County, on the North Side of the Main Road beginning to Proce∫sion the 2^d Tuesday in Decemb^r & finish the same by the last Day of March next.

Order'd that the above S^d Freeholders Proce∫sion Every Persons Land pursuant to the above ord^rs of Vestry and that they take & return an Acco^t of Every persons Land they Shall so Proce∫sion of the time when & of the Persons pre∫ent at the Same and of what Land in their Respective Precinct they Shall fail to Proce∫sion and the Reason of Such failiur to the next Vestry which shall happen after the last day of March next comming. And it is further Order'd that all the Freeholders of the Several Precincts above mentioned attend the above Said Proce∫sioners in their respective Precinct to perform the Proce∫sioning above Directed and the S^d Proce∫sioners are to take notice that if any Owner of any Land shall refuse to suffer his or her Land to be Proce∫sioned the Law requires that within ten Days after Such refusal they Certifie the same under their hands to the Church Wardens of the Parish.

	lb Tob^o
Order'd to Mr John Reade Minister	16000
Churchhill Jones Clk of the Vestry	800
Henry Towls Clk of the Middle Church	1200
Richd Steevens Clk of the Lower Chapple	1000
John Balwin Clk of the upper Chapple	1000

Keziah Ball Sexton of the Middle Church	600
Katharine Woods Sexton of the upper Chapple	500
George Barrick Sexton of the lower Chapple	500
Eliz^a Humphries	500
Ann Cooper	500
Rachel Baker	800
Ocany Palto	500

23900
lb Tob^o

(226) Brought over	23900
To Lettis Pateman	500
Margaret Bowman	200
Willm Crocker	500
To the Church wardens for the use of the Parish	12000
Willm Crocker further allow'd	300
Keziah Ball allow'd for Clearing the Church Yard	50
Katharine Woods further allow'd	50
John Williams allow'd for keeping Richd Bateman & John Carril 9 weeks	600
Doc^t John Mitchel allow'd as p^r Acco^t	800
John Dudley for keeping Elenor Keyton	800
Col Armistead Churchhill for Tarring the Church & Chapple	2000
Willm Robinson for painting the Church Gates	50
The Churchwardens to mend the Belfry	1000

42750

To 10 p^r C^t for Inspectors Notes	4275
Cask at 4 p^r C^t	1881
Salary at 4 p^r C^t	1881

50787

Christ Church Parifh	D^r	Con		C^r
	lb Tob°			
To Sundry Clames	50787	By 1193 Tithables at		lb Tob°
To a Depof: in the		43 p^d of Tob° p^r pole		51299
Collect^rs hands	512			

51,299

Order'd that John Robinson & John Walker Gen^t be Church-wardens this Insueing year.

Order'd that the said Churchwardens Collect 43 p^ds of Tob° p^r pole of the Several Tithables in this Parish and pay the same to the Parifh Creditors and that they agree with Workmen to repair the Bellfry as soon as pofsible.

Col. Armistead Churchhill Reports to this Vestry that he has Sold 12000^lb Tob° at 13 Shill & Eleven pence ½ p^r C^t amounting in the whole to £83: 15^s Current money which money the S^d Churchhill paid to m^r John More. And he likwise produced his Vouchers for his last years Collection, and it is Order'd that the S^d Churchhill pay to Capt Robt Gains £3: 5^s: 8 and to m^r Robt Price £8: 7: 6 out of the Money which is still remaining in his hands and his Own Acco^t is also allow'd which is £2: 1^s: 8½^d

John Reade

(227)   At a Vestry held for Christ Church Parifh in Midd^sx County the 12th Day of October 1736

Prefent

Mr John Reade, John Grymes Esqr, Edwin Thacker, Armistead Churchhill, Edmund Berkeley, Christopher Robinson, Thomas Price, John Robinfon, & George Hardin Gen^t

	lb Tob°
Order'd To Mr John Reade Minister	16000
Churchhill Jones Clk of the Vestry	800
Henry Towls Clk. of the Middle Church	1200
Richd Steevens Clk. of the Lower Chapple	1000
John Balwin Clk. of the Upper Chapple	1000
Keziah Ball Sexton of the Middle Church 9 months	450
Elizabeth Long Sexton of the S^d Church 3 months	150

Katharine Woods Sexton of the Upper Chapple   500
George Barrick Sexton of the Lower Chapple 6 months   250
Conſtance Alphin Sexton of the Sᵈ Chapple 6 months   250
Elizabeth Humphrys   500
Ann Cooper   500
Rachel Baker   800
Ocany Palto   500
Lettis Pateman   500
Margaret Bowman   200
John Goodwin for a Coffin for Richᵈ Bateman   75
Andrew Hardy for keeping a Child   75
John Lawson for a Coffin for Willᵐ Crocker   75
Elizabeth Crocker   300
Willᵐ Gardner for keeping a Child 10 Months   660
And the Sᵈ Gardner agrees to keep the Sᵈ Child the
Insueing year for 600ˡᵇ Tobᵒ
John Williams, for keeping Burying John Carrell   150
Ann Callehan   500
Elizabeth Humphrys, Junʳ for keeping a Bastard Child
4 months   250
Eustace Howard, for keeping a Baſtard Child 6 months 400
Capᵗ John Robinson, Collʳ of the last Levy his De-
linquents   993
Willᵐ Hammet for keeping Mary Butler   400
Capᵗ John Robinson for Cloths for the sᵈ Mary Buttler 100
To the Church Wardens for the use of the Pariſh   12000
Docᵗ Symmer for Cloths & Physick for Ann Kilshaw
Omitted in the year 1735   500
John Dudley for keeping Nelly Keyton 8 months   560
To the Church Wardens for to Tar the upper Chapple   1200
                                                     ─────
                                                     42838
To 10 pʳ Cᵗ for Inspectors notes on 42838 is   4283
To Caſk & Salary at 10 pʳ Cᵗ on Dᵒ is   4283
                                                     ─────
                                                     51404

lb Tob°

(228) Brought over			51404
Christ Church Parifh	D^r	Contra	C^r
To Sundry Clames	51,404	By a Ball. in the	
To Thomas French	249½	Coll^r hands	512
To Mary Guttery	249½	By 1158 Tithables at	
To Charles Forget	173	45^lb Tob° p^r pole	52110
To a Depofitum in the			
Coll^r hands	546		52622
	52,622		

Order'd That 499^lb of Tob° be Divided between Thomas French & Mary Guttery and to Charles Forget 173^lb of Tob° being part of the Depofitum in the Coll^rs hands.

Order'd That John Robinson & John Walker Gen^t continue Churchwarden this Insuing year. And it is Order'd that the S^d Church Wardens Collect 45^lb Tob° p^r pole of the several Tithables in this Parifh & pay the same to the Parifh Credit^rs

Order'd that the fines due to this Parish be Equally divided between John Chowning Elizabeth Terry and Mary Finley.

Ralph Wormely Gen^t is Elected Vestry Man in the rome of Sir William Skipwith Baronet.

John Reade

At a Vestry held for Chrift Church Parifh in Midd^sx County the 23^d Day of Novemb^r 1736

Prefent

John Reade, John Grymes Esqr, Rog^r Jones, Armistead Churchhill, Edmund Berkeley Henry Thacker, Christopher Robinson Thomas Price, John Walker, John Robinson and George Hardin Gen^t

Ralph Wormely Gen^t was this Day Sworn Vestry Man for this Parifh and took his place.

The Reverend Mr John Reade Informing the Vestry his Intention to leave the Parifh, being Chofen Minister of Stratton major Parifh in King & Queen It is Order'd that the Churchwardens write to Mr Bartho:* Yates to defire him immediately to come over.

* A note in pencil (and in a different hand) at the bottom of this page says "the son of the former Minister."--C. G. C.

This Day the Vestry agreed with the Reverend Mr Emanuel Jones to Preach in this Pariſh Every Friday at Each Church in turn and to be paid after the rate of Sixteen Thousand p^{ds} of Tob^o p^r year for the time he Serves.

Jno Reade

(229) At a Vestry held for Christ Church Parish in Midd^{sx} County the 13th Day of October 1737

Preſent

John Grymes Esqr Rog^r Jones, Edwin Thacker, Armistead Churchhill, Edm^d Berkeley, Henry Thacker, Christopher Robinson, Thomas Price John Walker, John Robinson, George Hardin, & Ralph Wormeley G^t

The Revd Mr Bartho: Yates being arrived this Vestry do unanimously choose him Minister of this Parish. And that the Church Wardens return the Revd Mr Emanuel Jones thanks for his faithfull Service.

A Letter from the Governour directed to the Church Wardens, preſented by Mr Yates was read. It is Ordered that the Church Wardens return his Honour thanks for his kind Letter.

	lb Tob^o
Ordered to Mr Emanuel Jones (by the conſent of Mr Read & Mr Yates	16000
Churchhill Jones Clk of the Vestry	800
Henry Towles Clk of the Middle Church	1200
Richd Steevens Clk of the lower Chapel	1000
John Balwin Clk of the upper Chapel	1000
Katherine Woods Sexto of the upper Chapel	600
Eliz^a Long Sexton of the Middle Church	500
Conſtance Alphin Sexton of the lower Chapel 6 months	250
Joseph Smith Sexton of the lower Chapel 6 months	250
Eliz^a Humphries	500
Ann Cooper	500
Rachel Baker	800
Ocany Panto	500
Lettis Pateman	300

Margaret Bowman	200
Eliz^a Crocker	300
Ann Callehan	500
Eliz^a Terry	300
Elenor Crosly for keeping Mary Buttler 9 months	300
Mary Buttler	200
Eliz^a Young	400
Katherine Woods for cleaning the Church yard	50
Charles Wortham for 3 Horse Blocks & Benches	600

27050
lb Tob°

(230) Brought over	27050
William Gardner for keeping a Parish Child	600
Doc^t Mitchel's Acco^t allow'd	125
Rog^r Cain for keeping John Smith	150
Capt Thos Price further allow'd for Tarring the Upper Chapel	300
Mr John Walker for Mending the Church Windows	100
The Churchwardens for the use of the Parish	2500
Capt John Robinson 3 Delinquents	180
Col Armistead Churchhill for Sundry Delinquents	975
The Church Wardens for the Maintainnance of Elenor Devoll	1200

	33180
Salary at 6 p^r C^t on 33180 is	1990
Cask at 4 p^r C^t on D° is	1327

	36497
10 p^r C^t on 36497 is	3649
William Lawson out of the Depo	41
Dorothy Chaney out of D°	31½
Elizabeth Humphries Junr the remaind^r	215½

lb Tob°	40434

lb Tobᵒ

Cʳ By 1172 Tithables at 34½ pᵈˢ of Tobᵒ pʳ pole   40434

Order'd That Rogʳ Jones & Edwin Thacker Genᵗ be Church-wardens this year, and that the sᵈ Ch: wardens receive 34½ pᵈˢ of Tobᵒ of the Several Tithables in this Pariſh, and pay the Same to the Several Creditors.

Order'd That the Churchwardens receive the fines due to this Pariſh and divid them between John Chowning Mary Finley and Mary Guttery.

Order'd That the Church Wardens Receive of John Moſley Two hundred and Thirty four pounds of Tobᵒ for his Levies in the year 1734.

Bartho: Yates

(231)   At a Vestry held for Christ Church Pariſh in Middˢˣ County the 12ᵗʰ Day of Octobʳ 1738

Preſent

Bartho: Yates, Rogʳ Jones, Edwin Thacker, Armistead Churchhill, Edmᵈ Berkeley, Henry Thacker, Christopher Robinson Thomas Price, John Robinſon George Hardin & Ralph Wormeley Genᵗ

	lb Tobᵒ
Order'd To Mʳ Bartho: Yates, Minister	16000
Churchhill Jones Clk. of the Vestry	800
Henry Towles Clk of the Middle Church	1200
Richᵈ Steevens Clk of the Lower Chapel	1000
John Balwin Clk of the Upper Chapel	1000
Katharine Woods Sexton of the upper Chapel	600
Elizᵃ Long Sexton of the Middle Church	600
Joseph Smith Sexton of the lower Chapel	500
Elizᵃ Humphries	500
Ann Cooper	500
Rachel Baker	800
Ocany Panto	500
Lettis Pateman	300
Margaret Bowman	200
Elizᵃ Crocker	300
Elizᵃ Young	400

Andrew Davis allow'd	60
Thomas Laughlin allow'd for removing of Wᵐ Greſom	200
To Dᵒ for keeping Elizᵃ Terry 4 months & Burying her	400
Edward Smith allow'd for a Coffin for Elizᵃ Terry	100
Elizᵃ Humphryes for keeping a Pariſh Child one year	600
To Dᵒ Omitted Last year for keeping the sᵈ Child	585
Willᵐ Davis for keeping Mary Weston one year	600
To Ball Col Thackers Accoᵗ Caſh 13/4 in Tobᵒ at 15/pʳ Cᵗ	95
Willᵐ Bristow for keeping Andrew South	600
Willᵐ Hammet for keeping Mary Buttler 10 month	400
The Church Wardens to Buy the sᵈ Mary Buttler Cloths	200

	29040
To Caſk at 4 pʳ Cᵗ on 29040ˡᵇ of Tobᵒ is	1161
	30201
To Salary at 6 pʳ Cᵗ on 30201ˡᵇ of Tobᵒ is	1812
	32013
To 10 pʳ Cᵗ on 32013 is	3201
Carried Over	35214 lb Tobᵒ
(232) Brought Over	35214
To Mary Guttrey	400
To 6 pʳ Cᵗ for Collecting the last 400ˡᵇ Tobᵒ	24
	35638
Order'd To Phillip Warwick out of the Depo:	10
To Churchhill Jones for one Quire paper	10
To Elizᵃ Long for a House Bruſh	16
To Frances Branch	299
To Salary at 6 pʳ Cᵗ on 356ˡᵇ of Tobᵒ the Depo: is	21
	35994

C^r By 1192 Tithables at 30^{lb} of Tob^o p^r pole is   35760
    By Col. Churchhill   234
                                                          ───────
                                                           35994

Order'd that Rog^r Jones & Edwin Thacker Gen^t be continued Church Wardens this year. And that the s^d Church Wardens receive 30^{lb} of Tob^o of the Several Tithables in this Parifh and pay the Same to the Several Cred^{rs}

Order'd that the Church Wardens Receive the fines due to this Parifh and Divide them between Mary Finly and Mary Guttery.

Order'd that Eliz^a Long be paid for a House Brufh, Churchhill Jones for a Quire of paper, and Phillip Warwick Ten p^{ds} of Tob^o out of the Dep^o and the Remainer be given to Frances Branch.

The Procefsioner's Returns was this Day Examin'd in prefence of the Vestry.

                                          Bartho: Yates

(233)   At a Vestry held for Christ Church Parish in Midd^{sx} County the 5th Day of September 1739

                        Present

Bartho: Yates, John Grymes Esqr Edwin Thacker, Christopher Robinson, John Robinson, John Walker, George Hardin, & Ralph Wormeley Gen^t

In Pursuance of an Order of Midd^{sx} County Court dated the 7th Day of Augst 1739 This Vestry have Divided this Parish in Several Precincts and have appointed two Freeholders of every Several precinct to Se all the Lands Procefsion'd within the said precincts as followeth

Ordered that Mr James Dudley, & Mr Peyton Dudley, Procefsion every persons Land between the lower end of the County and Maj^r Kemp's Mill, Crofs the Neck to Col. Churchhill's Creek beginning to Procefsion the Second Tuesday in October & finish the same by the last day of March next.

Order'd that Mr William Owen, & m^r John Davis, Procefsion Every persons Land between Maj^r Kemp's Mill & the piping Tree on the South Side of the Main Road beginning to procefsion the last Tuesday in Octob^r and finish the same by the last Day of March next.

Order'd that Mr Thomas Brummel & Mr John Fearn procefsion Every persons Land from Maj^r Kemp's Mill to the Piping Tree along Mr Ch^r Robinson's bounds to the River Side on the North Side of the Main Road beginning to Procefsion the last Tuesday in November & finish the Same by the last Day of March next.

Order'd that Mr Edward Clark & Mr John Smith (Popler) procefsion Every persons Land between the Piping Tree & Prittymans Roling Road from Rapp^a River to Piankatank beginning to Procefsion the 2^d Tuesday in Novemb^r & finish the same by the last day of March next.

Order'd that Mr John Smith (Aldin) & Mr Edward Dillard procefsion Every Persons Land between Prittymans Roling Road and the Main branch of Micklebourrough's Swamp including the Widow Cheedles plantation on the North Side of the Main Road beginning to Procefsion on the 2^d Tuesday in Decemb^r and finifh the same by the last Day of March next.

Order'd Mr Lawrence Orril & m^r William Daniel Procefsion Every persons Land between Prittyman's Roling Road and the new Dragon Bridg Road running from the Main Road to the Dragon on the South Side of the Main Road beginning to procefsion the 3^d Tuesday in Octob^{er} & finish the same by the last Day of March next.

Order'd that Mr John Segar & Mr John Macham procefsion Every persons Land between the lower end of the new Dragon Bridg Road and the Bryary Swamp thence to the Millstone Valley running from the Main Road to the Dragon (234) Dragon on the South Side of the Main Road beginning to Procefsion the last Tuesday in Octob^r & finish the same by the last Day of March next.

Order'd that Mr William Owin & Mr Harry George procefsion Every persons Land between the head of Col^o Thacker's Mill-Dam and the head of Parrotts Creek thence to the Millstone Valley on the North Side of the Main Road and from the said Road to the River beginning to proceſsion the 2ᵈ Tuesday in Novemb and finish the same by the last day of March next.

Order'ᵈ that Mʳ Garrott Daniel & Mʳ John Jones proceſsion Every persons Land between the Bryary Swamp, and from the Millstone Valley to the Dragon Swamp and the upper end of the County on the South Side of the Main Road beginning to proceſsion the last Tuesday in Novembʳ and finish the Same by the last Day of March next.

Order'd that Mʳ Thomas Mountague & Mʳ Charles Wortham proceſsion Every persons Land between the head of Parrott's Creek, and from the Millstone Valley to the Upper End of the County on the North Side of the Main Road beginning to proceſsion the 2ᵈ Tuesday in December & finish the same by the last Day of March next.

Order'd that the above said Freeholders proceſsion Every persons Land pursuant to the above Orders of Vestry and that they take & return an Account of Every persons Land they Shall so proceſsion, of the time when and of the persons preſent at the same, and of what Land in their reſpective Precinct they Shall fail to proceſsion and the Reaſon of Such failure to the next Vestry which Shall happen after the last Day of March next And it is further Order'd that all the Freeholders of the Several Precincts above mention'd attend the above said proceſsioners in their Respective precinct to perform the Proceſsioning above directed. And the Said Proceſsioners are to take notice that if the Owner of any Land Shall refuse to Suffer his or her Land to be proceſsion'd the Law requires that within ten Days after Such refusal they Certify the same under their hands to the Churchwardens of the Parish.

Richard Corbin Genᵗ is Elected Vestry Man in the room of Mʳ Rogʳ Jones Decd.

Bartho: Yates

(235)   At a Vestry held for Christ Church Parish in Middˢˣ County the 13ᵗʰ Day of October 1739

Preſent

Bartho: Yates, John Grymes Esqr Edwin Thacker, Armistead
Churchhill, Edmund Berkeley, Henry Thacker, John Robinson
& Ralph Wormeley Gent

Richd Corbin Gent was this Day Sworn Vestryman for
this Pariſh.

	lb Tobo
Ordered to Mr Bartho: Yates Minister	16000
Churchhill Jones Clk. of the Vestry	800
Henry Towles Clk. of the Middle Church	1200
Richd Steevens Clk. of the Lower Chapel	1000
John Baldwin Clk. of the Upper Chapel	1000
Katharin Woods Sexton of the Upper Chapel	600
Elizabeth Long Sexton of the Middle Church	600
Joseph Smith Sexton of the lower Chapel	500
Ann Cooper	500
Elizabeth Humphries	500
Rachel Baker	800
Ockaney Panto	500
Lettis Pateman	300
Margaret Bowman	200
Elizabeth Crocker	300
Churchhill Jones's Accot allow'd	166
Rachel Baker for keeping a Parish Child 8 months	375
William Hackney for conveying Mary Meggs & others	100
Eliza Humphries Junr for keeping a Parish Child	600
William Hammet for keeping Mary Buttler	400
Mary Buttler	200
John White allow'd	150
William Bristow for keeping Andrew South	400
Andrew South	200
Churchhill Jones for Glaſs for the lower Chapel	20
Churchwardens for Repairs of the Glebe & the floor of the Middle Church	3000
Mrs Sarah Yates for keeping Elenor Devol two years	1600

32011

Caſk at 4 p^r C^t	1280
Salary at 6 p^r C^t	1997
	35288
A depositum	922
	36210

lb Tob^o

Credit By 1207 Tithables at 30 pounds of Tob^o p^r pole   36210

(236)   Order'd that Ralph Wormeley & Richard Corbin Gen^t be Churchwardens this Insuing Year. and that the s^d Churchwardens receive 30 pounds of Tob^o of the Several Tithables in this Pariſh and pay the same to the Several Creditors.

Order'd that the Churchwarden Account for the Depositum in their hands at the laying of the next Levie.

Order'd that the Ch: warden pay John Lewis one Attorney's fee, and Grey Skipwith fifteen Shillings for Clk's fees out of the fines that are due to the Pariſh and the Remainder of the s^d fines being fourteen pounds and five Shillings be divided between Frances Branch Ann Dudley, Mary Finley, Mary Guthry, Mary French, Ann Rudd, and Mary Dobbs.

Bartho: Yates

(237)   At a Vestry held for Christ Church Parish in Midd^{sx} County the 9th Day of Octob^r 1740

Present

Bartho: Yates, John Grymes Esqr Edwin Thacker, Armistead Churchhill, Henry Thacker, Christopher Robinson Thomas Price & Richd Corbin Gen^t

	lb Tob^o
Order'd to Mr Bartho. Yates Minister	16000
Churchhill Jones Clk. of the Vestry	800
Henry Towles Clk. of the Middle Church	1200
Richd Steevens Clk. of the lower Chapel	1000
John Balwin Clk. of the Upper Chapel	1000
Katharine Woods Sexton of the Upper Chapel	600

Elizabeth Long Sexton of the Middle Church	600
Joseph Smith Sexton of the lower Chapel	500
Ann Cooper	500
Elizabeth Humphries	500
Rachel Baker	800
Ockaney Panto	500
Lettis Pateman	300
Margaret Bowman	200
William Hackney for conveying Ann Rudd & Children to Hampton	392
Doc^r Mitchell allow'd as p^r acco^t	1300
William Davis allow'd for two Horse Blocks	300
Mr James Reid allow'd as p^r Acco^t	120
Mary Sadler for Burying Charles Cooper	100
Capt Thomas Price Execut^r for Richd Greenwood	100
Margaret Bowman further allowd	200
Thomas Berry for keeping Elenor Devol	800
Robt Tureman for keeping & Burying Robt Harwood	400
William Hammet for keeping Mary Buttler 4 Months & Burying her	500
John Smith allow'd	30
Col^o Edwin Thacker allow'd as p^r Acco^t	240
Richd Steevens for keeping a Parish Child	600
	29561
C^r By Mr Christopher Curtis	537
	29024
Cask at 4 ℈^{r} C^t on 29024^{lb} Tob^o	1161
Salary at 6 p^r C^t on D^o	1741
A Depositum in the Coll^{rs} hands	730
	32656
	lb Tob^o
C^r By 1256 Tithables at 26^{lb} Tob^o p^r pole	32656

(238)   Order'd that Ralph Wormeley & Richd Corbin Gen^t be continued Churchwarden this insuing Year.

Order'd That the Churchwardens receive 26 pounds of Tob⁰ of the Several Tithables in this Parish and pay the same to the Several Creditors.

Order'd that the Churchwardens receive the fines that is due to the Parish & Divide the Same between Ann Dudley, Mary Finley, Mary Guthry, and Mary Dobbs.

Order'd that the Churchwardens Send for Three Common prayer Books for the use of the Churches.

Bartho Yates Minᵣ

(239)   At a Vestry held for Christ Church Pariſh in Middˢˣ County the 8ᵗʰ Day of October 1741

Present

Armistead Churchhill, Edmund Berkeley, Henry Thacker, Christopher Robinson, John Robinson, Tho: Price, George Hardin, Ralph Wormeley, & Richᵈ Corbin, Genᵗ

	lb Tob⁰
Order'd to Mᵣ Bartho. Yates Minister	16000
Churchhill Jones Clk. of the Vestry	800
Henry Towls Clk. of the Middle Church	1200
Richard Steevens Clk. of the lower Chapel	1000
John Baldwin Clk. of the Upper Chapel	1000
Samuel Woods Sexton of the upper Chapel	600
Elizabeth Long Sexton of the Middle Church	600
Elizabeth Smith Sexton of the lower Chapel	500
Elizabeth Humphries	500
Rachel Baker	800
Ockaney Panto	500
Lettis Pateman	300
Margaret Bowman	400
George Gues for keeping Elenor Devol	800
Lettis Pateman further allow'd	200
Reid & Cheap allow'd as pᵣ Accoᵗ	177
John Fearn Junᵣ allow'd as pᵣ Accoᵗ	80
Docᵗ Bird allow'd	800

26257

Cʳ By Christopher Curtis as pʳ Accoᵗ   330

                                                                25927
    To 4 pʳ Cᵗ on 25927 is   1037
    To 6 pʳ Cᵗ on Dᵒ is   1555
    To the Ch: Wardens for the use of the Parish   1500
    To 4 pʳ Cᵗ on 1500 is   60
    To 6 pʳ Cᵗ on Dᵒ is   90

                                                                30169
    A Depoſitum to be Accounted for by the Collʳ at
the laying of the next Parish Levy   623

                                                                30792
Cʳ By 1283 Tithables at 24ˡᵇ of Tobᵒ pʳ pole   30792
    (240)   Order'd that Henry Thacker & George Hardin Genᵗ
be Ch: Wardens this Insuing Year.
    Order'd that the Ch: Wardens receive 24ˡᵇ of Tobᵒ of the
Several Tithables in this Pariſh and pay the Same to the
Several Creditors.
                                                    A Churchhill
    At a Vestry held for Christ Church Parish in Middˢˣ County
the 7ᵗʰ Day of Octobʳ 1742
                        Preſent
    Barth. Yates, Edmᵈ Berkeley, Henry Thacker, Christopher
Robinson, John Walker, George Hardin & Thomas Price
Genᵗ
    Order'd to Mʳ Bartho: Yates Minister   16000
    Churchhill Jones Clk. of the Vestry   800
    Henry Towls Clk. of the Middle Church   1200
    Richᵈ Steevens Clk. of the lower Chapel   1000
    John Baldwin Clk. of the upper Chapel   1000
    Elizabeth Long Sexton of the Middle Church   600
    Judith Baldwin Sexton of the upper Chapel   600
    Elizabeth Smith Sexton of the Lower Chapel   500
    Elizabeth Humphries   500
    Rachel Baker   800

William Guthry for Keeping Ockaney Panto	800
Lettis Pateman	500
Margaret Bowman	400
George Gues for keeping Elenor Devol five months	400
Thomas Berry for keeping Dᵒ Seven months	581
Elizabeth Long for keeping Margaret Cambel	500
To the Churchwardens for the use of the Parish	3300
To the Churchwardens for Margaret Cambel	200
Edward Clark for keeping Margaret Bowman in 1740	400
William Bristow for keeping Dᵒ	400
Francis Loll allow'd as pʳ his Accoᵗ	140
John Crosfield allow'd as pʳ his Accoᵗ	500
mʳ Christopher Robinson allow'd for Glaſs	80

Capᵗ Thomas Price allow'd for five Copys of the
Acts of Aſsembly   200

                                                                      31401
                                                                      lb Tobᵒ

(241)   Brought over   31401
To Mʳ Richᵈ Corbin for three Common prayer Books
& one Bible for the use of the Churches   1000
To the Church Wardens for to Purchase three Sur-
plices for the use of the Parish   2000

                                                                      34401
Credit By Thomas Laughlin as pʳ accoᵗ 633
By William Guthry   560   1193

                                                                      33208
To Cask at 4 ℔ʳ Cᵗ on 33208 is   1328
To Salary at 6 ℔ʳ Cᵗ on Dᵒ is   1992
To a Depositum to be accounted for by the Collʳ at
the laying of the next Parish levie   665

                                                                      37193
                                                                      lb Tobᵒ
Credit By 1330 Tithables at 27½ pounds of Tobᵒ pʳ pole 37193

Order'd that Henry Thacker & George Hardin Gen[t] be continued Church Wardens this insuing year.

Order'd that the s[d] Churchwardens receive 27½ pounds of Tob[o] p[r] pole of the Several Tithables in this Parish and pay the same to the Several Creditors.

Order'd that Christopher Curtis late Coll[r] acco. with the Church Wardens for the fines in his hands that is due to the Parish.

Bartho Yates Min[r]

(242)   At a Vestry held for Christ Church Parish in Midd[sx] County the 24th Day of August 1743

Present

Bartho: Yates, John Grymes Esq[r], Armistead Churchhill, Henry Thacker, Christopher Robinson, John Robinson, John Walker, George Hardin, & Ralph Wormeley Gen[t]

In Pursuance of an Order of Midd[sx] County Court dated the 6th Day of July 1743 This Vestry have divided this Parish into Several Precincts and have appointed two Freeholders of Every Several Precinct to Se all the Lands Procefsioned within the said Precinct as followeth.

Order'd that m[r] John Berry & m[r] Will[m] Hill Jun[r] Procefsion Ever Person's Land between the lower End of the County and Maj[r] Kemp's Mill Crofs the Neck to Col[o] Churchhill's Creek and the line between Churchhill and S[r] Grey Skipwith beginning to Procefsion the Second Tuesday in October and finish the Same by the last Day of March next.

Order'd that m[r] Will[m] Owen, & m[r] John Davis Procefsion Every Person's Land between Maj[r] Kemp's Mill and the Piping Tree on the South Side of the Main Road. beginning to procefsion the last Tuesday in Octob[r] and finish the Same by the last Day of March next.

Order'd that Cap[t] John Robinson & m[r] Thomas Brummel Procefsion Every persons Land from Maj[r] Kemps Mill to the Piping-Tree along M[r] Christopher Robinson's bounds to the River on the north Side of the Main Road. beginning to procefsion the last Tuesday in November and finish the same by the last Day of March next.

Order'd that m^r Edward Clarke & m^r William Bristow Proceſsion Every persons Land between the Piping-Tree and Prittyman's Roling Road from Rapp^a River to Piank^t beginning to Proceſsion the Second Tuesday in November and finish the Same by the last Day of March next.

Order'd that m^r Edward Dillard, & m^r Robt Dudley Proceſsion Every persons Land between Prittymans Roling Road and the main branch of Micklebourrough's Swamp Including the Widow Cheedle's Plantation on the North Side of the Main Road beginning to Proceſsion the 2^d Tuesday in December and finish the same by the last Day of March next.

Order'd that m^r William Daniel Senr & m^r John Murry Proceſsion Every persons Land between Prittymans roling Road and the new Dragon Bridg Road running from the main Road to the Dragon on the South Side of the main Road beginning to proceſsion the third Tuesday in Octob^r and finish (243) The Same by the last Day of March next.

Order'd that m^r John Machen & m^r William Daniel proceſsion Every Persons Land between the lower end of the new Dragon Bridg Road and the Briery Swamp thence to the Millsone Valley, running from the Main Road to the Dragon on the South Side of the Main Road. beginning to Proceſsion the last Tuesday in October and finish the same by the last Day of March next.

Order'd that m^r James Cambel & m^r Humphrey Jones Proceſsion Every persons Land between the head of Col^o Thackers Mill-dam and the head of Parrotts Creek thence to the Millstone Valley on the North Side of the Main Road & from the said Road to the river. beginning to proceſsion the Second Tuesday in November and finish the same by the last Day of March next.

Order'd that m^r John Jones & m^r William Jones Proceſsion Every person's Land between the Bryery Swamp and from the Millstone Valley, to the Dragon Swamp and the upper End of the County on the South Side of the Main Road beginning to Proceſsion the last Tuesday in november and finish the same by the last Day of March next.

Order'd that mr Charles Wortham & mr Randolph Segar, Procefsion Every persons Land between the head of Parrott's Creek, and from the Millstone Valley to the upper End of the County, on the north Side of the Main Road beginning to procefsion the 2ᵈ Tuesday in December and finish the same by the last Day of March next.

Order'd that the above said Freeholders Procefsion Every person's Land pursuant to the above Orders of Vestry. and that they take and return an Account of Every perfons Land they Shall so procefsion, of the time when and of the Persons present at the same, and of what Land in their Refpective precinct they Shall fail to Procefsion, and the reafon of Such failure to the next Vestry which Shall happen after the last Day of March next and it is further Order'd that all the Freeholders of the Several Precincts above mention'd attend the above said Procefsioners in their respective precincts to perform the Procefsioning above directed. and the said Procefsioners are to take notice that if the Owner of any Land Shall refuse to Suffer his or her land to be procefsion'd the Law requires that within ten days after Such refusal they certifie the Same under their hands to the Churchwardens of the Parifh.

Bartho: Yates

(244)   At a Vestry held for Christ Church Parish in Middˢˣ County the 12ᵗʰ Day of Octobr 1743

Prefent

Barthᵒ Yates Edwin Thacker, Armistead Churchhill, Christopher Robinson, Henry Thacker, John Robinson, Thomas Price, George Hardin & Ralph Wormeley Genᵗ

Order'd to Mr Bartho: Yates Minister	16000
Churchhill Jones Clk. of the Vestry	800
Henry Towls Clk. of the Middle Church	1200
Richᵈ Steevens Clk. of the lower Chapel	1000
John Baldwin Clk. of the upper Chapel	1000
Elizabeth Long Sexton of the Middle Church	600
Judith Baldwin Sexton of the upper Chapel	600
Elizabeth Smith Sexton of the lower Chapel	500

Elizabeth Humphries	500
Rachel Baker	800
Lettis Pateman	500
Margaret Bowman	400
Thomas Berry for keeping Elenor Devol	1000
William Guthry for keeping Ockaney Panto	800
George Chowning for keeping Wm Carrell 2 months	200
Doc^t Symmer allow'd as p^r Acco^t	125
Doc^t Mitchel allow'd as p^r Acco^t	75
William Clowdas for keeping Maſsey House & paying the Doc^t	250
Christopher Curtis allow'd	27½
Anthony Smith allow'd as p^r Acco^t	112
George Barbee for making Seats for the lower Chapel	150
Capt Henry Thacker allow'd as p^r his Acco^t	424
Col^o Churchhill for 2 Bar: Corn for Eliz^a Roberts	128
Capt Hen: Thacker for 2 Bar: Corn for Patience Colley	128
	¦27319
Credit by the Coll^r	665
	26654
Caſk @ 4 p^r C^t on 26654 is	1066
Salary @ 6 p^r C^t on D^o	1599
	29319
A Depositum to be Accounted for by the Coll^r at the laying of the next Levy	21
lb Tob^o	29340
Credit By 1304 Tithables @ 22½ pounds of Tob^o p^r pole lb Tob^o	29340

(245)   Order'd that Mr James Jones be appointed Proceſsioner in the Room of Charles Wortham Decd.

Order'd that Edmund Berkeley & Thomas Price Gen^t be Churchwardens this Insuing year.

Order'd that the said Church Wardens receive 22½ pounds of Tob° pʳ pole of the Several Tithables in this Parifh and pay the Same to the Several Creditors.

Order'd that the fines that are due to the Parifh (being £6: 15) be divided between Mary Guthry, Ann Dudley, Patience Colly & Mary Blakey.

Christopher Curtis presented his Accoᵗˢ of the Fines that were due to the Parifh in the years 1739. 1740. & 1741 and they were Examined and Allow'd.

Barth° Yates Minʳ

(246)   At a Vestry held for Christ Church Parish in Middˢˣ County the 12ᵗʰ Day of October 1744

Prefent

Barth° Yates, Armistead Churchhill, Edmᵈ Berkeley, Henry Thacker, Christopher Robinson, John Robinson, Thomas Price and George Hardin Genᵗ

	lb Tob°
Order'd to Mʳ Barth° Yates Minister	16000
Churchhill Jones Clk. of the Vestry	800
Henry Towles Clk. of the Middle Church	1200
Richᵈ Steevens Clk. of the lower Chapel	1000
John Baldwin Clk of the Upper Chapel	1000
Elizᵃ Long Sexton of the Middle Church 5 months	250
Edward Whitaker Sexton of D° 7 months	350
Judith Baldwin Sexton of the Upper Chapel	600
Elizᵃ Smith Sexton of the lower Chapel	500
Elizᵃ Humphries	500
Rachel Baker	800
Letice Pateman	500
Margaret Bowman	400
Thomas Berry for keeping Elenor Devol	1000
William Guthry for keeping Okaney Panto	800
Mʳ William Armistead allow'd 5 levies Over Charg'd last year	112
Edward Whittaker for keeping & Burying Thomas Hammon	400
John Lawson for Burying Abraham More	200

Capt Tho: Price allow'd as p^r Acco^t 1140
Maj^r Edm^d Berkeley allow'd as p^r Acco^t 660
Doc^t John Strachey allow'd as p^r Acco^t 800
Curtis Hardee   30
Church-wardens for the use of the Parish   3000
                                                    _____
                                                         32042
   Credit by the Coll^r 21
                                                    _____
                                                         32021
Cask at 4 p^r C^t on 32021 is   1280
Salary at 6 p^r C^t on D^o is   1921
a Depositum to be accounted for by the Coll^r at the
laying of the next Levy   607
                                                         35829
                                                    _____
Credit. By 1327 Tithables at 27^{1b} Tob^o p^r pole   35829

(247) Order'd that Edmund Berkeley & Thomas Price
Gen^t be continued Church-wardens this Ensuing year.

Order'd that the s^d Church-Wardens receive 27^{1b} Tob^o p^r pole
of the Several Tithables in this Parish and pay the Same to the
Several Creditors.

Order'd that Okaney Panto be discharg'd from paying Parish
Levys.

Order'd that the fines that are due to the Parish (being
Thirteen pound) be divided between Mary Blakey, Patience
Colly, Mary Hennesey, Arthur Thomas, Mary Southern, Ruth
Howard, and the Church-Wardens for the use of Ann Dudley's
Children.

       Barth^o Yates Minister

At a Vestry held for Christ Church Parish in Midd^{sx} County
the 17th Day of Septemb^r 1745

       Prefent

Mr Barth^o Yates, John Grymes Esqr, Armistead Churchhill,
Edmund Berkeley, Henry Thacker, Christopher Robinson, John
Robinson, Thomas Price & Ralph Wormeley Gen^t

John Smith, Philip Grymes, Beverley Stanard and James Reid are Elected Vestrymen in the room of Edwin Thacker, George Hardin and John Walker Decd and Rich⁴ Corbin Genᵗ Who is Removed out of this Parish.

John Smith, Beverley Stanard and James Reid appear'd and took the Oath of Vestry Men Severally.

Barthᵒ Yates Minister

(248)   At a Vestry held for Christ Church Parish in Midd^{sx} County the 12ᵗʰ Day of Octobʳ 1745

Preſent

Barthᵒ Yates Minister John Grymes Esqʳ Armistead Church-hill Christopher Robinson, Thomas Price John Robinson Beverley Stanard and James Reid Genᵗ

Philip Grymes Genᵗ was this Day Sworn Vestryman for this Pariſh.

Order'd to Mʳ Barthᵒ Yates Minister	16000
Churchhill Jones Clk. of the Vestry	800
Henry Towles Clk. of the Middle Church	1200
Rich⁴ Steevens Clk. of the lower Chapel	1000
John Baldwin Clk of the Upper Chapel	1000
Edward Whitaker Sexton of the M[iddle] Church	600
Judith Baldwin Sexton of the upper Chapel	600
Thomas Sibley Sexton of the lower Chapel	500
Elizabeth Humphries	600
Rachel Baker	800
Lettice Pateman	500
Margaret Bowman	400
Thomas Berry for keeping Elenor Devol	1000
William Guthry for keeping Okaney Panto 5 months	333
William Guthry for burying Okaney Panto	200
Patrick Calleham for Clothing Catharine French	200
Elizabeth Roberts allow'd	300
Thomas Brumel for keeping an Orphan of Abraham More's	400
Margaret Bristow for keeping Margaret Bowman	400
Majʳ Edmund Berkeley as pʳ Accoᵗ	416

Edward Smith for keeping 5 Orphans Children of
Philip Brooks   800
  Charles Daniel alow'd as p^r Acco^t   50
The Church Wardens for Clothing the Orphans of
Philip Brooks   400
  Anthony Smith allow'd as p^r Acco^t   362
  Ann Johnſon allow'd   300
The Church Wardens for Willm Brooks Orphan of
Caleb Brooks   150
Willm Kidd for nursing a Child of William Wallas
7 months   468
  Capt Thomas Price as p^r Acco^t   390
The Church Wardens for Repairing the Gates of the
Several Church Yards, and Making a Well at the Glebe   3000

                                                   33169
(249)   Brought Over   33169
         Credit by the Collecter   607

                                                   32562
To Caſk @ 4 p^r C^t on 32562 is   1302
To Salary @ 6 p^r C^t on D^o is   1953
To a Depositum to be accounted for next Levy   66

                                                   35883
C^r By 1329 Tithables @ 27^{lb} Tob^o p^r Pole   35883
Order'd that John Smith & Beverley Stanard Gen^t be ap-
pointed Churchwardens this In[suing] year.
Order'd that the said Churchwardens receive 27^{lb} Tob^o p^r
pole of the Several Tithables in this Parish and pay the same
to the Several Creditors.
Order'd that the said Churchwardens let the freeschool Land
at Such terms as they shall think best.
Order'd that Capt Thomas Price diſtribute the fines in his
hands between Mary Blakey & Mary Hennesey.
The Several Proceſsioners returns was this Day Examined
in preſence of the Vestry.
                          Barth^o Yates Min^r

(250)   At a Vestry held for Christ Church Parish in Midd^sx
County the 8th Day of Octob^r 1746
Prefent

Bartho. Yates Minister, Armistead Churchhill, John Robinson, Thomas Price, John Smith, Philip Grymes, Beverley
Stanard, and James Reid Gen^t

Order'd to Mr Bartho Yates Minister	16000
Churchhill Jones Clk of the Vestry	800
Henry Towls Clk. of the Middle Church	1200
Richd Steevens Clk. of the lower Chapel	1000
John Baldwin Clk. of the upper Chapel	1000
Edwd Whitaker Sexton of the Middle Church	600
Judith Baldwin Sexton of the Upper Chapel	600
Thomas Sibley Sexton of the lower Chapel	500
Elizabeth Humphries	600
Rachel Baker	800
Letice Pateman	500
Margaret Bowman	400
Mary Brooks for keeping Elenor Devol	800
William Kidd for keeping an Orphan of Wm Wallas	600
Edwd Smith for keeping two Orphans of Philip Brook's	1000
Doc^t John Bird allow'd as p^r Acco^t	168
Daniel Stringer	100
Margaret Bristow for keeping Margaret Bowman	400
Beverley Stanard allow'd as p^r Acco^t	550
Mrs Eliz^a Hardin allow'd as p^r Acco^t	140
Mr John Smith allow'd as p^r Acco^t	854
John Matthewes for work done at the Middle Church and the lower Chapel	800
Thomas Brumel for keeping an Orphan of Abraham More and Clearing the Parish of any further Charge	800
Josep Small for keeping an Orphan of Caleb Brooks and Clearing the parish of any further Charge	100
Edwd Blackburn allow'd two Levis over Charg'd last year	54
John Jones allow'd	500

Mr Barth^o for Building a Tob^o house on the Glebe		2152
The Churchwardens for Clothing Ann Ridgway		400
To Mr Yates for allowance on the Transfer Notes paid by the Coll^r in discharge of his Salary		640
To Mr Yates for Difference paid the Inspection of 17 hh^d Tob^o @ 2/6		340
To Willm Macham for two Horse Block		240
		34638
(251)	Brought over	34638
	C^r By the Coll^r	66
		34572
Cask at 4 p^r C^t on 34,572 is		1382
Salary at 6 p^r C^t on D^o is		2074
A Depositum to be accounted for next levy		339
		38367

C^r By 1323 Tithables at 29 p^d Tob^o p^r pole   38367

Order'd that John Smith & Beverley Stanard Gen^t be continued Churchwardens this Ensuing year.

Order'd that the said Churchwarden's receive 29 pounds of Tob^o p^r pole of the Several Tithables in this Parish and pay the same to the Several Creditors.

Order'd that the Church Wardens provide Cushions for the Communion Table to the Church and Each Chapel.

Barth^o Yates Minister

(252)   At a Vestry held for Christ Church Parish in Midd^sx County the 1st Day of September 1747

Prefent

Armistead Churchhill, Christopher Robinson, Henry Thacker, John Robinson, Philip Grymes, John Smith, Tho: Price & Beverley Stanard Gen^t

In pursuance of an Order of Midd^sx County Court dated the 7th Day of July 1747 This Vestry have divided this Parish into Several precincts and have appointed two Freeholders of Every

Several Precinct to Se all the lands proceſsioned within the said precinct as followeth.

Order'd that mr John Berry & mr Christopher Miller Proceſsion every Persons Land between the lower end of the County and Majr Kemp's Mill Croſs the Neck to Colo Churchhill's Creek, and the line between Churchhill and Majr Edmd Berkeley. beginning to proceſsion the Second Tuesday in October and finish the same by the last day of March next.

Order'd that mr William Owen & mr Andrew Davis Proceſsion every persons Land between Majr Kemp's Mill and the Piping Tree on the South Side of the main road beginning to proceſsion the last Tuesday in October and finish the same by the last day of March next.

Order'd that Capt John Robinson & mr Jacob Stiff Proceſsion every persons Land between Majr Kemp's Mill to the Piping Tree along mr Christopher Robinson's bounds to the river on the North Side of the Main Road beginning to Proceſsion the last Tuesday in novembr and finish the same by the last Day of March next.

Order'd that mr William Bristow & mr Edwd Bristow Proceſsion every Persons Land between the Piping Tree and Prittyman's roling Road from Rappa to Piankt beginning to Proceſsion the Second Tuesday in november & finish the same by the last Day of March next.

Order'd that mr Edward Dillard & mr William Moulson Proceſsion Ever persons Land between Prittymans roling Road and the main branch of Micklebourrough's Swamp (including the Widdow Cheedle's Plantation) on the North Side of the main Road beginning to Proceſsion the Second Tuesday in Decembr and finish the same by the last Day of March next

Order'd that mr John Murry & mr Robt Daniel Proceſsion Every persons Land between Prittymans roling Road, and the new Dragon Bridg road running from the main road to the Dragon on the South Side of the main road beginning to proceſsion the third Tuesday in Novembr and finish the same by the last day of March next.

Order'd that m^r John Meacham & m^r James Daniel Proceſsion Every persons Land between the lower end of the new Dragon Bridg road and the Briery Swamp, thence to the Millstone Valley running from the main Road to the Dragon on the South Side of Main road beginning to proceſsion the Second Tuesday in Decemb^r and finish the same by the last day of March next.

(253) Order'd that Mr James Campble & Mr George Lee Proceſsion Every person's Land between the head of Col^o Thacker's Mill-dam and the head of Parrott's Creek, thence to the millstone Valley on the North Side of the Main Road and from the said road to the river beginning to Proceſsion the Second Tuesday in November and finish the same by the last day of march next.

Order'd that m^r William Jones & m^r Henry Daniel Proceſsion Every person's Land between the Briery Swamp, and from the millstone Valley, to the Dragon Swamp and the upper End of the County, on the South Side of the main road beginning to Proceſsion the last Tuesday in november and finish the same by the last Day of March next.

Order'd that m^r William Bewford & m^r Maſsey Yarrington Proceſsion Every person's Land between the Head of Parrott's Creek and from the Millstone Valley to the upper End of the County on the north Side of the Main road. beginning to Proceſsion the Second Tuesday in December and finish the same by the last Day of March Next.

Order'd that the above said Freeholders Proceſsion Every Persons Land pursuant to the above Orders of Vestry and that they take and Return an Account of every persons Land they Shall so Proceſsion of the time when and of the Persons present at the Same and of what Land in their respective precinct they Shall fail to Proceſsion and the reason of such failure t othe next Vestry which Shall happen after the last Day of March next. And it is further Order'd that all the Freeholders of the Several Precincts above mention attend the above said Proceſsioners in their respective precincts to perform the Proceſsioning above directed. And the said Pro-

ce∫sioners are to take notice that if the Owner of any Land
Shall refuse to Suffer his or her Land to be Proce∫sion'd the
Law requires that within ten days after Such refusal they
Certifie the Same under hands to the Church Wardens of
the Parish.

A Churchhill

(254)   At a Vestry held for Christ Church Parish in Midd^{sx}
County the 1st Day of Octob^r 1747

Pre∫ent

Bartho: Yates Minister Henry Thacker, Christopher Robinson, Thomas Price, John Robinson, Ralph Wormeley, John
Smith, Philip Grymes Beverley Stanard & James Reid Gent.

	lb Tob°
Order'd to Mr Barth° Yates Minister	16000
Churchhill Jones Clk. of the Vestry	800
Henry Towles Clk. of the Middle Church	1200
Richard Steevens Clk. of the lower Chapel	1000
John Baldwin Clk. of the Upper Chapel	1000
Edward Whitaker Sexton of the Middle Church	600
Elizabeth Forget Sexton of the Upper Chapel	600
Thomas Sibley Sexton of the lower Chapel	500
Elizabeth Humphries	600
Rachel Baker	800
Margaret Bowman	400
Mary Brooks for keeping Elenor Devol two months & Burying her	400
Margaret Bristow for keeping Margaret Bowman	400
William Robinson for keeping Catharine Brook one month & Burying her	400
Mary Rylee for keeping two Orphans of Philip Brooks seven months	600
James Smith for making a Coffin for Letice Pateman	80
Doc^t John Strachey on Acco^t of Thomas Pateman	61
Mr Robt Elliot allow'd as p^r his Acco^t	165
Mr Beverley Stanard allow'd the Ball^s of his Acco^t	50
William Bristow allow'd	40
Mr John Smith allow'd the Ball^s of his Acco^t	98

Mr Ralph Wormeley his Balls for the three Surplices	1000
William Moulson allow'd	64
The Churchwardens for Cloathing Willm Humphries	400
Doct Alexander Reade allow'd his acct	374
The Churchwardens to pay Richd Wiat his Accot when the work is finished	600
The Church Wardens for Making Well at the Glebe	3500
Mr Yates for allowance on the Transfer notes paid him by the Collr in discharge of his Salary	640
To Do for Differance paid the Inspection of 17 hhd @ 2/6	340
William Kidd for keeping an Orphan of Willm Wallis	600
	33312
	lb Tobo
(255) Brought Over	33312
To Tobo to be Sold and accounted for by the Church wardens to the next Vestry, towards building a new Glebe house	10000
	43312
Cr By the Collrs Accot	1258
	42054
To Cask at 4 pr Ct on 42054 is	1682
	43736
To Salary at 6 pr Ct 43736 is	2624
A depositum to be accounted for next Levy	526
	46886
	lb Tobo
Cr By 1379 Tithables at 34 pd of Tobo pr pole	46886

Order'd that Philip Grymes & James Reid Gent be appointed Churchwardens this Ensuing year.

Order'd that the Said Churchwardens Receive 34 pds of Tobo pr pole of the Several Tithables in this Parish and pay the same to the Several Creditors.

Order'd that Mr Beverley Stanard distribute the fines that is due to the Parish being Eight pound between Patrick Callahan, John Steward, David Snodgra$\int$s, Mary Brooks, Mary Matthews, Elizabeth Elliot, and William Crowdans.

Barth^o Yates Minister

(256)   At a Vestry held for Christ Church Parish in Midd^{sx} County the 3^d Day of Octob^r 1748

Pre$\int$ent

Bartho: Yates Minister, John Grymes, Armistead Churchhill, Edmund Berkeley, Henry Thacker, Christopher Robinson Thomas Price John Smith, John Robinson James Ried Gen^t

Order'd to Mr Barth^o Yates Minister	16000
Churchhill Jones Clk. of the Vestry	800
Henry Towles Clk. of the Middle Church	1200
Richd Steevens Clk. of the lower Chapel	1000
John Baldwin Clk. of the Upper Chapel	1000
Edwd Whitaker Sexton of the Middle Church	600
Eliz^a Forget Sexton of the Upper Chapel	600
Thomas Sibley Sexton of the lower Chapel	500
Elizabeth Humphries	600
Rachel Baker	800
Margaret Bowman	400
Margaret Bristow for boarding D^o	400
Mary Rylee for keeping two Orphans of Philip Brooks	1000
Church Wardens for Cloathing William Humphries	400
Willm Kidd for keeping an Orphan of William Wallas	600
William Hackney for boarding William Humphries	400
Francis Sykes for Burying George Morhead	200
The Revd Mr Yates for allowance on Transfer notes paid him by the Coll^r in discharge of his Salary	640
To D^o for difference p^d the Inspection of 17 hh^{ds} Tob^o @ 2/6	340
John Jones	500
Mary Shaw for keeping a Basterd Child for 6 months past	500
Andrew South for the Same Service	500

Willm Robinson for keeping a Child of Richd Bor-
roskell's one year   400
John Chowning Senr for keeping two Children of
James Overstreets one year   400
Thomas Price for his acco^t Clks Fees ag^st the Church-
wardens   230
James Ried Esqr for his acco^t £1. 1. 6 @ 12/6 in Tob^o   172
Alexand^r Frazier D^o   2. 11. 2   409
Saml Batchelder   2. 1. 6   332
Randolph Segar for his acco^t after having accounted
for Depositum   52
To the Churchwardens for the Rent of the Free
school land to be employ'd towards schooling of poor
children   500
To D^o to be Sold & accounted for towards building
a new Glebe House   10000
To be Sold and accounted for towards enlarging or
Building a Galary to the lower Chapel   5000

                                                                 46475
                                                             lb Tob^o
(257)   Brought over   46475
Cask @ 4 p^r C^t on 46475 is   1859
Salary @ 6 p^r C^t for Collecting 48334   2900
a Depoſitum to be accounted for next Levy   566

                                                                 51800

C^r By 1400 Tithables @ 37 pounds of Tob^o ℔^r poll   51800

Order'd that Philip Grymes & James Ried Esq^rs be Continued Church Wardens.

Order'd that the s^d Church Wardens receive 37^l Tob^o p^r
poll of the Several Tithables in this Parish and pay the Same
to the Several Creditors.

Order'd that the Church Wardens pay Mr Adam Ried fourteen Shillings and Six pence against Anne Cain out of the
Fines this Day accounted for to the Vestry being Ten pound

fifteen Shillings and that they distribute the Remaind[r] between Henry Emberson Ruth Overſtreet Patrick Calahan,
Joseph Humphries and Mary Matthews.

Order'd that the Church Wardens take Bond of the Pur-
chaser for the Produce of the Sale of the Ten Thousand
pound of Tob° Levy'd last year.

Barth° Yates Min[r]

(258)   At a Vestry held for Christ Church Parish in Midd[sx]
County the 2[d] Day of Octob[r] 1749

Preſent

Barth° Yates Minister, Armistead Churchhill, Edmund Berkeley, Henry Thacker, Thomas Price, Ralph Wormeley, Philip
Grymes, Beverley Stanard, & James Reid Gen[t]

	lb Tob°
Order'd to M[r] Barth° Yates Minister	16000
Churchhill Jones Clk of the Vestry	800
Henry Towles Clk. of the Middle Church 4 months	400
Charles Daniel Clk. of the Middle Church 8 months	800
Rich[d] Steevens Clk of the lower Chapel	1000
John Baldwin Clk. of the upper Chapel	1000
Edw[d] Whitaker Sexton of the Middle Church	600
Elizabeth Forget Sexton of the Upper Chapel	600
Thomas Sibley Sexton of the lower Chapel	500
Elizabeth Humphries	800
The Rev[d] M[r] Yates for allowance on Transfer notes paid him by the Coll[r] in discharge of his Salary	640
To D° for Differance p[d] the Inspection of 17 hh[ds] Tob° at 2/6	340
Margaret Bowman	400
Patrick Welch for keeping a bastard Child of Mary Redman's	300
Order'd George Guest to be levy free	
Henry Seers for keeping Catharine Watts	400
William Kidd for keeping Maſsey House 2 months & Burying her	400
George Blackley for keeping D° 2 months	200
William Croudas for keeping D° 2 months	200

Margaret Bristow for Boarding Margaret Bowman	400
John Jones for two years	1000
Docter Alexander Read	1100
George Daniel	600
William Kidd for keeping an Orphant of Willm Wallas's	300
Churchwardens as p^r Acco^t	816
Order'd Henry Emberson to be levy free	
John Chowning for keeping two Orphants of James Overstreets	1000
Mary Shaw for keeping a Bastard Child one year	500
Andrew South for keeping a Bastard Child one year	500
To the Church Wardens for three Fonts	1000
To D° for the rent of the Freeschool land to be Employ'd towards Schooling of poor Children	500
To Willm Buford, John Beaman, Edward Southarn, John Lee, William Cloudas, John Berry, Thomas Dudley, John Deagle, William Owin, James Gibson and William Haley, Patrolers each 37^{lb} Tob°	407
To the Churchwardens to be sold and accounted for towards building a new Glebe House	10000
To D° for Enlarging or building a Galary to the lower Chapel	5000
To the receiver for delinquents	404
	48407
Ca{k at 4 p^r C^t on 48407 is	1936
Salary @ 6 p^r C^t on 50343 is	3020
	53363
C^r By a depositum last year	566
	52797
To Mary Rylee for keeping two Children	1000
	53797

	lb Tob°
(259) Brought Over	53797
A Depositum to be accounted for next levy	179
	53976

lb Tob°

C^r By 1384 Tithables at 39 pound of Tob° p^r pole is   53976

William Churchhill Gent is Elected Vestry Man in the Room of John Grymes Esqr

Order'd that Christopher Robinson & William Churchhill Gen^t be appointed Churchwardens.

Order'd that the said Churchwardens receive 39^lb Tob° p^r pole of the Several Tithables in this Parish and pay the Same to the Several Creditors.

Order'd that the fines that are due to the Parish being £8. 5. 0 & 200^lb Tob° be devided between Mrs Mary Blackburn (on the acco^t of Eliz^a Roberts) George Guest, Henry Emberson and Mary Matthews and the Tob° to Ruth Overstreet.

Order'd that the Churchwardens Some time next Summer agree with Workmen to Build the Glebe House.

Barth° Yates Minister

(260)   At a Vestry held for Christ Church Parish in Mid^x County the 25th day of June 1750

Present

The Revd Bartholomew Yates Min^r Armistead Churchhill. Edmund Berkeley. Henry Thacker. John Robinson. Philip Grymes. John Smith. James Reid & William Churchhill Gentlemen of the Vestry

Ordered That Robert Elliot be Clerk of the Vestry he being first sworn & that the present Clerk take the records of the Vestry into his Custody.

Ordered That the Church Wardens give Notice in the publick Gazette that on the fifteenth day of Augt next the Vestry will agree (at Urbanna with Workmen) to build a Glebe House fifty foot long from out to out thirty foot wide two Story High the Walls Brick a flat Roof without Dormans and a

Cellar Thirty foot Square the Vestry will also agree either to make a Galery or build an addition to the lower Chappel.

Copia Testatur

Barth⁰ Yates Minʳ

At a Vestry held for Christ Church Parish on Wedensday the fifteenth day of August 1750

present

Armistead Churchhill Henry Thacker Christopher Robinson Thomas Price John Robinson Ralph Wormeley Philip Grymes James Reid Beverley Stanard and William Churchhill Gentlemen of the Vestry

ordered That the Gentlemen of the Vestry meet on the fourth day of October next at the Mother Church to agree with Workmen to build a Glebe House and also a Galery or make an addition to the lower Chappel, in the Notice given it is to be inserted that a considerable part of the money will be paid to the person who agrees for the same.

Copia Testatur

A Churchhill

(261)   (Blank.)

(262)   At a Vestry held for Christ Church Parish in Middlesex County the 5ᵗʰ day of Octʳ 1750

Present

The Revᵈ Bartholomew Yates Minʳ, Henry Thacker, Christopher Robinson, John Robinson, Philip Grymes John Smith, James Reid & Beverley Stanard Genᵗ

Ordered To the Revᵈ Bartholomew Yates Minʳ	16000
To D⁰ for allowance on Transfer Notes paid him by the Collector in discharge of his Salary	640
To D⁰ for the Inspection on 17 Hogsheads @ 2/6	340
To Robert Elliot Clerk of the Vestry	800
To Charles Daniel Clerk of the Mother Church	1200
To Richard Steevens Clerk of the lower Chappel	1000
To William Chowning Clerk of the upper Chappel	1000
To Edward Whitaker Sexton of the Mother Church	600
To Elizabeth Forget Sexton of the upper Chappel	600
To Thomas Siblee Sexton of the lower Chappel	500

To Elizabeth Humphreys	500
To Patrick Welsh for keeping a Bastard Child of *M. Redman	200
To Richard Daniel for keeping Margaret Bowman	300
To Mary Shaw for keeping a Bastard Child	250
To John Steevens for D°	400
To William Robinson for keeping Thoˢ Boreskill 2 years	800
To Henry Seers for keeping Katharine Watts & Cloathing her	800
To John Jones & his Wife	800
To John Burd	300
To Mary Rylee	700
To William Cardwell for keeping Mary Overstreet	400
To Thomas Price for making out 5 Acts of Aſſembly	180
To William Moulson for delinquents	260
To D° for the Quitrents of the Glebe land	110
To Arthur Dye	600
To Samuel Batchelder	150
To Elizabeth Baden	500
To Doctor John Symmer	252
To Alexander Frazier	134
To Christopher Robinson for 6 Bottles Claret	142
To Samuel Batchelder for burying William Cooper	200
To Curtis Hardee for mending Pughs &cᵃ in the upper Chapˡ	
To Josee Gore for making Forms at the lower Chappel	100
To Richard Daniel for burying Margaret Bowman	200
To the Church Wardens to be sold and accounted for to pay for Lead & Glass for all the Churches and the Glebe House	2000
To the Rent of the free School Land	500
To Cask at 4 ℔ Ct on 33508 pounds Tob°	1340
To Receivers Salary at 6 ℔ Ct on 34848 pounds Tob°	2090
	36938

* This name is very indistinct. I may not have read it correctly.—
C. G. C.

Per	Contra	Cr
By 1387 Tithables @ 26½ᵗᵇ Tob°		36755
By a ballance due to the Collector next year		183
		36938

(263)   Ordered That William Bristow son of Edward Bristow be levy free.

Ordered That Christopher Robinson and William Churchhill Gent. be continued Church Wardens and that they receive of every Tithable twenty six pounds and a half of Tobacco.

Ordered That the fine money being £3: 10: 0 be distributed between, George Guest & Mary Matthews

Copy attested by
Barth° Yates Min.

At a Vestry held for Christ Church Parish on Teusday the 25ᵗʰ day of June 1751

Present

The Revᵈ Bartholomew Yates Min Henry Thacker, Christopher Robinson, Edmund Berkeley, John Robinson Thomas Price Philip Grymes & James Reid Gent. of the Vestry

ordered That Mourning Richards be admitted to undertake the Building of the Glebe House upon the same Terms formerly agreed to by Stephen Johnston the said Johnston having demitted in his favour and the said Richards being willing to undertake the same and give sufficient security for the performance of the said work vzᵗ Major Richard Dunstan, Capᵗ Philip Johnston Capᵗ William Richards & Capᵗ Thomas Todd the work being to be performed according to the said Richards and his Securitys Bond and Articles.

Ordered That the said Mourning Richards be allowed for making a Flush Cellar under the whole House (besides the four hundred pounds agreed to by Stephen Johnston) the sum of twenty pounds.

ordered that the whole work be under the Inspection of Capᵗ Henry Thacker, Christopher Robinson Esq & the Honᵇˡᵉ Philip Grymes Esqʳ who are hereby desired to Inspect the same.

ordered That the said Mourning Richards have the sum
of two hundred and fifty pounds paid down upon his giving
security for the performance of the said work and the full
remainder in October one thousand Seven hundred and fifty
two at which time the work is to be fully compleated.

ordered That the Church Wardens send for a Cushion,
Pulpit Cloth Communion Cloth and a Pewter Flaggon for the
use of the upper Chappel and be allowed for the same.

Copy attested by

Barth° Yates Min

(264)   At a Vestry held for Christ Church Parish in Middlesex County the 4ᵗʰ day of September 1751

Present

The Revᵈ Bartholomew Yates Minister John Robinson
Thomas Price Philip Grymes Henry Thacker, John Smith
James Reid Beverley Stanard and William Churchhill Gentˢ
of the Vestry

In pursuance of an order of Middlesex County Court dated
the Sixth day of August one thousand Seven hundred and
fifty one This Vestry have devided the Parish into several precincts and have appointed two free holders of every several
precinct to see all the Lands procefsioned within the said
precincts as followeth

Ordered That Christopher Miller & Robert Elliot procefsion
every persons Land between the lower end of the County and
Robert Elliots Mill crofs the Neck to Col° Churchhills Creek
and the line between the said Churchhill and Col° Berkeley
begining to procefsion the Second Tuesday in October and
finish the same by the last day of March next.

Ordered That William Owen & John Smith Gent procefs
procefsion every persons Land between Robert Elliots Mill
and the piping Tree on the South side of the Main Road begining to procefsion the second Teusday in October and finish
the same by the last day of March next.

Ordered That John Robinson & Jacob Stiff procefsion every
persons Land between Robert Elliots Mill to the piping Tree
along James Scrosbys bounds to the River on the North side

of the Main Road begining to proceſsion the last Teusday
in November and finish the same by the last day of March
next.

Ordered That William Bristow & Edward Bristow proceſsion every persons Land between the Piping Tree and Prettymans Roleing Road from Rappahanock to Pyankitank begining
to proceſsion the second Teusday in November and finish the
same by the last day of March next.

Ordered That Edward Dillard & Henry Meikleborough proceſsion every persons Land between Prettymans Roleing Road
and the Main Branch of Meikleboroughs Swamp (including the
Widow Cheedles Plantation) on the north side of the Main
Road begining to proceſsion the second Teusday in December
and finish the same by the last day of March next.

(265)   ordered That John Murray & John Batcheldor proceſsion every persons Land between Prettymans Roleing Road
and the new Dragon Bridge Road runing from the Main Road
to the Dragon on the South side of the Main Road begining
to proceſsion on the third Teusday in November and finish
the same by the last day of March next.

Ordered That John Machen & James Daniel proceſsion
every persons Land between the lower end of the new Dragon
Bridge Road and the Briery Swamp thence to the Millstone
Valley runing from the Main Road to the Dragon on the
south side of the main Road begining to proceſsion the second
Teusday in December and finish the same by the last day of
March next.

ordered That George Lee & John Jackson proceſsion every
persons Land between the head of Colº Thackers Mill Dam and
the head of Parrots Creek thence to the Millstone Valley on
the north side of the Main Road and from the said Road to
the River begining to proceſsion the second Teusday of November and finish the same by the last day of March next.

ordered That Henry Daniel & Lewis Mountague proceſsion
every persons Land between the Briery Swamp and from the
Millstone Valley to the Dragon Swamp and the upper end
of the County on the South side of the Main Road begining

to proceſsion the last Teusday in November and finish the same by the last day of March next.

ordered That William Bewford & George Fearn proceſsion every persons Land between the head of Parrots Creek and from the Millstone Valley to the upper end of the County on the north side of the Main Road begining to proceſsion the second Teusday in December and finish the same by the last day of March next.

ordered That the above said Freeholders proceſsion every persons Land pursuant to the said orders of Vestry and that they take and return an account of every persons Land they shall so proceſsion of the time when and the persons present at the same and of what Land in their respective precinct they shall fail to proceſsion and the reason of such failure to the next Vestry which shall happen after the last day of March next.

(266) and it is further ordered that all the freeholders of the several precincts abovementioned attend the above said proceſsioners in their Respective precincts to perform the proceſsioning above directed and the said proceſsioners are to take notice that if the owner of any Land shall refuse to suffer his or her Land to be proceſsioned the Law requires that within ten days after such refusal they certify the same under their hands to the Church wardens of the Parish.

Barth° Yates Min^r

(267) At A Vestry held for Christ Church Parish in Middlesex County the 2^d day of October 1751

Present

Henry Thacker, Christopher Robinson, Edmund Berkeley, John Robinson Thomas Price, Philip Grymes, James Reid & John Smith Gent^s of the Vestry

Ordered	pounds of Tobacco
To the Revd Mr Bartholomew Yates	16000
To D^o for allowance on Transfer Notes paid by the Collector	640
To Robert Elliot Clerk of the Vestry	800
To Thomas Laughlin Clerk of the Mother Church	1200

To Richard Steevens Clerk of the lower Chappel   1000
To William Chowning Clerk of the Upper Chappel   1000
To Edward Whitaker Sexton of the Mother Church   600
To Thomas Siblee Sexton of the lower Chappel   500
To the Churchwardens for a ballance last year due to
them   183
To D° to be sold for discharge of the Glebe House
when finished   20000
To the Sexton of the upper Chappel   600
To Doctor Alexander Reade, in discharge of his ac-
count   1500
To Harry Seers for keeping Katharine Watts &
cloathing her   800
To James Reid Esqʳ his accᵗ   290
To Constant Hardee for keeping Alice Brooks   500
To the Sexton of the lower Chappel for mending
the Cushions   100
To Rebekah Hiptinstal for keeping Margaret Simpson   600
To John Bird   300
To William Robinson for keeping Thomas Boreskel
& releiving the Parish from any further charge   400
To Charles Forget for taking care of Margᵗ & Sarah
Emberson   500
To Ruth Overstreet for taking care of & burying
Jane Emberson   300
To Elizabeth Humphreys   500
To John Jones   500
To Mary Rylee for keeping two Orphans of Philip
Brookes   700
To William Cardwell for keeping Mary Overstreet   400
To Arthur Dye   600
To the Rent of the free school Land   500
To the Sherif for the Qᵗ Rents of the free school Land   110
To William Moulson for delinquents   79
To Alexander Murray for mending the Clerks Desk   50
To Cask at 4 ℔ cᵗ on 51,242 pounds of Tobacco   2049
To Receivers Salary at 6 ℔ Cᵗ   3197

To depositum to be accounted for next year   800

                                                    57288

℔ Contra   Cr

By 1364 Tithables at 42 pounds Tob° ℔ pole   57288

ordered That Christopher Robinson Esqʳ account with the next Churchwardens for the ballance of two thousand pounds of Tobacco levied (last year) for Lead and Glaſs for the Glebe and Churches the ballance being nine pounds & three pence half penny of which one pounds eleven shillings and eight pence is to be applyed toward Schooling poor Children.

                        turn over

(268)   ordered At the same Vestry as on the other side that Robert Elliot and Thomas Price pay unto the Churchwardens the money in their hands for Tobacco sold for building a Glebe House, Elliots sum being fifty eight pounds Seventeen shillings and ten pence, and Prices Sixty eight pounds fourteen shillings and four pence.

ordered That the fine money being two pounds ten shillings in the hands of James Daniel be divided between Ann Cain & Mary Matthews.

ordered That Armistead Churchhill and Henry Thacker Gentˢ be appointed Church wardens for the ensuing year and that they receive of every Tithable in this Parish forty two pounds of Tobacco.   Henry Thacker

(269)   At a Vestry held for Christ Church Parish in Middlesex County the 4ᵗʰ day of October 1752

                        Present

The Revᵈ Mʳ Bartholomew Yates Min. Henry Thacker Christopher Robinson, Edmund Berkeley Thomas Price Ralph Wormeley John Robinson Philip Grymes Esqʳ James Reid Esqʳ & John Smith Gentˢ of the Vestry

Ordered

To The Revᵈ Mʳ Barthᵒ Yates	16000
To Dᵒ for allowance on Transfer Notes	640
To Robert Elliot Clerk of the Vestry	800
To Thomas Laughlin Clerk of the Mother Church	1200

To Richard Steevens Clerk of the Lower Chappel   1000
To William Chowning Clerk of the upper Chappel   1000
To Edward Whitaker Sexton of the Middle Church   600
To Thomas Siblee Sexton of the lower Chapple   500
To the Sexton of the Upper Chapple   600
To the Rent of the free school Land   500
To the Sherif for the Quitrents of D°   110
To James Reid Esqr 168
To Alexander Frazier   144
To Capt Henry Thacker   100
To Doct^r Strachey   340
To Doct^r Reade   1658
To Joseph Holloway   688
To Harry Seers for keeping & Clothing Katharine
Watts   800
To Constant Hardee for keeping Alice Brookes   600
To Rebekah Hiptinstal for keeping Margaret Symson   600
To John Bird   600
To Ruth Overstreet for keeping Mary Overstreet   400
To Elizabeth Humphries   500
To Mary Rilee for keeping two Orphans of P:
Brookes   700
To Arthur Dye   600
To John Deagle for keeping an Orphan of H. Baden.
To D° for keeping an Orphan of John Steevens
one year   600
To the Widow Baden   800
To Thomas Pateman   600
To John Loyal   600
To Thomas Price out of the depositum as ℔ his acc^t 240½
To John Davis   602

    34650
To 4 ℔ Ct on 34650 for Cask   1386
To 6 ℔ C^t on 36036 for Collecting   2162

           Carried over   38198

(270)   At the same Vestry as on the other side

Christ Church Parish   D^r lb^s Tob^o

To sundry charges as on the opposite side   38198

                        Contra   C^r

By the last years depositum & Cask   832

By 1336 Tithables at 28½ ₩ pole   38076

By a depositum to be accounted for at laying the

next Levy   710

                                                           39618

Ordered that Henry Washington be Vestryman in the Room of Beverley Stanard removed out of the County.

Ordered That Armistead Churchhill & Henry Thacker Gent^s be continued Church Wardens for the ensuing year and that they receive of every Tithable 28½ pounds of Tobacco also that they receive the respective Ballances due from Robert Elliot and Thomas Price out of which money and that in the hands of John Smith & Col^o Churchhill Mourning Richards is to be paid a further sum of Seventy five pounds towards the Glebe House and the remainder to be accounted for at next Vestry.

Ordered That the Church Wardens take Bond and security of Thos Price for value of fourteen thousand six hundred and twenty one pounds of Tob^o at fourteen shillings and six pence ₩ hundred levied last year and the same to be accounted for to the Vestry./

                                        Barth^o Yates Min^r

(271)   At a Vestry held for Christ Church Parish in Middlesex on Monday the 4th day of June 1753

                        Present

The Revd Bartholomew Yates Min   James Reid

Armistead Churchill   Christopher Robinson

Thomas Price   John Smith

Philip Grymes   William Churchhill

                Gentlemen of the Vestry

ordered That the Churchwardens Immediately receive of Capt Thomas Price the sum of Thirty Seven pounds four

Shillings and three pence and of Armistead Churchhill Esqr the sum of forty three pounds nine shillings and Seven pence out of which sums they are to pay Mourning Richards Sixty eight pounds three shillings and one penny it being the ballance of Seventy five pounds (ordered to be paid him at a Vestry held for Middlesex County October the fourth one thousand Seven hundred and fifty two) as appears by his receipts now produced in Vestry.

Ordered also that the Church Wardens account for the Cash now in their hands being four pounds thirteen shillings and ten pence to the next Vestry and that it be remembered that the money formerly mentioned to be in the hands of John Smith Gent is included in Col° Churchhills sum of forty three pounds nine shillings and seven pence and the money mentioned in the hands of Robert Elliot is also included in the account of Capt Thomas Price for thirty seven pounds four shillings and three pence.

Barth° Yates Min^r

(272)   At a Vestry held for Christ Church Parish in Middlesex County the fifth day of October in the Year of our Lord one thousand Seven hundred and fifty three

Present
The Revd Bartholomew Yates Min

Henry Thacker	Ralph Wormeley
Christopher Robinson	Philip Grymes
Edmund Berkeley	James Reid
Thomas Price	William Churchhill
John Robinson	& Henry Washington

Gentlemen of the Vestry

Henry Washington Gent. having taken the Oaths appointed by Law and Subscribed to be conformable to the Doctrine of the Church of England took his Place as one of the Vestry.

Ordered	lb Tob°
To the Rev^r Bartholomew Yates Minister	16000
To D° for allowance on Transfer Notes	640
To Robert Elliot Clerk of the Vestry	1000
To Thomas Laughlin Clerk of the Mother Church	1200

To Richard Steevens Clerk of the lower Chappel   1000
To William Chowning Clerk of the Upper Chappel   1000
To Edward Whitaker Sexton of the Middle Church   600
To Thomas Siblee Sexton of the lower Chappel   500
To The Sexton of the Upper Chappel   600
To the Rent of the Free School Land   500
To the Sheriff for the Quitrents of D⁰   110
To James Reid Esq   750
To Doctor Alexander Reade   782
To Elizabeth Humphreys   500
To Alexander Frazier   350
To Elizabeth Baden   800
To Richard Wiat for making & mending the windows
of the Upper Chappel   200
To Thomas Siblee for keeping Thomas Roberts   240
To Armistead & William Churchhill Esqʳˢ   1150
To John Bird   600
To John Deagle for keeping John Steevens & to be
allowed no more   600
To Ann Grifsum for keeping Elizabeth Baden   800
To Harry Seers for keeping Katharine Watts one year   800
To James Hiptinstal for keeping Margaret Symson   600
To Constant Hardee for keeping Alice Brooks   600
To Ann Caine   500
                                                      _____
                        Carried over   32422

(273)   Ordered At the same Vestry as on the other side,
as follows vizᵗ   lb Tob⁰
To sundrys brought forward   32422
To Arthur Dye   600
To John Lyal   600
To George Daniel for Horse blocks & hanging Gates   200
To Capᵗ John Robinson in part for building a Stable   1800
                                                      _____
                                                        35622
To 4 ℔ Cᵗ for Cask on 35622 pounds Tob⁰   1424
To 6 ℔ Cᵗ for Collecting upon 37046 pounds D⁰   2222
                                                      _____
                                                        39268

℔   Contra   Cʳ
By Tobacco due from the Receiver as ℔ Moul-
sons account   559
By 1365 Tithables at 28 pounds Tobacco ℔ poll   39200
                                                    ──────
                                                     39759

Ordered That John Robinson and Henry Washington Gentˢ
be appointed Church Wardens for the ensuing year and that
they receive of every Tithable within this Parish twenty eight
pounds of Tobacco and that they account for a depositum of
four hundred and ninety pounds of Tobacco at the laying of
the next Levey.

Ordered That the Church Wardens receive of Capᵗ Thomas
Price the sum of fourteen pounds in part of his Bond and pay
the same to Capᵗ John Robinson in full for building a Stable
at the Glebe.

Ordered That the fine money in the hands of Capᵗ Henry
Thacker being fifty Shillings be given to Charles Forget.

                              Barthᵒ Yates Minʳ

(274)   At a Vestry held for Middlesex County being Christ
Church Parish the 1ˢᵗ day of April 1754
                         Present
          The Revᵈ Bartholomew Yates Minister

Henry Thacker   John Robinson
Christopher Robinson   James Reid   Gentˢ of the
Edmund Berkeley   John Smith   Vestry
                        Henry Washington

Ordered That the sum of eighty eight pounds three shillings
and a penny the ballance due to Mourning Richards for building the Glebe House be paid into the hands of the Church
Wardens as soon as the said House be finished and that they
pay the said Sum to the said Richards or his orders and take
his receipt in full for the same no orders to be accepted but
for Materials & provisions that are contracted for after the
date of Meʃsʳˢ Tunstalls and Johnsons Letters to the Vestry
bearing date Janʳʸ 29ᵗʰ & 30ᵗʰ 1754.

                              Barthᵒ Yates Min

(275)   At a Vestry held for Christ Church Parish in Middlesex County on the 2ᵈ day of October 1754
Present
The Revᵈ Bartholomew Yates Minʳ

Henry Thacker	Ralph Wormeley	
Christopher Robinson	Philip Grymes	Gentˢ of the
Edmund Berkeley	James Reid	
Thomas Price	John Smith	Vestry
John Robinson	Henry Washington	

Ordered

	lbˢ Tobacco
To the Revᵈ Bartholomew Yates	16000
To Dᵒ for allowance on Transfer Notes	640
To Robert Elliot Clerk of the Vestry	1000
To Thomas Laughlin Clerk of the Middle Church	1200
To Richard Steevens Dᵒ of the Lower Chappel	1000
To William Chowning Dᵒ of the Upper Chappel	1000
To Edward Whitaker Sexton of the Middle Church	600
To Thomas Sible Dᵒ of the lower Chappel	500
To Elizabeth Forget Dᵒ of the upper Chappel	600
To the Rent of the free School	500
To the Sherif for the Quitrents of Ditto	110
To Doctor Alexander Reade ℔ account	1370
To Elizabeth Baden	800

To Mourning Richards 180 pounds besides the 420 formerly paid him to be accounted for in Tobacco at 12/6 ℔ hundred when the Glebe House is compleatly finished & delivered & the Church Wardens relieved from their engagements to see the several accounts by them accepted paid & the Tobacco Collected   29000

To Henry Washington Gent	400

To John Robinson to pay James Reid & John Smith Gentˢ   1100

To Doctor John Symmer ℔ account	1400
To George Daniel for Blocks &cᵃ	600

To Mourning Richards for making a Door for the Middle Church &cᵃ   650

To Elizabeth Baden	1000

To John Bird	800
To Harry Seers for keeping Katharine Watts	800
To James Hiptinstal for keeping Margaret Symson to the last	600
To Elizabeth Forget for keeping Alice Brookes	600
To Ann Caine	500
To John Smith Adcock	200
To Arthur Dye	600
To John Lyal	600
To John Brim	450
To John Deacon for burying Thomas Meeks	300
To John Kilshaw for keeping John Steevens & burying him	600
To the Sherif for Delinquents	210
	65680
To 4 ℔ Cent for Cask	2627
To 6 ℔ Cent for Collecting	4098
	72405

Contra   Cr

By 1427 Tithables @ 50 pounds Tobᵒ ℔ poll	72777

Carried over

(276)   At the same Vestry as on the other side.

Ordered That John Robinson and Henry Washington Genᵗ be continued Church Wardens for the ensuing year and that they receive of every Tithable person in this Parish fifty pounds of Tobacco and account for the same and also for a depositum of three hundred & Seventy two pounds of Tobacco at the laying of the next Levy they having entered into Bond with security for performing the same.

That Henry Thacker Christopher Robinson and John Robinson Gentˢ receive the Glebe House when compleatly finished according to Mourning Richardss Bond and agreement.

That the fine money in the hands of William Moulson & Henry Washington being £ 5. 5 be devided between John Brim Ralph Watts & Charles Forget.

That no accounts be received except they be first settled & adjusted by the Church Wardens and attested by them.

Barth° Yates Min

At a Vestry Held for Christ Church Parish in Middlesex County the 1 day of September 1755

Present

The Rev⁴ Bartholomew Yates Min, Christopher Robinson, Thomas Price, John Robinson Ralph Wormeley, Philip Grymes, John Smith, James Reid William Churchhill & Henry Washington Gentlemen of the Vestry

In pursuance of an order of Middlesex County Court dated the 1ˢᵗ day of July 1755.

The Vestry have devided the Parish into several precincts and have appointed two Freeholders in every precinct to see all the Lands within the same proceſsioned as follows.

Ordered That Christopher Miller & Needles Hill proceſsion every persons Land between the lower end of the County and Robert Elliots Mill croſs the Neck to Col° Churchhills Creek and the line between the said Churchhill and Col° Berkeley begining to proceſsion the second Teusday in October and finish the same by the last day of March next.

That William Owen & John Smith Esq proceſsion every persons Land between Robert Elliots Mill and the Piping Tree on the south side of the Main Road begining to proceſsion the second Teusday in October and finish the same by the last day of March next.

That Majʳ John Robinson & Mʳ William Churchhill proceſsion every persons Land between Robert Elliots Mill to the Piping Tree along James Scrosbys bounds to the River on the North side of the Main Road begining to proceſsion the second Teusday in October and finish the same by the last day of March next.

That William Bristow & Thomas Laughlin proceſsion every persons Land between the Piping Tree and Prettymans Roling Road from Rappahannock to Pyankitank begining to proceſsion the second Teusday in October and finish the same by the last day of March next.

(277) Ordered That Henry Meikleborough & William Machen procefsion every persons Land between Prettymans Roling Road and the main branch of Meikleboroughs Swamp including the Widow Cheedles Plantation on the North side of the Main Road begining to procefsion the second Tuesday in October and finish the same by the last day of March next.

That John Murray & Robert Daniel procefsion every persons Land between Prettymans Roling Road and the new Dragon Bridge Road runing from the Main Road to the Dragon on the South side of the main Road begining to procefsion the second Tuesday in October and finish the same by the last day of March next.

That John Machen & William Daniel procefsion every persons Land from the lower end of the new Dragon Bridge Road and the Briery Swamp thence to the Millstone Valey runing from the Main Road to the Dragon on the South side of the Main Road begining to procefsion the second Tuesday in November and finish the same by the last day of March next.

That George Lee and John Mountague procefsion every persons Land between the head of Capt Henry Washingtons Mill Dam and the head of Parrots Creek thence to the Mill stone Valey on the North side of the Main Road and from the said Road to the River begining to procefsion the second Tuesday in October and finish the same by the last day of March next.

That Lewis Montague & John Bryant procefsion every persons Land between the Briery Swamp and from the Mill stone Valey to the Dragon Swamp and the Upper end of the County on the South side of the Main Road begining to procefsion the second Tuesday in November and finish the same by the last day of March.

That George Fearn & James M^{c}hann procefsion every persons Land between the head of Parrots Creek and the Mill stone Valey to the upper end of the County on the North side of the Main Road begining to procefsion the second Teusday in October and finish the same by the last day of March next.

That the above said Free holders procefsion every persons
Land pursuant to the said Orders of Vestry and that they
take and return an account of every persons Land they shall
so procefsion of the time when and the persons present at the
same and of what Lands in their respective precincts they
shall fail to procefsion and the reason of such failure to the
next Vestry which shall happen after the last day of March
next (278) and it is further ordered that all the free holders
of the several precincts before mentioned attend the said procefsioners mentioned before in their respective precincts to
perform the procefsioning above directed and the said procefsioners are to take Notice that if the Owner of any Land
shall refuse to suffer his or her Land to be procefsioned the
Law requires that within ten days after such refusal they
certify the same under their hands to the Church Wardens
of the Parish.

Barthᵒ Yates Minʳ

At a Vestry held for Christ Church Parish in Middlesex
County the first day of September one thousand Seven hundred and fifty five

Ordered

To the Revᵈ Bartholomew Yates	16000
To Dᵒ for allowance on Transfer Notes	640
To Robert Elliot Clerk of the Vestry	1000
To Thomas Laughlin Clerk of the Middle Church	1200
To Richard Steevens Clerk of the lower Chappel	1000
To William Chowning Clerk of the Upper Chappel	1000
To Edward Whitaker Sexton of the Middle Church	600
To Thomas Siblee Sexton of the lower Chappel	500
To Elizabeth Forget Sexton of the Upper Chappel	600
To the Rent of the free school Land	500
To the Quitrents of Ditto	110
To Elizabeth Humphreys	500
To John Bird	800
To Ann Caine	500
To Arthur Dye	600
To John Lyal	600

To John Bream for keeping his Daugh^rs Child	450
To John Smith Adcock	200
To Thomas Pateman	500
To Mary Brookes for keeping Elizabeth Dobbins	800
To Edward Ware for burying Ann Thomson	100
To Henry Seers for keeping Katharine Watts	800
To Elizabeth Gest	200
To Ralph Watts Sen.	250
To Doctor Alexander Read	495
To Alexander Frazier	122
To Mr John Smith	189
To Mr James Reid	380
To Constant Hardee for keeping Alice Brookes	600
To Robert Elliot ballance of Delinquents	28
To Doctor John Symmer	1550
To Thomas Brummel for keeping Eliz^a Baden	416

	33220
To 4 ꝑ Cent for Cask	1328¾

	34548¾
To 6 ꝑ Cent for Collecting	2073

	36621

Contra   C^r

By 1432 Tithables @ 26 each   37232

(279)   Ordered That Col° Edmund Berkeley and Capt Thomas Price be appointed Church Wardens for the ensuing Year and that they receive of every Tithable person within this Parish 26 pounds of Tobacco and pay the same to the respective Creditors and also that they account for a depositum of 611 pounds of Tobacco at the laying of the next Levey they first entering into Bond for the performance of the same.

Ordered That John McNeal be allowed out of the Depositum fifty pounds of Tobacco it appearing to the Vestry he was twice listed as a Tithable last year.

Ordered That Capt Thomas Price be allowed also out of the depositum fifty four pounds of Tobacco for making out Copies of the Lists of Tythables.

Ordered That the fine money being fifty shillings in the hands of Robert Elliot for Jean Kellys fine be devided between John Bream Senr & charles Forget.

Ordered That the Church Wardens let the money left by Col° William Churchhill for the use of this Parish (now in the hands of Capt Thomas Price) to Interest.

Barth° Yates Min^r

(280)   At a Vestry held for Christ Church Parish in Middlesex County the 6th day of October 1756

Present

The Revd Bartholomew Yates Minister

Henry Thacker	Armistead Churchhill	
Christopher Robinson	Philip Grymes	
Edmund Berkeley	James Reid	Gentlemen of
Thomas Price	Henry Washington	the Vestry
John Robinson		

Ordered	lb Tob°
To the Revd Bartholomew Yates	16000
To Ditto for allowance on Transfer Notes	640
To Robert Elliot Clerk of the Vestry	1000
To Thomas Laughlin Clerk of the middle Church	1200
To Richard Steevens Clerk of the lower Chappel	1000
To William Chowning Clerk of the Upper Chappel	1000
To Edward Whitaker Sexton of the Middle Church	600
To Thomas Siblee Sexton of the lower Chappel	500
To Elizabeth Forget Sexton of the Upper Chappel	600
To the Rent of the Free School	500
To the Sherif for the Quitrents of Ditto	110
To Elizabeth Humphreys	600
To John Bird	800
To Arthur Dye	600
To John Bream Senr	600
To John Loyal	400
To John Smith Adcock	200

To Elizabeth Gest	200
To Thomas Pateman	500
To Mary Brookes for keeping Elizabeth Dobbins	800
To Henry Seers for keeping Katharine Watts	800
To Ralph Watts Senr	250
To Constant Hardee for keeping Alice Brookes	600
To Elizabeth Wood for keeping John Spotiswood 7 months	350
To James Hiptinstal for William Bests Levey	26
To William Hackney for his Negroe George twice listed	26
To John Lewis being a patroler	26
To James Gardner one Levey	26
To Elizabeth Hackney for keeping John Holmes	180
To Christopher Miller for making a Coffin and burying John Holmes	108
To Richard Wyat for mending the upper Chappel Windows & Glebe	216
To James Reid ℔ account	1023
To Doctor Alexander Reade ℔ his account	1282
To Major John Robinson for mending the middle Church windows	60
To Capt Henry Washington for Lead & Glaſs	21
(281) Orders of the Vestry as on the other side continued	32244
To Col^o Edmund Berkeley for John Raffes Children	300
	32544
To 4 ℔ Cent for Cask	1301¾
	33845¾
To 6 ℔ Cent for collecting	2030¾
	35876½
Contra C^r	
By last years depositum	507
By 1475 Tithes at 24 pounds Tobacco each	35400½
	35907½

Ordered That Col⁰ Edmund Berkeley & Capt Thomas Price be continued Church Wardens for the ensuing year and that they receive of every Tithable person within this Parish twenty four pounds of Tobacco and pay the same to the Respective Parish Creditors and also that they account for a depositum of thirty one pounds of Tobacco at the laying of the next levey they first entering into Bond for the performance of the said office.

Ordered That the Church Wardens view the Kitchin & Dairy at the Glebe and employ Workmen to either repair the same or build new ones as they shall think proper.

Ordered That the Church Wardens send for three Prayer Books for the use of the Churches and also that they buy a new Register Book.

Barth⁰ Yates Min^r

(282)   At A Vestry held for Christ Church Parish in Middlesex County the 5th day of October 1757

Present

The Revd Bartholomew Yates Min^r Armistead Churchhill Henry Thacker Edmund Berkeley Christopher Robinson Thomas Price John Robinson Philip Grymes James Reid and John Smith Gentlemen of the Vestry

	lb Tob⁰
Ordered	
To the Revd Bartholomew Yates	16000
To Ditto for allowance on Transfer Notes	640
To Robert Elliot Clerk of the Vestry	1000
To Thomas Laughlin Clerk of the middle Church	1200
To Richard Steevens Clerk of the lower Chappel	1000
To William Chowning Clerk of the Upper Chappel	1000
To Edward Whitaker Sexton of the Middle Church	600
To Thomas Siblee Sexton of the lower Chappel	500
To Elizabeth Forget Sexton of the Upper Chappel	600
To the Rent of the Free School Land	500
To the Sherif for the Quitrents of Ditto	110
To Elizabeth Humphreys	600
To John Bird	800
To Arthur Dye	600

To Thomas Pateman	500
To Mary Brookes for keeping Elizabeth Dobbins	800
To John Bream for keeping Richard Bream	600
To John Loyal	400
To John Adcock Smith	200
To Henry Seers for keeping Katharine Watts	800
To Ralph Watts Senr	250
To James Daniel for account of Ralph Watts	158
To Constant Hardee for keeping Alice Brookes	600
To Elizabeth Wood for keeping John Spotiswood	350
To James Reid ℔ account	984
To Alexander Frazier ℔ Ditto	196
To Judith Brummell for keeping John Palmer	350
To Robert Elliot for delinquents	417
To Doctor Alexander Reade ℔	327
To Francis Potter for keeping John *Uriee	300
To William Moulson for delinquents	233
To John Hardee for keeping a Child of John Sanders's	50
To John Fox for keeping Ann Cotes & paying the Midwife	250
To Col° Edmund Berkeley for a Coffin & burying Ann Ruffe	108
To John Greenwood William Daniel & Charles Lee Patrolers 24 each	72
To William Bristow Ditto	26
To Edward Bristow Ditto	26
To John Deacon for keeping an Orphan Child of Robert Bonds	250
To John Lewis attorney for sundry fees	400
To be leavied and sold to pay Maj^r Robinsons acc^t being £51. 1. 0 and the overplus for Repairs done to the upper Chappel to T: Price	7000
	36797

* Note. This name is hard to decipher. I may have read it incorrectly.—C. G. C.

lb Tob°

(283)   At a Vestry held as on the Other side to sundrys brought forward   36797
Ordered To the Estate of Samuel Batcheldor Deceased for work done at the Middle Church   246
To Cap⁺ Thomas Price for two years Lists of Tithables   108

                                                        37151
To 4 ℔ C⁺ for Cask   1486

                                                        38637
To 6 ℔ C⁺ for Collecting   2318

                                                        40955
                Contra   C⁻
By 1446 Tithables @ 28½ pounds of Tobacco each   41211
Ordered That Ralph Wormeley and John Smith Gent⁵ be
appointed Church Wardens for the ensuing year and that
they Collect from every Tithable person in this Parish twenty
eight and a half pounds of Tobacco and pay the same to the
several persons for whom it is ordered and also that they account for a depositum of two hundred and fifty six pounds
of Tobacco at the laying of the next Levey they entering into
Bond for the performance of the said Office.

Ordered That the Church Wardens view the Kitchin at the
Glebe and either repair the old Dwelling House or agree with
Workmen to build a new one as they shall think proper.

Ordered That the Church Wardens send for three Prayer
Books for the use of the Churches and also that they buy a
new Register Book.

Ordered That the Church Wardens take Bond and security
in behalf of the Vestry for the money left by Col° William
Churchhill for the use of the Parish.

                            Barth° Yates Min⁻

N. B. Some mistakes having been made in the addition
and for other reasons the Vestry appointed another day for

their meeting to lay the Levey as is done on the other side which see.

(284) At a Vestry held for Christ Church Parish in Middlesex County the 1ˢᵗ day of Novʳ 1757

present

The Revᵈ Bartholomew Yates Henry Thacker Edmund Berkeley, Christopher Robinson Thomas Price John Robinson James Reid William Churchhill and Henry Washington Gentlemen of the Vestry

Ordered	lb Tob°
To the Revᵈ Bartholomew Yates	16000
To Ditto for allowance on Transfer Notes	640
To Robert Elliot Clerk of the Vestry	1000
To Thomas Laughlin Clerk of the Mother Church	1200
To Royal Richard *Steevens Clerk of the lower Chappell	1000
To William Chowning Clerk of the Upper Chappell	1000
To Edward Whittaker Sexton of the Mother Church	600
To Thomas Siblee Sexton of the lower Chappell	500
To Elizabeth Forget Sexton of the upper Chappell	600
To the Rent of the free School Land	500
To the Sherif for the Quitrents of Ditto	110
To Elizabeth Humphreys	600
To John Bird	800
To Arthur Dye	600
To Thomas Pateman	800
To Mary Brooks for keeping Elizabeth Dobbins	800
To John Bream for keeping Richard Bream	600
To John Loyal	400
To John Adcock Smith	200
To Henry Seers for keeping Katharine Watts	800
To Ralph Watts Senʳ	250
To James Daniel for Account of Ralph Watts in Cash £ 1 ‖ 16 ‖ 5	218
To Constant Hardee for keeping Alice Brookes	600

* Note. Under the word Steevens can be read (with some difficulty) the name Allen.—C. G. C.

To Elizabeth Wood for keeping John Spotiswood   700
To James Reid for Account in Cash £ 7 || 18 || o   948
To Alexander Frazier ⅌ Ditto   1 || 11 || 11   192
To Judith Brummell for keeping John Palmer   350
To Robert Elliot for Delinquents   417
To Doctor Alexander Reade £ 3 || 1 || 6   369
To Francis Potter for keeping John Urie   300
To William Moulson for Delinquents   233
To John Hardee for keeping a Child of John Sanders's   50
To John Fox for keeping Ann Cotes & paying the
Midwife   250
To Col⁰ Edmund Berkeley for making a Coffin &
burying Ann Ruffe   108
To John Greenwood William Daniel & Charles Lee
patrolers each 24   72
To William and Edward Bristow 26 each   52
To John Deacon for keeping an Orphan Child of
Robert Bonds   250
To John Lewis Attorney for sundry fees   400
To be levied & sold to pay Major John Robinson for
shingling the lower Chappell £ 51 || 1 || o & the Church
Wardens to pay the ballance for repairs done the Upper
Chappell   7000
To the Estate of Samuel Batcheldor Deceased   246
To Capᵗ Thomas Price for 2 years Lists of Tithables   108
                                                      ─────
                                                     41863
                                                   lb Tob⁰

(285)   Ordered as on the Other side brought forward 41863
To 4 ⅌ Cᵗ on the above for Cask   1674
To 6 ⅌ Cᵗ for Collecting   2612
                                                      ─────
                                                     46149
              Contra   Cʳ
By 1446 Tithes @ 32 pounds of Tobacco each   46272
Ordered That Ralph Wormeley & John Smith Gentlemen
be appointed Church Wardens for the ensuing Year and that

they receive from every Tithable person in this Parish thirty two pounds of Tobacco and pay the same to the sundry Creditors for whom it is levied and also that they Account to the Vestry at laying the next Levey for a depositum of one hundred and twenty three pounds of Tobacco they entering into Bond for the performance of the said office.

Ordered That the Church Wardens view the Kitchin at the Glebe & either repair the old Dwelling House for a Kitchin or agree with Workmen to build a New one as they shall think proper.

Ordered That the Church Wardens send for three prayer Books for the use of the Churches and also that they buy a New Register Book.

Ordered That the Church Wardens take Bond and Security in behalf of the Vestry for the Money left by Colo William Churchhill for the use of the Parish.

Bartho Yates Minr

Truly copied by Robert Elliot Clerk of the Vestry.

(286)   At a Vestry held for Christ Church Parish in Middlesex County the 4th day of October 1758

Present

[One inch of blank space here.—C. G. C.]

In pursuance of an order of Middlesex County Court dated [Date not given.—C. G. C.]

The Vestry have devided the Parish into several Precincts and have appointed two Freeholders in every Precinct to see all the lands within the same procefsioned as follows.

Ordered That [This and the following blank spaces are blank in the original.—C. G. C.] procefsion every persons Land between the lower end of the County and Robert Elliots Mill crofs the Neck to Colo Churchhills Creek and the line between the said Churchhill and Colo Berkeley begining to procefsion the second Teusday in October and finish the same by the last day of March next.

Ordered That [   ] procefsion every persons Land between Robert Elliots Mill and the piping Tree on the south side of the Main Road begining to procefsion the last Teusday in October and finish the same by the last day of March next.

Ordered That [   ] proceſsion every persons Land from Robert Elliots Mill to the Piping Tree along James Scrosbys bounds to the River on the North side of the Main Road begining to proceſsion the last Teusday in November and and finish the same by the last of March next.

Ordered That [   ] proceſsion every Persons Land from the Piping Tree and Prettymans Rolling Road from Rappahanock to Pyankitank begining to proceſsion the second Teusday in November and finish the same by the last day of March next.

Ordered That [   ] proceſsion every persons Land from Prettymans Rolling Road and the Main Branch of Mickleboroughs Swamp including the widow Cheedles's Plantation on the North side of the Main Road begining to proceſsion the second Teusday in October and finish the same by the last day of March next.

Ordered That [   ] proceſsion every persons Land from Prettymans Rolling Road and the New Dragon Bridge Road runing from the Main Road to the Dragon on the south side of the Main Road begining to proceſsion the last Teusday in October and finish the same by the last day of March next.

Ordered That [   ] proceſsion every persons Land from the lower end of the New Dragon Bridge Road and the Briery Swamp thence to the Millstone Valey runing from the Main Road to the Dragon on the south side of the Main Road begining to proceſsion the second Teusday in November and finish the same by the last day of March last.

Ordered That [   ] proceſsion every persons Land from the head of Capt Henry Washingtons Mill Dam & the Head of Parrots Creek thence to the Mill Stone Valey on the North side of the Main Road & from the said Road to the River begining to proceſsion the second Teusday in

October & finish the same by the last day of March next.

(287)   At a Vestry as on the other side

Ordered That [   ] proceſsion every persons Land from the Briery Swamp and the Millstone Valey to the Dragon Swamp and the upper end of the County on the south side of the Main Road begining to proceſsion the second Teusday of November & finish the same by the last day of March next.

Ordered That [   ] proceſsion every persons Land between the head of Parrots Creek and the Millstone Valey to the upper end of the County on the North side of the Main Road begining to proceſsion the third Teusday in October and finish the same by the last day of March next.

Ordered That the above said Freeholders proceſsion every persons Land pursuant to the said Orders of Veſtry and that they take and return an Account of every persons Land they shall so proceſsion of the time when & the persons present at the same and of what Lands in their respective Precincts they shall fail to proceſsion and the reason of such failure to the Next Vestry which shall happen after the last day of March Next and it is further ordered that all the Freeholders of the several Precincts before mentioned attend the said proceſsioners mentioned before in their respective Precincts to perform the proceſsioning as above directed and the said Proceſsioners are to take Notice that if the Owner of any land shall refuse to suffer his or her Land to be proceſsioned the Law requires that within ten days after such refusal they Certify the same under their hands to the Church Wardens of the Parish.

(288)   At A Vestry held for Christ Church Parish in Middlesex County the 4 day of October 1758

Present

The Revᵈ Bartholomew Yates Minister Armistead Churchhill, Henry Thacker Christopher Robinson John Robinson James Reid John Smith William Churchhill & Henry Washington Gentˢ of the Vestry

	lb Tob⁰

Ordered

	lb Tob°
To the Revᵈ Bartholomew Yates	16000
To Ditto for allowance on Transfer Notes	640
To Robert Elliot Clerk of the Vestry	1000
To Thomas Laughlin Clerk of the Mother Church	1200
To Royal Richard Allen Clerk of the lower Chappell for the time he served	333
To William Chowning Clerk of the Upper Chappell	1000
To Edward Bristow Sexton of the Mother Church	600
To Thomas Sibley Sexton of the lower Chappell	500
To Elizabeth Forget Sexton of the Upper Chappell	600
21873	

	£	
To John Smith Esqʳ for Lead & Glass	£ 3:15: 0	
To Ditto for 3 bottles Red Wine	0:12: 0	
To Ditto for a Register Book	1 :10: 0	
To Ditto for 3 prayer Books for the use of the Churches as ℔ Mʳ Edward *Hhawes's Account Sterling	2: 8: 7	
To 50 ℔ Cent advance upon the above article	1: 4: 3½	
	9: 9:10½	

To James Reid Esqʳ ℔ Account	4: 4: 0
To Alexander Frazier ℔ order of Ralph Wormeley Esqʳ	5: 9: 3½
To Doctor Alexander Reade	8: 1: 9
To William Roane for puting up Benches at the Upper Chappell	1 :10: 0
	28 :14 :11

To Richard Steevens's Heirs as late Clerk of the lower Chappell	667
To the Rent of the free School Land	500
To the Sheriff for the Quitrents of Ditto	110
To John Adcock Smith	600

* Note. Or Athawes's. The name is difficult to decipher.—C. G. C.

To Ann Bird for account of her late husband   135
To Constant Hardee for keeping Alice Brookes   600
To Henry Seers for keeping Katharine Watts   800
To John Brame for keeping Richard Bream   600
To Elizabeth Wood for keeping John Spotiswood   600
To Arthur Dye   800
To Mary Brookes for keeping Elizabeth Dobbins   800
To Ralph Watts Sen͘ʳ   400
To Judith Brummell for keeping John Palmer   350
To the Clerk of the County for making out Lists of
Tithables   54
To James Bristow 1 levey overcharged last year   32
To Robert Stamper 1 Ditto   32
To the Collectors for last years Delinquents   224
To Elizabeth Gest   600
To the Church Wardens to pay of sundry money debts
and to account for the ballance in case there is no Law
to discharge the same at two pence ⅌ pound   605
To Patrick Calahann for his sons Levey who went a
Soldier   32
To John Greenwood William Daniel and Charles Lee
Patrolers 32 each   96

      To sundrys carried over   30510
(289)   At the same Vestry as on the other side   lb Tobacco
Ordered To sundrys brought over from the other side   30510
To 4 ⅌ Cᵗ for Cask   1220
To 6 ⅌ Cᵗ for Collecting   1904

                                                   33634
      ⅌   Contra   Cʳ
By 1425 Tithables @ 23½ pounds Tobacco each   33487
By last years depositum   123
By due to the Collector   24

                                                   33634

Ordered That John Smith Gent: pay the sundry persons
following the sums following out of the £14: 4: 1½ in his
hands & 605 pounds of Tobacco levyed at two pence ℔ pound
vizt

To James Reid Esqr	£ 4: 4: 0
To Alexander Frazier	5: 9: 3½
To Doctor Alexander Reade	8: 1: 9
To William Roane	1 :10: 0
	19: 5: 0½

Ordered That Ralph Wormeley & John Smith Gent^s be
continued Church Wardens for the following year and that
they receive of every Tithable person within this Parish twenty
three and a half pounds of Tobacco and pay the same to the
sundry Parish Creditors.

Ordered That the Church Wardens pay Christopher Curtis
and William Roane the sum of sixty pounds being one half of
the money agreed upon for Building a Kitchin & Dairy at the
Glebe and that they be allowed to take up Money upon Interest
for that use when the work is finished.

Ordered That the Fine money being in the hands of John
Smith William Churchhill and William Moulson Gent^s amount-
ing to five pounds be given to John Bream Senr £ 1: 5: 0
Edward Whitaker £ 1: 5: 0 Rebekah Sanders £ 1: 5: 0 and
Ann Bird £ 1: 5.

Barth° Yates Min^r
Truly copied by
Robert Elliott Clk Vestry

(290)   At A Vestry held for Christ Church Parish in Middlesex County the 7th day of Augt 1759

Present

Armis^d Churchhill Henry Thacker, Christopher Robinson,
Ralph Wormeley, Thomas Price, James Reid John Smith &
Henry Washington Gent^s of the Vestry

Ordered that in pursuance of an order of Middlesex County
Court bearing date at Urbanna June 5th 1759. The Parish be
devided into several Precincts and that the several Freeholders

hereafter Named see all the Lands within the same procef̄-sioned as followeth vizᵗ

Ordered That Needels Hill & Thoˢ Hardin procef̄sion every persons Land between the Lower end of the County and Robert Elliots Mill crof̄s the Neck to Colᵒ Churchhills Creek and the Line between the said Churchhill and Colᵒ Berkeley begining to procef̄sion the second Teusday in October and finish the same by the 21ˢᵗ day of March next.

Ordered That* John Smith Esqʳ & Thoˢ Kemp procef̄sion every persons Land between Robert Elliots Mill and the Piping Tree on the South side of the Main Road begining to pro-cef̄sion the last Teusday in October & finish the same by the 22ᵈ day of March Next.

Ordered That John Robinson & Will: Churchill procef̄sion every persons Land from Robert Elliots Mill to the Piping Tree along James Scrosbys bounds to the River on the North side of the Main Road begining to procef̄sion †begining to procef̄sion the Last Teusday in November and finish the same by the 23ᵈ day of March next.

Ordered That Thoˢ Laughlin & James Wortham procef̄sion every persons Land from the Piping Tree & Prettymans Roling Road from Rappahanock River to Peankitank begining to procef̄sion the second Teusday in November and finish the same by the 24ᵗʰ day of March next.

Ordered That Henry Meikleborough & Henry Tuggle pro-cef̄sion every persons Land between Prettymans Roling Road and the Main Branch of Mickleboroughs Swamp including the Widow Cheedles Plantation on the North side of the Main Road begining to procef̄sion the first Teusday in December & finish the same by the 25ᵗʰ day of March next.

Ordered That John Murray & Willᵐ Roan procef̄sion every persons Land between Prettymans Roling Road and the New Dragon Bridge Road runing from the Main Road to the

* Note. Just below the name John Smith Esqʳ, but half erased, can be read the name Needles Hill. Just above the name Thoˢ Kemp, but half erased, can be read the name Willᵐ Owen.—C. G. C.

† This and the two following words half erased in original.—C. G. C.

Dragon on the South side of the Main Road begining to proceſsion the 3 Teusday in October and finish the same by the
26 day of March next.

Ordered That Willm Daniel & James Daniel proceſsion
every persons Land between the lower end of the New Dragon
Bridge Road and the Briery Swamp thence to the Millstone
Valey runing from the Main Road to the Dragon on the south
side of the Road begining to proceſsion the last Teusday in
October & finish the same by the 27th day of March next.

(291)   Ordered That Morris Smith & Wm Montague proceſsion every persons Land between the head of Capt Henry
Washingtons Mill Dam and the head of Parrots Creek thence
to the Mill Stone Valley on the North side of the Main Road
to the River begining to proceſsion the 2^d Teusday in November and finish the same by the 28th day of March next.

Ordered That Lewis Montague & Reuben Skilton proceſsion every persons Land between the Briery Swamp from the
Millstone Valley to the Dragon Swamp & the Upper end of
the County on the South side of the Main Road begining to
proceſsion the last Teusday in November & finish the same
by the 29 day of March next.

Ordered That George Fearn & James M^chan proceſsion
every persons Land between the head of Parrots Creek from
the Millstone Valley to the upper end of the County on the
North side of the Main Road begining to proceſsion the second
Teusday in December & finish the same by the last day of
March next.

Ordered That the above Named Freeholders proceſsion every
persons Land pursuant to the above order of Vestry & that
they take & return an account of every persons Land they
shall so proceſsion the time when and the persons present at
the same; what Lands in their Precincts they shall fail to proceſsion and the reason of such failure to the next Vestry
which shall happen after the last day of March next ensuing.
and it is further ordered that all the Freeholders of the several Precincts above mentioned attend the above said proceſsioners in their respective precincts to perform the proceſ-

sioning above directed and the said proceſsioners are to take Notice that if the Owner of any Land shall refuse to Suffer his or her or their Land to be proceſsioned the Law requires that within ten days after such refusal they certify the same under their hands to the Church Wardens of the Parish.

A Churchhill

(292)   At a Vestry held for Christ Church Parish in Middlesex County the 5ᵗʰ day of October 1759

at which were present

Armistead Churchhill, Christopher Robinson, Edmund Berkeley, John Robinson, Ralph Wormeley, John Smith & James Reid Gentˢ of the Vestry

Ordered	lb Tobᵒ
To the Revᵈ Mʳ Bàrtholomew Yates Minister	16000
To Ditto for allowance on Transfer Notes	640
To Robert Elliot Clerk of the Vestry	1000
To Thomas Laughlin Clerk of the Mother Church	1200
To Royal Richard Allen Clerk of the lower Chappel	1000
To William Chowning Clerk of the Upper Chappel	1000
To Edward Bristow Sexton of the Mother Church	600
To Elizabeth Forget Sexton of the Upper Chappel	600
To Thomas Siblee Sexton of the lower Chappel	500
To the Rent of the free School Land	500
To the Sherif for the Quitrents of Ditto	110
To John Smith Adcock	600
To Joseph Hardee for keeping Alice Brooks	600
To Henry Seers for keeping Katharine Watts	800
To John Bream for keeping Richard Bream	600
To Elizabeth Wood for keeping John Spotiswood	600
To Arthur Dye	800
To Mary Brooks for keeping Elizabeth Dobbins	800
To Ralph Watts Senʳ	600
To the Clerk of the County for making out lists of Tithables	54
To Elizabeth Gest	600
To William Moulson for a delinquency last year	24
To George Chowning for taking care of Susanna Carroll	200

To John Bream for keeping and burying Penelope
Bream   200
  To Thomas Siblee for keeping John Neal 2 Months   200
  To John Deagle for burying Elizabeth Humphreys   200
  To Rebekah Sanders   500
  To Daniel Stringer for John Kidds Levey last year   23
  To Thomas Sanders for a Levey overpaid in 1757   28
  To be sold and the Money accounted for to the
Church Wardens to pay Money debts and the Glaziers
account not delivered in   23000

                                                            53579
To 4 ℔ Cent for Cask   2143

                                                            55722
To 6 ℔ Cᵗ for Collecting   3343

                                                            59065

         ℔   Contra   Cʳ
By 1459 Tithables at 40 pounds Tobacco ℔ Poll   58360

(293)   At the same Vestry as on the other side
     Ordered   £   S   D
To Alexander Frazier ℔ Account   ‖ 2 ‖ 8
To Doctor Alexander Reade ℔ Ditto   10 ‖ 15 ‖
To James Gibson for his Wifes keeping Ja-
cob Urie 2 years   8 ‖
To George Daniel ℔ account   4 ‖ 12 ‖
To John Smith Esqʳ ℔ Ditto   3 ‖   6 ‖
To Ralph Wormeley Esqʳ for 5 dozen of
Red Wine   7 ‖ 10 ‖
To William Roan for building a Kitching &
Dairy at the Glebe Principal and Interest 126 ‖

                                    £ 160 ‖ 5 ‖ 8
Ordered That Philip Grymes & James Reid Esqʳˢ be appointed Church Wardens for the ensuing Year and that they
receive of every Tithable person within the Parish 40 pounds

of Tobacco and pay the same to the several Parish Creditors deducting out of the twenty three thousand above levyed Seven hundred and five pounds of Tobacco which the proportion falls short of the debts.

A Churchhill

(294)   At a Vestry held for Christ Church Parish in Middlesex County the 1ˢᵗ day of October 1760

At which were present The Revᵈ Mʳ Bartholomew Yates Minister Christopher Robinson, Henry Thacker, John Robinson, Ralph Wormeley, Philip Grymes John Smith & James Reid Gentlemen of the Vestry

	lbˢ Tobᵒ
Ordered	
To the Revᵈ Mʳ Bartholomew Yates Minister	16000
To Ditto for allowance on Transfer Notes	640
To Robert Elliot Clerk of the Vestry	1000
To Thomas Laughlin Clerk of the Mother Church	1200
To Royal Richard Allen Clerk of the lower Chappell	1000
To William Chowning Clerk of the Upper Chappell	1000
To Edward Bristow Sexton of the Mother Church	600
To Elizabeth Forget Sexton of the Upper Chappel	600
To Thomas Siblee Sexton of the lower Chappel	500
To the Rent of the free School Land	500
To the Sheriff for the Quit-rents of Ditto	110
To John Smith Adcock neceſsarys by application to the Church Wardens	

To Joseph Hardee for keeping
Alice Brooks & Edward Ware to
keep her for the future   600
    To Arthur Dye and his wife   1000
    To Rebekah Sanders   500
    To Elizabeth Wood for keep-
ing John Spotiswood   600
    To Mary Brookes for keeping
Elizabeth Dobbins   800
    To the Clerk of the County for
making out Lists of Tithables   54
    To William Gardner for taking
care of Elizabeth Gest & burying
her   100   & £ 1 || 5 || 10½
    To Henry Anderson   800
    To Judith Brumel for keeping
John Palmer   350
    To Thomas Siblee for keeping
Ann McCormack 8 months   2 || 8 || 6
    To James Hiptinstall for burying John Neal   0 || 15 || 0
    To John McNeal for account of John Urie   2 || 0 || 0
    To Doctor Alexander Reades Estate   3 || 18 || 9
    To James Reid for so much paid by him
upon account of Thomas Moxam to John Davis   8 || 0 || 0
    To John Daniel for keeping Thomas
Moxam 3 months   1 || 10 || 0
    To Elizabeth Bream for keep-
ing Richard Bream (& to be
bound out)   600
    To Alexander Frazier for account of
Ann McCormack   1 || 0 || 0
    To Capt John Gordon for account of
Thomas Moxam   0 || 4 || 9
    To James Reid for 5 dozen of Wine bought
of Thomas Brereton   7 || 0 || 0
    To Henry Seers for keeping Katharine
Watts & a Coffin   66

To James Gibson for keeping Jacob Urie
(& to be bound out)   4 || 0 || 0

lbˢ Tobº 28620   £32 || 12 || 10½

(295)   At a Vestry as on the other side
lbˢ Tobaº
         Ordered
To sundrys brought forward   28620   £32 || 12 || 10½
To Robert Murray for account
of Robert Bond's Orphan   400
To be sold to pay Money debts
and accounted for by the Receiver
to the Church Wardens   718

                                    29738
To 4 ₱ Cent for Cask   1189½

                                    30927½
To 6 ₱ Cent for Collecting   1855½

                                    32783
         Contra   Cʳ
By 1437 Tithables @ 22½ pounds
of Tobacco ₱ Poll   32332
By a delinquency to be allowed the
Collector at laying of the next Levey   451

                                    32783
         Ordered
That James Reid Esqʳ receive of Benjamin
Rhodes for his Fathers Smiths Tools   4 || 0 || 0
That Thomas Price pay the Church Wardens
for a Fine   2 || 10 || 0
That the Church Wardens account for a Bill
paid for a Fine   0 || 10 || 0

That the Church Wardens account for the
ballance of money in the hands of the last
years Collector being   25 ‖ 5 ‖ 3

That John Sanders Sen[r] be allowed out of
the Fine money and Rhodes's Tools   1 ‖ 0 ‖ 0

That William Sanders be allowed out of Ditto 1 ‖ 0 ‖ 0

That the Widow Heyley have the remainder
of Ditto being   5 ‖ 0 ‖ 0

Ordered That Philip Grymes & James Reid Esq[rs] be continued Church Wardens for the ensuing year and that they
receive of every Tithable Person within this Parish 22½
pounds of Tobacco & pay the same to the several Parish Creditors and also that they be allowed the above ballance of four
hundred and fifty one pounds of Tobacco at the laying of the
next Levey.

Barth° Yates Min[r]

(296)   At a Vestry held for Christ Church Parish in Middlesex County the 24th day of November 1761

At which were present

The Rev[d] M[r] Bartholomew Yates Minister Armistead
Churchhill Edmund Berkeley, Christopher Robinson, John Robinson Philip Grymes John Smith and Henry Washington Gent[s]
of the Vestry

Ordered	lb[s] T°
To the Revd M[r] Bartholomew Yates Minister	16,000
To Ditto for allowance on Transfer Notes	640
To Robert Elliot Clerk of the Vestry	1000
To Thomas Laughlin Clerk of the Mother	1200
To Royal Richard Allen Clerk of the Lower Chappell	1000
To William Chowning Clerk of the Upper Chappell	1000

To Edward Bristow Sexton of
the Mother Church   600
To Elizabeth Forget Sexton of
the Upper Chappell   600
To Thomas Siblee Sexton of the
Lower Chappell   500
To the Rent of the Free School
Land   500
To the Sheriff for Quitrents of
Ditto   110
To the Clerk of the County for
making out Lists of Tithables   60
    To Arthur Dye and his Wife   1000
    To Doctor Philip Fercharson ꝑ
account   £ 3 ‖ 3 ‖ 6½
To the Collector for last years
delinquency   563
    To Rebekah Sanders   800
    To John Wharton   500
To Thomas Siblee for keeping
and burying Ann McCormack   900
    To Elizabeth Bream   500
    To Doctor Symmer ꝑ account   4 ‖ 0 ‖ 0
    To James Reid for sundrys found
John Adcock Smith   5 ‖ 16 ‖ 4
To Elizabeth Forget for keeping
Elizabeth Robson & Child 5 months   500
To the Church Wardens to lay
out for Harry Andersons Children   500
To the Church Wardens to buy
neceſsarys for Nelly Booth   500
To John Adcock Smith neceſ-
saries as the Church Wardens shall
think proper.
To be levied and accounted for
(by the Parish Collector) to the
V e s t r y towards repairing the

Churches buying a Surplace and paying the money Debts	15000

	43973 & £12 ‖ 19 ‖ 10½
To 4 ℔ Cᵗ for Cask	1759

	45732
To 6 ℔ Cᵗ for Collection	2744

	48476
To depositum to be accounted for at laying the next Levy	441

	48917

(297)   At the same Vestry as on the other side

lb Tobacco

To sundrys brought forward   48917 & £12 ‖ 19 ‖ 10½
                    Contra   Cʳ
By 1415 Tithables @ 34½ pounds
of Tobacco ℔ Poll   48917

Christopher Curtis Gent is this day chosen and elected Vestryman in the Room of Thomas Price Gent decd.

Christopher Robinson and William Churchhill are appointed Church Wardens for the ensuing year.

Ordered that the fine money in the hands of Philip Grymes Esqʳ being fifty shillings be devided between John Lyal and Elizabeth Healey.

Ordered That Robert Daniel be appointed Receiver and that he Receive of every Tithable person within this Parish thirty four and a half pounds of Tobacco and pay the same to the several Parish Creditors.

Ordered That the said Receiver give Bond and security for the due performance of his Office to the Church Wardens.

Barthᵒ Yates Minʳ

At a Vestry held for Christ Church Parish in Middlesex County the 15ᵗʰ day of April 1762

At which were Present

The Revd Mr Bartholomew Yates Min^r Armistead Churchhill, Henry Thacker, Christopher Robinson, Ralph Wormeley,
John Smith James Reid, William Churchhill, & Henry Washington Gent^s of the Vestry

Ordered That the Church Wardens agree with Workmen to
make all the single Pews in the lower part of the Middle
Church into double ones also that they alter the two upper
Pews as they shall see proper and repair the other Churches.

Ordered That Robert Murray make Steps & such repairs
at the Glebe House as Mr Yates shall direct him & bring in
his account to the Church Wardens who are desired to pay the
Account out of the Tobacco levied for repairing the Churches.

Gawin Corbin Esqr is elected & chose a Vestryman in the
Room of Philip Grymes Esqr decd

Barth^o Yates Min^r

(298)   At a Vestry held for Christ Church Parish in Middlesex County the 6th day of October 1762

At which were present

The Revd Mr Bartholomew Yates Minister, Armistead
Churchhill Edmond Berkeley, Henry Thacker Christopher Rob-
inson, John Robinson Ralph Wormeley, John Smith, William
Churchhill, Henry Washington Gent^s of the Vestry

Ordered	lb Tob^o
To the Revd Mr Bartholomew Yates Minister	16000
To Ditto for allowance on Trans-fer Notes	640
To Robert Elliot Clerk of the Vestry	1000
To Thomas Laughlin Clerk of the Mother Church	1200
To James Hiptinstal Clerk of the Lower Chappel	1000
To William Chowning Clerk of the Upper Chappel	1000

To Edward Bristow Sexton of the
Mother Church   600
To Elizabeth Forget Sexton of the
Upper Chappel   600
To Thomas Siblee Sexton of the
Lower Chappel   500
To the Rent of the Free school Land   500
To the Sheriff for the Quitrents of
Ditto   110
To the Clerk of the County for
making out Lists of Tithables   60
To Arthur Dye and his Wife   1000
To Christopher Robinson Church-
warden for Wine for the use of the
Churches from William Moulson ℔ acc\ᵗ   £ 2 ‖ 11 ‖ 0
To Dᵒ for Pork for John Smith
Adcock ℔ Dᵒ   3 ‖ 15 ‖ 0
To Dᵒ for Cloathes and Neceſ-
sarys for Dᵒ ℔ Dᵒ   1 ‖ 13 ‖ 8
To George Daniel for the Quitrents
of the Glebe Land & Taxes 2 years   2 ‖ 7 ‖ 6
To William Churchhill Churchwar-
den for a Lock for the Linnen Chest
at the Lower Chappel   0 ‖ 3 ‖ 6
To Dᵒ for Wine for the use of the
Churches   2 ‖ 8 ‖ 0
To Elizabeth Brame   800
To Mary Brookes for keeping Eliz-
abeth Dobbins   800
Ordered That the Collector pay
Ditto for last years keeping the same
800ˡᵇ Tobᵒ @ 2ᵈ ℔ pound
To Rebekah Sanders   800
To Elizabeth Wood for keeping
John Spotiswood last year 800 pounds
of Tobᵒ to be paid by the Collector
@ 2ᵈ ℔ pound

To Edward Ware for keeping Alice
Brookes last year 800ᴸᵇ Tobᵒ to be paid
by the Collector at 2ᵈ ℔ pound

To Ditto for keeping the said Alice
Brookes this year   600

To the Church Wardens to buy nec-
eſsaries for Nelly Booth   500

	lb Tobᵒ	27710	£12 ‖ 18 ‖ 8
			lb Tobᵒ

(299)   To sundrys brought   lb Tobᵒ
forward from the other side   27710 £12 ‖ 18 ‖ 8

To Christopher Robinson Church
warden for a Surplice   6 ‖ 10 ‖ 0

To Edward Bristow for a Dial Post
at the Mother Church   0 ‖ 5 ‖ 0

To Colᵒ Armistead Churchhill for
Rebekah Sanders Medecines   1 ‖ 12 ‖ 0

To 4 ℔ Cᵗ for Cask on the above
Tobacco   1108 £21 ‖ 5 ‖ 8

                                28818
To 6 ℔ Cᵗ for Collecting   1729

                                30547
To depositum to be accounted for
next year   176

                                30723
          Contra   Cʳ
By last years depositum   441
By 1442 Tithables @ 21 pounds
Tobacco each   30282

                                30723

Ordered that Christopher Robinson & William Churchhill be continued Churchwardens for the Ensuing year.

Robert Daniel Gent is elected a Vestryman in the Room of Christopher Curtis Gent who refuses to serve.

Ordered That the Fine money in the hands of George Daniel & Christopher Robinson Gent. being £7 || 12 || 6 be devided between the Widows Robson & Smith to them £3 || 15 & to Joseph Crosly £1 || 17 || 6 & the other remaining £ 1 || 17 || 6 to any poor person the Church Wardens shall think proper.

Ordered that the Church Wardens lay out for Harry Andersons Children five hundred pounds of Tobacco.

Ordered That the above depositum of 176 pd˙ of Tobacco be paid to George Daniel and the ballance of his account being 100 pounds of Tobacco be paid him by the Church Wardens in money.

Ordered That Lewis Mountague Gent be appointed Receiver & that he receive of every Tithable person within this Parish 21 pounds of Tobacco & account to the Church Wardens for the payment of the same to the several Parish Creditors.

Ordered That the said Receiver give Bond & security to the Church Wardens for the due performance of his Office.

Barthᵒ Yates Minʳ

(300) At a Vestry held for Christ Church Parish in Middlesex County the 14 day of Septʳ 1763

Present

Henry Thacker, Christopher Robinson, John Robinson, Ralph Wormeley John Smith, William Churchhill, Henry Washington & Robert Daniel Gentlemen of the Vestry

In pursuance of an Order of Middlesex County Court dated the 7ᵗʰ day of June 1763 The Vestry have devided the Parish into several Precincts and appointed two freeholders in every Precinct to see all the Lands procefsioned within the said Precincts as followeth

Ordered That Needels Hill & Joseph Batchelder procefsion every persons Land between the lower end of the County and Robert Elliots Mill crofs the Neck to Mʳ Churchhills

Creek and the line between the said Churchhill and Col⁰
Berkeley begining to proceſsion the second Tuesday in October
and finish the same by the last day of March next.

That John Smith & Thoˢ Kemp proceſsion every persons
Land between Robert Elliots Mill and the Pipeing Tree on
the South side of the Main Road begining to proceſsion the last
Tuesday in October and finish the same by the last day of
March next.

That Willᵐ Churchhill & Wᵐ Stiff proceſsion every persons
Land between Robert Elliots Mill and the Pipeing Tree along
Mʳ James Scrosbys bounds to the River on the North side of
the Main Road begining to proceſsion the first Tuesday in
November and finish the same by the last day of March next.

That Jaˢ Wortham & Thoˢ Wortham proceſsion every persons Land between the Pipeing Tree and Prittymans Roleing
Road from Rappahanock River to Peankitank begining to proceſsion the second Tuesday in November & finish the same
by the last day of March next.

That Henry Tuggle & John Dillard proceſsion every persons Land between *the Pettymans Roleing Road and the Main
branch of Meikleborough Swamp (including the Plantation
which belonged to the Widow Cheedle) on the North side of
the Main Road begining to proceſsion the third Tuesday in
November and finish the same by the last day of March next.

That John Murray & †J Batchelder proceſsion every persons Land between Prettymans Roleing Road and the New
Dragon Bridge Road runing from the Main Road to the
Dragon on the South side of the said Road begining to proceſsion the last Tuesday in November and finish the same by
the last day of March next.

---

* This word is half erased in the original.—C. G. C.

† Apparently the letter N has been written over the letter J; but it
is impossible to say with certainty what the letter is. In any case, however, the J (which is plainly to be read) was written by mistake, and
without erasing it the clerk endeavored to cover it up by a substitute
initial.—C. G. C.

(301)   Ordered

That Jaˢ Daniel & John Sword proceſsion every persons Land between the lower end of the New Dragon Bridge Road and the Briery Swamp from thence to the Millstone Valley runing from the Main Road to the Dragon on the south side of the Main Road begining to proceſsion the first Tuesday in December and finish the same by the last day of March next.

That Maurice Smith & Wᵐ Segar proceſsion every persons Land between the Head of Capᵗ Henry Washingtons Mill Dam and the Head of Parrots Creek from thence to the Millstone Valley on the North side of the Main Road and from the said Road to the River begining to proceſsion the second Tuesday in December and finish the same by the last day of March next.

That Lewis Mountague & Chˢ Lee proceſsion every persons Land between the Briery Swamp and from the Millstone Valley to the Dragon Swamp and the upper end of the County on the south side of the Main Road begining to proceſsion the third Tuesday in December and finish the same by the last day of March next.

That Jaˢ Mᶜhan & George Warwick proceſsion every persons Land between the Head of Parrots Creek and from the Millstone Valley to the upper end of the County on the North side of the Main Roade begining to proceſsion the fourth Tuesday in December and finish the same by the last day of March next.

Ordered That the aforesaid Freeholders proceſsion every persons Land pursuant to the above orders of Vestry and that they take and return an account of every persons Land they shall so proceſsion of the time when and of the persons present at the same and of what Lands they shall fail to proceſsion in their respective precincts and the reason of such failure to the next Vestry which shall happen after the last day of March next. and it is further ordered that all the Freeholders of the several precincts above mentioned attend the said proceſsioners in their several precincts respectively to perform the proceſsioning as above mentioned and directed; and the said proce∫sioners are to take notice that if the owner of any Land shall refuse to suffer his or her Land to be proce∫sioned the Law requires that within ten days after such refusal they certify the same under their hands to the Churchwardens of the Parish.

(302) Robert Daniel Gent: Took the Oath of a Vestryman and took his place in the Vestry accordingly.

Robert Elliot is chose a Vestryman in the Room of A Churchhill Esqʳ decd.

Henry Thacker

At A Vestry held for Christ Church Parish in Middlesex County the 4ᵗʰ day of October 1763

At which were present

The Revᵈ Mʳ Bartholomew Yates Minister, Henry Thacker, Christopher Robinson, John Robinson, Ralph Wormeley, William Churchhill, Henry Washington, Robert Daniel & Robert Elliot Gentlemen of the Vestry

Ordered	lb Tobᵒ	L. S. D.
To the Revᵈ Mʳ Bartholomew Yates	16000	
To Dittᵒ for allowance on Transfer Notes	640	
To Robert Elliot Clerk of the Vestry	1000	
To Thomas Laughlin Clerk of the Mother Church	1200	
To William Chowning Clerk of the Upper Chappel	1000	
To James Hiptinstall Clerk of the Lower Chappel	1000	
To Edward Bristow Sexton of the Mother Church	600	
To Elizabeth Forget Sexton of the Upper Chappel	600	
To Thomas Siblee Sexton of the Lower Chappel	500	
To the Rent of the Free School Land	500	

To the Sheriff for the Quitrents of Ditt°	110			
To the Clerk of the County for Lists of Tithables	60			
To Arthur Dye and his Wife	1000			
To the Sheriff for Quitrents & Taxes of the Glebe Land		£ 2 ‖	7 ‖	6
To Charles Roane for Board of John & Edward Barden		6 ‖	15 ‖	o
To Elizabeth Allen for keeping Mary Overstreet	100			
To Nicholas Jacob for his charges about Jacob Rice & Child	800	1 ‖	18 ‖	o
To William Churchhill Esqʳ ℔ Accᵗ		5 ‖	9 ‖	o
To William Bristow for Horse Blocks		o ‖	7 ‖	6
To Edward Bristow for Ditt°		o ‖	7 ‖	6
To the Church wardens for Harry Andersons Children	500			
To Samuel Wortham ℔ Accᵗ		o ‖	5 ‖	o
	25610	17 ‖	9 ‖	6

(303)   At the same Vestry held for Christ Church Parish as on the other side

Ordered	lb Tob°			
To sundrys brought forward	25610	£17 ‖	9 ‖	6
To Capᵗ Robert Daniel for Adcock Smith ℔ Accᵗ		3 ‖	13 ‖	2½
To James Daniel		o ‖	3 ‖	o
To Doctor Philip Fercharson		3 ‖	10 ‖	3
To Edward Ware for keeping Alice Brookes & Burying her	400			
To Mary Brookes for keeping Elizabeth Dobbins	800			
To Elizabeth Bream	800			
To John Hardee & his Wife for keeping Elizabeth Gardner	800			
To John Yarrington ℔ Account		2 ‖	o ‖	o

To John Daniel for keeping Kath-
arine Alstone half a year   400
To the Church Wardens for the use
of Eleanor Booth   500
   To Christopher Robinson Esqʳ ⅌ Accᵗ   1 ‖ 6 ‖ 5
   To William Churchhill Esqʳ ⅌ Dᵒ   11 ‖ 3 ‖ 6
To John Newcomb for taking care
of Jacob Rice   4 ‖ 0 ‖ 0
   To the Sheriff for Delinquents   766½
   To Rebekah Sanders   800

Ordered That Robert Daniel &
Robert Elliot be Church Wardens for
the ensuing year.

That the Fine money in the hands
of Christopher Robinson Esqʳ be
given to Joseph Crosley being   0 ‖ 10 ‖ 0
   To the Widows Robson & Smith   4 ‖ 0 ‖ 0

That the money Debts be paid out
of the money remaining in the hands
of the late Church Wardens

                     30876½ £47 ‖ 5 ‖ 10½
To 4 ⅌ Cᵗ for Cask   1233
To 6 ⅌ Cᵗ for Collecting   1927
To depositum to be accounted for
to the Church Wardens   1013½

                     35050
           Contra   Cʳ
By last years depositum in the
hands of the Sheriff   176
By 1484 Tithables @ 23½ lb
Tobᵒ each   34874

                  35050 £47 ‖ 5 ‖ 10½
Ordered That Lewis Mountague Gent: be appointed Receiver of the Parish Levy & that he receive of every Tithable

person within this Parish 23½ lb Tob° and that he give Bond & security to the Church Wardens for the due performance of the same & account for the depositum in his hands being 1013½ lb Tob° to the Church Wardens.

James Mills Gent: is Elected & chose Vestryman in the Room of James Reid Esqʳ decd.

Barth° Yates Minʳ

(304)   At a Vestry held for Christ Church Parish in the County of Middlesex the 9ᵗʰ day of October 1764

At which were present

The Revᵈ Mʳ Bartholomew Yates Minʳ, Henry Thacker, Edmund Berkeley Christopher Robinson, John Robinson, Ralph Wormeley, Robert Daniel & Robert Elliot Gentˢ of the Vestry

Ordered	lb Tob°
To the Revᵈ Mʳ Bartholomew Yates	16000
To D° for allowance on Transfer Notes	640
To Robert Elliot Clerk of the Vestry	1000
To Thomas Laughlin Clerk of the Mother Church	1200
To William Chowning Clerk of the Upper Chappel	1000
To James Hiptinstall Clerk of the Lower Chappel	1000
To Edward Bristow Sexton of the Mother Church	600
To Elizabeth Forget Sexton of the Upper Chappel	600
To Thomas Siblee Sexton of the Lower Chappel	500
To the Rent of the Free School Land	500
To the Sheriff for the Quitrents of Ditto	110
To the Clerk of the County for Lists of Tithables	60
To Arthur Dye and his Wife	1000
To William Kidd for the Board of John & Edward Barden	1200
To be paid Christopher Robinson Esqʳ for an Ideot son of William Kidd	500
To Nicholas Jacob for taking care of Jacob Rices Child	500
To Mary Ann Deagle for keeping James Somers 6 Month	400
To Rebekah Deagle	500

To John Hardee for keeping Elizabeth Gardner   800
To the Church Wardens for the use of Eleanor Booth   500
To the last years Receiver for Delinquents   309
To Rebekah Sanders   800
To Mary Brookes for keeping Elizabeth Dobbins   500
To Paul Philpotts Senr 800
To James Wortham for Patrolers   94
To be sold to pay former Debts & for the use of the
Parish & the money arising therefrom to be paid to the
Church Wardens who are to account for the same to the
Vestry   1000

                                                    ―――――
                                                    41113
To 4 ⅌ Cent for Cask   1644
To 6 ⅌ Cent for Collecting   2565
                                                    ―――――
                                        Totall   45322

                      Contra   C^r
By 1418 Tithables @ 32 lb Tob^o ⅌ Poll   45376
Ordered that the ballance be accounted for by
the Receiver at laying of the next Levy being   54
That the fine money in the Hands of Robert
Daniel Gent James Wortham & Edward Ware
to be paid to the Church Wardens   £ 7 || 10 || 0

   (305)   At the same Vestry as on the other side
Ordered That the Church Wardens pay the
Widows Robson & Smith forty shillings each
out of the Fine money & distribute the ballance
as they shall think proper.
   That the late Receiver pay the Rent of the
Free School Land being 520 lb Tob^o to the
Church wardens.
   To the Sheriff for Quitrents & taxes of the
Glebe land   £ 1 || 3 || 9
   To Alexander Frazier by account   0 || 10 || 0
   To John Daniel for Katharine Allstone   3 || 15 || 6

To John Newcomb in full of his account for Jacob Rice	2 ǁ	7 ǁ	0
To Mary Brookes ballance of a former account	3 ǁ	18 ǁ	8
To Mrs Price for Funeral charges of Joseph Crosley	1 ǁ	10 ǁ	0
To Edward Bristow for finding a Lock for the Church Chest	0 ǁ	2 ǁ	6
To John Adcock Smith to be paid Robert Daniel Gent	2 ǁ	1 ǁ	11
To Robert Daniel Gent. by Account	7 ǁ	15 ǁ	3
To D^o for Joseph Crosley by D^o	0 ǁ	17 ǁ	11
To D^o for account of Thomas Ogilvie	2 ǁ	6 ǁ	6

£26 ǁ 9 ǁ 0

Ordered That John Robinson Gent. be appointed Receiver of the Parish Levy and that he receive of every Tithable person within this Parish thirty two pounds of Tobacco & pay the same to the persons for whom it is levyed (he first giving Bond & security to the Church-Wardens for the due performance of the same) also that he be allowed the ballance in Tobacco being fifty four pounds at the laying of the next Levy.

That Robert Daniel & Robert Elliot Gent^n be continued Church Wardens for the ensuing year.

Barth^o Yates Min^r

*At a Vestry held for Christ Church Parish in Middlesex County At Which Ware Present

The Revd Bartho: Yates, Minister Edmond Berkeley Christopher Robinson Ralph Wormley John Smith William Churchill, Robert Daniel James Mills & Lewis Mountague Gen^t of the Vestrey

(306)   At a Vestry held for Christ Church Parish in Middlesex County on Wedensday the 17th day of July 1765

Present

The Revd Bartholomew Yates Min^r, Henry Thacker, Christopher Robinson, John Robinson, Ralph Wormeley, John Smith

---

*This entry is scratched over and partly erased in the original.— C. G. C.

Robert Daniel & Robert Elliot Gent[n] of the Vestry

The returns of the proceſsioners were this day examined in presence of the Vestry.

Ordered That the Church Wardens pay Robert Murray out of the Tobacco levyed & sold for the use of the Parish the sum of forty two pounds five shillings in full for work done at the Glebe House.

Ordered That the former Receiver of the Parish Levy pay the Tobacco due for the Rent of the Free School Land for the years 1762 & 1763 & also the 1013½ pounds of Tobacco in his hands not accounted for to the present Church Wardens.

That Richard Watts account for Glaziers work done at the Churches amounting to £3 || 10 || 0 be paid by the Church Wardens.

Barth[o] Yates Min[r]

(307) At a Vestry held for Christ Church Parish in the County of Middlesex the 21st day of October 1765

At which were present

The Rev[d] M[r] Bartholomew Yates Min[r], Christopher Robinson, Edmund Berkeley, John Robinson, Ralph Wormeley, John Smith, Robert Daniel & Robert Elliot Gent[n] of the Vestry

	lb Tob[o]
Ordered	
To the Rev[d] Bartholomew Yates Minister	16000
To Ditto for allowance on Transfer Notes	640
To Robert Elliot Clerk of the Vestry	1000
To Thomas Laughlin Clerk of the Mother Church	1200
To William Chowning Clerk of the Upper Chappel	1000
To James Hiptinstall Clerk of the Lower Chappel	1000
To Edward Bristow Sexton of the Mother Church	600
To Elizabeth Forget Sexton of the Upper Chappel	600

To Thomas Siblee sexton of the Lower Chappel	600				
To the Rent of the Free School Land	500				
To the Sheriff for the Quitrents of Ditto	110				
To the Clerk of the County for Lists of Tithes	60				
To John Smith Esqʳ by accounts given in		4 ‖	7 ‖	6	
To Thomas Whilley			4 ‖	6	
To Smith South for keeping Mary Curtis five Weeks		1 ‖	0 ‖	0	
To Doctor Robert Spratt by Account		12 ‖	12 ‖	9	
To Johannah Dunlevy for the care of Sarah Summers	1500				
To Mʳ Alexander Frazier by Account		1 ‖	8 ‖	6	
To Rebekah Deagle	500				
To Rebekah Sanders	800				
To William Segar by Account		1 ‖	0 ‖	0	
To Frances Ogilvie	500				
To John Kidds Children	800				
To the Sheriff for Delinquents	544				
To Arthur Dye and his Wife to be paid Robert Daniel	1000				
To the Sheriff for the Quitrents of the Glebe Land		2 ‖	7 ‖	6	
To Nicholas Jacob for himself & Jacob Rices Child	800				
To John Hardee and Wife for keeping Elizabeth Gardner	800				
To Paul Philpots Senʳ	800				
To John Smith Adcock to be paid Robert Daniel		3 ‖	5 ‖	0	
To William Kidd for John Kidds Children to be paid Dᵒ		2 ‖	18 ‖	0	
To Frances Ogilvie to be paid Ditto		2 ‖	4 ‖	6	

To 4000 lb Tob° to pay money
Debts   4000

            Carried over   35354   31 ‖ 8 ‖ 3

(308)   At the same Vestry as on the other side
To sundrys brought over   35354   31 ‖ 8 ‖ 3
To 4 ℔ Cᵗ for Cask   1414
                               _____
                               36768
To 6 ℔ Cᵗ for Collecting   2206
                               _____
                               38974
            Contra   Cʳ
By 1439 Tithables @ 27 lb Tob°
℔ Poll   38853
To be accounted for to the Collec-
tor at the laying the next Levy   121
                               _____
                               38974

Ordered That Lewis Mountague Gent be appointed Vestryman in the Room of Henry Washington Gentⁿ decd.

Ordered That Edmund Berkeley and James Mills Gentⁿ be
appointed Church Wardens for the ensuing year.

Ordered That John Robinson Gent be appointed Receiver
*for the ensuing year of the Parish Levey and that he receive
of every Tithable person within this Parish twenty seven
pounds of Tobacco & pay the same to the severall persons for
whom it is levied (he first giving Bond & security to the
Church Wardens for the due performance of the same) also
that the Deficiency being 121 lb of Tobacco be accounted for
to him at laying of the next Parish Levy.

                                    Barth° Yates Minʳ

(309)   At a Vestry held for Christ Church Parish in Middlesex County on Tuesday the 23ᵈ day of December 1766

_____

* This and the three words next following are scratched through in
the original but are still legible.—C. G. C.

At which were present

The Rev⁴ M⁻ Bartholomew Yates Minister, Edmond Berkeley, Christopher Robinson, Ralph Wormeley, William Churchhill, Robert Daniel, Robert Elliot, Gawin Corbin & James Mills Gentⁿ of the Vestry

	lb Tob°			
Ordered				
To the Rev⁴ M⁻ Bartholomew Yates Minister	16000			
To Ditto for allowance on Transfer Notes	640			
To Robert Elliot Clerk of the Vestry	1000			
To Ditto ⅌ account	238			
To Thomas Laughlin Clerk of the Mother Church	1200			
To William Chowning Clerk of the Upper Chappell	1000			
To James Hiptinstall Clerk of the Lower Chappell	1000			
To Edward Bristow Sexton of the Mother Church	600			
To Elizabeth Forget Sexton of the Upper Chappell	600			
To Thomas Siblee Sexton of the Lower Chappell	500			
To the Rent of the Free School Land	500			
To the Sheriff for Quitrents of Ditto 23388	110			
To Ann Dye	800			
To the Sheriff for Quitrents of the Glebe Land & Taxes		£ 2 ‖ 7 ‖ 6		
To Col° Edmond Berkeley ⅌ account		6 ‖ 14 ‖ 3		
To John Humphreys for Steps at the Lower Chappell		0 ‖ 5 ‖ 0		
To George Daniel for ballance of his account		2 ‖ 5 ‖ 11		

To Garret Tool for charges of Ann
Hog & burying her   2 ‖ 6 ‖ o
   To Mary Curtis   500
   To Thomas Siblee   200
   To James Mills ℈ Account   18 ‖ 19 ‖ 3½
   To Frances Ogilvie   500
   To Rebekah Sanders   800
   To Nicholas Jacob for himself &
Jacob Rices's Child   800
   To John Hardee & Wife for keep-
ing Elizabeth Gardner   800
   To Paul Philpotts Senr   800
   To William Kidd & keeping John
Kidds Children   800
   To Eleanor Booth   500
   To Mr Yates for pailing in a Gar-
den 708 feet at the Glebe   35 ‖ 8 ‖ o
   To Ditto for building a Corn House
at D°   3 ‖ 10 ‖ o
   To Johannah Dunlevy for keeping
Sarah Summers   1000
   To be levied & accounted for by
the Collector to pay money Debts
&c^a   8000

                     38888 71   15   11½
4 ℈ Cent: for Cask   1555

                     40443
6 ℈ Cent: for Collecting   2426

                     42869

Ordered That James Mills Esqr be Collector of the Parish
Levy and that he receive of every Tithable person within this
Parish 28½ lb Tob° & account to the sundry persons for whom
the same is Levied.

(310)   At the same Vestry as on the other side
    Ordered   lb Tob°
To sundry Tobacco & Money ac-
counts as before   42869 £71 ‖ 15 ‖ 11½
          Contra   C^r
By ballance due the Parish from
Robert Daniel Gent   5 ‖ 2 ‖ 1

                          66 ‖ 13 ‖ 10½
By 1446 Tithables @ 28½ each   41211
By ballance due the Collector   1658

                      42869

Ordered That James Mills Esqr be Collector of the Parish
Levy and that he receive of every Tithable Person within the
same 28½ pounds of Tob° and account for the same to the
sundry persons for whom the same is levied also ordered that
the Receiver give Bond for the due Collection of the same
in the Clerks Office.

Ralph Wormeley Junr Esqr is Elected a Vestryman in the
Room of Henry Thacker Gent: Deceased.

Ordered That the Present Church Wardens agree for a
Work House and a proper person to look after and take care
of the poor.
                        Barth° Yates Min^r

At a Vestry held for Christ Church *Church Parish in the
County of Midd^x the 1st day of July 1767 at Which Ware
Present

The Revd Bartho Yates Min^r Edmund Berkley Christopher
Robinson Ralph Wormley John Smith William Churchil
*James *Mills Robert Daniel James Mills & Lewis Mountague
Gen^t Vestrymen

In Pursuance of an Order of Middlesex County Court dated
at Urbanna on Tuesday the second day of June 1767

Order^d That Needlis hill & Joseph Batcheldor Proceſsion
Every Persons Land between the Lower End of the County

---

* These words erased in original but still legible.—C. G. C.

and Mʳˢ Elizᵃ Elliotts Mill Crofs the Neck to Mʳ Churchills
Creek and the Line Between the sᵈ Churchel and Colᵒ Berkley
begining to Procefsion the Second Tuesday in Octoʳ and to
finish the same by the Last day of March Next.

Orderᵈ Thoˢ Kemp & William Owen do Profsefsion Every
Persons Land between Mʳˢ Elizᵃ Elliotts Mill and the Pipeing
tree on the South Side of the Main Road beginning to Procefsion the second Tuesday in October and to finish the same
by the Last day of March Next.

Orderᵈ That William Stiff and David Barwick do Profsefsion Every Persons Land Between Mʳˢ Elizᵃ Elliotts Mill
and the Piping Tree a Long Mʳ James Scrosbys bounds to
the River on the north side of the main Road begining on the
secon[d] Tuesday in Otober And finish yᵉ same by yᵉ Last
of March Nex[t].

(311) Ordered That James Wortham & Edward Bristow
Procefsion Every Persons Land between the Piping Tree and
Pretymans Rowling Road from Rappahannock River to Piankitank begining to Procefsion the Second Tuesday in October
and to finish the same by the Last day of March Next.

Ordered That Henry Tuggle and John Dillard Procefsion
Every Persons Land Between Prettymans Rowling Road and
the Main branch of Mickleborough's Swamp (including the
Plantation Which belong to the Widdow Cheedle) on the North
Side of the Main Road, begining to Procefsion on the Second
Tuesday in October and to finish the same by the Last day
of March Next.

Ordered That John Murray and William Roan Procefsion
Every Persons Land between Pretimans Rowling Road and the
New Draggon Bridge Runing from the Main Road to the
Draggon on the South Side of the Main Road, begining to
Procefsion on the Second Tuesday in October and to finish the
same by the Last day of *October March Next.

Ordered That John Swoard and *James *Daniel Henry
Shapord Procefsefsion Every Persons Land between the Lower
End of the New draggon Bridge Road and the Bryary Swamp
from thence to the Mill stone Valley Runing from the Main

Road to the Draggon on the south side of the Main Road begining to Procefsion the second Tuesday in October and to finish the same by the Last day of March Next.

Ordered That Maurice Smith & Wm Seagar Procefsion Every Persons Land between the head of Mr Charles Nelson's Mill Pond and Parrotts Creek from thence to the Millstone Valley on the North side of the Main Road and from the s^d Road to the River begining to Procefsion on the second Tuesday in October And to finish the same by the Last day of *October March Next.

(312) Ordered That Jeremiah Shapord & John Clark Procefsion Every Persons Land between the Bryery Swamp and from the Mill Stone Vallie to the Draggon Swamp and the Upper End of the County on the South Side of the Main Road begining to Procefsion the Second Tuesday in October and to finish the same by the Last day of March Next.

Or^d that James Machan & George Warwick Procefsion Every Persons Land between the head of Parrots Creek and from the Millstone Valley to the Upper End of the County on the North Side of the Main Road begining to Procefsion the Second Tuesday in October and to finish the same by the Last day of March Next.

Ordered that the aforesaid freeholders Procefsion Every Persons Land Pursuant to the Above Orders of Vestery and that they take And Return An Account of Every Persons Land they shall so Procefsion of the time When and the Persons Present at the same and of What Land they shall fail to Procefsion in their Respective Precincts and the reason of such failure to the Next Vestery Which Shall happen after the s^d Last day of March Next and it is further Ordered that all the freeholders of the Severall Precincts Above Mentioned Attend the said Procefsioners in their Severall Precincts Respectively to Perform the Procefsioning As Above Mentioned and Directed; and the s^d Procefsioners are to take Notice that If the Owner of Any Land Shall refuse to Suffer his or her Land to be Procefsioned as the Law Directs that within ten

---

* Scratched through in original but still legible.—C. G. C.

Order'd that Lewis Mountague be Appointed Clerk
this Vestry

Phillip Grymes Gen[t] is Appointed Vestryman in [the]
of Robert Elliott Gen[t] d[ecease]d

Barth[o] Yates Min[ister]

At a Vestry held for Christ Church Parish in the Co[unty]
of Middlesex on Tuesday the first Day of Dec[r] 1767 at Which [were]
Present The Rev[d] Barth[o] Yates Minister, John Robinson,
William Churchhill Robert Daniel, James Mills
Gawin Corbin, & Lewis Mountague, Gent[n] of the Vestry
Charles Nelson & Augustin Smith is Elected Vestry[man and]
Present Charles Nelson & Augusten Smith Gen[tn] Vestry

We of this Vestry According to an Act of Assembly have
Subscribe'd that We are Conformable to the Doctrines of [the]
Church of England and the discipline thereof To Witne[ss]
Our hands.

John Robinson   John Robinson
Will Churchhill   Will Churchhill
Robert Daniel   Robert Daniel
James Mills   James Mills
Gawin Corbin   Gawin Corbin
Lewis Mountague   Lewis Mountague
Cha[s] Nelson   Cha[s] Nelson
Augustine Smith   Augustine Smith
Nov[r] 1[?] 176[?]   Philip L Grymes
Philip L Grymes

PAGE 313 OF THE MANUSCRIPT

Days after Such Refusal they Certifie the same to the Church wardins of the Parish.

(313)   Order^d that Lewis Mountague be Appointed Clark of This Vestery.

Phillip Grymes Gen^t is Appointed Vesteryman in the Room of Robert Elliott Gen^t decd.

Barth° Yates Min^r

At a Vestery held for Christ Church Parish in the County of Middlesex on Tuesday the first Day of Decr 1767 at Which Ware Present. The Revd Barth° Yates Minister, John Robinson William Churchhill Robert Daniel, James Mills Gawin Corbin, & Lewis Mountague, Gen^{tn} of the Vestery

Charles Nelson, & Augustin Smith is Elected Vesterymen. Present Charles Nelson & Augustin Smith Gen^{tn} Vesterymen.

We of this Vestery According to an Act of Aſsembley have Subscribed that We are Conformable to the Doctrine of the Church of England and the discipline thereof As Witneſs Our hands.

John Robinson	John Robinson
Will Churchhill	Will Churchhill
Robert Daniel	Robert Daniel
James Mills	James Mills
Gawin Corbin	Gawin Corbin
Lewis Mountague	Lewis Montague
Chas Neilson	Chas Neilson
Augustine Smith	Augustine Smith

Novr 15. 1768

Philip L. Grymes	Philip L Grymes

(314)   At The same Vestery as on The Other side
        Ordered

To The Revd Barth° Yates Minister	16000
To Ditto Allowance for Transfar Notes	640
To Lewis Mountague Clk of the Vestery	1000
To Thomas Laughlin Clk of the Mother Church	1200
To William Chowning Clk of the Upper Church	1000
To James Hiptinstall and Roger Blackburn Clks of The Lower Church to be Paid According to time	1000

To Edward Bristo Sexton of the mother Church	600
To Eliz* Forgett Sexton of the Upper Church	600
To Thomas Sible Sexton of the Lower Church	500
To The Rent of the free School Land	500
To the Sherieff for Quitrents of ditto	110
To The Clk of the County for the List of Tithables	60

23210

To Charles Medeares		100
To William Guthrey		100
To Richard Wiatt	£ 5 ‖ 0 ‖ 0	
To the Church Wardins to Repair the Gleeb	5 ‖ 0 ‖ 0	
To Ellener Booth		500
To The Church Wardins for Mary Curtis		800
To Eliz* Brumwell		1200
To George Don lavy	1 ‖ 0 ‖ 0	

Agree'd With Dormon Darby to keep Anthony Fisher
for the Ensuing Year 800 to Be Levied Next Vestery
if he be Living

Order^d

To Judith Brumwell	300
To Rebecca Saunders	800
To Thomas Sibble	500
To Nicho* Jacobs for himself & Jacob Rice's Children	800
To Eliz* Forgett	500
To Sarah Proster for Eliz* Rupston and Child	500
To Paull Phillpotts	800
To John Hardee and Wife to keeping Eliz* Gardner	500
To William Kidd & keeping Jn° Kidd's Children	1200

To Rachel South for keeping Josep
Bishops Child   350

       Carried over Cash   £11 ‖ 0 ‖ 0   8950

       Carried Over Tobacco   32160
(315) Brought Over   £11 ‖ 0 ‖ 0   32160
To Joanna Dun lavy   1000
To William Saunders for keeping
Mary Lake   300
To James Mills Gen^{tn} as ℈ Acc^t 24 ‖ 10 ‖ 2
To William Chowning as ℈ Acc^t 10 ‖
To Tobias Allen for the Care of
John Smith   1 ‖ 11 ‖ 6
To Doct^r Robt Spratt   9 ‖ 0 ‖ 9
To Henry Va∫s for John Saunders   300
To Andrew Low   1 ‖ 11 ‖ 3
To George Daniel for Delinquents   675
To The Collector as by Acc^t &
Delinquents   1065
By a Deposi^m in Cash in
the Collectors hands 7 ‖ 18 ‖ 0¾
By the Collector
for fines   5 ‖

       12 ‖ 18 ‖ 0¾   48 ‖ 3 ‖ 8   35500
To the Collector to Sell to Pay
Cash Debts   4000
To 4 ℈ C^t for Cask   1580
To 6 ℈ C^t for Collecting   2464   8044

                            43544
By 1454 Tithables at 30 Each   43620
Order^d That James Mills Gen^{tm} be Appointed Collector of
this Present Le[vy].

Ord⁴ That The Parish Collector Collect *Collect of Every Tithable 30 ᵗᵇ Tob°

Ord⁴ That the Collector Give bond & security to the Church Wardins.

Gawin Corbin & Augustin Smith are Appoint Church Warde[ns] for the Insuing Year.

Ord⁴ That The Church Wardins Provide Such Surplises and Table Linen as Shall be Necefary for the Churches.

Ord⁴ That The Overplus of The Tob° Levied for the *free *School *Land Quitrents of the free School land be Accounted for at the Laying of the Next Parish Levey.

Barth° Yates

(316) Mr. Robert Yates Minister of Middlesex Parish from May 1699 to May 1702 returned to England in bad health.

In †1403 Mr Bartholomew Yates (probably his son) succeeded him After 14 years of faithful ministering they increased his salary 4000 weight of Tobbacco fearing to lose him to York Hampton & renewed his Glebe House. He died in 1734 being minis 31 years They sent over for one of his sons then receiving his education in England. The Rev⁴ Mr Read & Jones supplied the parish for two years untill he came. His name also Bartholomew he was the minister untill 1767 according to the Vestry book which was filled or the rest torn off I can find no other Vestry book

The Father son & Grandson ministers from 1699 to 1767 & perhaps more   *By *a *list *I *have

In the year 1754 we find a William Yates minister in Glocester supposed to be the son of Bartholomew Yates

---

* These words scratched through in original, but still legible.—C. G. C.
† Evidently a mistake for 1703.—C. G. C.

NOTES

NOTES

The MS. page numbers—which are not a part of the original record, but were supplied by the transcriber—are shown thus (1) in the printed volume.

Blank spaces —— generally enclosed within brackets, sometimes (e. g., on pages 35 and 40) unenclosed —— denote something left out by mistake of the writer of the MS, or something erased or otherwise illegible, or something written on a part of the page that has been worn away by time or use.

The circumflex accent appearing in the printed volume over certain letters of certains words (e. g., the letter m in the word sume on page 1.) and occurring thus, or as a straight line, in the MS. indicates a contraction or unusual form of spelling.

Page 2. (MS. page 1.)

"Vestry Mens Oath &c". The explanation of the fact that we find in the Vestrymen's Oath (which occurs on page 1. of the MS., between items dated 1663 and 1664 respectively) a reference to Christ Church Parish, whereas that parish was not established until 1666, is as follows.

The extant MS. Vestry Book, while containing (copies of) records going back to 1663, was first written in in the year 1701 or 1702. [See page 93. (MS. page 109), note of copyist John Nash, written subsequent to Nov. 20, 1701.] The clerk, John Nash, evidently made use of the first convenient blank space he had (which happened to be part of page 1.) to record the form of oath which all vestrymen then (i. e., in 1701) were required to take before entering upon the duties of their office. In 1701 the form of oath to be taken naturally contained the words Parish of Christ Church.

Page 5. (MS. page 5.)

"General Vestry"; i. e., a vestry consisting of the members of the vestries of the two parishes of Lancaster and Peanckatanck.

Page 7. (MS. page 6.)

"County List"; i. e., List of tythables in that part of Lancaster County lying south of the Rappahannock.

Page 8 (MS. page 7.)

"30th of January An. 1666". According to the modern way of reckoning this date should read January 30, 1667.

Page 12. (MS. page 11.)

"lower pish"; i. e., that part of the parish which formerly had been the Parish of Peanckatanck.

Page 19. (MS. page 19.)

The first reference to Middlesex County by name is dated Sep. 5, 1672. See cut facing this page.

Page 20. (MS. page 19.)

From the figures given at the bottom of this page, it appears that in the year 1672 Christ Church Parish contained 571 persons subject to the payment of parish and county taxes (i. e., by or on account of whom taxes were payable.

Page 24. (MS. page 23.)

The memorandum note, by the copyist, John Nash, written at the bottom of MS. page 23, is interesting and (perhaps) significant in view of the date, 1676—the year of Bacon's Rebellion.

Page 46. (MS. page 48.)

"Repaireing the Housen". Note the unusual plural form *housen* for *houses*.

Page 126. (MS. page 140.)

On this and the following page are given the building specifications for the yet standing Christ Church, Middlesex County, Va. See frontispiece.

Page 148. (MS. page 152.)

"the Piping Tree". In *Old King William Homes and Families* (P. N. Clarke, Louisville, 1897), occurs the following: "This report" (i. e., a report of the Smithsonian Institute by John Garland Pollard, of Richmond) "also explains the origin of the curious name of 'Piping-tree Ferry'. At a council between the whites and Indians the pipe was passed around on the ratification of the treaty, after which it was deposited in a hollow tree near by. Ever afterward when the whites disregarded their agreement they were reminded by the Indians of the 'Pipe-in-tree'."

The above explanation is ingenious, and would perhaps be convincing but for the fact that in the Colony of Virginia there were certainly three —and probably many more—places called by the name of the Piping (or Pipeing, or Pipe-in-) Tree; e. g., the Pipe-in-Tree Ferry on the Chickahominy, the Piping Tree Ferry over the Pamunkey, and the Piping Tree in Middlesex County. If at the conclusion of every treaty with Indians a pipe was placed in a tree, Mr. Pollard's explanation of the origin of the name Piping Tree might be considered plausible, but otherwise not.

Another possible explanation has been suggested to the transcriber by Dr. W. G. Stanard, of the Virginia Historical Society. Dr. Stanard calls attention to the fact that in the colonial period the verb *to pipe* was used as the equivalent of the modern verbs *to whistle* and *to blow*. If then the name Piping Tree were always associated with a ferry, the explanation would be that on this spot stood a tree to which was attached a whistle or horn to be blown by travellers as a signal to the ferryman that they were waiting to cross the stream. Against this explanation, however, there must in fairness be admitted the fact that so far as the "Piping Tree" frequently mentioned in this book is concerned there is nothing in the book to indicate whether it was the name of a ferry or not.

Page 197. (MS. page 188.)

"Act for the better and more effectual Improveing the Staple of Tobacco". The wording of this Act (which is given in *Hening* by title only) was first published in full in *The Virginia Magazine of History and Biography*, vol. xx, page 158 (1912).

Page 339. (MS. page 313.)

It is interesting to note that the names appearing in the first column of subscribers to the Oath of Conformity are autograph signatures. See cut facing this page.

List of Names of the Incumbents of Christ Church Parish, giving page on which each name first appears.

*The Rev. Mr. Morris, page 2.

†The Rev. Mr. Cole, page 5.

The Rev. Mr. John Shepherd, page 12.

The Rev. Mr. Duell Pead, page 41.

The Rev. Matthew Lidford, page 71.

The Rev. Mr. Samuel Gray, page 71.

The Rev. Mr. Robert Yates, page 86.

The Rev. Mr. Bartholomew Yates, page 96.

‡The Rev. Mr. John Reade, page 238.

The Rev. Mr. Bartholomew Yates, page 244.

* Mr. Morris was the first incumbent of Christ Church Parish. He had previously been the incumbent of Lancaster and Peanckatanck Parishes. —C. G. C.

† Mr. Cole was a predecessor of Mr. Morris in Lancaster and Peanckatanck Parishes, which when combined formed Christ Church Parish. He was of course, technically speaking, never the incumbent of Christ Church Parish.—C. G. C.

‡ Mr. Reade is included in the list because of the fact that he was in charge of the parish for about two years. Technically speaking he was not incumbent of the parish in the sense that the other clergymen in the list were.—C. G. C.

List of Names of Occasional (or Supply) Preachers in Christ Church Parish, giving page on which each name first appears.

The Rev. Mr. Superias, page 11.

*(The Rev.) Mr. John Davis, page 41.

The Rev. Mr. Clack, page 68.

The Rev. Mr. Booker, page 68.

The Rev. Mr. Emanuel Jones, page 245.

* Mr. Davis is mentioned but once in the Vestry Book in connection with the function of preaching. That he was a regularly ordained minister cannot be proved from the single entry on page 41. The John Davis whose name appears frequently later on in the book was probably a different person.—C. G. C.

List of Names of Physicians and Surgeons occurring in this Book, giving page on which each name first appears.

Dr. Rose, page 10.
Dr. Wm. Poole, page 28.
Dr. Robert Boodle, page 40.
Dr. Stapleton, page 45.
Dr. Tankerley, page 81.
Dr. Wm. Oastler, page 83.
Dr. Robert Deputy, page 88.
Dr. Lomax, page 91.
*Nathaniel Juice, page 101.
*John Gibbs, page 113.
Dr. Baker, page 115.
Dr. Crannavett, page 115.
Dr. Thornton, page 124.
Dr. Lewis Tomkins, page 151.
Dr. Wallford, page 160.
Dr. Mark Bannerman, page 200.
Dr. James Boyd, page 223.
Dr. John Symmer, page 231.
Dr. John Mitchell, page 241.
Dr. Bird, page 255.
Dr. John Strachey, page 263.
Dr. Alexander Reade, page 271.
Dr. Philip Fercharson, page 317.
Dr. Robert Spratt, page 332.

* I am not at all sure that Nathaniel Juice and John Gibbs were regular physicians. Probably they were not.—C. G. C.

List of Names of Surveyors and of Surveyors of the Highways occurring in this Book, giving the page on which each name with title first appears.

Col. John Catlett, page 10.
Mr. George Morris, page 10.
Mr. Edwin Thacker, page 57.
Mr. Harry Beaverley, page 98.

List of Subscribers

List of Subscribers

Adams, Prof Arthur; Hartford, Conn.

Ancell, Rev. B. L.; Yangchow, China.

Barnhill, Mrs. John F.; Indianapolis, Ind.

Battle, Mrs. Geo. Gordon; New York, N. Y.

Blackwell, Mr. Henry; New York, N. Y.

Bristow, Mr. M. E.; Richmond, Va.

Brooke, Dr. T. V.; Sutherlin, Va.

Bruce, Senator Wm. Cabell, Baltimore, Md.

Bryan, Mr. John Stewart, Richmond, Va.

Carpenter, Mr. H. W., Brookfield Center, Conn.

Cary, Mr. Hunsdon; Richmond, Va.

Chamberlayne, Mrs. Jno. Hampden; Richmond, Va.

Chowning, Mr. Carroll C.; Urbanna, Va.

Claiborne, Mr. W. S.; Monteagle, Texas

Davie, Mr. Preston; New York, N. Y.

Davies, Mr. H. Thornton, Manassas, Va.

Drybread, Mrs. J. G.; Franklin, Ind.

Eggleston, Dr. J. D.; Hampden-Sidney, Va.

Embrey, Mr. Alvin T.; Fredericksburg, Va.

Fauntleroy, Miss Juliet; Alavista, Va.

Fishburn, Mr. J. B.; Roanoke, Va.

Gordon, Mr. Armistead C.; Staunton, Va.

Gordon, Mr. Jas. W.; Richmond, Va.

Gordon, Mr. R. Latimer; Richmond, Va.

Gray, Mr. Palmer; Richmond, Va.

Gregory, Mr. Geo. C.; Richmond, Va.

Grinnan, Judge Daniel; Richmond, Va.

Harrison, Mr. Fairfax; Belvoir, Va.

Henderson, Mrs. Helen S. T.; Lynchburg, Va.

Hiden, Mrs. R. W. Newport News, Va.

Hill, Mr. Albert H.; Richmond, Va.

Hinkle, Prof. Wm. J.; Auburn, N. Y.

Holliday, Mr. J. S.; Indianapolis, Ind.

Jackson, Mr. H. W.; Richmond, Va.

Jones, Mr. T. Catesby; New York, N. Y.

Jones, Mr. W. Mac; Richmond, Va.

Joynes, Mr. Levin; Richmond, Va.

Kemper, Mr. E. H.; Alexandria, Va.

Lamb, Mrs. E. T.; Norfolk, Va.

McCandlish, Mr. F. S.; Fairfax, Va.

McFall, Mr. James; Pittsburgh, Pa.

McGuire, Mr. M. M.; Richmond, Va.

McKinney, Mrs. Roy W.; Paducah Ky:

McNeill, Mrs. W. S.; Richmond, Va.

Michael, Mr. C. Edwin; Roanoke, Va.

Miller, Mr. Rudolph P.; New York, N. Y.

Myers, Mr. Lilburn T.; Richmond, Va.

Nicklin, Mr. J. B., Jr.; Chattanooga, Tenn.

Patton, Miss Nancy L.; Richmond, Va.

Payne, Mr. Brooke; Fredericksburg, Va.

Payne, The Hon. John Barton; Washington, D. C.

Peterkin; Mrs. Geo. W.; Parkersburg, W. Va.

Robins, Dr. Charles R.; Richmond, Va.

Robinson, Miss Agnes C.; Washington, D. C.

Scott, Mrs. Thos. B.; Richmond, Va.

Sheppard, Mrs. H. D.; Hanover, Pa.

Slemp, The Hon. C. Bascom: Washington, D. C.

Smith, Mr. H. M., Jr.; Richmond, Va.

Smith, Dr. Jas. H; Richmond, Va.

Smith, Mr. Jno. Augustine; New Orleans, La.

Stewart, Miss A. C.; Brook Hill, Va.

Stewart, Miss E. H.; Brook Hill, Va.

Stewart Mr. J. Adger; Louisville, Ky.

Stewart, Miss L. W.; Brook Hill, Va.

Stewart, Miss Norma; Brook Hill, Va.

Stone, Mr. Edward L.; Roanoke, Va.

Stone, Miss Lucy P.; Hollins, Va.

Tennant, Mr. W. Brydon; Richmond, Va.

Thomas, Dr. Jno. N.; Pineville, La.

Thruston, Mr. R. C. Ballard; Louisville, Ky.

Todd, Mrs. G. Carroll; Washington, D. C.

Tyler, Dr. Lyon G. Holdcroft, Va.

Valentine, Mrs. E. V.; Richmond, Va.

Valentine, Mr. Frederick S.; Richmond, Va.

Valentine, Mr. G. G.; Richmond, Va.

Valentine, Mrs. G. G.; Richmond, Va.

Walker, Mrs. J. A.; Brownwood, Texas

Waller, Mr. E. P.; Schenectady, N. Y.

Walters, Mr. J. S. T.; Baltimore, Md.

Watson, Mrs. A. M.; Louisville, Ky.

Wayland, Dr. John W.; Harrisonburg, Va.

Weddell, Consul General A. W.; City of Mexico, Mexico

Wellford, Dr. B. R.; Richmond, Va.

Whitty, Mr. T. H.; Richmond, Va.

Wiggins, Mrs. Joseph P.; Indianapolis, Ind.

Williams, Mr. E. Randolph; Richmond, Va.

Williams, Mr. Lewis C.; Richmond, Va.

Williams, Mr. Thos. C.; Richmond, Va.

Wood, Mrs. Wm. P.; Richmond, Va.

Woodward, Rev. E. L., M. D.; Richmond, Va.

Wormeley, Mr. Carter W.; Richmond, Va.

BOOK-STORES

The Bell Book and Stationery Co.; Richmond, Va.

Hunter & Co.; Richmond, Va.

Presbyterian Committee of Publication; Richmond, Va.

LIBRARIES

Bridgeport Public Library and Reading Room; Bridgeport, Conn.

Detroit Public Library; Detroit, Mich.

Hampden-Sidney College; Hampden-Sidney, Va.

Handley Library; Winchester, Va.

Historical Memorial, and Art Department of Iowa; Des Moines, Iowa.

Historical Society of Pennsylvania; Philadelphia, Pa.

Indiana State Library; Indianapolis, Ind.

Jones Memorial Library, Lynchburg, Va.

Kenmore Association; Fredericksburg, Va.

Lawson McGhee Library; Knoxville, Tenn.

Library of Congress; Washington, D. C.

Long Island Historical Society; Brooklyn, N. Y.

Los Angeles Public Library; Los Angeles, Calif.

National Society of Daughters of the American Revolution; Washington, D. C.

Nebraska State Library; Lincoln, Nebraska

Newberry Library; Chicago, Illinois

Newport News Public Library; Newport News, Va.

Norfolk Public Library; Norfolk, Va.

North Carolina State Library; Raleigh, N. C.

Ohio State Library; Columbus, Ohio

Peabody Institute; Baltimore, Md.

Theological Seminary of Virginia; Alexandria, Va.

University of North Carolina; Chapel Hill, N. C.

University of Virginia; University, Va.

Virginia Diocesan Library; Richmond, Va.

Virginia Historical Society, Richmond, Va.

Virginia State Library; Richmond, Va.

Wallace Library; Fredericksburg, Va.

West Virginia, Dept. of Archives and History; Charleston, W. Va.

West Virginia Historical Society; Morgantown, W. Va.

William and Mary, Library of the College of; Williamsburg, Va.

INDEXES

Index of Names of Persons

Adcock;—164, 170; John Smith,—291, 295, 296, 311, 313, 320, 332; Sarah,—159[2]

Aker; Ralph,—113

Alden (Aldin, Alldin); Ellianor.—65; Jno.—149, 167, 178, 184

Allen (Allin); Eliz^a—326; Rich^d—181; Royal Rich^d—301, 306, 311, 313, 316; Tobias,—341

Alphin; Constance,—243, 245

Alstone (Allstone); Katharine,—327, 329

Anderson; Henry (Harry),—314, 317, 322, 326; W^m—164, 165

Anderton; Geo.—19

Anne; Edwd—66, 67

Appleton; Jno.—5, 6

Armistead (Armstead); Mr.—109; Henry,—147, 152, 156, 162; W^m—262

Athawes; Edwd—306

Axe; Geo.—17, 20, 21, 24[2], 25, 26, 27, 29

Baden; Eliz^a—278, 288[2], 290[2], 295; H.—285; Widow,—285

Baker; D^r—115, 117[2], 124; Avarilla,—117, 123; Rachel,—223, 227, 229, 231, 236, 241, 243, 245, 247, 252[2], 254, 255, 256, 261, 262, 264, 266, 270, 272; Ralph—113; Robt—215; W^m—165

Baldwin (Baldin, Balwin); Jno.—227, 229, 231, 236, 240, 242, 245, 247, 252, 253, 255, 256, 260, 262, 264, 266, 270, 272, 274; Judith,—256, 260, 261, 264, 266; W^m—4

Ball (Bawl); Edwd—89[2], 94, 143, 151, 154, 156, 159, 164, 169, 174, 178, 180, 181, 186, 200, 203, 207; Henry,—117, 124, 134, 137, 142, 223, 227; Keziah,—210, 217, 220, 222, 227, 229, 231, 236, 241[2], 242

Bannerman; Mark,—200, 207, 217

Barbee; Geo.—261; W^m—148, 166

Barden; Edwd—326, 328; Jno—326, 328

Barnes; Henery,—117

Barnet; Christopher,—109

Barwick (Barrick, Berwick, Berrick); David,—18, 20, 28, 29, 60, 337; Geo.—134, 149, 167, 175, 184, 199, 206, 209, 236, 241, 243

Baskett (Basket); Henry,—87, 91, 134, 137, 142, 152, 159; Honora (Honor, Honour),—117, 124, 134, 137, 142, 152, 155, 159, 165, 169, 174, 178[2]

Batchelder (Batcheldor, Batcheller); J.— 323; Jas.—222; Jno—281; Joseph,—322, 336; Saml—165, 169, 175, 213, 225, 230, 273, 278[2], 300, 302; W^m—169, 174, 178, 181, 186, 200, 203, 207, 210

Bateman; Rich^d—241, 243

Beaman; Jno.—275

Bendall; Jas.—105

Berkeley (Berkley, Barkley, Bearkley); Col.—280, 292, 303, 309, 323, 337; Maj.—229, 232, 234; Edm^d—138, 147, 152[2], 156, 157, 158, 159, 162[3], 163, 166, 215, 217, 218, 219, 220, 224[2], 227[2], 228, 229, 230[2], 231[2], 233, 234, 235[2], 236, 238, 242, 244, 245, 247, 252, 255, 256, 261, 262, 263[3], 264, 268, 272,

274, 276, 279, 282, 284, 287, 289, 290, 295, 296, 297, 298², 299, 301, 302, 311, 316, 319, 328, 330, 331, 333, 334², 336

Berry; Jno.—198, 258, 268, 275; Thos.—254, 257, 261, 262, 264

Best; Wm—297

Bevan; Jno.—152

Beverley (Beverley); Mr—17, 95; Robt—7, 8³, 10, 12, 15, 16, 18², 19, 21, 22, 24, 26, 27, 28³, 30², 31, 32, 33², 34, 45, 46; Harry,—93, 96, 98, 99, 100, 101², 104, 106, 109, 110, 111, 112, 114, 116, 118², 119, 121, 122³, 123², 124, 125, 128, 131, 133, 134, 136², 137, 138, 141, 143, 145, 148, 150, 151², 152, 157, 158², 162, 163, 164, 166, 169, 172⁶, 173⁷, 174⁴, 177, 180, 183, 187

Biggs; Robt—101, 102, 104

Bird (Burd); Dr—255; Ann,—307, 308; Jno.—105, 169, 174, 178, 266, 278, 283, 285, 288, 291, 294, 296, 298, 301

Bishop; Joseph, 341

Blackburn (Blackbourne); Edwd —266; Mary,—276; Roger,— 339; Wm— 141², 142, 148, 166, 184, 198, 199, 202, 207

Blackley; Geo.—274

Blackmore; Jas.—23²

Blake (Blaike); Jno.—9, 10, 17, 26², 28, 29³, 30²

Blakey; Mary,—262, 263, 265

Blalke; Jno.—31

Blewford; Eliza—91, 94; Thos.— 214, 217

Bohannah; Jno.—222

Bond; Robt—299, 302, 315

Boodle; Dr Robt—40³, 47, 60², 64, 67

Booker; (the Rev.?) Mr—68

Booth; Eleanor (Nelly),—317, 321, 327, 329, 335, 340

Borden; Thos.—211

Boreskel (Boreskill, Borroskell); Richd—273; Thos.—278, 283

Boswell; Mr—4; Edwd—2, 3, 6

Bowman; Margaret,—201, 204, 205, 207, 222, 223², 227², 229², 231², 236, 241, 243, 246, 247, 252, 254² 255, 257², 261, 262, 264², 266² 270², 272, 274, 275, 278²

Boyd; Dr Jas.—223

Branch; Frances,—248, 249, 253

Branshaw; Chas.—91 96³; Mary,— 96

Bream (Brame, Brim); Eliza— 314, 317, 320, 326; Jno.—291², 295, 296², 299, 301, 307, 308, 311, 312; Penelope,—312; Richd— 299, 301, 307, 311, 314

Brereton; Thos.—314

Bridge; Francis,—22, 25³, 26

Bristow (Bristo, Bristoll); Mr— 100, 101, 106; Edwd—268, 279, 281, 299, 302, 306, 311, 313, 317, 320, 321, 325, 326, 328, 330, 331, 334, 337, 340; Jas.—307; Jno.— 93, 94², 96, 102, 104, 109², 112, 114, 115, 116, 117², 123, 134, 136, 137, 142, 151; Margaret,—264, 266, 270, 272, 275; Mary,—221; Nicholas,—178, 180; Wm—248, 252, 257, 259, 268, 270, 279, 281, 292, 299, 302, 326

Brocas; Capt—5

Bromel; Elenor,— 218, 221, 223, 227, 229, 231

Brooks (Brookes), Alice,—283, 285, 288, 291, 295, 297, 299, 301, 307, 311, 314, 321², 326; Caleb,— 211, 265, 266; Catharine (Catherine),—113, 270; Jeffrey,—51; Jonathan,—159; Mary,—266, 270, 272, 295, 297, 299, 301, 307, 311, 314, 320, 326, 329, 330; Philip,— 265², 266, 270, 272, 283, 285; Sarah,—105, 113; Thos.—94, 97; Wm—89, 159, 165, 265

Browne; Jas.—115

Brumwell (Brummel, Brummell, Brumel); Eliza—340; Judith,—299, 302, 307, 314, 340; Thos.—239, 250, 258, 264, 266, 295

Bryant (Briant); Jno.—226, 230, 293

Buford (Beuford, B e w f o r d); Eliza—97, 102, 105; Henry,—168; Wm—269, 275, 282

Burk (Birk); Jno.—134, 151², 152

Burnham; Lt Col.—26; Jno.— 18, 19, 24, 25², 27, 30; Rowland,—3

Burtin; Isaack,—208

Butcher (Bucher); Wm— 6, 8², 10², 11, 13²

Butler (Buttler); Mary,—243², 246², 248², 252², 254

Cain (Caine); Anne,—273, 284, 288, 291, 294; Roger,—246; Wm —229, 231, 236

Callahan (Calleham, Callehan); Ann,— 218, 224, 243, 246; Patrick,—264, 272, 274, 307

Cambel (C a m p b l e); Jas.—259, 269; Margaret, 257²

Cambridge (Cambridg); Ann,—220; Edmd—151

C a n n a d y (Cannedy, Canida); Alice,—97; Edwd—181; Eliza,—118; Kathrine,—181

Cant; Jno.—49³ 58, 66, 69², 70, 72, 73, 74, 77

Cardwell; Wm—278, 283

Carroll (Carrell, Carril); Jno.—241, 243; Susanna,—311; Wm—261

Cary; Oswald,—36, 37, 40, 43, 44, 46, 50, 52, 56², 57, 58², 62

Catlett (Catlitt); Jno.—10,11

Chaney; Dorothy,—246

Cheap;—255

Cheedle (C h e d l e); Hannah,—136, 142, 151, 156, 159; Jno.—91,

94; Widow,—198, 202, 206, 209, 216, 223, 225, 239, 250, 259, 268, 281, 293, 304, 309, 323, 337

Chichley; Lady Agatha,—38; Sir Henry,—5, 15, 16³, 17, 18², 24⁴, 25, 30

Chilton; Peter,—94

Chipsey; Edmd—65

Chowning (Chewning); Mr—14; Geo.—198, 226, 261, 311; Jno.—244, 247, 273, 275; Richd—294; Robt—1, 2, 3², 4, 8, 15; Thos.—13; Wm—277, 283, 285, 288, 290, 296, 298, 301, 306, 311, 313, 316, 319, 325, 328, 331, 334, 339, 341

Churchill (Churchhill, Churchel); —234, 258, 268, 280, 292, 303, 309, 323, 337; Col.—223², 236, 249, 261, 286, 287; Esqr—102, 104²; Madam,— 124, 142, 151²; Madam Eliza—151³, 163²; Mr—100²; Armistead,—209, 215, 217, 218², 219, 220, 221, 222, 224, 227, 228, 231, 233², 234, 235², 237³, 238, 241, 242⁴, 244, 245, 246, 247, 252, 253, 255, 256, 258, 260, 262, 263, 264, 266, 267, 270, 272, 274, 276, 277², 284, 286², 287, 288, 296, 298, 305, 308, 311², 313, 316, 319², 321, 325; Eliza—132², 137²; Wm—43², 44, 45, 46, 47³, 48, 50², 56, 58², 59, 60, 63, 66³, 67², 68, 69, 70, 72, 79, 80, 81, 82, 83², 85, 87², 88², 90, 91², 92², 93³, 94, 95⁴, 96², 97, 99, 100³, 101, 102², 103, 104², 106, 107, 108², 132², 135, 157, 178, 276³, 277, 279, 280, 286, 287, 288, 292², 300, 301, 303, 305, 308, 309, 318, 319², 320, 322², 323, 325, 326, 327, 330, 334, 336, 339²

Clack; Mr—68

Clark (Clarke); Edwd—225, 230, 239, 250, 257, 259; Jno.—122, 123², 124, 127, 128, 172², 173, 338; Thos.—200

Clay; Mary,—76, 78, 79, 83, 85, 87, 89, 91, 94, 97, 103, 105, 109, 113, 114, 117, 124, 134, 137, 142, 151, 155; Widow,—81

Clowdas (Cloudas, Croudas, Crowdans); Wᵐ—261, 272, 274, 275

Cock; Mʳ—4, 14, 24; Maurice,—64, 66², 68², 69, 72, 73, 75, 76, 77, 78, 80; Nicholas,—2. 3², 5, 8, 10, 12, 16, 17, 21², 23, 28, 33, 37², 38, 39, 44, 47, 48

Coffley (Coffle); Mary,—203², 204², 207, 211³

Coggin (Cogin, Coging, Cocking); Jno.—25, 26, 27, 29

Cole; Mʳ—5

Collins; Jno.— 28, 29

Colly (Colley); Patience,— 261, 262, 263

Comberland; Gabriell, 9

Cooper; Ann,— 183, 203, 217, 220, 223, 227, 229, 231, 236, 241, 243, 245, 247, 252, 254; Chas.— 169, 187, 200, 204, 254; Wᵐ—278

Corbin (Corban);—118, 119, 122; Col.—16, 17, 19, 121; Esqʳ—24; Mʳ—4, 6, 87; Gawin (Gowen), —85, 86, 87, 89, 90², 93³, 94, 100, 101, 104, 109, 115, 116, 118, 119, 122², 123, 319, 334, 339³, 342; Henry,—1⁴ 2², 3³, 4⁴, 5, 6, 7, 8², 9, 10², 11, 12, 13, 15, 16, 18, 21, 22, 24, 35²; Richᵈ—251, 252, 253², 254, 255, 257, 264

Cosley; Mary,—200

Cotes; Ann,—299, 302

Crank; Thos.—65

Crannavett; Dʳ—115

Creeke; Henry,—35

Crisp (Chrisp); Thos.—80, 81, 83, 86, 87, 89, 90²

Crocker; Elizᵃ—243, 246, 247, 252; Wᵐ—227, 229, 231, 235, 236 241², 243

Crosfield; Jno.—257

Crosly (Crosley); Elenor,— 246; Joseph,—322, 327, 330²

Crutchfield; Wᵐ—211

Cummins (Cumings, Comings); Angelo,—169, 174, 178

Curlis (Curliss); Elizᵃ—169², 174, 178, 181; Mercy,—112; Michael, —103, 104, 109, 112

Curtis (Curtice); Mʳ—4, 5, 6; Christopher,—254, 256, 258, 261, 262, 308, 318, 322; Jas.—45, 49, 149; Jno.—3², 4², 5, 6, 8, 11, 12, 13², 116, 138, 143, 183, 201, 204, 205³, 207, 209, 211, 212², 216, 217, 219, 224², 227, 229, 236; Mary,—332, 335, 340; Rice,—185, 214², 217

Daniel (Daniell); Chas.—265, 274, 277; Garrott (Garrot, Garrit),—214, 216², 226, 230, 240, 251; Geo.—275, 288, 290, 312, 320, 322², 334, 341; Henry,—269, 281; Jas.— 149, 167, 184, 188, 198, 202, 206, 209, 213, 216², 219, 225, 269, 281, 284, 299, 301, 310, 324, 326, 337; Jno.—314, 327, 329; Richᵈ—117, 151, 200, 203, 207², 278²; Robᵗ—77, 92, 93², 101, 104, 106, 107, 109, 111, 112, 116, 118², 122, 123², 125, 133, 135, 136, 137², 139, 141, 143, 144, 145, 150, 158, 163, 166, 169, 172³, 173, 174, 175, 178, 184, 187, 268, 293, 318, 322², 325², 326, 327, 328, 329, 330⁴, 331², 332², 334, 336², 339³; Widow,— 218; Wᵐ—43² 44, 46, 50⁴, 51, 52, 56, 58, 61, 63, 66², 69², 70, 72, 74², 78, 79, 80, 81, 211², 239, 250, 259², 293, 299, 302, 307, 310

Darby; Dorman,—340

Davidson; Robᵗ—229

Davis (D a v i e s) ; Alice,—178 ;
Andrew,—248, 268 ; Eliz^a— 183 ;
Henry,—71, 81 ; Jno.—41, 149,
151, 225, 230, 249, 258, 285,
314 ; W^m—187, 248, 254
Day ; Jno.—124
Deacon ; Edward,—299 ; Jno.—291,
302
Deagle ; Jno.— 275, 285, 288, 312 ;
Mary Ann,—328 ; Rebekah,—
328, 332
Degee ; Jno.— 142, 187
Deputy ; Dr Robt—88
Deverdale ; Jone,— 45, 46, 47, 59,
83 ; Jno.—81
Devoll (Devol) ; Elenor,—246, 252,
254, 255, 257, 261, 262, 266, 270
Diggs (Digg) ; Jno.— 149, 175
Dillard ; Edwd—239, 250, 259, 268,
281 ; Jno.—323, 337
Dobbins ; Eliz^a— 295, 297, 299,
301, 307, 311, 314, 320, 326, 329
Dobbs ; Mary,—253, 255
Docker ; Edwd—95, 96, 100, 102,
104^2, 109, 110, 112, 114, 117, 124
Dodson ; Francis,—84, 138 ; Mabel,
—159 ; Nathaniel,—104 ; Rachel,
—207
Don lavy ; Geo.—340
Dos ; W^m—156
Dowrey (Dowrie) ; Eliz^a—45, 49^2
Dudding ; Humphrey,—51
Dudley ; M^r—6, 14, 18, 23, 24 ;
Ann,—253, 255, 262, 263 ; Jas.—
213, 238, 249 ; Jno.—241, 243 ;
Peyton,—249 ; Robt—36, 39^2, 43,
50^2, 51, 52, 56, 58, 60, 61, 62,
66, 69, 70, 72, 73, 74, 77, 78,
80, 81, 84, 87^3, 259 ; Thos.—78,
275 ; W^m—6, 8, 15, 16^3, 20^2, 21^2,
23^2, 66
Dunkington ; Ann,—83
Dunlevy (Dunlavy), J o a n n a
(Johannah) ;—332, 335, 341
Dunstan ; Richard,—279

Dye ; Ann,—334 ; Arthur,—278,
283^6, 285, 288, 291, 294, 296,
298, 301, 307, 311, 314, 317,
320, 326, 328, 332

Eberson ;—235
Eddington ; Eliz^a—60
Edey ; Christopher,—34
Effingham ;—43
Elliott (Elliot) ; Anthony,—7 ;
Eliz^a—272 ; Robt—270, 276, 277,
280, 282, 284^3, 286, 287^2, 290,
294, 295, 296^2, 298, 299, 301,
302, 306, 308, 311, 316, 319,
325^3, 327, 328^2, 330, 331^3, 334^2,
339
Emberson ; Henry,—274, 275, 276 ;
Jane,—283 ; M a r g a r e t,—283 ;
Sarah,—283
Etrage ; Katherine, 34
Evans ; Edwd—40

Falkner ; Thos.—222
Fearn ; Geo.—282, 293, 310 ; Jno.—
213, 217, 225, 230, 255 ; Thos.—
250
Fercharson ; Dr Philip,— 317, 326
Field ; Thos.—164
Finley (Finly, Finlee) ; Mary,—
183, 205, 222, 224, 235, 238,
244, 247, 249, 253, 255
Finnick (Finick) ;Mary,—204^2, 207
Fisher ; Anthony,—340 ; Jas.—187,
200 ; Rich^d—85
Floyd ; Jane, 89, 90
Folke ; Andrew,—91
Fomett ; Jno.—102
Forget ; Chas.—244^2, 283, 289, 291,
296 ; Eliz^a—270, 272, 274, 277,
290, 291, 294, 296, 298, 301,
306, 311, 313, 317^2, 320, 325,
328, 331, 334, 340^2
Fox (Foxe) ; Jno.—299, 302 ;
Owen,—47

Frazier; Alex^r—273, 278, 285, 288, 295, 299, 302, 306, 308, 312, 314, 329, 332

Freeman; Ann,—183

Freestone, (Freeston, Freston); Geo.—169, 174, 178; Mary—76, 182

French; Catharine,—264; Mary,—253; Thos.—244²

Fricston; Henry,—45

Furnett; Jno.—117

Furrell; Ann,—117

Gailbraith; Robt—167

Gaines (Gains, Gaynes); Henry,—234, 235; Robt—235², 237, 242

Gardner (Gardiner); Ann,—160; Eliz^a—326, 329, 332, 335, 340; Jas.—297; W^m—142, 243², 246, 314

Gayre; Jonathan,—156, 159, 161, 164, 169

George; Harry,—250; Rich^d—239

Gest; Eliz^a—295, 297, 307, 311, 314

Gibbs; Gregory,—23; Jno.—113², 115, 160, 165, 178; Mary,—207

Gibson; Jas.—275, 312, 315

Gillet; Rebecca,—222

Gilliam; Robt—60

Goodloe; Henry,—150, 168

Goodridge; Rebecca,—31

Goodwin; Geo.—240; Jno.—243

Gordon (Gorden, Gordin); Jno.—71, 314; W^m—15, 16³, 50, 52, 71, 212

Gore (Goar); Joseph,—135, 148, 166, 184, 206, 278

Gott; Edwd—95

Goulder; Christopher,—38, 39, 47²

Graves; M^r—134, 144; Alex^r—126, 129³, 130², 131³, 136, 138, 143², 155, 172³, 173³, 174, 211, 222

Gray; Saml— 71, 74, 75⁴, 77³, 78², 79², 80, 81², 83², 86²; W^m—211

Greenwood; Jno.—299, 302, 307; Rich^d—254

Gresom; W^m—248

Griffin; Thos.—108, 115

Grissum; Ann,—288

Grymes; 202², 206², 234; Col.—114, 216², 219, 234; M^r—53, 209²; Jno.— 77, 78², 79, 80², 81, 82, 84, 87², 89, 90, 93³, 95², 96, 99, 100², 101, 102², 105, 106, 107, 112², 123, 125², 128, 129², 131, 133, 139, 144, 145, 146, 147, 150, 153, 157², 158², 161³, 163⁴, 164, 165, 166, 169, 170², 171³, 172, 173³, 174³, 175, 177², 180, 181, 182, 183², 186, 197, 199, 200, 201², 202, 203³, 204², 205², 206, 208², 209, 210, 215², 217, 219, 220, 222, 224, 227², 229, 231, 233, 234, 235³, 237², 238², 242, 244, 245, 249, 252, 253, 258, 263, 264, 272, 276; Philip,—264², 266, 267, 270, 271, 273, 274, 276, 277², 279², 280, 282, 284, 286, 287, 290, 292, 296, 298, 312, 313, 316², 318, 319, 339³

Guest (Gues); Geo.—255, 257, 274, 276, 279

Guilliams; Robert,—45

Guthrey (Guthry, Gutterey, Guttery, Guttry); Jno.—178, 181, 222²; Mary,—238, 244², 247, 248, 249, 253, 255, 262; W^m—174, 257², 261, 262, 264², 340

Hackey; Ann,—204

Hackney; Eliz^a—297; W^m—252, 254, 272, 297

Haines; Chas.—156; Sarah,—155², 156

Haley; W^m—275

Hammet; W^m—243, 248, 252, 254

Hammon; Thos.—262

Handson; Rich^d—78

Hardee; Avarila,—222; Constant, —283, 285, 295, 297, 299, 301, 307; Curtis,—263, 278; Jno.— 299, 302, 326, 329, 332, 335, 340; Jos.—185, 188, 202, 206, 212, 220, 222², 311, 314

Hardin (Harding); Eliz^a—266; Geo.—148, 166, 184, 198, 202, 206, 209, 210, 216, 219, 235³, 242, 244, 245, 247, 249, 255, 256², 258², 260, 262, 264; Thos.— 309

Hardy; Andrew,—243

Harrin; Jonathan,—95

Harvie; Joseph,—28, 29², 31², 33², 34, 35², 37, 38, 40, 45², 46, 47, 49³, 51, 56, 58

Harwood; Robt—254

Haslewood; M^r—12; Jno.—3, 5, 7, 8, 10, 13, 15, 16

Head; Jno.—74

Healey; Eliz^a—318

Hennesey; Mary,—263, 265

Herne, (Hearn); Jno.—211; Isabell (Isable),—160, 165, 169, 174, 181, 182, 186, 187, 200, 203, 207, 210; W^m—117, 155, 160, 165, 169

Heyley; Widow,—316

Heyward; Mrs.—63; Thos.—61², 62

Hhawes; Edwd—306

Hicks; Jno.—151, 153, 154, 161

Hill; Ann (Anne),—175², 178, 181, 187, 200, 203, 207², 211; Needles (Needels, Needlis),—292, 309², 322, 336; Rich^d—155, 215; W^m —159, 164, 169, 258

Hipkins (Hipkings); M^r—144; Andrew,—170, 199; Jno.—128, 129⁴, 130², 131, 134, 137, 143, 146², 151, 152, 154, 155, 160, 165, 172², 173², 174, 181, 204, 207, 211

Hiptinstall (Hiptinstal); Jas.—288, 291, 297, 314, 319, 325, 328, 331, 334, 339; Rebekah,—283, 285

Holloway; Joseph,—285

Hog; Ann,—335

Holderness; Robt—174

Holmes; Jno.—297²; Robt—156, 159

Hopkins; Joseph,—34

Horne; Frances,—118, 124²

Hornsbee; Marmaduk,—7

House; Massey,—261, 274

Howard; Eustace,—243; Francis Lord——Baron of Effingham,— 42; Ruth,—263

Hoyls; Jno.—113

Hudle; Mary,—109

Hughs; M^r—13²; Rich^d—9, 11

Humphreys (Humphres, Humphris, Humphrys, Humphries, Humphryes, Humfreys); Eliz^a—178, 181, 186, 200, 203, 207, 210, 217, 220, 223, 227, 229, 231, 236, 241, 243², 245, 246, 247, 248, 252², 254, 255, 256, 261, 262, 264, 266, 270, 272, 274, 278, 283, 285, 288, 294, 296, 298, 301, 312—Jno.—9², 11, 223, 234; Joseph,—211, 223, 274; Robt— 134, 151; W^m—271, 272²

Hundle; Jeffery,—137

Hunt; Matthew,—136

Hutson; Mary—49², 51, 56

Hyde; Jonathan,—183

Ingram; Anne—113; Jno.—151, 155; Mary,—160; Sarah,—137², 142, 151, 159³, 160²

Ingwell; Henry,—178

Jackson; Jno.—281

Jacob; Nicholas,—326, 328, 332, 335, 340

Jacobus; Joseph,—136

James; Robt—113, 114, 117, 124, 134, 137, 142, 151, 156

Jaxson; Ellianor,—84

Jeffreys; Sir Jeoffery,—102

Jemson; Jas.—170

Jennings (Jenings); Eliza—138; Geo.—155, 159, 160

Jervis; Jno.—170

Johnson ;—289; Ann—265; Arthur, —163, 164², 169; Jonathan,—198

Johnston; Philip,—279; Stephen,— 279³

Jollye; Dudly,—105

Jones; Mrs—62, 63; Rev. Mr—342; Churchhill (Churchill),—180 181, 186, 198, 200², 202, 203, 206, 207, 209, 210, 217, 219, 220, 222, 225, 227, 229, 230, 231, 236, 238, 240, 242, 245, 247, 248, 249, 252³, 253, 255, 256, 260, 262, 264, 266, 270, 272, 274; E m a n u e l,—245³; Evan,—101; Humphrey,—7, 8³, 9, 10, 15², 16, 21, 25², 27², 30², 31, 32², 33, 35, 43, 149, 167, 185, 189, 214, 216, 220, 226, 239, 259; Jas.—261 Jno.,—183, 211, 217, 221, 223, 227, 240, 251, 259, 266, 272, 275, 278, 283; Joshua,—221; Matthew, —34; Rice,—231; Roger,—125², 128, 133, 135², 136, 137, 138, 139, 141, 144, 145, 146, 147, 148, 150, 153, 154, 156, 157, 158, 160, 161, 162, 163, 164², 165, 166, 169, 171, 174, 177, 180, 181, 183², 186, 188, 197, 199, 200, 201², 202, 203, 204³, 205³, 206, 209, 210², 215, 216, 219, 222, 227, 228, 229, 231, 233, 235², 237, 238, 244, 245, 247², 249, 251; Rowland,—156; Wm—259, 269

Jordan; James,—113

Juice; Nathaniel,—101,105

Kelly; Jean,—296

Kelshaw (Kilshaw, Kilsha); Ann, —243; Christopher,—113², 183, 186; Jno.—291; Mary,—200, 203, 204, 207, 210, 212, 217, 218, 220, 223

Kemp; Mr—65², 107; Col.—109, 142; Lt. Col.—90³; Major,— 228²; Matthew,—30, 31, 32, 36, 37³, 39, 41, 44, 46, 48, 50, 56, 57, 58, 59, 60⁴, 61, 62², 63⁴, 64³, 66, 69, 70, 72, 74, 77, 78, 79, 80², 81², 83, 87², 89, 90, 91, 92, 93³, 94, 96³, 98, 100, 101, 102, 106², 107, 109, 110³, 112, 114, 116², 117, 118², 123, 124, 125², 128², 129³, 130², 132², 133², 134, 135, 139, 141, 144, 145, 148, 170, 171³, 172³, 173², 174, 175, 176², 177³, 179, 180², 181, 183, 186, 187, 188⁵, 197, 199⁷, 200, 201, 202, 203², 205², 207, 208², 209, 210, 212², 215, 217, 219, 220, 221², 222; Nathaniel,—43; Richd —93, 95, 96², 99, 100, 101, 102, 103⁴, 104, 105, 106², 107², 109², 110, 111⁶, 112, 113³, 114, 115, 116, 117, 118, 119, 122; Thos.— 309, 323, 337

Keyton; Elenor (Nelly),—241, 243

Kidd (Kid); Jno.—312, 332², 335, 340; Thos.—101, 103, 109, 112, 124; Wm—265, 266, 271, 272, 274, 275, 328², 332, 335, 340

Kilbee; Christopher,—200; Richd— 100; Wm—83, 92, 93, 96, 99, 102, 103

King (Knig); Alice,—117², 124

Knight; Robt—222

Lake; Mary,—341

Lane; Henry,—103, 105

Lark; Jno.—210, 217, 220, 222, 227, 229

Laughlin; Thos.—248, 257, 282, 284, 287, 290, 292, 294, 296, 298, 301, 306, 309, 311, 313, 316, 319, 325, 328, 331, 334, 339

Lawrence; Jno.—124, 137, 142

Lawson; Jno.—243, 262; Wm—130, 131, 246

Leach; Mr—6; Wm—7, 8, 10, 11, 13

Lee; Chas.—142, 151, 299, 302, 307, 324; Geo.—269, 281, 293; Jno.—275; Thos.—114

Lestridge; Elizⁿ—40; Katherine—40^2

Lewis; Jas.—164; Jno.—207, 211^2 217, 221^2, 253, 297, 299, 302

Lidford; Lettice,—74; Matthew,—71, 72^3, 73, 74^2, 75

Lindsey; Jno.—22

Loe; Samuel,—115, 117, 179, 204

Loll; Francis,—257

Lomax (Loemax); Dr—91; Jno.—132^2, 133^3, 135

Long; Daniel,—31; Elizⁿ—242, 245, 247, 248, 249, 252, 254, 255, 256, 257, 260, 262

Love; Nicholas,—63, 64, 67^2

Low; Andrew,—341

Loyal (Loyall, Lyall); Jno.—285, 288, 291, 294, 296, 299, 301, 318; Ralph,—155, 160

Macham; Jas.—184, 209, 214, 216, 220; Jno.—250; Wm—267

Machan; Jas;—338

Machen; Jno.—259, 281, 293; Thos.—198, 202; Wm—293

Mackernet (Macknerent, Mackneret, Macknerett); Jno.—20, 21, 24; Old,—23

Macktyre (Mactire, Mactyer, Mectyre, Meektyre, Mcktyre); Hugh,—105, 155, 159, 165, 169, 174, 178, 187

Mahaffey; Robt—211, 217, 220

Mainwell (Manel, Manell, Mannell, Manuell), Dorothy,—87, 109, 112, 114, 115, 117, 124, 134, 137, 142, 151, 155

Mainⁱⁱ; Robt—28

Man; Jno.—30, 31, 32, 33, 41, 43, 44, 48, 52

Marcum; Wm—118

Marston (Marstin, Mastin); Mr—100, 106; Jno.—94, 174, 211, 217, 220; Thos.—67, 68, 69, 71^2, 73, 75, 76^2, 78, 79^2, 80, 81, 83, 86, 87, 89, 90^2, 94, 96

Matthews (Matthewes); Jno.—266; Mary,—272, 274, 276, 279, 284; Samuel,—67

Mayo; Ann,—155, 159, 164; Valentine,—151

Mazy; Alice,—154, 155, 156^2, 159, 164, 169; Ralph,—123, 134, 137, 141, 143, 151, 154

MccCarty (MckCarty, Maccartey); Chas.—159, 160^2, 165^3, 169, 174, 175, 178

McCormack; Ann,—314^2, 317

McCurdy (MccCurdy); Archible,—221, 223, 227, 229, 231, 236

Mchan (Mchann); Jas.—293, 310, 324

McNeal; Jno.—295, 314

Meacham; Jno.—239, 269

Mealer; Nicholas,—236

Medeares; Chas.—340

Meecham; Jas.—124, 137, 149, 167

Meggs; Mary,—252

Meeks; Thos.—291

Michaell; Edwᵃ—19

Mickleborough (Meikleborough, Mickleburrough); Edmᵈ—112, 114, 117, 124, 176; Henry—281, 293, 309; Tobias—92

Middleton; Mary—165; Susannah —175

Miller; M^r—14, 22; Christopher—268, 280, 292, 297; Patrick—6, 8, 11, 97^2, 100, 101

Mills; Jas.— 328, 330, 333, 334, 335^2, 336^3, 339^3, 341^2

Minor; Dorothy—115

Mins; Thos.—32

Mitchell (Mitchel); D^r (Dr Jno.) —241, 246, 254, 261

Molloughon; Eliz^a (Eli)—124^2, 143

Moor; Jno.—234^2

More; Abraham—262, 264, 266; Jno. 242

Morgan (Morgaine); M^r—12; David—148, 159, 163, 164, 169; Eliz^a—159, 175

Morhead; Geo.—272

Morrey; M^r—14

Morris; M^r—2^2, 4, 6^2, 7; Geo.—10, 11; Rich^d—6, 9

Mosely (M o s e l y e, Mosley, Mosly); Jno.—198, 225, 247; Marvell—119, 122

Moulson (Molson); 289; Rich^d—178, 181, 186, 200, 203, 207, 210, 217; W^m—268, 271, 278, 283, 291, 299, 302, 308, 311, 320

Montague (Mountague); Jno.—293; Lewis—281, 293, 310, 322, 324, 327, 330, 333, 336, 339^5; Thos.—150, 168, 185, 198, 214, 217, 226, 230, 240, 251; W^m—89, 226, 230, 310

Moxam (Moxom, Moxum);—136; Eliz^a—136; Easton—137; Thos. —136, 314^3

Mullins (Mullen); Mary—212^2, 215

Mumpus;—89

Murray (Murrey, Murry); Alex^r —283; Jno.—136, 259, 268, 281, 293, 309, 323, 337; Robt—315, 319, 331; Sarah—178

Musgrave (Mustgrave); Michael —59, 64, 69, 71, 73, 76

Nash; Jno.—64, 66, 69, 70, 71, 72, 73, 74, 75, 77, 78, 79, 80, 83, 87, 92, 93, 94, 97

Neal; Jno.—312, 314

Needles; Dorothy—116; Jno.—7, 8^2, 10^2, 11, 12^2, 13^3, 15^2, 21, 25^2, 27^2, 33

Neilson (Nelson); Chas.—339^4

Newberry; Agnis—204^2, 207; W^m —101

Newcomb; Jno.—327, 330

Nicholls (Nichols); Henry—3^2; Jno. 45, 51

Nicholson; Francis—99, 100

Nickcolls; Eliz^a—183

Norman; Henry—32; Mary—47, 51^2, 56^2, 64; Thos.—32, 35, 40, 45, 47, 57, 59, 65, 67, 68, 73, 83

Northey; Sir Edwd— 99^3, 102

Norton; Peter—156

Oastler; W^m—83

Obrissell; Thos.—47

Ogivie; Frances—332^2, 335; Thos. —330

Okill, Jno.—138

"Old John"—117

Orrill (Orril); Lawrence (Larrance)—225, 230, 239, 250

Overstreet; Jas.—273, 275; Mary —278, 283, 285, 326; Ruth—274, 276, 283, 285

Owen; Augustin—151; Jno.—116^2, 118^2, 123, 130, 131, 133^2, 136^2, 138, 141^2, 142^3, 151, 152, 153, 154, 156, 159, 161, 164, 169, 174, 178; W^m—213, 225, 227, 229^4, 230, 231^2, 236^2, 238, 249, 250, 258, 268, 275, 280, 292, 309, 337

Paffatt; Rich^d—130, 131

Palmer; Jno.—299, 302, 307, 314

Palto (Panto) ; Occaney (Occany, Ocany, Ockaney, Okaney)—224, 227, 229, 231[2], 236, 241, 243, 245, 247, 252, 254, 255, 257, 261, 262, 263, 264[2]

Parrott (Perrott, Parrot) ; M^r—6, 12, 13; M^rs—142; Rich^d—1, 2, 3, 4, 5, 6, 9, 15, 16, 18, 21, 24[2], 25[4], 26, 27[3], 28[2], 29, 32[2], 33, 35[2], 36, 37, 38, 39, 43, 44, 48, 63, 67, 74, 159, 167, 185, 189, 198, 202, 206, 209, 214, 216[2], 223

Pate ; Thos.—42[3]

Pateman; Lettis—218, 224, 227, 229, 231, 236[2], 241, 243, 245, 247, 252, 254, 255[2], 257, 261, 262, 264, 266, 270; Thos.—270, 285, 295, 297, 299, 301

Pead; Duell (Duel, Deuel)—41, 43[2], 44[5], 46[4], 48[2], 50[2], 51, 52[2], 53, 56[3], 58, 60, 63[2], 64[2], 65, 66[2], 69, 70, 71[2]

Pearce (Peirce) ; Edwd—47, 156

Pendergest; Edwd—170

Perry; Micajah—70; Robt—220, 222; W^m—26

Petty; M^r—45

Philpotts (Phillpotts, Philpots) ; Paul—329, 332, 335, 340

Pickett; Henry—4[2]

Pinnill; Eliz^a—224

Poole; Sarah—91[2], 92; W^m—28, 30, 34, 38, 39, 47[2]

Porter; Eliz^a—238; Francis—218

Potter; M^r—4, 6, 10; Col.—19[2]; Cuthbert—1[2], 2, 3, 4[2], 5[2], 6, 7[2], 8[3], 10[2], 11, 12[2], 13, 15, 16, 18, 19, 37, 38, 39, 41, 43, 44, 46; Francis—299, 302

Press; Bridget (Bridgett)—59, 60, 64, 65, 67[2]

Preston; Mary—180

Price; M^rs—330; Jno.—155, 177, 186, 188, 197, 199[2], 202; Robt—28, 30, 36, 37, 39, 43, 45, 46, 48, 50, 62, 242; Thos.—228[4], 229[2], 230, 231, 232, 233[2], 234, 235, 238, 242, 244, 245, 246, 247, 253, 254, 255, 256, 257, 260, 261, 262, 263[3], 264, 265[2], 266, 267, 270, 272, 273, 274, 277, 278, 279, 280, 282, 284[3], 285, 286[4], 287[2], 289, 290, 292, 295, 296[3], 298[2], 299, 300, 301, 302, 308, 315, 318

Privett, Jane—39

Probart (Provert) ; W^m—102, 105

Proster; Sarah—340

Purcell; Patrick—238

Purton (Purtin) ; Jno.—146, 151, 156, 160, 164, 169, 174, 176, 178, 181

Purvis; Geo.—170; Jno.—162, 169; Mary (Ma)—155, 156, 160, 165, 169, 174

Quarles; Jno.—211

Raffe; Jno.—297

Ransford; Rich^d—97, 100

Ranstead; Mary—159, 160, 164, 169, 175; Rich^d—91[3], 92, 94, 102, 104[2], 109, 110, 113, 114, 117, 124, 134, 137

Read; Rev. M^r—342

Reade; Dr Alex^r—271, 275, 283, 285, 288, 290, 295, 297, 299, 302, 306, 308, 312, 314; (Rev.) Jno.—238[3], 240, 242[3], 244[3], 245[2]

Redman; Mary—274, 278

Redmond; Abigall—65

Reeves; M^r—14; Geo.—19

Reid ;—255; Jas.—229, 231, 254, 264[3], 266, 270, 271, 272, 273[2], 274, 276, 277[2], 279, 280, 282,

283, 284, 285, 286, 287, 288,
289, 290², 292, 295, 296, 297,
298, 299, 301, 302, 305, 306,
308², 311, 312, 313, 314², 315,
316, 317, 319, 328

Reynald (Reynalds) ; Richᵈ—102,
116

Rhodes (Rhods, Roads) ;—316 ;
Benjamin—315 ; E z e k i a s—89 ;
Geo.—84 ; Her ;—231 ; Jno.—167,
184, 199, 213, 216, 217, 219

Rice ; Jacob—326, 327, 328, 330,
332, 335, 340

Richards ; Mourning—279⁴, 280,
286, 287, 289², 290², 291 ; Wᵐ—
279

Richardson ; Peter—47

Ridgway (Ridgaway) ; Ann—267 ;
Jno.—83, 85 ; Margery—87, 89

Ried ; Adam—273

Risque (Risq) ; Jas.—137, 153, 154

Roane (Roan) ; Chas.—326 ; Michⁱ
—222 ; Wᵐ—306, 308², 309, 312,
337

Roberts ; Elizᵃ—261, 264, 276 ;
Thos.—288

Robertson ; Wᵐ—99

Robeson ; Jno.—160 ; Wᵐ—159,
165

Robey ; Mʳ—64

Robinson ; Mʳ—22, 33, 35, 69, 71 ;
Mʳˢ—48² ; Major—299 ; Ann—
53⁴, 54, 55⁴ ; Christopher—30, 31,
32, 33², 34, 35³, 37², 38, 39,
46, 49, 50, 55², 56², 57, 58³, 59, 60,
61, 62, 63, 66², 69, 70², 92, 106²,
107², 109, 110, 111, 112, 113,
114³, 115, 116, 118, 124, 135,
177², 180, 181, 182, 183⁴, 186,
187, 188³, 197, 199², 200², 202,
205³, 207, 217, 231, 233², 235²,
236, 237³, 238, 239, 242, 244,
245, 247, 249, 250, 253, 255,
256, 257, 258², 260, 262, 263,

264, 267, 268, 270, 272, 276,
277², 278, 279³, 281, 284², 286,
287, 289, 290, 291, 292, 296,
298, 301, 305, 308, 311, 313²,
316, 318, 319², 320, 321, 322³,
325, 327², 328², 330², 331, 334,
336 ; Jno.—104, 105, 106, 107,
109, 110, 111, 112, 114², 115²,
116², 118, 119, 122², 123², 125³,
128³, 129³, 130², 131, 132², 133³,
134², 144, 145, 146, 147², 148,
150, 152², 153, 154², 155, 156,
157⁴, 158² 161, 162³, 163³, 164,
165², 169², 170, 171⁴, 172⁴, 173,
174², 175, 176⁴, 177³, 178, 179,
180, 181², 183³, 186, 187, 188,
197, 199, 200, 203, 205², 206,
235³, 237, 242², 243², 244², 245,
246, 247, 249, 252, 255, 258²,
260, 262, 263, 264, 266, 267,
268, 270, 272, 276, 277³, 279,
280², 282, 284, 287, 288, 289³,
290², 291², 292², 296, 297, 298,
301, 302, 305, 309, 311, 313,
316, 319, 322, 325, 328, 330²,
331, 333, 339³ ; Mary—200² ;
Richᵈ—15, 16, 18², 21², 23, 25³,
27², 30³, 31, 32³, 33, 35², 36, 37,
38, 39³, 40, 41, 43², 44², 46³,
48², 50², 51, 53⁴, 54, 55⁵, 56, 58²,
61, 62, 65, 66, 70 ; Wᵐ—241, 270,
273, 278, 283

Robson ; Elizᵃ—317 ; Widow—322,
327, 329

Rose ; Dʳ—10, 17 ; Henry—113

Ross ; Andrew—31 ; Ann—47 ;
Daniell—151²

Row (Roe) ; Dorothy—203 ; Jno—
113, 143, 146, 151², 156, 160,
161, 164, 169, 174, 178, 180,
181, 186

Rudd ; Ann—253, 254

Ruff ;—71 ; Ann—299, 302

Rupston ; Elizᵃ—340

Ryan; Edmᵈ—100
Rylee (Rilee); Mary—270, 272, 275, 278, 283, 285

Sadᵗer; Mary—254
Sandeford (Sandiford); Jno.—64, 95, 96
Saunders (Sanders); Edmᵈ—85, 88, 112, 114, 117, 123, 134, 137² 142; Jno.—181, 299, 302, 316, 341; Rebekah—308, 312, 314, 317, 320, 321, 327, 329, 332, 335, 340; Thos.—312; Wᵐ—316, 341
Scarbrough; Jno.—11, 15², 16
Scrosby; Jas.—280, 292, 304, 309, 323, 337
Seager (Segar); Mʳˢ—75; Ann—75²; Jno.—150, 168, 185, 187, 188, 198, 202, 206, 209, 214, 216, 220, 239, 250; Oliver—137², 138, 141, 142, 143, 145, 147, 148, 150, 152², 153, 154, 155, 156, 157, 158², 160, 163, 164, 166, 169, 170, 171², 172², 173, 174, 175, 176², 177, 179, 186, 200, 201² 202, 203², 204³, 206, 207, 209, 210, 217, 218², 219, 220, 221, 222, 224, 227, 228; Randolph —66², 67, 68, 69, 70, 71, 72, 260, 273; Wᵐ—150, 168, 185, 198, 202, 206, 209, 214, 216, 217, 220, 324, 332, 338
Seers; Henry (Harry)—274, 278, 283, 285, 288, 291, 295, 297, 299, 301, 307, 311, 314
Shapord; Henry—337; Jeremiah—338
Shaw; Mary—272, 275, 278
Sheilding (Scheilding); Thos.—19, 20
Shelton; Ralph—214, 216²; Susanna—231
Shepherd (Sheppard, Shepard); Mʳ—12, 13⁵, 14², 15, 16, 17, 18³,

19, 20², 22, 23, 24, 31, 33, 39, 155; Frances—45, 47, 49², 51, 56; Jno.—21³, 23², 24², 25³, 26², 27³, 29⁵, 30³, 31², 32², 33³, 35³, 36³, 37, 38², 39, 40, 41, 54, 64, 213; Mary— 105
Sherman; Anne—103; Edwᵈ—108
Sherwood; Wᵐ—70
Shilton; Zebulon—205
Shippey; Richᵈ—19
Sibley (Siblee); Thos.—264, 266, 270, 272, 274, 277, ¦283, 285, 288², 290, 294, 296, 298, 301, 306, 311, 312, 313, 314, 317², 320, 325, 328, 332, 334, 335, 340²
Siddon, Edwᵈ—91
Silvester; Alice—94, 96, 97, 103, 105², 109, 113, 114, 115², 142², 151
Simpson (Symson); Ann—78, 79, 81; Margaret—283, 285, 288, 291
Sittern (Sitterne); Edwᵈ—160, 165
Skeeres; Jno.—67
Skilton; Reuben—310
Skipwith; Sir Gray (Grey)—6², 8, 13, 253, 258; Sir Wᵐ—72, 73, 74, 77, 80, 82, 83, 84², 87³, 89 90, 93², 96², 99, 100³, 101, 112, 114², 115³, 116², 118, 123, 125² 133, 135², 136², 138², 141², 143, 144, 145², 146², 147², 148², 150, 154, 155, 157, 158, 161, 162, 163, 164, 166, 169, 171², 172, 174, 177², 179², 181, 182², 183, 186², 188, 197, 199⁴ 200, 205², 210, 213, 215, 217, 219, 220, 227, 228, 231, 233², 235, 244
Slaughter (Slauter); Annᵉ 32, 35², 73, 76, 78², 79, 81; Dorothy—85, 88, 89; Ellianor—82, 83, 88
Sloper;—23
Small; Joseph—266

S m i t h (Smyth) ; Capᵗ—117 ;
Adcock—326 ; Alexʳ—18, 23, 32,
34, 35, 36, 39², 41, 43, 66, 69² ;
Anthony—261, 265 ; Augustin (e)
—339⁴, 341 ; Edwᵈ—210, 213, 216,
219, 225, 230, 248, 265, 266 ;
Elizᵃ—255, 256, 260, 262 ; Gregory—239 ; Henry—151 ; Jas—84,
134, 142, 149, 167, 184, 188,
198, 202, 206, 209, 216, 270 ;
Jno.— 16, 17, 18, 20, 23, 74²,
77, 78, 79, 81, 82, 83, 84², 85²,
87², 89, 90, 91, 93³, 96, 99, 100,
101, 102, 103, 104, 106, 107²,
108, 109², 110, 111³, 112, 113,
114, 115³, 116, 118², 119, 122,
123³, 125, 128³, 129, 131, 132,
133², 135, 136, 139, 141, 142,
143³, 144², 145, 146², 147, 148,
149, 150, 153³, 154, 157, 158²,
162, 163, 164, 166, 167, 168,
169, 171, 172², 174, 177³, 178,
179², 180² 181, 182², 183³, 184,
186, 187, 188, 189, 197, 198,
199, 200, 201, 202², 203², 205³,
206², 208, 209², 213, 215, 216²,
220, 225², 230², 239, 245, 250²,
254, 264², 265, 266², 267²,270²,
272, 276, 277, 280², 282, 284,
286², 287, 289, 290², 292², 295,
298, 300, 302, 306, 308⁴, 309,
311, 312, 313, 316, 319², 322,
323, 330², 331, 332, 336, 341 ;
Jno. Adcock—299, 301, 306, 317²,
330 ; Joseph— 49², 245, 247, 252,
254 ; Michaell—124, 134, 137, 142,
151, 155, 165 ; Morris (Maurice)
—310, 324, 338 ; Robᵗ—6², 8², 10²,
1ᵗ ᵥ2ᵗ, 13ᵗ, 14³, 15³, 16², 19³,
21, 25, 27, 30, 31, 32³, 33², 34,
35, 36, 37², 38³, 39, 40², 41, 43,
44, 46, 47, 48, 50 ; Thos.—158 ;
Widow—322, 327, 329
Snodgrass, David—272

South ; Andrew—248, 252², 272,
275 ; Jno.—183 ; Rachel—341 ;
Smith—332
Southern (Southarn) ; Edwᵈ—275 ;
Jno.—207 ; Mary—263
Southworth (Southward) ; Grace
—178 ; 181, 187² ; Jno.—187, 230,
235
Spencer ; Thos.—34
Spicer ; Thos.—12
Spotiswood ; Jno.—297, 299, 302,
307, 311, 314, 320
Spratt ; Robᵗ—332, 341
Stamper ; Jno.—28, 56 ; Mary—
224 ; Powell—155, 159 ; Robᵗ—
307 ; Widow—235
Stanard (Stannard) ; Mʳ—81, 155,
222² ; Beverley (Beverly)—264³,
265, 266², 267², 270², 272, 274,
277², 280, 286 ; Wᵐ—100, 103,
112, 113, 135, 155, 183, 208,
209, 210, 211, 212², 215, 217,
218² 219, 220, 221, 222, 224, 228,
229
Stapleton, Dʳ—45, 75 ; Mʳ—83, 89 ;
Thos.—75², 84, 85 ; Wᵐ—221,
223
Stephens (Stevens, Steevens) ;
Jno.—278, 285, 288, 291 ; Richᵈ—
91, 174, 178, 181, 186, 200, 203,
207, 210, 217, 220, 222, 227,
229, 231, 236, 240, 242, 245,
247, 252, 253, 254, 255, 256,
260, 262, 264, 266, 270, 272,
274, 277, 283, 285, 288, 290,
294, 296, 298, 306 ; Royal Richard
—301
Steward ; Jno.—272
Stiff ; Jacob—187, 225, 230, 239,
268, 280 ; Wᵐ—323, 337
Stone ; Wᵐ—40²,47
Strachey ; Dʳ—285 ; Jno. 263, 270
Strastow ;—26
Stringer ; Daniel—266, 312

Summers   (Sumers,   Sumors);
    Eliz͏ª—155, 159, 165, 169, 174,
    178, 187; Jas.—328; Sarah—332,
    335
Superias (Superious); M͏r—11, 40
Sutton;   Christopher—184,   225,
    230; Dorothy—45, 49, 50; Jno.—
    19, 59, 64²; Mary—45
Sword; Jno.—324, 337
Sykes; Francis—272
Symmer;   D͏r—243, 261, 317; Jno.
    —231, 236, 278, 290, 295
Symonds, Margarett—117, 123
Syms; Thos.—117

Tankerley; D͏r—81
Taylor; Jane—212
Terry; Eliz͏ª—235, 244, 246, 248²
Teston, Mary—34
Thacker; M͏r—4; Col—248; Edwin
    —57, 58², 72, 73, 74, 78, 79, 80²,
    81, 83², 84, 87², 89, 90², 93³,
    94, 96, 100, 187, 188, 197, 199²,
    203, 205², 207², 208², 209, 210,
    212⁴, 215, 217, 219, 220, 222,
    224, 227, 228, 229, 231, 233,
    235, 237, 242, 245, 247², 249²,
    252, 253, 254, 260, 264; Henry—
    2, 7, 8², 10, 12, 15², 16, 21, 22,
    72, 73, 74², 77, 78, 79, 80, 81²,
    82, 83², 84, 87, 89², 90, 93³, 96,
    97, 101, 102, 104, 106², 107, 109,
    111⁴, 112, 114², 115, 187, 198,
    199², 211², 215², 219, 220, 221²,
    222, 223, 224², 227², 228, 229,
    231, 233, 235, 237, 238, 244, 245,
    247, 252, 253, 255, 256², 258²,
    260, 261², 262, 263, 267, 270,
    272, 274, 276, 277², 279², 280,
    281, 284³, 285, 286, 287, 289²,
    290, 291, 296, 298, 301, 305,
    308, 313, 319², 322, 325², 328,
    330, 336; Rich͏ᵈ—6

Thackston; Eliz͏ª—69, 71
Thilman; Paul—95²
Thomas; Arthur—235, 263
Thompson;—21; Mary—51, 56, 59,
    65, 67, 71, 73; Old—23; Rob͏t—
    18, 20, 24; W͏ᵐ—73
Thomson; Ann—295
Thornton; D͏r—124, 143²
Todd; Thos.—279
Tompkins   (Tomkies);   D͏r—151,
    155, 160, 164; Lewis—162, 175,
    181, 187, 204, 207²
Tool; Garret—335
Towles (Towls, Toles); Henry—
    229, 231¦, 236, 240, 242, 245,
    247, 252, 253, 255, 256, 260,
    262, 264, 266, 270, 272, 274;
    Stokely (Stockle, Stokley)—165,
    167, 184, 213
Townsend; Thos.—102
Towser; Henry—88
Trigg;   A b r a h a m—137,   142;
    Daniell—47, 51
Tuggle (Tugle); Henry—149, 167,
    184, 202, 206, 209, 213, 216²,
    220, 309, 323, 337
Tunstall;—289
Tureman; Rob͏t—254

Underwood;   Nathan—101,   102,
    104², 105, 106, 109, 112², 114,
    116, 117², 123, 134, 137, 138
Urie (Uriee); Jacob—312, 315;
    Jno.—299, 302, 314

Vallott; Claud—71
Vass; Henry—341
Vause; Jno.—1, 2, 4, 5, 8, 12²,
    15, 16², 17, 18, 21, 22, 25², 27²,
    28, 30², 31, 66², 68, 70
Vivion;   Eliz͏ª—181; Jno.—135,
    142², 176², 177

Wacomb (Wacum, Wakum) ; 116, 137, 142, 143², 151

Wade, Geo.—112

Wading (Wadding) ; Mr—12, 13; Geo. 7², 8², 10, 13

Wait ; Richᵈ—160

Walker ; Geo.—175, 200, 204, 211, 221, 223², 227, 229, 231² ; Jas.—114, 117, 118, 119, 121, 122³, 123, 135, 136, 138, 141, 143², 145, 146, 147², 150, 152², 153, 154², 155, 156², 157⁵, 158³, 160², 162⁴, 163² 164, 165, 166², 168, 169, 170³, 172, 176, 177 ; Jno.—235, 238, 242, 244², 245, 246, 249, 256, 258, 264 ; Richᵈ—178 ; Sarah—112, 113

Wallford ; Dr—160, 170

Wallis (Wallas) ; Wm—113, 265, 266, 271, 272, 275

Walters ; Elizª—40 ; Wm—40²

Ware ; Edwᵈ—295, 314, 321, 326, 329

Warren ; Richᵈ—200

Warwick (Warrick) ; Geo.—324, 338 ; Phillip—248, 249 ; Richᵈ—105, 109 ; Thos.—15, 16³

Washington ; Henry—286, 287², 289², 290², 291², 292, 296, 297, 301, 305, 308, 316, 319², 322, 325, 333

Watkyns ; Ann—89

Watson ; Thos.—45

Watts (Watt) ; Hannah—102, 105, 109 ; Hugh—91, 94, 97², 113 ; Jane—19 ; Katharine (Catharine)—274, 278, 283, 285, 288, 291, 295, 297, 299, 301, 307, 311, 314 ; Ralph—291, 295, 297, 299², 301², 307, 311 ; Richᵈ—34, 39, 45, 46, 51, 56, 59, 64, 67, 331 ; Wm—36

Webster ; Jno.—97, 103, 105, 109, 113, 115, 117, 124

Weekes ; Mr—6, 12 ; Abraham—1, 2, 3³, 4, 5, 7, 8, 11, 12, 15, 16, 21, 25², 27, 29, 32, 33, 35, 39, 44, 46, 50², 52², 56, 58, 63, 66 ; Francis—57, 58², 60, 61, 63, 72, 84², 86, 96 ; Hobbs—149

Welch (Welsh) ; Patrick—274, 278

West ; Nicholas—32, 73, 76²

Weston ; Mary—248

Wharton ; Jno.—317 ; Thos.—55

Whilley ; Thos.—332

White ; Elizª—113 ; Jno.—151, 252 ; Thos.—115, 148

Whittaker (Whitaker) ; Capt—24, 33 ; Dr—16, 20 ; Edwᵈ—262², 264, 266, 270, 272, 274, 277, 283, 285, 288, 290, 294,ᶦ 296, 298, 301, 308 ; Walter—15², 24, 25, 27², 28, 31, 32, 33, 35, 38, 39, 41, 43, 44, 46

Wiat (Wiatt, Wyat) : Richᵈ—271, 288, 297, 340

Williams ; Andrew—54 ; Geo.—24, 26 ; Jno.—21, 124, 178, 181, 187, 223, 241, 243

Williamson ; Andrew—20 ; Charity—81, 84, 86, 89, 91², 94 ; Robᵗ—149⁴, 167⁴, 168, 184³, 185², 213, 214³

Willis ; Mr—10, 14, 87 ; Richᵈ—56, 57, 58², 60, 61, 62, 65⁵, 66, 74, 77², 79, 80², 81, 82, 84, 86, 87³, 88, 89 ; Thos.—1, 2, 3, 4, 5, 8², 10, 11, 12

Wilson ; Thos.—48

Wingar (Winger) ; Ann—64, 175, 181, 182, 186, 200, 203, 207

Winn ; Richᵈ—103, 113

Wise ; Wm—89

Wood ; Elizª—297, 299, 302, 307, 311, 314, 320 ; Wm—178², 180

Woods; Katharine (Katherine)—
236, 241², 243, 245, 246, 247,
252, 253; Samuel—255; Wᵐ—
181², 186, 200, 203, 204, 207²,
210, 217, 220, 223, 227, 229, 231

Woodward (Woodward) ; Bridget
—71, 73, 76, 78, 79

Wormeley (Wormely, Wormley,
Wormly) ;—234, 235 ; Col.—20,
47, 59, 213, 225 ; Mʳ Secretary—
84; Christopher—8³, 10, 12², 13,
15², 16, 18, 21, 24, 25², 27²,
28, 30, 31, 32, 33, 35, 36, 37,
38, 39, 41, 44, 49, 60, 61², 62,
63, 69, 79, 80 ; Jno.—139, 141²,
143, 145, 146, 148, 150, 153,
154, 156, 158, 163, 164, 166,
169, 172, 174, 177², 179², 180,
181, 182², 183³, 186, 188³, 199,
200, 203, 205², 206, 208² ; Ralph—
18, 19, 24², 25², 26², 27, 30,
31, 32, 38², 41, 44, 61², 62, 63,
69², 70, 71, 77, 78, 79, 80, 84,
86, 118, 119, 123, 125², 128³,
129, 131, 132³, 133², 135, 136,
137, 141, 244², 245, 247, 249,
252, 253, 254, 255, 258, 260,
263, 270, 271, 274, 277, 284,
287, 290, 292, 300, 302, 306,
308², 311, 312, 313, 319², 322,
325, 328, 330², 331, 334, 336² ;
Wᵐ—70 72, 73², 74, 77, 78²,
84, 86, 87²

Worth ; Thos.—10

Wortham; Chas.—246, 251, 260,
261 ; Geo.—117, 118², 119, 122,
123, 125², 128², 129², 130², 131,
132², 133², 134, 135², 136², 137,
138, 141, 143, 144, ¦146, 147,
148, 150, 152², 153², 154², 155³,
157², 158, 162, 163, 169, 171,
172², 173, 174, 175, 177², 180,
183, 186, 188, 197, 199, 200,

202, 203, 205², 206, 209, 210,
215, 217, 219², 220, 222², 224,
227, 229, 231², 233 ; Jas.—309,
323, 329², 337 ; Jno.—17, 18², 20,
21, 22², 24, 43², 44, 45, 46, 48,
50², 56, 58, 61, 62, 63, 66², 69²,
70 ; Samuel—326 ; Thos.—323

Wortley (Worsele) ; Frances—59,
64²

Yarrington ; Jno.—326 ; Massey—
269

Yarro (Yarrow) ; Mary—183, 188,
215

Yates ; Mʳ—141, 143, 154, 161, 171 ;
Mʳˢ — 238 ; Bartholomew — 96,
100⁴, 101, 102⁴, 104², 106, 107,
109², 110, 111, 112², 114², 115,
116², 117, 118, 119, 122, 123²,
125, 128, 131, 133³, 135, 136³,
137², 138, 141², 143, 144, 145,
146, 147, 148, 150², 153, 154²,
157², 158, 159, 162³, 163, 164²,
166, 169³, 171, 172, 174², 175,
176, 177⁴, 178², 180, 181², 182³,
183², 186², 188³, 197, 199, 200²,
201, 202, 203², 205³, 207, 208,
209, 210², 212, 215, 217², 218²,
219, 220², 222⁴, 224², 227², 228,
229³, 230, 231², 233, 235, 236,
237, 238, 244, 245³, 247³, 249²,
251, 252², 253³, 255², 256², 258²,
260³, 262³, 263², 264³, 265, 266²,
267⁴, 270², 271, 272⁴, 274⁴ ,276²,
277³, 279², 280², 281, 282, 284², 286,
287³, 289³, 290², 292², 294², 296³,
298³, 300, 301², 303, 305, 306,
308, 311, 313², 316³, 318, 319⁵,
322, 325², 328³, 330³, 331³, 333,
334², 335, 336², 339³, 342⁴ ; Robᵗ—
86, 87⁴, 89², 90⁴, 92, 93, 94, 95,
342 ; Sarah—252 ; Wᵐ—342

Young ; Elizᵃ—246, 247

Geographic Index

Brandon (Brandon Plantation),—198

Brandon Road,—198

Briary (Bryary) Swamp [The],—149, 150, 167, 168, 185², 198, 214², 225, 226, 239, 240, 250, 251, 259², 269², 281², 293², 304, 305, 310², 324², 337, 338

Churchhill's (Churchill's) Creek [sometimes Col., sometimes Mʳ], —148, 166, 184, 198², 202², 206, 209, 213, 216², 219², 225, 238, 249, 258, 268, 280, 292, 303, 309, 322, 337

Curtice's (Curtis's) Mill Dam [Mr. Rice],—214²

Dragon [The],—149³, 167², 184, 185, 214², 225², 239², 250³, 259², 268, 269, 281², 293², 304², 310², 323, 324, 337, 338

Dragon Bridge [The],—138, 198, 202, 206, 209, 216², 220

Dragon Swamp [The],—150², 168², 185², 198, 214², 226, 240, 251, 259, 269, ᵇ281, 293, 305, 310, 324, 338

Elliott's Mill [Mr. Robert],—280³, 292³, 303², 304, 309³, 322, 323², [Mrs. Elizᵃ],—337³

England,—69, 205, 342

Essex County,—132

Gardner's Swamp,—198

Gloucester,—342

Grimes line [Mr.],—53

Hampton,—254

Harwood's Pattent,—5

Indian Field [The Small],—5

Kemp's Mill [generally Col. or Major or Mr.],—148², 149, 166², 167, 184³, 198³, 202², 206, 209, 213³, 216², 219², 225³, 238², 239, 249², 250, 258³, 268³

King and Queen County,—244

Lancaster County,—5

Lancaster Parish,—1, 5³, 6², 8

London,—70

Mickleborough's Swamp [The word Mickleborough is spelled in a variety of ways],—225, 239, 250, 259, 268, 281, 293, 304, 309, 323, 337

Middle Plantation Church,—4, 6, 7, 12

Millstone Valley [The],—149², 150², 167², 168², 185⁴, 198², 214⁴, 225, 226³, 239², 240², 250², 251², 259³, 260, 269⁴, 281³, 282, 293⁴, 304², 305², 310⁴, 324⁴, 337, 338³

My Lady's Bridge,—198

Neck [The],—72, 148, 166, 184, 198, 202, 206, 209, 225, 238, 258, 268, 280, 292, 303, 309, 322, 337

Nelson's Mill Pond [Mr. Charles], —338

New Bridge [The],—198, 202, 206, 209

New Bridge Road [The],—198, 202, 206, 209

New Dragon Bridge [The],—216, 220, 337

New Dragon Bridge Road [The], —216, 220, 225^2, 239^2, 250^2, 259^2, 268, 269, 281^2, 293^2, 304^2, 309, 310, 323, 324, 337

Nimcock Creek,—53^2

Parrot's (Parrott's, Perrott's) Creek,—149, 150, 167, 168, 185^2, 198^2, 214^2, 226^2, 239, 240, 250, 251, 259, 260, 269^2, 281, 282, 293^2, 304, 305, 310^2, 324^2, 338^2

P e a n c k a t a nck (Pyanckatanke, Pyancketancke, Pyancktanke) Parish,—4, 5^3, 6, 8

P e a n k a t anke (Pyanckatancke) Church,—17, 63

Peankitank (Piankatank, Piankitank, Pyankitank),—167, 184, 202, 206, 209, 213, 216, 219, 225, 239, 250, 259, 268, 281, 292, 304, 309, 323, 337

P y a n c k a tanck (Pyanckatanke) Precinct,—14, 16

Pipeing (Piping) Tree [The],— 148, 149^2, 166, 167^2, 184^3, 213^3, 225^3, 239^3, 250^3, 258^2, 259, 268^3, 280^2, 281, 292^3, 303, 304^2, 309^3, 323^3, 337^3

Pipers Spring,—107^2

Prettyman's (Prittyman's),—198, 202, 206, 209, 216

Prettyman's (Prittyman's) Landing,—216, 220

Prettyman's Quarter,—138

Prettyman's (Pretiman's, Pretyman's Prittiman's, Prittyman's) Rolling (R o l e i n g, Rowling) Road,—149^3, 167^3, 184^3, 213^3, 225^3, 239^3, 250^3, 259^3, 268^3, 281^3, 292, 293^2, 304^3, 309^3, 323^3, 337^3

Rappahannock River,—167, 184, 202, 206, 209, 213, 216, 219, 225, 239, 250, 259, 268, 281, 292, 304, 309, 323, 337

River [The],—149^3, 150^2, 167^2, 168^3, 185^4, 198, 214^4, 226, 240, 251, 258, 259, 268, 269, 280, 281, 292, 293, 304^2, 309, 310, 323, 324, 337, 338

Robinson's Mill Dam [Mr. Christopher],—149^2, 167^2, 184, 185, 213, 214; [Henry],—168^2, 185^2

Rose Gill Creek,—53

Slash [The],—168^2, 185^2, 214^3

Stratton Major Parish,—244

Sunderland Creek,—3

Thacker's Mill [Major, Col.],— 198^2, 202^2, 206^2, 209^2, 216^2, 220^2

Thacker's Mill Dam [Col.],—226, 239, 250, 259, 269, 281

Thicket (Thickett) Plantation,—5^2

Urbanna,—122, 125, 128, 276, 308, 336

Washington's Mill Dam [Capt. Henry],—293, 304, 310, 324

Wormley's bounds [Col.],—149, 167, 184

York Hampton Parish,—177

Topic Index

Act of Assembly,—1, 13², 32, 41, 52, 197, 202, 205, 209, 219, 339

Addition to minister's salary,—177, 178, 180, 182, ¡188, 201, 205, 208, 212, 218, 221, 224, 229, 230, 233, 237

Appointments to parish offices,— 176, 182

Articles of Faith,—2

Assembly [Grand or General],—6, 13, 180

Bastard Children; Bastardy,—20, 21, 26², 27, 28, 29, 31², 32⁴, 34⁴, 35⁵, 36, 40², 45, 46, 47, 49, 51, 56, 59, 63, 67², 68², 69, 71, 73, 76, 78, 83, 84, 85, 90, 91, 94, 97², 101, 102, 103, 105², 109², 183, 203, 212², 243, 272, 274, 275, 278

Canons of Church of England,—2

Casting lots,—3

Church (buildings, land, furniture, ornaments, books, plate, linen, etc.),—3, 5², 6², 15, 18, 19, 37, 43, 120, 123, 126, 128, 139, 144, 162², 163, 170, 171², 227, 233², 237², 275, 280, 298, 300, 303, 342

Church of England,—2, 70

Church Wardens (election of; when and where sworn in; accounts, duties, and salaries of, etc.),—37, 62², 63, 64, 65, 88, 144², 153, 157², 164, 171, 177, 179, 212

Clerks (of churches and of vestry),—14, 61⁴, 62, 92, 101

Contractors,—12, 129, 130

Corn (Three barrels of) paid as a fine,—235

County Courts,—5, 19

Disagreement between minister and vestry,—31

Fines for various offences,—4, 19, 27², 65, 157, 158², 183, 188, 222, 235, 244, 258, 273

Firm name,—255

Free School,—50, 71, 265, 273, 294², 296², 298², 301², 306², 311², 313², 317², 320², 325, 326, 328², 329, 331, 332², 334², 340², 342

Gazette [The],—276

Gifts and Bequests (to the parish or to individual churches),— 3, 25, 27, 35, 50, 52, 69, 70, 71, 132, 162, 163, 178, 296, 303

Glebe,—10, 11, 18, 57, 58, 171, 218, 219, 320, 326, 329, 332

Highways,—52, 98

Inspectors notes,—228, 230, 232, 243

King's land,—57

Marriage licences,—41, 42, 43

Masters of families,—22

Masters of servants,—17

"Middlesex County" or "Middlesex Parish" (used as equivalent of

"Christ Church Parish"),—23, 73, 77, 78, 287, 289, 342

Ministers (engagement, induction, dismissal, duties, perquisites, obligations, and salary of, etc.)—5, 6, 9, 13⁴, 16, 18, 21, 22, 29, 38, 39, 40, 46, 68, 100, 102, 143, 205, 238

Morals (proceedings against parents of bastards),—49, 62, 90

Note by copyist,—24

Oaths (forms of and references to),—2, 8³, 19

Officials :

Attorney General,—99

Bishop of London,—69, 162

Clerk of Assembly,88

Clerk of the Council,—99

Commissary,—70

Governor,—22, 30, 59, 100, 101, 189, 238, 245

Governor and Council,—8, 10, 11

King Charles II,—53

King William III,—70

Lieutenant Governor, Council, and Burgesses,—189

Queen Mary,—70

Secretary (of the Colony?),—59

Opinions :

of Attorney General,—98

of Governor,—18,19

Parish :

Accounts,—122, 135, 138

Bounds (settling of),—4

Levy (collection of),—65, 114

Precincts (division into),—138

Records,—1, 77, 92, 303

Union,—4, 6,

Patrollers,—275, 299, 302, 307, 329

Pensioners' allowances cut 20 per cent,—153

Permissions (to build additions to churches),— 234³

Petitions (to Grand Assembly),—13, 180

Poor [The] ; Binding out,—4, 115, 136²

Medical attention to, and general support of,—4, 10, 12, 17, 26, 28, 32, 34, 38, 40, 45, 80, 88, 92, 113, 165

Proceeds from fines distributed among,—158, 188, 235, 247, 249, 253, 255, 262, 263, 265, 272, 274, 276, 279, 284, 289, 291, 296, 308, 318, 322, 327, 329

Schooling of,—273, 275, 284

Work House for,—336

Presentation to Governor for Induction of Minister,—100

Prices :

of Corn,—261

of Tobacco,—230, 233, 237, 242

Processioning and Processioners,—92, 104, 148², 166, 168, 177, 183, 199, 200, 216, 220, 224, 230, 231, 238, 249², 258, 265, 267, 280, 292, 303, 308, 322, 331, 336

Quarterly sermons,—136

Quitrents,—306, 311, 313, 317, 320², 326², 328, 329, 332², 334², 340, 342

Quorum,—15, 36, 61

Readers,—9, 10, 11, 12, 13, 22

Rebellion (Bacon's),—25

Relief from paying levies (to certain persons for service rendered),—22, 29, 38, 64, 211, 297, 307

Religious instruction of children and servants,—44

Sacrament of the Lord's Supper,—44

Servant Maid,—26

Sheriff (as collector of parish fines),—23

Slaves (Act concerning trial of),—
189, 190, 191, 192, 193, 194,
195, 196, 197
Special sermon,—44
Suits (law and chancery),—65,
161, 171, 212

Titled persons (first reference to
in each case),—5, 6, 38, 42, 72,
99, 102, 258
Tobacco :
Counting,—197, 202, 203, 205,
209, 215, 219
Inspection,—267, 271, 272, 274,
277
Paid as parish levy to be of
growth of the parish,—111
Transfer notes,—267, 271, 272,
274, 277, 282, 284, 287, 290,
294, 296, 298, 301, 306, 311,
313, 316, 319, 325, 328, 331,
334, 339

Vestry :
Certify as to character of the
Rev. Bartholmew Yates,—188
Clerk of ordered to wait on Capt.
Robert Daniel,—139
Contribute personally to minis-
ter's salary,—14

Disagree over money matters,—
173
Election of Church Wardens,—
104
Fined for absence from meeting,
—27
Four or five members to consti-
tute a quorum,—15, 61
General Vestry,—5
Meeting place,—61
Order building overseers to act,
—158
Sign letter of thanks for gift of
bell,—162
Special meeting,—172
Vestryman does piece of work
for the church at his own
charge,—171

Warehouses (Law to prevent burning of),—152
Waste Land,—58, 59
Women Sextons,—156, 200, 203,
207, 210, 217, 220, 222, 227,
229, 231, 236, 241, 242, 243,
245, 247, 252, 253, 254, 255,
256, 260, 262, 264, 266, 270,
272, 274, 277, 294, 296, 298,
301², 306, 311, 313, 317, 320,
325, 328, 331, 334, 340

www.ingramcontent.com/pod-product-compliance
Lightning Source LLC
Chambersburg PA
CBHW070539270326
41926CB00013B/2147